China versus the US, World Bank and IMF in Sub-Saharan Africa

World Scientific Series in Multinational Investment and Business

Print ISSN: 2631-6587
Online ISSN: 2631-6595

This focused Series explores multilateral investments in business and political environments, especially in emerging and transitional markets, small states or dealing with emergent technologies, where such investments have unpredictable consequences for multinational business and society.

Multinational corporations, governmental and non-governmental organizations negotiate complex market and policy environments at the local, national, and global levels. These environments create global opportunities and impose global obligations. By focusing on emerging and transitional markets and technologies, the Series hopes to explore how global business environments are evolving through processes that involve actors at various levels with implications for policy and practice.

The series editors can be reached at uhaley@asia-pacific.com and gthaley@asia-pacific.com.

Published:

Vol. 2 *China versus the US, World Bank and IMF in Sub-Saharan Africa*
by Lynne Ciochetto

Vol. 1 *Storytelling in the Global Age: There is No Planet B*
by David M. Boje

World Scientific Series in Multinational Investment and Business

Volume 2

Series Editors **Usha C. V. Haley** & **George T. Haley**

China versus the US, World Bank and IMF in Sub-Saharan Africa

Lynne Ciochetto
Massey University, New Zealand

World Scientific

NEW JERSEY • LONDON • SINGAPORE • BEIJING • SHANGHAI • HONG KONG • TAIPEI • CHENNAI • TOKYO

Published by

World Scientific Publishing Europe Ltd.
57 Shelton Street, Covent Garden, London WC2H 9HE
Head office: 5 Toh Tuck Link, Singapore 596224
USA office: 27 Warren Street, Suite 401-402, Hackensack, NJ 07601

Library of Congress Cataloging-in-Publication Data
Names: Ciochetto, Lynne, author.
Title: China versus the US, World Bank and IMF in Sub-Saharan Africa /
Lynne Ciochetto, Massey University, New Zealand.
Description: Hackensack, NJ : World Scientific, 2023. |
Series: World scientific series in multinational investment and business, 2631-6587 ; 2 |
Includes bibliographical references and index.
Identifiers: LCCN 2022021003 | ISBN 9781783266678 (hardcover) |
ISBN 9781783266685 (ebook) | ISBN 9781783266692 (ebook other)
Subjects: LCSH: China--Foreign economic relations--Africa, Sub-Saharan. |
Africa, Sub-Saharan--Foreign economic relations--China. |
United States--Foreign economic relations--Africa, Sub-Saharan. |
Africa, Sub-Saharan--Foreign economic relations--United States. |
International Monetary Fund--Africa, Sub-Saharan. | World Bank--Africa, Sub-Saharan.
Classification: LCC HF1604.Z4 A35743 2023 | DDC 337.51067--dc23/eng/20220615
LC record available at https://lccn.loc.gov/2022021003

British Library Cataloguing-in-Publication Data
A catalogue record for this book is available from the British Library.

For any available supplementary material, please visit
https://www.worldscientific.com/worldscibooks/10.1142/P999#t=suppl

Desk Editors: Aanand Jayaraman/Geysilla Jean

Typeset by Stallion Press
Email: enquiries@stallionpress.com

About the Author

Lynne Ciochetto's publishing background is interdisciplinary. Her academic background began with sociology and development studies and then moved on to graphic design. After post-graduate studies in Switzerland, she worked in design education. Early research papers reflected an interest in the cultural impact of western advertising in emerging economies. Her first book was *Globalisation and Advertising in Emerging Economies: Brazil, Russia, India and China* (2011). Interest stimulated by negative media reports on China in Africa led to a paper *Impact of China on Sub-Saharan Africa's Ability to Work Towards a Sustainable Future*, in the *Journal of Global Studies* (2014). This book is a broader investigation into the dynamics of external influences on contemporary Sub-Saharan Africa, measured in terms of the triple bottom line — people, profit and planet.

Contents

About the Author		v
Chapter 1	Introduction	1
Chapter 2	Sub-Saharan Africa After 2000	15
Chapter 3	China After 2000	69
Chapter 4	The United States, World Bank and International Monetary Fund After 2000	89
Chapter 5	China in Sub-Saharan Africa Since 2000	113
Chapter 6	The Impact of the US, the World Bank and IMF on Sub-Saharan Africa Since 2000	157
Chapter 7	Conclusion	211
References		221
Index		279

Chapter 1

Introduction

Initially, the idea for this book was to answer the question: What is China doing in Africa? During my previous 10 years' research into China's economic development (Ciochetto, 2005, 2011, 2014), I had not encountered any mention of Africa but constantly came across articles in the Western media criticising China's behaviour in Sub-Saharan Africa (SSA). When I began to investigate China's presence in this region after 2000, I realised the bigger story was what the West had been doing there for centuries, and especially since 1945. I also came to understand the dynamics of US influence on the policies of the World Bank (WB) and International Monetary Fund (IMF) — the Bretton Woods Institutions (BWIs) — and how detrimental those combined influences have been on SSA. The underlying assumption of the book is that the US dominates the WB and IMF as it does the World Trade Organisation (WTO), and that these multilateral organisations act as US government proxies (Meltzer, 2000; Touissant, 2014). As most Organization for Economic Corporation and Development (OECD) countries and bilateral lenders tend to fall in line with American policies, this group, along with Western multinational corporations and the international financial sector, has been clustered together under the term 'the Washington Consensus' (Williamson, 2004).

The book explores development in SSA through the relationships the region has with the United States and the BWIs, and China. Designations of the SSA region vary depending on the organisation. I have adopted the United Nations Development Program (UNDP) designation, which includes 46 of the nations in the African continent, excluding Algeria, Djbouti, Egypt, Libya, Morocco, Somalia, Sudan and Tunisia (UNDP, 2018). The first part of the book explores what has been happening in SSA, China and the US and BWIs since 2000. The second half of the book assesses the impact of China and the US/BWIs on SSA. Each chapter ends with an evaluation of that impact. The final chapter compares briefly the impact of China's activities on SSA with those of the US and BWIs.

Each chapter is divided into the three key areas of the triple bottom line model — people, profit, and planet. Politics and human development are explored under the category 'people', economic variables under 'profit', and 'planet' covers environmental issues. Economic development, GDP and growth figures are assessed in terms of their impact on human development and the environment. I have adopted a human development perspective that prioritises human progress, environmental sustainability and economic development over economic growth and corporate interests.

This book advocates a more nuanced approach to understanding contemporary China, not as a monolithic entity but as a complex array of interests and agents that are reflected in a diversity of practices. According to an expert on China, Martin Jacques, there is no unified Chinese 'African policy' and no unified 'state' that Chinese companies represent (2012). A more finely calibrated approach to contemporary China and its activities is more appropriate to the context of contemporary geopolitical relations. My aim is to contribute to the body of evidence supporting a more balanced view of China's external activities in order for the West to engage more effectively with China in the future (Brautigam, 2010, 2011; Brautigam & Hwang, 2016; Huang, 2013; Keet, 2010; Stahl, 2016; Taylor, 2009). I also want to shed light on the activities of the US and BWIs in the region, and contribute to the body of evidence on how harmful these activities have been. These institutions need to comply with international regulations, as does China and other nations as well as the international financial community.

The sequence of the book is as follows. The second chapter discusses the changes in SSA after 2000, while Chapters 3 and 4 explore consecutively the changes in China and the US and BWIs since 2000. Later chapters examine the impact of China on SSA (Chapter 5) and the US and BWIs on SSA (Chapter 6). The final chapter provides a brief comparison of the impact on SSA of China versus the US and BWIs.

Chapter 2 provides an overview of contemporary SSA in the context of significant events in the 20th century. Most nations in SSA won their independence in the two decades after 1957. In the early years of independence, many of the nations experienced social and economic growth. African leaders tended to favour a gradualist approach to development. This position was articulated in the Lagos Plan of Action in 1980 (Irele & Jeyifo, 2010). In the 1960s and early 1970s, commodity prices were high and SSA nations were encouraged to borrow freely. The WB was the main lender and it significantly increased its lending in the 1970s. The IMF and aid donors also began lending to SSA at this time. When an international economic downturn occurred in the late 1970s, almost all nations had trouble repaying their debts. By this time, most countries in SSA were dependent on borrowed funds to function. Indebted countries started to lose their political and economic sovereignty when lenders and donors made the supply of further funds conditional on the imposition of neoliberal policies known as Structural Adjustment Policies (SAPs). Such policies included the privatisation of state assets, economic deregulation, privatising social services and reducing the state. These policies were promoted as a means of stimulating economic development and high growth rates, but this failed to materialise. Debt levels were so high that debt servicing took up large proportions of government incomes, and for the next 20 years — the 1980s and 1990s — social and economic development stagnated. It is significant that most of the debt was illegitimate debt, loans to totalitarian rulers who suppressed populations and expropriated the money. The pressure to sell state assets enabled acquisitions by foreign corporations, especially in the resource extraction sectors. Economic deregulation made it easier for corporations to avoid taxes and spirit profits offshore. The same neoliberal policies caused social harm in SSA nations by cutting subsidies, lowering wages and opening countries to international free markets, while upholding subsidies entrenched in the G7 and other affluent nations. These neoliberal policies persisted in various guises over the following decades, including the Highly Indebted Poor Country Initiative (HIPCI) of the BWIs in 1996, and in 2005, the Multilateral Debt Relief Initiative (MDRI). Neoliberal policies continue to be part of US and BWIs lending and aid conditions as well as for the other members of the Washington Consensus.

After 2000, there was a spurt in economic growth in SSA stimulated by Chinese demand for resources. By 2011, *The Economist* was writing about 'Africa Rising' (2011). Though the Western media was enthusiastic, the high growth rates did not dramatically improve human development or reduce the number of people living in poverty. Few Africans benefited from these economic changes because of corporate tax evasion, made easier through economic deregulation. The illegal financial outflows by Western corporations have been the most damaging occurrence in SSA since 2000. Global Financial Integrity (GFI), the Washington DC-based think tank, estimated that illegal financial outflows between 2005 and 2014 were between $36 and $69 billion, the highest from any region worldwide (Clough, 2017a). This has created a severe lack of capital for development, one of the most pressing problems facing SSA countries apart from internal issues, such as corruption and poor governance. SSA's economic position would be much better if illegal financial flows could be stopped. The region would benefit hugely from much more stringent corporate regulations, both foreign and local. This 'stolen' money would have made a major contribution to development in SSA.

Chapter 3 — China after 2000 — explores recent changes in China, based on the economic transition of the previous two decades. China remains a totalitarian state, ruled by its Communist Party since 1950. China's economic transition began in the 1980s and accelerated in the 1990s. By the early 2000s, 400 million people had been lifted out of poverty, one of the greatest social transformations in world history, although freedom of speech, democracy and human rights are still absent in contemporary China. The country achieved its social transition under the umbrella of totalitarian rule, the 'China Model'. The Chinese have also attained rapid economic development in a very short period of time. Following the disasters of Mao's leadership when millions died in famines, and the chaos of the Cultural Revolution, China embarked on a conversion to 'market socialism' or 'socialism with a capitalist face'. Communist Party leaders explored ways to embrace the capitalist economy without relinquishing political control of the Communist Party. The recent nature of China's economic and social transition means the memory of its experience of colonialism and its former political weakness is still fresh. The country has not forgotten the lessons it learnt from its own economic development, and this knowledge is valuable for other developing economies. China remains a society in transition, and millions of its rural people have been bypassed by development which in China has proceeded in stages and experimentally: disbanding agricultural communes and the 'iron rice-bowl' system, establishing special export processing zones on the eastern seaboard, and building infrastructure, industrialisation and export market expansion in the 1990s. Private capitalist enterprises were permitted and then foreign companies allowed entry. China learnt from joint ventures with these companies, acquiring foreign technology and improving the quality of Chinese products. It also borrowed from the WB. Other changes have included encouraging China's major companies to expand outwards, combining state-owned enterprises (SOEs) for core industries, and extension of the private sector.

Chinese leadership has been seeking to regain the position of major international power it lost in the 19th century. This achievement has been remarkably rapid. After 2000, Chinese foreign policy became more outward looking with the 'Go Global' strategy, followed by the 'One Belt One Road' project, renamed the 'Belt and Road Initiative' in 2016 (China Policy, 2017). China's spectacular growth continued for the first decade of the new century but slowed in 2011 as it began to feel the effects of the global financial crisis (GFC) and its exports contracted. Though China's growth rates have been declining, they remain much higher than in the US. Prins considers the Chinese response to the GFC and economic downturn by building infrastructure that will be used in the future, to be healthier than the US response which was to bail out banks, in effect rewarding their poor behaviour (2014a). The major downside to China's spectacular economic achievements has been the havoc unregulated development has wreaked on the environment and accompanying human costs. The absence of democracy and of human rights, especially for minority groups, are major problems for the country.

Chapter 4 explores the US and the BWIs after 2000 in the context of the history of the previous 50 years. After US assistance enabled its allies to win the Second World War (WW2), the US entered a period of triumphalism and optimism. The decades after 1960 were a time of strong economic development, technological innovation and rapid social change. On the strength of having the largest economy in the world, the US has dominated the international economy since 1945 and also politically dominated Western capitalist nations and multilateral institutions. It made some concessions to the welfare state in the 1950s and 1960s, but these were less extensive than those in Europe. The oil crisis in the 1970s — resulting from its support of Israel in conflicts in the Middle East — provided a sharp reality check, revealing its energy dependence and the vulnerability of the economy. As budgets tightened, leaders embraced the new political–economic ideology of neoliberalism. Neoliberal policies were adopted domestically and imposed internationally, through US influence in the BWIs, the Development Assistance Committee (DAC) group of aid donors and the Paris Club group of creditors. Within the US poverty rates and inequality increased while unemployment rose as manufacturing relocated to countries with cheaper labour, in particular to China. When manufacturing moved offshore, the financial sector became more economically important and the digital technology sector emerged. The relaxing of corporate regulations under neoliberalism encouraged financial speculation and unethical behaviour, bringing on a series of financial crises, the most spectacular being the GFC in 2008–2009. Corporate political power in the US increased in the neoliberal era, accompanied by a growth in lobbying and the size of campaign donations. The power of fossil fuel and the banking sectors grew. The military–industrial complex also grew more powerful after 2000 when President Bush embarked on the 'War on Terror'. Military expenditure increased dramatically, causing the US economy to fall into deficit. China began to invest in the US economy, and soon the US had a large trade deficit with China. Earlier environmental gains were undermined when the fossil fuel sector was allowed exemption from Environmental Protection Agency regulations. The US energy sector was transformed with the expansion of 'fracking', the extraction of gas from shale by injecting a toxic mix of chemicals into the ground, which increased domestic energy production but has caused significant health and environmental damage. The US has one of the largest per capita ecological footprints, due to high levels of energy use and the emergence of a culture dominated by consumerism. It has one of the highest levels of carbon emissions per capita. At the same time, the US fossil fuel sector has been very influential in funding media campaigns denying the realities of contemporary climate and environmental crises. The US has been slow to acknowledge the climate crisis and has not stepped up to take a leadership role. Since 2000, the international economic power balance has changed, and the Chinese economy is likely to overtake the US economy in the near future. China is also taking a more prominent international role, which challenges US dominance.

Chapter 5 — China in SSA after 2000 — explores the rapid and extensive expansion of Chinese activities into SSA post 2000. China has been involved with Africa since the late 1950s, soon after the Communist Party came to power. In the early decades, the relationship was primarily political. China wanted recognition and support for its 'One China' policy and identified with countries who were trying to break free from colonialism and the capitalist system. China supplied development assistance to Ethiopia and Tanzania, along with military assistance to Mozambique and Angola during their wars of independence. African countries supported China's application to the UN in 1971 when it became interested in becoming an international player. China joined the WB and the IMF in 1980 and the WTO in 2001. China also saw itself taking a lead in representing developing nations. From its own recent development experience, China felt it had significant development expertise to offer Africa.

In the 1990s, China's need for resources expanded and it began importing resources from SSA. This demand pushed up resource prices and stimulated an economic boom in SSA after 2000. A number of SSA countries had very high levels of economic growth at this time. China's relations with Africa changed after it launched its 'Go Global' policy in 2000, transforming its aid model from the provision of grants to mostly advancing concessional and commercial loans and bartering resources for infrastructure. China has never claimed to be altruistic in its international economic relations; it doesn't even like the term 'aid' as it implies an unequal relationship between donor and recipient. China's development assistance through loans, aid and expertise is not altruistic but rather based on the concept of 'win–win', bringing benefits to both sides. This is particularly true of resources for infrastructure deals. Such infrastructure projects are tied to Chinese companies and the funds paid in China, never reaching SSA, thus circumventing any disappearance or appropriation of funds. Central to the Chinese model is the idea that economic development is the key to the reduction of poverty. The focus on economic development is shared by the West but their approaches are quite different. Central to China's economic development was the reform of agriculture to increase productivity and the recognition that infrastructure was essential to economic development. These are areas the West has neglected in SSA for decades, whereas China was happy to comply with government requests and begin building infrastructure throughout SSA. It also provided loans without the many conditions that accompanied Western aid and loans as well as 'resource for infrastructure' exchanges.

Also, China has treated African leaders with respect, demonstrating that respect through the frequent visits by Chinese leaders. China has brought many benefits to Africa, and rather than undermining development with cuts to subsidies, tariffs, and privatising water, health and education, it has supplied services that have assisted with development: medical assistance and personnel, training and education opportunities in China, agricultural centres and training in Africa and much needed infrastructure (Brautigam, 2009). The Chinese government has not been aggressive in the pursuit of land acquisition in SSA, perhaps realising there has been enough negative publicity about China's presence in Africa. China has been responsible for environmental issues, land dispossession for infrastructure and resource acquisitions. China has granted debt relief to very low-income nations (a similar group to the WB's HIPCI) for concessional and no-interest loans. Debt relief comes without conditions. Commercial loans have to be repaid (Brautigam, 2009).

As SSA economies began to slow down after 2011, many increased their borrowing from China. In recent years, SSA's debt to China has grown and could cause problems in the future, although that debt in 2017 was still only 20 percent of the region's overall debt (Jubilee Debt Campaign, 2018). China may have imperial ambitions (Jacques, 2012) as indicated in the poorly named 'One Belt One Road' strategy in 2013, and there has been a lot of negative reporting about China's activities in SSA, but the conclusion of this study is that China's presence in SSA has been overwhelmingly positive and has assisted economic development and brought many benefits to the people.

The underlying assumption of Chapter 6 — the US and BWIs in SSA after 2000 — is that the US dominates the WB and IMF along with the WTO. Both the WB and the IMF are based in Washington, and the head of the WB is chosen by the US. The WB was the largest lender for development in the 20th century (Hertz, 2004) and has continued to be so since 2000 (Brautigam & Hwang, 2016). The lending policies of these organisations have reflected the economic models currently in vogue in American economics, but the main focus has always been economic growth. The BWIs have imposed development policies on SSA since the late 1950s, chiefly through the selection of development projects they are prepared to fund and their influence over government finance ministries. The US and the BWIs have also contributed aid to SSA. US corporations have likewise had a significant impact on SSA. Some have operated there since 1900, but most, in particular the oil companies, expanded their influence after 1950. The enforced sales of state assets under neoliberal policies enabled more foreign ownership of African resources. The other multilateral partner that reinforces the US agenda is the WTO, whose main impact is from its unequal subsidies and tariff policies.

SSA has been losing out to Europe and the US for centuries. The 19th century industrial revolution in Great Britain and the US was significantly supported by profits accumulated during the African slave trade, the first great tragedy inflicted on Africa. Then, the Berlin Conference of 1884 created the great African carve-up, where the boundaries of today's nation states were drawn up, without any African input. Local people were completely unrepresented. Colonial governments wrested as much wealth as they could from their colonies and transferred it back to Europe, maintaining only minimal spending in the colonies themselves. Education and health services were provided for colonists but for very few Africans. As independence movements emerged in the 20th century, the colonial powers tried to hold on to their colonies. The decimation caused by two major wars in Europe, however, weakened the hold of these external minorities who ruled by force and repression, and most SSA countries gained independence between the 1950s and the 1970s. By 1990, only Namibia was still a colony (of South Africa). The black African people of South Africa remained subject to internal colonisation and did not have a political voice until 1994.

The West soon found it was cheaper to maintain economic than political control of former colonies. Continued relationships with these colonies led to the emergence of the 'development sector', ideologically driven by economists of the WB and the IMF, both located in Washington. The key mechanisms of lending, debt and debt servicing enabled the BWIs to exert political and economic control over SSA nations. Patterns of lending and aid were always paternalistic. African people were not asked what they wanted but told what would be good for them. Lenders and aid donors set the rules and defined the projects they would fund. A key characteristic of the development sector has been the high turnover, almost every decade, of 'fashionable' theories for achieving development and aid (Brautigam, 2009). Over sixty years of US/BWIs development policies and projects have failed to eliminate poverty in SSA, which remains the poorest region in the world.

During the first buoyant years in the early decades of independence, developing countries were encouraged to borrow freely to stimulate economic development. The economic crisis of the 1970s left such countries indebted and facing rising interest rates. Governments depended on borrowing in order to function. As the main lender, the WB was able to dictate conditions for further loans. These conditions reflected the current ideological fashion for political and economic neoliberalism. SAPs became the new mantra in the late 1970s, and stringent policies were imposed in the name of economic growth. These policies included cutting back the state, selling off state assets (privatisation), cutting subsidies and tariffs to allow maximisation of the 'free market' and loosening regulations. Foreign corporations and banks were the main beneficiaries. In SSA, these policies intensified the stagnation of economic and human development through the 1980s and into the 1990s. Debt levels increased to the point where countries were borrowing to service debt. A growing international movement led by non-government organisations (NGOs), in particular Jubilee South, called for debt cancellation. The WB and IMF responded with the HIPCI in 1996. Most of the nations in the programme (nearly 40) were SSA countries. The initiative increased pressure on governments to sell state assets, deregulate economies and cut subsidies and tariffs. These neoliberal policies enabled corporations to acquire more assets in SSA, while the less restrictive regulatory environment enabled a vast increase in illegal financial flows (IFFs) out of SSA. After 2000, when new NGOs conducted more detailed research into financial transactions, the extent of these illegal financial flows was revealed to be higher than aid coming into the region (Curtis, 2017). Global Financial Integrity (GFI), an American NGO that investigates illicit financial flows between countries, discovered that 87% of illegal financial flows globally between 2005 and 2014 was from trade misinvoicing by multinational companies. The organisation estimated illegal financial flows out of SSA during this period to have been between $36 billion and $69 billion (Clough, 2017a). SSA's economic development has been held back by the theft of the value of its resources. This region has been and continues to be exploited by the West, the BWIs, the WTO and the Paris Club of creditors and corporations. If multinational corporations paid the actual taxes they owed, local governments would have vastly more funds to spend on social services and economic development.

Evaluation of the roles of China versus the US and the BWIs in SSA is summarised in Chapter 7 (conclusion). Both China and the West have been driven by the desire to acquire resources from Africa. China has been a significant actor in SSA only since the 1990s, and it has expanded its economic and political, but not its military, presence into almost every nation in the region. After 2000, China's negotiations were dominated by the exchange of resources for infrastructure, arrangements that meant countries in Africa did not amass huge debt burdens. A change in direction was indicated at the 2015 Forum on China–Africa Co-Operation (FOCAC) meeting when China increased its financial pledges. Concerns were raised that SSA may have taken on loans it is not able to repay (Brautigam & Hwang, 2016). In general, China's policies have been more sympathetic to what African leaders wanted. It has supplied massive amounts of infrastructure which, apart from the building of dams, the West was less willing to provide. China has also tried to stimulate agriculture and industry and has helped provide training and educational opportunities for African people both in Africa and China. The China–Africa Research Initiative (CARI) has documented many of these projects (CARI, n.d.a). Where China shares many of the faults of the West is in the environmental impacts of their infrastructure projects, especially their dams. There have been high incidences of corruption in their tendering processes.

The US, WB and IMF have supplied aid and loans to Africa since nations gained their independence. They have been responsible for stifling social and economic development in Africa for decades. The neoliberal policies the US and BWIs have imposed since the 1980s have resulted in the sale of Africa's key assets to corporations. Profits were then transferred out of Africa through various methods of tax evasion. The less restrictive regulatory environment, another neoliberal policy, made these transfers easier. Corporate illegal financial flows out of Africa accelerated after 2000 (Curtis, 2017). Neoliberal policies — privatisation of education, health and water — forced on SSA nations have held back human development. Independent internal evaluations of WB and IMF aid and lending practices have revealed high levels of project failure and corruption, and policies that benefit foreign corporations more than aid recipients (Hertz, 2004; Easterley, 2007; Independent Evaluation Office (IEO), 2007; Woods, 2008; Bretton Woods Project, 2019). Sufficient operational flaws have been revealed that critics from both the right (Easterley, 2007; Bandow, 2012) and the left (Bond, 2006, 2007; Bello, 2000; Danaher, 2004) have advocated for the WB and IMF to cease to exist but their lending ability is irresistible to borrowers and they seem to be able to survive any setback.

1.1. A Note on Sources

My thanks go to Walter Rodney for his pivotal book, *How Europe Underdeveloped Africa* (1981), which first awakened my interest in African development. The initial inspiration for my book came from a World Sociology Conference in Durban in 2006 where I heard Samir Amin speak, and where I attended a presentation by Patrick Bond and promptly bought his book, *Looting Africa* (2006). Patrick Bond's work has been a constant inspiration and is reflected throughout the references in this book. My other key source on China in SSA has been Deborah Brautigam and her book *Dragon's Gift* (2009), again constantly referred to in this book. The excellent work since carried out by Deborah Brautigam, now director of the CARI at John Hopkins University, and her researchers, has been central to the chapter on China's activities in SSA.

As the WB has set itself up as the knowledge bank of development (Klein, 2006), its data on development remain the most comprehensive available, and despite my criticisms of the bank, I am appreciative of the information it provides. I think it is worthwhile to use the same data to assess the policies of the WB and the IMF. Since the late 1970s, the WB itself has been driven by an ethnocentric, ideological, economic determinism, fixated on neoliberal recommendations. How the WB works reflects the vested interests, goals and agendas of the international financial sector and political-economic agenda of Western powers rather than its espoused motto of creating a 'World Without Poverty' (WB, n.d.). Outcomes have caused arrested human development and economic stagnation. Sometimes, projects have also resulted in environmental devastation. The US is the largest economy in the world, which has translated into political domination over the capitalist world since the end of World War II.

This political domination has been facilitated by the enormous influence of the WB and the IMF, which in turn are dominated by the US through the strength of its voting power and power of veto. With the largest military, military spending and arms exports, the US has reinforced its position as the world's policeman. Other major powers tend to follow the lead of the US because they share the same interests (Goldman, 2005). Is it too late to make the WB and IMF democratic?

Though the data produced by the WB is extensive, it can be questioned on methodology and accuracy. According to the economist Sanjay Reddy, the World Development Report 2006 provides a good example of the inherent bias in its information gathering processes. It often relies on questionable indicators and analytical tools; for example, 'more secure property rights' as judged by foreign investors are used as proxy for 'quality of institutions. The intellectual basis is weak, contents are not adequately completed, prescriptions are often questionable or of limited practical value' (Reddy, cited in Bond, 2006). WB data is used to justify policies, but often their own reports reflect the flaws in their own policies. Justifying the structural adjustment programmes was one such exercise. There was a high turnover of neoliberal or SAPs success stories as successes were often short-lived. The WB has never acknowledged the role neoliberal SAPs have had in reinforcing poverty and undermining development in SSA.

Another site that provides useful environmental data is the Global Footprint Network. It has developed key tools to assess environmental health, including the ecological footprint calculators and biocapacity reserves. The ecological footprint measures the ecological assets a population requires to produce the natural resources it consumes and to absorb its waste, while the biocapacity represents the productivity of a population's ecological assets. If the ecological footprint exceeds the region's biocapacity, it is in ecological deficit and has to meet its demand by importing, liquidating its own ecological assets and/or emitting carbon dioxide into the environment. The world slipped into negative capacity in 1970. The world average per capita biocapacity in 2016 was 1.7 hectares (Global Footprint Network, n.d.a).

1.2. Notes on Terminology

My focus is on SSA, but sometimes data and figures cited refer to Africa as a whole and include North Africa. The US and Chinese government data tend to include all of Africa, while the WB often uses the term 'Africa' for SSA. This is made clear in the text.

Terms 'TNC' and 'MNC': Most references to major international corporations use a mix of transnational corporations (TNCs) and multinational corporations (MNCs). The term multinational corporations (MNCs) seems to have eclipsed TNCs in recent years and will be used even if the term 'TNC' is used in reference material.

All dollar figures represent US dollars.

1.3. Defining 'Aid'

Another contentious topic central to the book is that of 'aid', starting with its definition. The term 'aid' covers a spectrum of definitions depending on the organisation. It is termed 'overseas development assistance' (ODA) in the US and comes under United States Agency for International Development (USAID). For the Development Assistance Committee of the OECD (DAC), aid or overseas development assistance must provide economic and social benefits, and any loans must include a 25% grant component (i.e., 75% can be interest-bearing loans). Aid does not include military assistance or humanitarian assistance (OECD, n.d.). The US includes military assistance and humanitarian assistance as aid, as well as debt relief (USAID, n.d.a). The amount of China's aid has been hotly contested. China includes military assistance as aid and excludes donor administrative costs but not debt relief (Carter, 2017).

For the figures for China's aid, I rely on the CARI data rather than the AidData project. Deborah Brautigam, Director of the International Development Program and CARI at Johns Hopkins University, has pointed out that the figures cited by AidData rely heavily on media reports which can tell users only that projects were announced and not whether they were actually carried out. Some of the early figures were based on policy commitments rather than actual money spent (Brautigam, 2013). Since its first release of data in 2013, AidData has diversified its sourcing. About half of its data now come from media reports while the rest come from Chinese and other government documents, international organisations and academic papers. On average, AidData has calculated that each project cited is backed up by three different sources (Constantaras, 2016).

1.4. The Climate Crisis

In 2019, *The Guardian Weekly* stated that the paper was going to change the way it talked about the environment, updating its style guide to accurately describe the environmental crisis facing the world. It, therefore, would replace the term 'climate change' (a passive and gentle term) with 'climate emergency, crisis or breakdown'. 'Global heating' would be used instead of 'global warming' (Carrington, 2019).

Another contentious term is that of 'developing' nation. Hans Rosling has challenged the use of the term, claiming that 'poor developing nations' no longer exist as a group. Rather than a binary framework 'developed/undeveloped or developing' or 'low income/high income', he proposes a four-tier model based on income level. He claims only nine percent of the world live in extreme poverty. He describes extreme poverty as living on $1 per day: life is precarious; people grow their own food; have no running water and no transport and firewood is used for fuel; cooking is on a fire; the same diet is eaten all the time except when there is no food; there is no health care and when people get sick from curable illnesses, they die (2018). Unfortunately, the majority of the people in SSA still live in extreme poverty or in the second income level. While there are groups at levels 3 and 4 in every country, these are a small minority. Though Rosling's point is useful, the terms 'developing nation', 'poor nation' and 'low-income' nations are still common in development literature and I have used them throughout the book.

Abbreviations

BRICS	Brazil Russia India China South Africa
CARI	China–Africa Research Institute
CIA	Central Intelligence Agency
DAC	Development Assistance Committee (OECD)
EU	The European Union
FAO	Food and Agriculture Organisation
FOCAC	The Forum on China–Africa Co-Operation
G7	The US, the UK, Germany, France, Japan, Italy, and Canada
G8	The US, the UK, Germany, France, Japan, Italy, Canada, and Russia (until 2014)
GDP	Gross Domestic Product
GFC	Global Financial Crisis
GFI	Global Financial Integrity
GHG	Greenhouse Gases
GNI	Gross National Income
GPF	Global Policy Forum monitors the work of the UN bodies and global policymaking
IEA	International Energy Agency
IMF	International Monetary Fund
IPCC	Intergovernmental Panel on Climate Change
HIPCI	Highly Indebted Poor Country Initiative
MDGs	Millennium Development Goals
MDRI	Multilateral Debt Relief Initiative
MGI	McKinsey Global Institute
NEPAD	New Partnership for Africa's Development
NGO	Non-Government Organisation

OECD	Organisation for Economic Development
PPP	Private-Public Partnership
SAL	Structural Adjustment Loans
SAPs	Structural Adjustment Policies
SDG	Sustainable Development Goals
SOE	State Owned Enterprise
SSA	Sub-Saharan Africa
UN	The United Nations
UNCTAD	United Nations Conference on Trade and Development
UNDP	United Nations Development Program
UNESCO	United Nations Educational, Scientific and Cultural Organisation
UNFCCC	United Nations Framework Convention on Climate Change
UNODC	United Nations Office on Drugs and Crime
USAID	United States Agency for International Development
US Census	United States Census
USODA	United States Overseas Development Assistance
WB	World Bank Group
WTO	World Trade Organisation

Chapter 2

Sub-Saharan Africa After 2000

External agents have been exploiting Sub-Saharan Africa (SSA) since the beginning of the slave trade. The agents of contemporary exploitation include multilateral and bilateral agencies, governments through their aid and loans and multinational companies. Key tools of recent exploitation have been the leveraging of debt and the imposition of neoliberal policies. Local elites implemented the neoliberal policies in order to continue borrowing (Bond, 2006). SSA has also been subject to evolving 'fashions' in development theory and practise, dominated by the World Bank (WB) and International Monetary Fund (IMF) (the Bretton Woods Institutions or BWIs). Since the late 1970s, the result of these policies has been to increase the net outflow of wealth from Africa (Action Aid, 2005).

SSA has abundant natural resources but they benefit few people, and poverty levels are high. Since 2000, creditors have continued to mandate various iterations of neoliberal policies that they have been imposing since the late 1970s. Many countries in SSA had high growth rates after 2000, but standards of living did not improve at the same rate (Bond, 2017a). Much of the wealth created was transferred out of SSA through legal and illegal financial flows (Curtis, 2017; Clough, 2017). Continued foreign exploitation of SSA in the 21st century means that the region continues to 'lose out' in the global economy, failing to benefit from the value of its own resources (Oxfam International, 2018a). Natural capital accounting has been adopted by the UN and the WB as an economic tool that can help measure the full extent of a country's natural assets, linking the economy, ecology, and environment (Sieber, 2015). Though natural capital accounting is inherently problematic because it monetises the natural world which has intrinsic value far beyond its monetary value (Monbiot, 2018), it does provide an indication of the losses from resource depletion. Using this measure, the WB estimated that the average decline in per capita African net wealth attributed to the extraction of 'natural capital'— minerals, energy, and forest products — was 12% in

2010 (WB, 2014b). In 2012, the Gaborone Declaration for Sustainability in Africa adopted by nations in SSA incorporated natural capital accounting as an assessment tool (Bond, 2018).

2.1. People: Politics and Human Development

The number of nations included in the SSA region differs according to the organisation doing the counting. The WB includes 48 nations in SSA (WB, n.d.b2), while the United Nations Development Programme (UNDP) lists 46 nations (UNDP, 2018). The latter reference is used here. Many of these nations are small with populations under two million people: in contrast, the 10 largest countries account for 59% of the population. After 2000, the population of SSA grew rapidly from 667.7 million to 1 billion people in 2016 (WB, n.d.b2). SSA accounts for 13.6% of the global population, roughly equivalent to the 1.03 billion population in the high-income nations. Because economic size rather than population is related to power, SSA's bargaining position in international organisations is weak because its total GDP is only a tiny percentage of world GDP (WB, n.d.a2, n.d.b2). As other developing nations have become stronger, SSA's position has further weakened.

2.1.1. *Politics*

The development of the state in SSA has been moulded by historical experience, beginning with the precolonial political systems, which were then distorted by nearly 100 years of colonialism. During the period when nations became independent, many newly independent governments were undermined by external intervention, particularly from former rulers, and some became embroiled in Cold War hostilities by proxy. The Western model of the state, based on a 'hegemonic bourgeoisie grounded in solid and independent economic base and successfully engaged in the private accumulation of capital', is absent in SSA (Taylor, 2009). The nature of the state in SSA resembles neither the West nor the regimes of Asia, communist or otherwise. Rather, they are more like quasi-states than democratic entities (Jackson, 2005 cited in Taylor, 2009). Taylor considers that in the West, the moral and political models transcend economic and corporate interests and create an 'ethico-political framework.' In SSA, there emerged an 'unstable, personalised system of domination' characterised by clientism and neopatrimonialism. Ruling elites in Africa lack hegemonic power, and the power of the ruling class is dependent on capturing the state (Taylor, 2009). Soon after the years of nationalist struggles and independence, countries 'collapsed into autocracy.' Political rule and elections reflected a combination of control and patronage rather than the will of the people. Governance and domination were based on the threat of violence. These conditions undermined development as the top priority of governments was to stay in power. In many of these 'quasi-states,' control was imposed by force and not maintained throughout the whole country (Taylor, 2009). External development agencies did not understand that when leaders proclaimed commitment to development and negotiated for development assistance with international organisations, they were not necessarily ready and willing to implement development policies (Taylor, 2009). Corruption flourished in the quasi-states and civil society was repressed. This is one of the reasons development did not happen. Other contributing factors were paternalism, economic determinism and a high turnover of development models and prescriptions that came from institutions in Washington (Brautigam, 2009).

Instability in the SSA region meant that when the 'Failed States Index' was established in 2005, states in SSA dominated the list (Amburn, 2009). In 2000, there were armed conflicts in nine countries: Democratic Republic of the Congo (DRC), Sudan, Liberia, Burundi, Rwanda, Somalia, Uganda, Ethiopia/Eritrea and Congo-Brazzaville (Ismi, 2002). Since then, SSA has continued to be the most war-torn region in the world. The index, renamed the 'Fragile' States Index in 2014, continues to be dominated by countries in Africa. In 2016, there were still many nations that did not have a state government that controlled the entire country. Political instability is particularly common in resource-rich countries, what has become known as the 'resource curse.' The characteristics of fragile states cover a spectrum from social issues (demographic pressures, massive displacement of refugees, vengeance seeking, chronic and sustained human flight), economic factors (uneven economic development along group lines and economic decline) to political issues (criminalisation and/or de-legitimisation of the state, deterioration of public services, arbitrary suspension of the law, security forces operating as a state within a state, factionalised elites and intervention of external political agents) (Freedom House, 2016). In 2016, SSA continued to dominate the Fragile States Index with six out of the eight countries classified as 'Very High Alert' nations (South Somalia (1), South Sudan (2), Central African Republic (3), Sudan (4), Chad (7) and Democratic Republic of the Congo (DRC) (8)) and six in the 'High Alert' category (Guinea (12), Nigeria (13), Côte d'Ivoire (14), Burundi (15) and, jointly in 16th place, Zimbabwe and Guinea Bissau) (Fund for Peace, 2016). These 12 nations account for 41% of the region's population (US Census International Data, 2019). A large number of countries with resource-curse profiles have totalitarian governments. There are high levels of corruption in resource-rich countries. The ruling elites expropriate the country's wealth and use it to arm the military, repress the population and enrich themselves. The elites also use wealth for patronage. These governments are more interested in maintaining control than improving human development, raising standards of living, investing in health services or developing the economy to provide jobs and taxes. In countries experiencing conflict and instability, growth rates are often weak and erratic. Where countries have high-value resources, the growth rates may be high but are accompanied by economic stagnation and high international debt. Because little effort goes into development, high levels of poverty and extremes in inequality translate into low levels of human development.

Not all resource-rich countries are fragile states. Only three of the eight countries in SSA benefitting from the recent oil boom (Chad, Sudan and Nigeria) are 'fragile states'; the others are not (Angola, Gabon, Equatorial Guinea, São Tomé and Cameroon) (Fund for Peace, 2016). Human development levels are low in the resource-rich countries (UNDP, 2016). Corruption deprives the local people of benefits from the sale of natural resources in all countries in SSA, not just the fragile states (Chêne, 2010). The BWIS introduced good governance as a loan condition in the 1990s. A decade later, Easterley found that the concept of good governance had achieved very little with no obvious improvement in governance in countries that borrowed money (2007).

2.1.1.1. *The road to democracy*

The absence of democracy in SSA has had economic implications. A long-term (30-year) international study of democracy and economic development in 184 countries concluded that increased democracy can contribute to a 20% increase in GDP. Democracy has had positive effects on economic reforms, private investment and the size and capacity of government, and can lead to a reduction in social conflict. All of these factors contributed to economic growth. The most important variable was the increase in liberties (Acemoglu *et al.*, 2014). A strong legal system is also an important part of good governance, social justice and the equitable distribution of a country's resources. Unsurprisingly, higher human development ratings tend to accompany good governance; however, China's rapid social and economic transition is evidence that social and economic development can occur without democracy but with a strong government. Good governance is closely related to a strong civil society.

A number of generations have been born since SSA countries gained independence. In the decade after 2000, there was optimism about political change, the growth of civil society along with stable economic and social development, and much talk of 'Africa Rising' (*The Economist*, 2011; *Time Magazine*, 2012). In 2010, researchers at McKinsey Global Institute (MGI) reported a decline in internal hostilities and an expansion of democracy in many countries (Leke *et al.*, 2010). In the same year, Radelet identified 17 countries at the forefront of democratisation in SSA. He saw democracy as the key pre-condition for future development and he believed that the emergence of a new generation of leaders, whom he called the 'cheetah' generation, was particularly significant. He did acknowledge there was more evidence of expanding democratic institutions than the actual practise of democracy, but people had more say in choosing their leaders than they had in the past. The number of democratically elected leaders increased from three in 1989 to 23 in 2008. As well as the expansion of democracy he noted improvements in economic policies, a decline in debt and poverty and the introduction of new technologies (2010). By 2016, this earlier optimism had evaporated as economic growth had slowed for a number of years and SSA's debt was increasing. Patrick Bond has challenged the concept of 'Africa Rising' (2017a) that had been popular earlier in the decade.

The Mo Ibrahim Foundation audits democracy in Africa using a five-stage scale. It focuses on what happens between elections in terms of safety and the rule of law, participation by citizens, human rights and sustainable human development. In its study of African governance in 2015, no country qualified as a democracy (ranking 80–100), but the overall trend was moving that way. At the top of the 2016 list were Mauritius and Botswana (79.9), while at the bottom was

Somalia (8.5) and South Sudan (19.9) (Vuylsteke, 2017). Though progress towards democracy was flawed, there were fewer internal coups in 2015 than there had been in 2000 (Freedom House's Freedom in the World Report 2016, cited in *The Guardian*, 2016). Another measure, the Economic Intelligence Unit's Democracy Index, used four categories of democracy to explore the political spectrum in SSA: full, flawed, hybrid and authoritarian. Only Mauritius qualified as a full democracy in 2015 (2016). Mauritius is neither a typical state in SSA nor a role model. With a population of 1.2 million in 2016, it functions as a tax haven facilitates money laundering, illegal and legal funds transfers and enables the exploitation of its regional partners.

2.1.1.2. *SSA's voting power*

Votes in the WB and IMF were allocated at the end of the Second World War. At the time, SSA was still colonised and had no votes. Since independence, nations in SSA continued to lack political power in international organisations, a reflection of the region's economic size rather than the size of its population. SSA's economy, valued at $1.5 trillion in 2016 (WB, n.d.b2), comprised only 1.97% of the global economy, compared to the US with 25% valued at $19.06 trillion (Central Intelligence Agency (CIA), 2019a) and China's 28% at $21.74 trillion (CIA, 2019b). Similarly, China's votes also do not reflect the size of its GDP or population. In 2000, just under 50 countries in SSA, approximately one-seventh of the world's population, were represented in the BWIs by two directors, while the eight wealthy countries had directorial roles, and the US maintained its veto power with more than 15% of the votes (Bond, 2017a). In 2015, the voting power of the BRICS (Brazil, Russia, India, China and South Africa) in the IMF was increased, while SSA lost more votes, Nigeria (–41%), Namibia (–26%) and Gabon (–26%). Even though South Africa was a member of the BRICS, its votes were reduced by 21% (Bond, 2017a, 2017b). In the WTO, voting and decisions are made by consensus, requiring unanimity in voting, unlike the WB and IMF where power is delegated to a board of directors or the head of the organisation (World Trade Organisation (WTO), 2018). SSA now has more bargaining power in the WTO than in the IMF (Weisbrot & Johnson, 2016), but not enough to affect unequal policies on subsidies. The interests of SSA nations are further weakened by the fact that South Africa represents them in international organisations. South Africa is not a true representative of the rest of the region. It tends to play a comprador role acting as a proxy for Western interests as well as a base for the expansion of multinational companies in SSA. South African companies also play a role in the exploitation of resources elsewhere in Africa (Bond, 2006, 2017b). In terms of revenue and subscribers, the main local telecommunications company to have emerged in SSA is the South African company MTN. This organisation operates in a predatory manner similar to foreign companies (Kembaro, 2012). An example of this wider chain of exploitation is the US company Walmart, which has a majority ownership of the South African company Massmart. By leveraging economies of scale, it can undercut producers in other countries and undermine residual basic needs production in the region (Bond, 2017a).

2.1.1.3. *Loss of political sovereignty*

One of the most significant political events in SSA in the late 1970s was the loss of state sovereignty in the countries that had borrowed from the WB in previous decades. The majority of countries in the region were in this position. Many of the newly independent SSA states had favoured a state-driven development model, complemented with funds borrowed from the WB, as well as aid from OECD countries. This approach was characterised by economic planning, import-substitution-industrialisation, price controls, credit rationing, state-owned enterprises and government control of agricultural marketing (Van de Walle, 2001; Lofchie, 1994; Killick, 1989; Waterbury, 1999; cited in Woods, 2009). Once nations became indebted in the late 1970s, they wanted to address the debt crisis with a gradualist approach, articulated in the Lagos Plan of Action set out by the Organisation for African Unity in 1980. Leaders wanted to shift nations away from their dependence on the export of basic raw materials, which 'had made African economies highly susceptible to external developments' (Irele & Jeyifo, 2010).To achieve this goal, the plan focused on increasing Africa's self-reliance, promoting industrialisation and building up regional and sub-regional cooperation and integration. The state was seen to have a central role in development, in direct contrast to the premise of the WB that the state was a hindrance and the market should play the central role (Mkandawire & Soludo, 1998). The cases of China and other East Asian nations provide ample evidence of success. What African leaders wanted was swept aside and they became subject to the conditions imposed by BWI lenders who had embraced the current neoliberal political and economic policies of the US government under President Reagan. African nations have been subject to these conditions ever since.

2.1.1.4. *Governance and corruption*

Corruption is a major problem throughout SSA. Transparency International defines 'corruption' as 'the abuse of entrusted power for private gain. It can be classified as 'grand, petty and political, depending on the amounts of money lost and the sector where it occurs' (2019). In many SSA countries, governments are not accountable to the people, the judiciary is not independent and justice is not equal. SSA also suffers from international corruption. During the Cold War, Western governments, BWIs and multinational companies were all complicit in propping up notorious leaders with aid, loans and military assistance. Poor governance was perpetuated by bribes and ongoing lending. Loans were often given in the full knowledge that they would not or could not be repaid (entrapment) (Perkins, 2004a). According to the 2004 Global Corruption Report, Botswana was the least corrupt country in SSA and Nigeria the third most corrupt country in the world (Jerome *et al.*, 2005). In 2016, the Global Corruption Index showed that 11 out of the 20 nations at the bottom of the list were in SSA, with Somalia (ranked 176) and South Sudan (175) at the bottom. Nigeria ranked 136 (Transparency International, 2017). Where corruption is endemic in fragile states like the DRC, the problems are multifaceted and cannot be changed merely by policy changes. Change needs to be far reaching throughout many sectors. High levels of corruption are closely related to low levels of human development. Expropriated funds are used to repress the population and enrich individuals.

'Balance of payments leakages', including the expropriation of government revenues, loans and aid and along with bribery, have been the most common forms of high-level local corruption in SSA. Foreign corporations are involved with bribery and payments to local officials. Misinvoicing of trade and tax avoidance by foreign corporations have been responsible for most of the illicit financial flows out of SSA in recent decades. According to Global Financial Integrity (GFI), fraudulent misinvoicing of trade accounted for 87% of global illicit financial outflows over the 2005–2014 period. During that time, total global illicit financial flows (outflows plus inflows) grew at an average rate of between 8.5% and 10.1% a year. 'Illicit financial outflows from SSA ranged from 5.3% to 9.9% of total trade in 2014, a ratio higher than any other geographic region studied' (Salomon & Spanjers, 2017).

The resource extraction sectors are notorious for corruption and collusion with governments throughout SSA. Oil companies in Nigeria have colluded with the government to repress opposition to the environmental damage caused by oil extraction in the Niger Delta. The most notorious case of human rights abuse was when the Nigerian government put to death members of the Movement for the Survival of the Ogoni People (MOSOP) who were protesting against Shell in the 1990s. This prompted an international backlash against the company (Frynas, 2001).

2.1.1.4.1. Case study: South Africa

Corruption is one of the main reasons holding back development in South Africa. In 2015, South Africa was named the 7th worst country for IFF, amounting to an average loss of $21 billion annually (Kar & Spanjers, 2015). PricewaterhouseCoopers named Johannesburg's corporate elite as the most corrupt corporate class in the world in 2014 and 2016 based on these criteria: money laundering, bribery and corruption, procurement fraud, asset misappropriation and cybercrime (PriceWaterhouseCoopers, 2016). The parastate energy corporation Eskom Power exemplifies many of South Africa's problems. Corruption and incompetence are damaging the economy because the company cannot guarantee a continuous supply of power. Eskom is overstaffed and inefficiently run. Attention to plant maintenance has been poor and expropriation of funds has been a major problem. One of its most notorious contracts was a deal made in 1993 with South Africa's largest energy consumer — BHB Billiton — to deliver energy until 2025 at a price lower than it costs Eskom to produce it, a net loss to the company (Gosling, 2019). The WB funded the Eskom Power project to the building of two coal-fired power stations: Medupi and Kusile. Part of the total funding of $110 million was approved in 2010. Production was meant to commence in 2012 and 2014, but the plants were not completed by 2016 (WB, n.d.i2). When early problems emerged, they were not sorted out. Eskom took over the management of part of the project — dam building — because no one else would take it on, but they did not have the expertise for the undertaking. Eskom has had major debt repayment problems (Gosling, 2019). Another South African parastate company, Transnet, had major corruption problems in the Durban container port expansion. The project had to be put on hold because of corruption in both lending and locomotive acquisitions. Tenders had been inflated to provide kickbacks for the Gupta brothers who were business associates of President Zuma (Bond, 2017a).

Most foreign corporations in the region have their corporate headquarters in South Africa. After 1994, more South African corporations began expanding northwards. The activities of South African politicians and companies were often accompanied by 'extreme exploitation of nature and society' (Bond, 2018). The activities of mining companies were particularly despicable. During the brutal civil war in DRC, the South African company AngloAshantiGold, which owned Mongbwalu mine in eastern DRC, collaborated with local warlords responsible for many civilian deaths and major environmental damage. The film 'The Curse of Gold' documented these impacts. In the film, the company defended itself from criticism from NGO Human Rights Watch (*ibid*).

A common form of corporate corruption in SSA is the channelling of profits through tax havens. South Africa's MTN cell phone service earned high profits in Nigeria, Uganda and South Africa and channelled them offshore through financial offices in Mauritania and Dubai. Corporate income tax rates in Mauritania are 3%, with no tax on capital gains (Bond, 2017d). The chairperson of MTN was Cyril Ramaphosa, the deputy president of South Africa after 2014. He also held 9% shares in Lonmin when it was using 'sham' marketing in Bermuda as a means of tax avoidance. Under Ramaphosa's responsibility in 2007, Lonmin raised a WB credit line of $100 million to build 5,000 housing units but only three were actually built (Bond, 2017a). Ramaphosa was also on the board of Lonmin during the Marikana mining strike in 2012. He was instrumental in requesting the police to take more action at the mine, and the next day, 34 miners were shot (Bond, 2014a). The miners were not armed and were protesting for a living wage of $1520 a month (Bond, 2018b). President Jacob Zuma's government was also complicit in protecting the private interests of political allies in neighbouring countries. When South African troops were protecting a property owned by Zuma's nephew Khulubuse in DRC, they did not intervene to stop a nearby massacre of civilians (Alison, 2016 cited in Bond, 2018).

2.1.2. *Human development*

The agreement of 189 members of the United Nations to the 'Millennium Development Goals' (MDG) in 2000 was evidence that decades of Western efforts to promote development had failed to address key issues in human development. Nowhere was this more evident than in SSA. Aims of the MDG included eradication of extreme poverty and hunger, provision of universal primary school education, promotion of gender equality and empowerment of women, reduction of child mortality, improving maternal health, combatting diseases (including HIV/AIDS and malaria) and ensuring environmental sustainability (AidWatch, 2013). The process of establishing the goals reflected the paternalistic nature of the development sector. External actors defined the goals, identified the priorities and decided how they would be met. By the end of the programme in 2015, SSA was the region least successful in meeting the goals. The key reason for failure was the ongoing effects of the imposition of neoliberal policies by the nations, institutions and corporations that held SSA's debt.

By 2000, 38 nations in SSA had endured more than two decades of trying to comply with structural adjustment conditions imposed by creditors. The poorest indebted nations were in the process of implementing further neoliberal policies to qualify for debt relief under the 1996 Highly Indebted Poor Country Initiative (HIPCI). High levels of debt servicing are directly related to inadequate provision of social services, poor health levels, poverty and political instability (Hertz, 2004). After 2000, human development in the region began to improve after stagnating for nearly two decades. In 2000, the regional Human Development Rating was 0.421, increasing to 0.523 by 2015, but SSA continued to lag behind the rest of the world (UNDP, 2016). The development sector continued to evolve its definitions and policies. The UNDP expanded its definition of development to include human development and poverty reduction along with economic growth. The definition for poverty broadened to take in social factors as well as income under the term 'multidimensional poverty' (2015). In a comparison of average gains in human development between 1990 and 2015, countries in SSA held the 19 lowest places in the world (UNDP, 2016). In 2016, the criteria for human development were broadened again. The term 'sustainable human development' included social, economic and environmental sustainability. Only two small countries in SSA were classified as having high human development, Seychelles (population 0.95 million) and Mauritius (population 1.2 million) in 2015 (WB, n.d.b2). Nine countries had medium human development (Botswana 108, Gabon 109, South Africa 119, Cabo Verde 122, Equatorial Guinea 135, Ghana 139, Zambia 139, SãoTomé and Principe 142 and Kenya 146) with a HDI ranking between 147 and 107 in 2015. The remaining 35 nations had low levels of human development (UNDP, 2016). Environmental degradation, climate change, natural disasters, epidemics and conflicts have also held back human development in SSA (UNDP, 2016).

The historical legacies of violence, discrimination and human rights abuses have held back human development in SSA. The victims of human rights abuses have a right to compensation. The loans and assistance given to totalitarian rulers made the lenders complicit in those crimes. In 2002, a group of 168 South Africans sued 20 banks and corporations that did business in South Africa during the apartheid era in the US federal court. The plaintiffs alleged that the participation of the defendant companies in key industries during the apartheid era made them complicit in the commission of abuse against black Africans. The plaintiffs were victims of human rights abuses such as extrajudicial killings, torture and rape. The nine banks were Barclays, National Bank, Citigroup, Commerz Bank, Credit Suisse, Deutsche Bank, Dresdener Bank, JP Morgan and UBS ANG. After a long judicial process, most of the allegations were not upheld. In February 2012, the plaintiffs reached a settlement with General Motors and eventually only the IBM and Ford cases were tried. These were dismissed in 2015 (Business and

Human Rights Resource Centre, n.d.). The structural imbalances of the apartheid system have persisted in the post-apartheid era. There are more black people in power but inequality remains and the system still discriminates against the poor both economically and in the delivery of social services.

2.1.2.1. *Poverty*

Between 2000 and 2015, SSA remained the most impoverished region in the world. Though GDP per capita increased between 1998 and 2008, little trickled down to the general population (Bond, 2017a). While growth rates were high until 2011, there was little improvement in human development. High population growth offset reductions in poverty (Bond, 2017d). In 2010, in collaboration with the Oxford Poverty & Human Development Initiative (OPHI), the UNDP broadened its definition of poverty beyond income levels (such as $1 per day). The 'Human Poverty Index' was renamed the 'Global Multidimensional Poverty Index' for the 2010 report. Aspects of multidimensional poverty, health, education and standards of living were evaluated against 10 criteria: child mortality, nutrition, years of schooling, school attendance, cooking fuel, toilet access, water, electricity and types of floors and assets (*The Economist*, 2010). Broad-based regional averages conceal vast differences between countries and also inequality within countries. Most of the world's hungriest and poorest people live in rural Africa. The number of undernourished people in SSA increased from 203.6 million in 2000–2002 to 220 million in 2014–2016, though the percentages showed a decrease from 30% to 23.2% (Food and Agricultural Organization (FAO), International Fund for Agricultural Development (IFAD) and WFP, 2015).

When the UN released its final progress report on the MDGs in July 2015, many of the goals had not been reached in SSA, particularly the first goal, reducing poverty. There had been reductions in child mortality. Even though the percentage of those living in poverty had fallen from 57% in 1990 to 41% in 2015, rapid population increases offset these small gains. Numbers living in poverty increased from 290 million in 1990 to 408 million 25 years later (Goldberg, 2015; WB, n.d.b2). Those living in rural areas are more likely to be living in multidimensional poverty (74%) than the 31% living in urban areas. Gender also plays an important role. Households headed by women were even poorer than those headed by males. People living in areas of conflict were also particularly at risk of falling into multidimensional poverty (UNDP, 2016). The failure to reduce poverty in Africa called into question the effectiveness of 50 years of external aid and development.

2.1.2.2. *Health*

Advances were made in healthcare provision in SSA during the 1960s and 1970s, but these were stifled or reversed under structural adjustment conditions which mandated eliminating healthcare subsidies, privatising health services and introducing user charges. By 1998, 75% of all loans to SSA required the expansion of user fees (Colgan, 2002). Life expectancy in Africa dropped by 15 years between 1980 and 2000 (UNICEF, 'Balance sheet of human progress in Africa' 2000 cited in Colgan, 2002). The ongoing burden of debt repayments after 2000 continued to impact the ability of governments to provide health services. When a petition for debt relief was presented to the US Congress in 1999, one of the key justifications was that debt repayments exceeded health and education expenditure in many SSA countries (Njehu, 1999). In 2005, when the G8 debt relief reduced $4 billion of Zambia's debt, the government was able to provide free health care. In Zambia, there were only 600 doctors, 24 pharmacists and no psychiatrists. The ratio of doctors to population was 1 to 14,000 people (BBC World News, 2006). Zambian healthcare has continued to improve, and by 2016, researchers were recommending that other countries in SSA follow some of the initiatives undertaken in Zambia (Kipp *et al.*, 2017).

The AIDS epidemic in SSA has highlighted problems in the health sector. AIDS is a major health problem and SSA has the highest number of cases in the world. Approximately 25.5 million people lived with HIV in 2016. East and South Africa had the highest rates (7.1%), but more people there were taking antiviral drugs (45%). In West and Central Africa where occurrence rates were much lower (2.2%), only 12% were taking antiviral drugs. Nigeria had a relatively low incidence rate of 3.5%, but because of the large population, that percentage equalled 3.2 million people with HIV, 51% of them on anti-retroviral treatment. The AIDS epidemic created other problems and intensified rural poverty. Large numbers of children lived with HIV, and an estimated 10.6 million children were orphaned by AIDS. Nigeria had 2.6 million such orphaned children (UNAIDS Prevention Gap Report 2016, cited in AVERT, 2018).

In 2000, AIDS medication cost $10 thousand per patient per year because of corporate patent monopolies. Medication was unaffordable for most people. At that time, the NGO Treatment Action Campaign (TAC) was demanding access to retroviral medications. Prime Minister Mbeki denied the link between HIV and AIDS and accused TAC of being a front for international pharmaceutical companies and the CIA (Geffen, 2010). Expensive antiretroviral drugs came down in price as a result of international campaigns and public protests. In 2001, the campaign for patent exemptions for essential medicines was successful at the WTO Doha summit (Bond, 2018a). South Africa restricted the availability of protective drugs for women during labour until 2003 and did not introduce a national adult AIDS campaign until the following year (Boseley, 2008). In 2008, a Harvard study estimated that as many as 365,000 people died unnecessarily because Mbeki's policies denied antiretroviral drugs to AIDS patients and to infected pregnant women to prevent their passing on the condition to their babies (Dugger, 2008). It was now possible to produce generic medicines and deliver free treatment to nearly four million patients. National life expectancy in South Africa increased from 52 to 64 between 2004 and 2017 (Bond, 2018a).

Another source of health problems is directly related to privatisation policies. The privatisation of water was added to structural adjustment loan conditions in the 1990s. The privatising of water excluded the poor from access to clean water in Africa where water-borne diseases were a major source of disease (Colgan, 2002). South Africa was one of the first countries in which the WB introduced water privatisation. When prices went up, many people could not afford to pay and were disconnected. This lack of clean water caused an outbreak of cholera in

KwaZulu Natal (Bond, 2014a). Though the Ebola outbreak was a major issue that received a lot of international media attention, the rates of death were far lower than those for diseases such as diarrhoea and dysentery (United Nations, 2015). Dysentery is a major but preventable health problem in SSA, particularly among children. The solution is the provision of safe drinking water. After 2000, only 24% of the population had access to improved drinking water (MDG Monitor, 2016).

The MDG for health were only partially achieved in SSA. Even though the prevalence of the three major diseases (respiratory diseases, malaria and HIV) decreased, the region still accounts for most global cases and deaths. Child mortality figures have dropped but not those for maternal mortality (MDG Monitor, 2016). High rates of child and maternal mortality at childbirth persist. In 2015, there were 551 deaths per 100,000 women. Another indication of underdevelopment — the birth rate for adolescent women aged between 15 and 19 years — was also high, 103 births per 1,000 (UNDP, 2016). There was a 52% drop in mortality rates for children from 179 to 86 per 1,000 births, but the goal — of reducing the number of deaths of under five-year-olds by two thirds — was not reached (Goldberg, 2015). Malaria continues to be a major problem in Africa even though the global incidence of the disease has dropped to 37%. Most of the world's malaria cases occur in 17 countries (80%), most in Africa.

2.1.2.3. *Education and literacy*

There are great variations in levels and quality of education throughout SSA (Graetz *et al.*, 2018). According to United Nations Educational, Scientific and Cultural Organization (UNESCO), 38% of African adults cannot read (153 million people) and female literacy is much lower than male literacy (UNESCO, 2016). The provision of good quality education is crucial to future economic development and social transformation. Though levels of literacy have improved in SSA, the region still lags behind other areas of the world. Rates for educational completion remain low (MDG Monitor, 2016). The education sector was undermined by structural adjustment policies which insisted on cuts to education funding and the introduction of fees (Colgan, 2002). In 2015, only 20% of African nations reached the MDG education target. Primary school completion rates were only 67%, so a third of children continued to leave school early. In the age bracket 15–24, the literacy rate was 75% in 58% of African countries. Only Chad, Ivory Coast and Niger had rates below 50% (MDG Monitor, 2016). The quality of education remains an issue in many parts of SSA.

At the other end of the educational spectrum, the region faces a major problem of 'brain drain.' Many skilled people leave to seek employment elsewhere (Bond, 2006). In 2008, an estimated 300,000 professionals lived and worked outside Africa. Between 1990 and 2008, an average of 90,000 professionals left SSA each year. There were two types of migration patterns: those going offshore to developed nations and those moving within the region. The latter group often move away from areas of conflict or poverty to economically stronger or politically stable areas. Losses in the health sector are a particular problem (Shinn,

2008). The African diaspora is a significant source of remittances sent back to the region. According to the WB, $20 billion in remittances was sent back to SSA in 2007, amounting to more than FDI and slightly less than foreign aid. Nigeria was receiving $2.5 billion annually in this way (Shinn, 2008). The economic downturn in recent years has seen a reduction in remittances (WB, n.d.d2).

2.1.2.4. *Labour and employment*

Poverty in SSA since 2000 has been closely tied to low wages, high levels of unemployment and underemployment. In 2012, only 29% of Africa's labour force had stable, wage-paying jobs (Leke *et al.*, 2014). One of the worst countries for unemployment is South Africa, with a rate of 26.7% in 2016, ranking 200th in the world. Rates are much higher among black males (CIA, 2019c). The highest levels of poverty are among rural workers who make up 65% of the labour force, though agriculture contributes only 32% of regional GDP. Rural workers include a wide spectrum from small-holder farmers to labourers in plantations and agri-businesses and casual labour. According to the International Labour Organisation (ILO), these workers do not earn a living wage and their working conditions are not reasonable or fair. Much agricultural work is seasonal and insecure. Agriculture also has a significant gender imbalance. Women make up 43% of the rural labour force but are particularly disadvantaged because they have less access to land, credit, education and technology (Pye-Smith, 2012). Improving productivity in rural areas would help raise these people out of poverty as well as diversify the economy and meet local food needs (Pearce, 2012).

In comparison to agriculture, employment levels in mining and resource extraction are relatively small and not proportional to the sector's contribution to GDP. Ownership in the resource sector throughout SSA is dominated by foreign or South African corporations. Neoliberal policies have kept wages low, though they are still higher than those in agriculture. Working conditions are poor and often dangerous. Miners are captive to the high prices set by mining companies for goods sold in mining communities. In 2011, thousands of workers in the resource sector were laid off after a dramatic slump in commodity sector prices (Bond, 2017d). The infamous Marikana strike against Lonmin in August 2012 began as a protest for a living wage and was a response to wage increases given to the white administrative staff. After 18 years of political freedom, South African miners were still living in poverty (Bond, 2014a).

SSA has the highest incidence of child labour in the world; approximately 20% of its children (72.1 million) work as slaves (UNDP, 2015). An estimated 31.5 million children worked in hazardous conditions in 2016. Child labour actually increased between 2012 and 2016. Most child labourers (85%) work in agriculture (61.4 million), another 11% work in the service sector (8.7 million) and 4% work in industry (2.7 million). The age of child labourers in Africa is very low (ILO, 2016). Many involved in hazardous work are on family farms. Child labour is prevalent in cocoa farming in the two main cocoa-producing countries of Ghana and Côte d'Ivoire (Ryan, 2011). Child labour is also used wherever tobacco is grown. One of the main tobacco-producing countries in SSA is

Malawi, also one of the poorest nations. Many children have to work to help their parents meet quotas, often without payment. Some work 12-hour days. The children also get poisoned by the high intakes of nicotine which they absorb from the tobacco plants (Palitza, 2011).

2.1.2.5. *Human trafficking and slavery*

Human trafficking is a major problem in SSA. In the 2017 US Trafficking in Persons Report, no African country qualified as 'tier 1.' Most nations in SSA fell into 'tier 2', with governments making efforts to comply with regulations but not meeting minimum standards. The worst African offenders were grouped in 'tier 3', not fully meeting the Trafficking Victims Protection Act's (TVPA) minimum standards and not making significant efforts to meet them. These countries included Burundi, Central African Republic, Comoros, Democratic Republic of the Congo, Congo, Equatorial Guinea, Eritrea, Guinea, Guinea-Bissau, Mali, Mauritania, South Sudan and Sudan. They are grouped with China, Russia, Iran and North Korea (US Department of State, 2017). Globally, 71% of the victims of trafficking are women and children, with one-third being children (21%), but in SSA, 66% of the victims are children. Female victims tend to be marketed for sexual slavery or marriage, while men and boys are used for exploitative work. In the mining industry, victims are used as soldiers, porters and slaves (United Nations Office of Drugs and Crime (UNODC), 2016). Rape is another form of exploitation common in countries in conflict.

An estimated 6.2 million people were enslaved in SSA in 2016, approximately 13.6% of the world's total enslaved people. The Walk Free Foundation conducted surveys in Ghana, Nigeria, South Africa and Ethiopia. Slavery in those countries takes the form of forced marriage and forced labour. The highest rates are in Central African Republic, DRC, Somalia, South Sudan, Sudan and Mauritania (Global Slavery Index, 2017). The abduction of children to become soldiers is another form of slavery. SSA has the highest number of child soldiers in the world. In states in conflict like DRC, many children are forced into becoming soldiers. Even when they are rescued, they face abuse and stigma (Bonney, 2016). Some multinational companies have been complicit in slavery. In 2005, the rubber company Firestone was taken to court in the US for practising slavery in its plantations in Liberia (Rizvi, 2005).

2.1.2.6. *Migrant labour*

A major cause of social dislocation in SSA is the lack of employment, which forces men to migrate in search of work in cities and neighbouring countries. When families are separated, extra burdens fall on the women left behind who have to work and raise children on their own (UNDP, 2015). Migrant labour also plays a major role in the spread of AIDs. The number of people migrating in SSA increased from 13.2 million in 2008 to 15.9 million in 2014, of these 8.3 million were migrant workers (ILO, 2015). International migration from SSA increased by 31% between 2010 and 2017. The number of migrants living outside their home countries reached 25 million in 2017. Migration destinations have also changed. In the 1990s, 75% of people migrated to other countries in SSA, but that figure had dropped to 68% by 2017. More migrants now leave for the EU, Norway and Switzerland (17% in 2017) as well as the US (Connor, 2018).

2.1.2.7. *Social change*

As the middle classes expanded after 2000, a slow transformation in the social structure took place (Kharas, 2010). The middle classes, defined as living on $4–20 a day, live mainly in the cities. They are spread unevenly throughout the region. An estimated third of the population in South Africa is middle class, compared to five percent in Kenya and Niger. Increased availability of education and economic opportunities has contributed to this expansion (African Economic Outlook, 2016). The chief economist at the African Development Bank has been more optimistic. In 2013, he claimed that a third of Africans were middle class living on incomes between $2 and $20 per day. Of that third, 20% were spending $2–4 and 13% were spending $4–20 a day. That is not enough to live on in Africa's cities today. The data also revealed that numbers living on over $20 a day were declining (Bond, 2017a).

One of the significant characteristics of the region is its young age profile. There are potential future benefits in this young population as populations elsewhere are ageing, particularly in India and China. Population densities in SSA are relatively low. A youthful labour force has economic potential if production could be transferred from countries with ageing populations. There are nearly 500 million people in the region of working age, and Africa's population is estimated to rise to 2.478 billion — 25% of the world's population — by 2050 and reach 39% by 2100 (United Nations Department of Economic and Social Affairs (DESA), 2015). By 2040, Africa's labour force will be bigger than China's and India's combined (Leke *et al.*, 2010). There is potential for investment to be diverted from Asia and for SSA to take over the manufacturing role that Asia and China have dominated since the late 1980s. For such an economic transformation to take place poverty needs to be reduced along with improvements in education and skills (Leke *et al.*, 2010). If social and economic development occur the projected population increases may not, as family sizes tend to fall when incomes rise (Rosling, 2018).

The rapid growth in inequality is another problem SSA is facing. This growth has been faster than the expansion of the middle classes, particularly in the cities. The average per capita income of the poorest 20% in SSA has dropped significantly, which undermines social and political development (Sundaram *et al.*, 2011). According to the Inequality Index using the Palma ratio, SSA has four of the five most unequal countries in the world. South Africa is the most unequal nation in the world followed by Namibia (2nd), Botswana (4th) and Central African Republic (5th) (Barr, 2017). Incongruously, South Africa had one of the highest human development ratings in the region in 2015 (0.666) and ranked 119th in the world (UNDP, 2016). In an effort to address historical inequality and economic transformation, and increase black participation in the economy, the South African government introduced Black Economic Empowerment (BEE) in

2003. This code promoted black ownership of companies, but rather than empowering the poor, it was the already wealthy who benefitted. Cyril Ramaphosa was one of the most prominent beneficiaries. He was a member of the original committee that drafted the bill. Over the next decade, Ramaphosa was elected to various executive and non-executive positions in the largest firms listed on the Johannesburg Stock Exchange. The roles he occupied helped favour these companies with government contracts and level their BEE status (News 24, 2015). He became president in 2018 when President Zuma resigned.

Rapid, unplanned and chaotic urban development has occurred recently in SSA. The urban population in the whole of the African continent grew from 28% in 1980 to 40% in 2010. Cities have become a destination for the poor. Most of the urban population (62%) live in slums with inadequate housing, poor sanitation, insufficient services and without access to clean water. They are at future risk from the effects of the climate crisis. There are high levels of insecure employment, unemployment and underemployment in the slums of major cities. Crime rates are also high. Despite these challenges, levels of poverty are lower in the cities than in the countryside (UNDP, 2016).

2.1.2.8. *Conclusion*

The imposition of structural adjustment policies (SAPs) in SSA was in essence (rather than in law) a crime against humanity. After 20 years of SAPs, in 2001, 381 million of the 682 million population lived in absolute poverty, a 200% increase on 1994 numbers (including population increases). Life expectancy dropped by 15% and at age 47 was the lowest in the world, 40% of the people were malnourished and 47% were without safe drinking water. In 42 of the poorest countries, healthcare spending declined by 50%, leading to a health crisis — rising health problems including AIDS deaths and infection rates — akin to genocide. From 1986 to 1996, spending on education in SSA declined (Ismi, 2002). SSA's political sovereignty and human development since 2000 continued to be compromised by external conditionalities resulting from debt burdens and neoliberal loan conditions. The SSA region was still in the straitjacket of indebtedness to the US and BWIs, and other members of the Washington Consensus. It remains subject to the neoliberal policies imposed by lenders. Human development continues to be held back by these prescriptions which forbid subsidies for health and education and tariffs to protect local producers. Since 2000, the region has seen a higher incidence of peaceful transitions of power and evidence of progress towards democracy. SSA had some of the highest growth rates in the world in the decade after 2000 and there was optimism that Africa was on the brink of major social transition but hopes faded in the next decade. Incidents of corruption are still widespread. Some of the most damaging impacts on human development are caused by the burdens of debt repayment and tax avoidance by foreign corporations. Despite the rhetoric of Africa rising, there have only been small improvements in human development. A reduction in poverty rates has been offset by population increases and the actual numbers living in poverty have risen. Levels of human development and social justice are much better measures of national well-being than economic growth has been widely acknowledged since 1990 (UNDP, 1990). SSA still has the highest levels of poverty in the world and was the region where MDG achievements were least successful. Ongoing economic stagnation does not bode well for human development in the region.

2.2. Profit

In 1981, at the start of the structural adjustment period, Walter Rodney described what had been happening in Africa as 'Growth without development' — profit going abroad, with dependency and reinforced underdevelopment increasing at home (1981). Rodney could not have envisaged the way in which the global economy would develop and how the international balance of power would intensify these processes in Africa after the 1970s. The imposition of neoliberal policies caused social and economic stagnation (underdevelopment) as well as enabled a vast increase of legal (profits) and illegal financial outflows (IFF) from Africa. Today, SSA is both 'more integrated into the global economy and more marginalised' through these IFF (Ndikumana, 2017). There has been a change in external attitudes towards SSA in the 21st century. In 2000, *The Economist* ran a lead article called 'Hopeless Africa' (2000). After 2010, the tone of external reporting changed to talk of 'Africa Rising' (*The Economist*, 2011; *Time Magazine*, 2012). Optimism about SSA's fortunes was short-lived, however, as the region began to experience the effects of the international economic downturn through reduced demand for its resources after 2011.

In the 1970s, governments in SSA depended on borrowing to function. After the debt crisis in 1982 when commercial loans dried up, countries turned to the WB and IMF, who assumed a new 'saviour status' (Hertz, 2004). The WB had previously loaned for specific projects but now broadened its lending to non-specific loans. Staff at the BWIs were pressured to lend and keep lending, and job security and promotion were dependent on meeting loan targets. Hertz considers this to be one reason the WB funded so many unsound projects at this time (2004). Indebted governments had to comply with lender demands — implementing structural adjustment policies (SAPs) — before further loans were advanced. The rationale for the imposition of SAPs was that they would stimulate growth and enable debt repayment. Countries were advanced loans to service debt and to implement BWIs policies. SAPs were imposed on most (38) of the nations in SSA. These conditions included fiscal austerity (cutbacks to reduce budget deficits and create space for multinationals), privatisation, deregulation and trade liberalisation (Halifax Initiative, 2004). Structural adjustment loans came with as many as a hundred conditions (Hertz, 2004). The BWIs were supported in structural adjustment programmes by the broader Washington Consensus of multilateral organisations, the Paris Club of creditors, OECD aid donors (DAC), and international financial institutions, all of whom imposed neoliberal conditions on their aid and loans. Multinational companies also supported the policies which brought them benefits.

BWI programmes and loan conditions evolved over the decades. During the 1990s, the WB became the largest lender for water privatisation, and most WB loans after 1998 included water privatisation conditions (Barlow & Clarke, 2004b). The result of these policies was two decades of economic stagnation in SSA. Countries did not manage to achieve economic development and repay their loans. The policies undermined economic development in many cases. During the 1990s, there was a rising tide of criticism of structural adjustment and protests at G7, BWIs and WTO meetings around the world. The WB was criticised as providing 'defensive lending', simply supplying money so previous loans could be paid back as countries continued to be given loans whether or not there was evidence of policy improvement (Easterley, 2007). The same criticism applies to the IMF which was originally established to assist with temporary financial relief in order to ensure international financial stability. By the 1980s, the institution was making loans continuously available for countries with 'unpayable debts' (Sachs, 2002). The WB admitted in 2002 that the first 20 years of structural adjustment loans had not promoted economic growth (WB, 2002, cited in Easterley, 2007). Even the IMF admitted that 'adjustment policies while beneficial in the long run may adversely affect certain segments in the short run' (cited in Hertz, 2004).

2.2.1. *Economic profile*

There are vast differences in the profiles and sizes of individual economies within SSA, which are not evident in regional economic averages. National economic profiles are the product of a complex mix of variables: natural resources, climatic factors, politics, leadership, historical legacies and current relationships, as well as international demand for key exports. There are also extreme differences in the size of countries in the region, geographically, economically and in terms of population. Nigeria, South Africa and Angola are the largest economies with combined GDP in 2016 of $822.4 billion, 54.8% of the GDP of SSA (GDP figures in 2016: SSA ($1.5 trillion), South Africa ($295.7 billion), Nigeria ($404.6 billion) and Angola ($122.1 billion) (WB, n.d.b2). Population size impacts GDP per capita rates, which are low in most SSA countries. Large national GDP figures are not correlated here with low levels of poverty or inequality. Nigeria has the largest GDP, but its GDP per capita of $6,100 in 2016 was one of the lowest in the world. Around 40% of the population was living in poverty, and inequality is a major problem (CIA, 2020a).

In 2000, the GDP of nations in SSA was significantly smaller than that in other regions, and growth rates were also lower. After 2000, SSA had some of the highest growth rates in the world. At that time, six of the 10 fastest growing economies in the world were in Africa: Angola, Nigeria, Ethiopia, Chad, Mozambique and Rwanda. Their growth rates averaged 8% (*The Economist*, 2011a). By the end of the decade, the Western financial media were changing their stories. Both *The Economist* (2011) and *Time Magazine* (2012) ran 'Africa Rising' cover stories, and *The Economist* was 'regretting' having labelled Africa 'the hopeless continent' (*ibid*). The MGI was also reporting favourably

(Leke *et al.*, 2010). Goldman Sachs was encouraging investment — 'Africa's Turn: Now is the time to invest in Africa' (The Fletcher School, 2012). The views of the foreign investment sector do not, however, represent the reality of people's daily lives. Patrick Bond has challenged the concept of 'Africa Rising' as it was based only on the healthy growth rates and increasing GDP per capita. Human development indicators provided contrary evidence that much else had changed in SSA. High growth rates contributed little to economic development because they were based on resource extraction which was primarily in the hands of foreign or South African companies. Most of the profits were exported, and companies avoided paying appropriate taxes or reinvesting them in the local economy (2017a).

Although GDP per capita in SSA increased between 2000 and 2016, because of comparable increases elsewhere, SSA's GDP as a percentage of world GDP increased by a small amount — from 1.1% to 1.2% (World GDP was $33.5 trillion in 2000 and $75.8 trillion in 2016) (WB, n.d.a2). This economic imbalance continues to be reflected in economic and political relationships. The West does not listen to poor countries. The West sets the aid and trade rules and Africa gets what the West decides to give it (Bolton, 2008). Once African countries became indebted to the West, they lost both their political and economic sovereignty. The West has continued to inflict loan conditions and trade rules through the BWIs, WTO and bilateral aid partners, conditions that benefit them and exploit SSA. Neoliberal policies have contributed to a net transfer of wealth out of SSA primarily through illegitimate financial outflows and corporate tax evasion.

2.2.2. *Economic growth*

SSA's change of economic fortunes in the first decade of the 21st century was the result of a rise in world commodity prices because of increasing demand from China. According to recent WB data, SSA's average annual growth rate between 2001 and 2012 was 4.6%, something that had not occurred since the average growth rate of 4.7% between 1961 and 1970. Between 1980 and 2000, growth rates dropped to an average of 2.7% (Lopes, 2013), but from 2000 to 2008, the region had some of the highest growth rates in the world, with real GDP rising by 4.9%, more than double the rates of the 1980s and 1990s (WB, n.d.b2). This high growth has been accompanied by significant increases in regional and national GNI per capita rates. SSA's GDP was valued at $368 billion in 2000; GNI per capita (Atlas method) was $604, and in 2016, its GDP was valued at $1.49 trillion, a decline from $1.77 trillion in 2014. GNI per capita in 2016 was $1,516 (Atlas method), a 300% increase in 2000 (WB, n.d.b2). 'The Atlas method smooths exchange rate fluctuations using a three-year moving average, price-adjusted conversion factor' (WB, n.d.c1 data).

Resource exports were the reason behind the high growth rates in SSA after 2000 (Songwe & Winter, 2012). Most growth was in the resource extraction sectors, which were primarily owned by foreign companies since the sale of state assets under the structural adjustment policies (Melzter Commission, 2000; Structural Adjustment Participatory Review International Network

(SAPRIN), 2004). Researchers at the MGI saw differently. In 2010, they considered only one-third of the increased growth rates after 2000 resulted from higher resource prices and related government spending. The other two-thirds came from internal structural changes and changes in the wholesale, retail, transportation, telecommunications and manufacturing sectors. Urbanisation had stimulated the construction of roads, buildings and water systems. Other positive economic changes included inflation rates dropping from 22% in the 1990s to 8% after 2000, a 25% reduction in foreign debt and a reduction in budget deficits by 66%. They considered African governments to have adopted neoliberal policies to energise markets, privatise state-owned enterprises, increase the openness of trade, lower corporate taxes, strengthen regulatory and legal systems and provide critical physical and social infrastructure. Economic growth accelerated across the continent in 27 of the 30 largest economies. Countries with and without significant resource exports had similar GDP growth rates. They also saw growth rates as the source of improvements in human development, poverty reduction, health and education (Leke *et al.*, 2010). The same MGI researchers analysed country profiles in terms of the diversity of the economies and differentiated oil exporters from the rest. South Africa was considered the only diversified economy; the other two categories were those transitioning to diversity and pre-transition economies (*ibid*). In 2016, the MGI recommended that governments address the continent's productivity and drive growth by focusing on six priorities: mobilising more domestic resources, aggressively diversifying economies, accelerating infrastructure development, deepening regional integration, expanding education and ensuring healthy urbanisation (2016). The MGI reports reflected advice from a financial advisory perspective rather than that of human development. Financial advisors focused on investment opportunities for clients and ignored the impact of external pressures like debt servicing, SAPs and even the impact of fluctuating demand from China on SSA.

Between 2002 and 2011, world commodity prices increased up to 380% (Bond, 2017f). In 2011, those international commodity prices dropped dramatically when reduced demand for Chinese goods flowed through to a reduced need for imported resources. There was a reduction in trade credit, foreign investment and aid in Africa after the GFC. Remittances also went down. Fluctuations in commodity prices were reflected in fluctuating growth rates. In 2009, regional growth rates declined to 2.8% and then climbed to 5.3% in 2013 (IMF, 2014). The WB growth figures for 2013 are slightly different with growth rates of 4.9% in 2013, 4.5% in 2014 and a further decline in 2015 to 3.0% (WB, 2016a). By 2016, growth had slowed to 1.3% (WB, 2017b). Economic growth in that year was the lowest for more than 20 years, down to 1.5% from 5% in 2011 (IMF, 2017c). In some years, countries in SSA had very low or negative growth rates. In South Africa, growth rates were 1.3% in 2015, 0.6% in 2016 and 1.3% in 2017 (CIA, 2019c). Oil exporters suffered a drop in growth rates from an average of 7.3% between 2000 and 2010 to 4% between 2010 and 2015, while non-oil exporting countries improved from 4.1% between 2000 and 2010 to 4.4% between 2010 and 2015 (MGI, 2016).

2.2.3. *Sector profiles*

2.2.3.1. *Resource extraction*

Most economies in SSA are reliant on one or two exports. The exemption is South Africa which has a more diversified economy although it still relies heavily on resource exports. Around half of the economies in SSA are dependent on resource exports, while the rest rely on agricultural exports. Many governments do not own the resource assets but depend on company taxes as their main form of income. Other governments are in joint ventures with foreign companies (Angola and Nigeria). Resource extraction is capital intensive and is dominated by foreign multinational companies that operate in relatively concentrated, self-contained enclaves. Resource extraction can continue even where there is civil unrest (Ferguson, 2005). In recent years, foreign companies have been hiring private security firms like Haliburton to protect their assets and ensure continuity of operations.

The resource extraction sector is characterised by a lack of transparency, the hiding of large profits and rampant corruption, and it is where most illegal financial flows and tax evasion occur. The term 'resource curse' refers to the profiles of the many countries reliant on mineral and oil exports. A relatively small rent-seeking elite has captured the vast wealth derived from resources. These 'resource curse' countries tend to have high rates of poverty, violence, crime and civic unrest (Shaxon, 2007). The WB Report 'Where is the Wealth of Nations?' identified the largest resource exporters — Nigeria, Zambia, Mauritania, Gabon, Congo and South Africa — as being characterised by stagnant savings and low capital accumulation (WB, 2005). The oil-exporting countries earn the most revenues, but because of corruption, they also are some of the most indebted.

Because economies remained locked into a small number of exports, large foreign multinational companies are politically important to governments. In South Africa, the locally owned multinational companies have similar political power and are also influential throughout the region. Collusion between multinational companies and governments is common. The lack of transparency enables the payment of bribes and the theft of public money by local officials and politicians, and governments have sided with companies against the interests of the people. The Nigerian government has always had close ties with major oil companies operating in the Niger Delta. This was the government that ordered the deaths of the Ogoni activists, including Ken Saro-Wiwa, protesting against Shell in the 1990s (The Goldman Environmental Prize, 1995). Similarly, at the Lonmin Mine during the Marikana mining dispute in 2012, vice president and board member Cyril Ramaphosa called in the South African police who shot 34 miners (Bond, 2018a).

2.2.3.2. *Manufacturing*

According to the World Economic Forum, manufacturing in SSA made up 10% of GDP in the 1970s. This had not changed by 2013. Africa's share of global manufacturing meanwhile had gone down from 3% in the 1970s to 2% (Newman *et al.*, 2017). There was limited expansion in light industry in SSA in the years after independence. In the 1960s and 1970s, China funded many aid projects, establishing small import substitution industries in many countries. They found that workers did not work as hard as in China, productivity was lower and the workforce was less educated. Furthermore, when projects were handed over to local people, the projects failed. Textile production in many SSA countries, especially the cotton-producing countries of Malawi, Tanzania, Zimbabwe and Kenya, contracted in the 1990s. Few of these countries were exporting (Brautigam, 2009). Manufacturing was undermined by the removal of tariffs under the SAPs. Locally produced products were undercut by cheap foreign imports (Dembele, 2004). Brautigam considers that the BWI liberalisation policies played a far greater role in this situation than competition from Chinese exports. The export of used clothes to Africa from the US was another contributing factor in the decline of the African textile industry (2009).

Recently, the annual growth in manufacturing (3.5%) in SSA has been higher than the global average, increasing from $72 billion in 2005 to $157 billion in 2014. Manufacturing exports doubled from $50 billion in 2005 to more than $100 billion in 2014. Many countries have also seen an increase in foreign direct investment (FDI). Countries in SSA are exporting more to each other, increasing from 20% of exports in 2005 to 34% in 2014. More exports are also going to countries in Asia (Overseas Development Institute (ODI), 2016). Output per person in manufacturing continues to be low, a third of the average for developing countries, but still five times higher than in agriculture. Manufacturing exports are 10% of the developing country average (Newman *et al.*, 2017). The MDG ignored work and employment, but 'decent work and economic growth' (Goal 8) was introduced as one of the 2015 SDG's (United Nations, n.d.). Only one in five people in Africa are in the wage economy, so building up manufacturing is crucial to increasing jobs and promoting economic diversification.

2.2.3.3. *Agriculture*

A number of SSA nations continue to be primarily agricultural exporters. In many of these countries, agricultural products accounted for 30–53% of GDP in 2014 (Kenya, Tanzania, Malawi, Mali, Ethiopia and Chad) (Schuttenheim, 2018). Between 1966 and 1970, Africa was self-sufficient in food and a food exporter. Since then, agricultural development in SSA has been distorted by the imposition of neoliberal policies. The emphasis on export-driven agriculture under structural adjustment policies increased local food insecurity and reduced diversity and self-sufficiency. Production for the local market was neglected (Bello, 2008). Lifting of price controls increased fertiliser prices, and simultaneously, agricultural credit systems and subsidies were cut back. This led to reduced fertiliser use, lower yields and lower investment (Bello, 2008). By 2009, usage by African farmers of fertilisers was one-tenth the global average per hectare (Toulmin, 2009). Africa has been a net importer of agricultural products since the 1970s and a net importer of food since the 1980s. Between 1980 and 2007, net food imports rose annually by 3.4% as productivity stagnated and the population grew. Many countries have been increasingly dependent on imported food, which was relatively cheap when it came from countries where agriculture is subsidised. When food prices increased in 2008, importing food became problematic as other sectors of the economy were often not earning enough to pay for these imports (Rakotoarisoa *et al.*, 2011). By 2008, Africa was importing 25% of its food (Bello, 2008). Agricultural productivity continues to be low even compared to other developing nations. Any expansion in production has been the result of growth in cropping areas rather than mechanisation or labour productivity which has only marginally improved in the previous 30 years. There are also high losses after harvesting. Fertiliser use remains very low compared to other regions. Most crops are rain-fed and levels of irrigation are also low. There is an urgent need for more education, research and development expenditure (OECD & FAO, 2016).

The majority of the population in SSA still work in agriculture (65%) but the region's agriculture has never been very productive or competitive (Pye-Smith, 2012). Small-holder farming is the traditional African production model, and there are around 33 million farms (80%) smaller than two hectares. Agricultural work is labour-intensive with little use of mechanisation or technology. Productivity levels and income levels are low. Employment is also insecure. Agriculture may employ the majority of people, but the sector gets little government funding and is chronically undercapitalised (Cotula *et al.*, 2009). Governments in SSA have neglected agriculture. Agricultural spending has only slightly increased, from 2.3% of GDP in the 1980s to 4.6% after 2000, which is lower than that in other countries (IMF, cited in Fan & Saurkar, n.d.). The SSA regional average hides great variations, some countries spending much more and others less.

Trade liberalisation has also been detrimental to agriculture in SSA. WTO trade rules allowed wealthy countries to subsidise their own agricultural production while cutting subsidies for farmers in SSA. The US offloaded its cotton at 25–55% of the cost of production which destroyed producers in West and Central Africa (Bello, 2008). The focus on exports bypasses many working in agriculture in remote areas with poor transportation links. Another issue with concentrating on export-driven agriculture is that any lending is directed to these crops (for example, the cocoa industry in Ghana) and the rest of the sector is ignored (Anyinam, 1994). Another unanticipated problem was the imposition of the same policies on many countries producing similar crops. This led to overproduction, triggering international price collapses and further reducing government incomes. Ghana's successful expansion of cocoa production led to a 48% drop in the international price of cocoa between 1986 and 1989. In 2002–2003, a collapse in coffee prices contributed to another food emergency in Ethiopia (Bello, 2008). Uganda was the first country to qualify for debt relief under the HIPCI, but benefits were soon wiped out by the drop in coffee prices (Isar, 2012).

The high percentage of the population who work in agriculture are the poorest people in the region. Improving agricultural productivity is essential to reducing poverty in SSA. If small holders were more productive, they could feed the local population and reduce reliance on food imports. In 2003, the African Union set up the Comprehensive Africa Agriculture Development Programme (CAADP) as part of the New Partnership for Africa's Development (NEPAD). The set target for governments was to spend 10% of GDP on agriculture each year. By 2009, only seven out of 37 countries had reached this target. The Economic Community of West African States (ECOWAS) nations made the most progress in reaching the targets. Agricultural spending in the Sahel region and in less developed countries was heavily dependent on foreign aid. At the G7 summit in L'Aquila in 2008, $22 billion was pledged for sustainable agricultural development and to ensure adequate food aid assistance between 2009 and 2012 (G7 Research Group, 2009). One year later, it was reported by Action Aid that less than a third of the funding pledged was new funding, over and above the funding for 2006–2008, and some countries, such as Italy, had reduced their agricultural aid (The Chicago Council on Global Affairs, 2010). FAO reported in 2017 that in Africa between 2001 and 2017 expenditure on agriculture declined from 3.66% to 2.30% of GDP (FAO, 2019).

There have been some agricultural export success stories in SSA. In Kenya, farmers managed to sell to British supermarkets by making contract deals with big companies. They are earning a good income. Despite criticisms of the carbon footprint of transporting these products, the footprint is still less than that created by production in the heated greenhouses of Europe (Pearce, 2012a). This is unlikely to provide a model for the wider sector. The Kenyan flower industry has been held up as another success story for export-led growth in a new product area, but this has been disastrous for workers. There are many downsides to this sector. It is dominated by Kampala elites who operate in much the same way as the former colonists. They squeeze as much profit from workers, pay the lowest possible wages and ignore the environmental impacts of the industry (Amoding & Wass, 2015).

The FAO study of agriculture in SSA concluded that there is an urgent need to reinstate and expand the public services supporting agriculture. Key priorities include research and extension services, irrigation and power supply, rural roads, storage facilities, education and health care. Putting in place the infrastructure to connect farmers to markets is expensive because population density is low. Transport costs are even higher in the landlocked countries where 40% of agricultural land is located. High transport costs can make up 77% of the value of exports (FAO, 2009). Many of these problems have been made worse by the structural adjustment policies enforced by the BWIs, along with the unequal trade rules enforced by the WTO. These have been harmful to agriculture in SSA by opening up local markets to foreign competition while denying SSA access to the EU and US markets.

2.2.3.4. *Services*

SSA has had an infrastructure deficit since the colonial era. It suffers from shortages in a wide range of services. National road and rail systems are based on the systems built by colonists to facilitate resource exports. These continue to be the principal transport links. The main arteries lead from the interior to the coast, and internal linkages between nations continue to be poor. Better links between countries within SSA are vital to the promotion of regional trade. With only a brief interval after independence before structural adjustment policies were imposed, there was little time to address infrastructure deficits. Since then, countries have spent so much on debt servicing there has been little money for infrastructure. After 2000, the African Union and NEPAD prioritised the building of infrastructure as essential for economic development. Apart from the building of dams, requests for infrastructure were ignored by the West (Brautigam, 2009). When China came looking for resources in the 1990s, they quickly responded to requests for infrastructure, and after 2000, many contracts were resource-for-infrastructure exchanges.

The energy sector has attracted the most BWIs lending. Most of these loans are intended to serve the interests of corporations and the business sector. Notable examples include the funding of the Bujagali dam in Uganda and Eskom coal-fired power plants. The WB assisted the building of two of the biggest coal-fired plants in the world: the Medupi and Kusile plants. The 28 corporations in South Africa's Energy Intensive Users Group consume approximately 44% of Eskom's energy production (Bond, 2018). Of this group, 48% are in mining and quarrying and 27% in manufacturing. The group claims it contributes over 20% of South Africa's GDP (Energy Intensive Users Group of South Africa, 2019). There have been ongoing problems with both plants. They were behind schedule, over budget and have continued to operate poorly. Electricity shutdowns are still common (Compton, 2019). Problems with Eskom reflect the 2014 and 2016 Price Waterhouse Coopers' Economic Crimes surveys, which identified the South African corporate elite as the world's most corrupt (Price Waterhouse Coopers, 2014, 2016). Though the stated objective of the Bujagali dam project in Uganda was the provision of low-cost electricity to Uganda, most of the population were not on the grid. Energy prices increased. Alternative energy options to the big dam solution were not explored (Irigoyen, 2017).

Services provided by foreign companies — such as banking and insurance — have prioritised the interests of the corporate sector. Banking systems throughout the region are weak or absent, especially in rural areas. Africa has the lowest level of banking penetration in the world, a ratio of five banks per 100,000 people in most countries, with South Africa the exception, at 17 banks per 100,000 people. Demand for banking services has been driven by the need to transfer remittances. With the large numbers of migrant workers, mobile banking has accelerated dramatically. This became possible before the advent of smartphones (Chironga *et al.*, 2018). The telecommunications sector has expanded rapidly in SSA since 2000. Mobile phones have had a major impact on everyday life by providing basic services. Apart from improving communications in a region where landline provision was poor, mobile phones have made huge differences to SSA's chronically underresourced banking and health sectors. The health sector has a shortage of health professionals and many people live at a distance from health clinics. Mobile phones are used to provide services to the ill, including sending reminders to patients to take their medication. Phones are also used to help fieldworkers diagnose other illnesses and offer treatment at a distance from hospitals (Kembaro, 2012).

Kenya had one of the fastest uptakes of mobile phones in the developing world, with 75% of the population owning a mobile phone by 2012. Rural people's lives have changed rapidly since then. These phones were not usually smartphones. Pioneering work in providing mobile banking occurred in Kenya. The text-based payment system M-Pesa was launched in 2007 and by 2011 was providing M-banking services to more than 70% of the adult population. Kenya has one of the highest levels of M-banking in the world. According to the IMF in 2011, M-Pesa processed more transactions a day than Western Union did globally. Mobile phones were also used by rural farmers to market their products. Instead of taking long journeys to markets, they were able to optimise market opportunities by identifying supply and demand shortages via their phones. They were then able to travel to sell products where demand or prices were higher. A text-based app called M-Farm has enabled subsistence farmers to post their produce for sale on the web and find buyers more easily. They were also able to bargain collectively (Gatehouse, 2012).

2.2.4. *Trade*

SSA suffers from unequal trade relationships because the international trade system is biased in favour of the US and G7. The BWIs and WTO imposed trade liberalisation on SSA (removing subsidies, enforcing asset sales and deregulation of economies) without implementing the same policies in the high-income nations. Free trade agreements imposed as part of structural adjustment loan conditions demanded the opening of markets, extensive intellectual property rights and investment protection (Action Aid, 2005).

The profile of SSA's trading partners has changed since 2000. Its major trading partners in the 20th century were the US and the EU, but trade with China began to increase in the 1990s. In 2009, China overtook the US as the region's largest trading partner. Trade figures peaked in 2011 and then ebbed as demand from China slowed. The value of SSA's external trade increased from $151 billion in 2000 to $739 billion in 2011 and then dropped to $381 billion in 2016 (WB, n.d.d2). SSA's trade was only 1.1% of world trade in 2016 (WB, n.d.e1). After having healthy trade balances in the first decade, exports declined, and by 2016, SSA had a trade deficit with China (China Africa Research Initiative (CARI), 2018a). The US continued its trade deficit with Africa over the same period because of its oil imports, but that deficit has contracted significantly (US Census Bureau, 2020). SSA's external trade continues to be dominated by primary resources, oil, minerals, agricultural products and textiles.

2.2.5. *Financial inflows*

Though it is often pointed out that aid and finance from China are difficult to unravel (Brautigam, 2009), the same can be said about loans and aid from the West, which is a mix of bilateral and multilateral aid (grants and low-interest loans) and various forms of commercial loans. The OECD definition of aid specifies that it takes the form of grants and concessional loans. Specifically excluded are military aid and promotion of donors' security interests along with 'transactions that have primarily commercial objectives such as export credits' (2019). The mix is blurred by the amounts of tied aid, debt relief (phantom aid) and export credits. Inward finance to SSA includes FDI, loans (commercial, bilateral and multilateral), aid (bilateral and multilateral) and remittances from abroad. The international economic downturn has reduced the amount of remittances.

2.2.5.1. *Commercial loans and export credits: Bilateral, multilateral and commercial loans*

The cause of SSA's debt problems has been in borrowing more than its capacity for repayment. Lenders must share the blame. Most SSA loans have never been fully repaid. One exception was Angola which repaid its loans soon after 2004 with its expanding oil revenues (Brautigam, 2009). Loans to governments in SSA have come from many sources. Concessional loans have been part of the aid from bilateral and multilateral lenders to low-income countries, while other loans are at commercial rates. The OECD Development Assistance Committee (DAC) definition of aid includes interest-bearing loans, 25% of the aid must be a grant (n.d.a.). Commercial banks have also supplied loans. The BWIs have been the major source of finance for SSA since the 1960s, particularly the WB, and much of that finance is obtained through selling bonds. Early loans to Africa had very low interest rates until the 1970s when rates spiked with the oil crisis. Early commercial lending to Africa was more restrained but by 1982 had reached 35% of African debt (Hertz, 2004). Export credit agencies encouraged commercial banks to lend to developing nations by guaranteeing the loans if the country defaulted, the loan being folded into the nation's bilateral debt. Commercial loans meant paying commercial interest rates (rather than lower levels of bilateral and multilateral lending), which increases debt (Hertz, 2004). The government guarantee leaves the door open for irresponsible lending. In the 1970s, Western banks were awash with funds and the WB also encouraged generous private lending; in fact, employee bonuses were awarded based on the amount of loans they facilitated. In the 1980s, the IMF also increased its lending to developing countries (Hertz, 2004).

2.2.5.2. *Aid, Official Development Assistance (ODA) grants and concessional loans*

At the end of the Cold War in the 1990s, foreign aid to SSA dipped. It then increased from $13.05 billion in 2000 to $40.25 billion in 2008. Aid continued to rise reaching $47.33 billion in 2011 and then contracting to $44.293 billion in 2016 (WB, n.d.d2). Except for 2005 and 2006 when more aid went to Asia, Africa was the largest recipient of foreign aid in the world between 2001 and 2014. Allocation differences between Asia and Africa levelled out in 2014 when both received 33% of total DAC aid (OECD, 2016). Despite the increasing amounts of ODA, aid per capita in Africa actually declined after 2011, from $52.4 to $46 per capita in 2016, because the population increased (WB, n.d.e1). That year, Africa received $52 billion in aid, 32% of the $163 billion figure for total aid (OECD, 2018). The balance was made up of smaller donations. In 2016, the major aid donors to Africa were the US ($9.8 billion, 20%), the EU ($6.3 billion, 13%), IDA ($5.8 billion, 12%), the UK ($3.8 billion, 8%) and Germany ($34.1 billion, 7%). The top recipients in Africa were Ethiopia ($4.1 billion), Nigeria ($2.5 billion), Tanzania ($2.3 billion), Kenya ($2.2 billion) and Egypt ($2.1 billion)

(OECD, 2018). Total aid figures are misleading. According to NGO Action Aid, the $69 billion in aid given to SSA in 2003 was reduced to $27 billion by the time the variables such as 'tied aid' (attached to donor country products) and debt relief were considered. The transaction and administrative costs of paying out aid funds are also deducted and can be as high as 14% of the total aid allocated. These factors benefit the donor. Aid often includes technical assistance by Western experts (as much as 25%) to facilitate detrimental processes like privatisation and monetary conditions. When Action Aid investigated the per capita figures for aid in 2003, they found that the countries at the lowest end of the Human Development Index were not getting more aid (cited in Bond, 2006). Easterley confirmed this in 2007. The Commission for Africa has claimed that only a small percentage of aid is technically without ties, with the US and Italy the worst 'tied aid' offenders (cited in Bond, 2006). Non-delivery of aid is also a major problem. An NGO survey by One International in 2010 revealed funding gaps in the $25 billion in aid committed by the G8 between 2005 and 2010 to Africa. A number of countries had failed to meet commitments (UN Non-Government Liaison Service, 2010).

2.2.5.3. *Remittances*

Migrant workers contribute significantly to SSA's balance of payment figures through the remittances they send home. These play an important role, particularly in the Horn of Africa. The foreign diaspora also contribute remittances. The amount of remittances has increased since the 1970s, and the WB estimated that remittances in 2007 reached $20 billion, higher than that of FDI and nearly equal the amount of aid to SSA. Nigeria with the largest population receives the most remittances in the region, on average $2.5 billion annually. In 2000, remittances in Ethiopia were almost equivalent to earnings from coffee exports (Shinn, 2008). That year, the value of remittances was $4.8 billion, increasing to a peak in 2015 of $42.5 billion and then declining to $38.4 billion in 2016 (WB, n.d.e1). A different set of figures from the NGO sector estimated that $31 billion sent in remittance in 2015 was approximately equivalent to the profits exported by multinational companies, of $31.2 billion (Curtis, 2017).

2.2.5.4. *Foreign Direct Investment (FDI)*

According to Oxfam, 'international investment plays a vital role in development and poverty reduction. Investment can improve livelihoods and bring jobs, services and infrastructure when it is managed responsibly within the context of an effective regulatory framework' (2011). Before independence, most investments in Africa were foreign. On the eve of independence, most countries experienced a flight of capital and investment. After independence, African governments offered incentives to encourage companies to return, including co-financing, tax holidays, protection and repressive labour laws, but foreign investment was still restrained and there was no option to the 'state taking charge of the development process' (Mkandawire & Soludo, 1998). For the last 50 years, foreign investment has been lower in SSA than in Asia. In the decades of independence, many foreign investors were not interested in Africa as, apart from resource extraction, it was seen as too risky. Though it required large investments, resource extraction attracted most foreign investments in SSA because the profits were high. During the structural adjustment decades, much FDI was purchasing assets that governments were being pressured to sell. Some of the highest levels of FDI occurred in South Africa in the late 1990s, but it was more of an accounting exercise than a new investment. It was investment from South African companies that had relocated to London after 1994 when Mandela came to power (Bond, 2006). FDI in the region increased, rising from $6.8 billion in 2000 to a high of $42.8 billion in 2011 and then declining to $31 billion in 2016, approximately 25% of all financial inflows (WB, n.d.g). By 2016, China had become the largest single source of foreign investment in SSA. Since 2005, it had invested in 293 FDI projects involving an investment of $66.4 billion (Xingua, 2017).

2.2.5.5. *Bartering resources for infrastructure*

Though not strictly direct investment, China has been supplying services in exchange for urgently needed infrastructure in SSA since 2000. For many years, foreign donors and investors were not interested in infrastructure projects apart from the building of dams. In resource-rich countries, China exchanged infrastructure for resources or provided loans with resources as collateral. The money effectively stayed in China, paid to Chinese corporations who then did the work. This profited Chinese corporations who were building the infrastructure and providing the resources that China needed, particularly oil. The first large infrastructure project undertaken was assisting with the rebuilding of Angola at the end of the civil war. From 2004, a series of similar arrangements were made with other resource-rich countries (Brautigam, 2011).

2.2.6. *Financial outflows*

2.2.6.1. *Legal financial outflows*

SSA suffers from a net outflow of funds. Between 1970 and 2002, the region received $294 billion in disbursements and paid $268 billion in debt servicing but remained with a debt stock of $210 billion. Discounting interest and interest on arrears, further payment of the outstanding debt would represent a reverse transfer of resources (UNCTAD, 2004). Financial outflows increased after 2000. In 2015, loans to Africa amounted to $32.8 billion (Curtis, 2017), while $18 billion was paid out in interest on debt and principal payments (Curtis, 2017). In 2015, African countries received about $19 billion in aid but more than three times that amount, $68 billion, was taken out of Africa through capital flight and corporate capital transfers, legal or illegal (Curtis, 2017).

Legal financial outflows (LFFs) include debt servicing, loan repayments and corporate repatriation of profits (often from companies bought cheaply under the structural adjustment requirements). Profits have increased because these companies could keep paying low wages and regulatory frameworks were lighter under the structural adjustment programmes. Neoliberal policies persisted and were expanded under the conditions of debt relief in the HIPCI from 1996 to 2017 and the Multilateral Debt Relief Initiative (MDRI) (2005–2017).

2.2.6.2. *Illegitimate financial outflows*

There are high levels of corruption in SSA, and illegal outflows of funds have played a major role in the African continent's lack of economic development. During the Cold War years, corrupt politicians were responsible for most of the illegal flows, transferring expropriated funds to foreign bank accounts (Ayittey, 1994). Sustained illicit outflows have turned Africa into a net creditor to the rest of the world (Adow, 2014). Foreign governments, multinational organisations and corporations as well as local politicians have all been guilty of corrupt behaviour. Governments lending or providing aid to corrupt and brutal leaders are complicit in their activities. Neoliberal policies have also played a role in illegitimate financial flows. Financial deregulation made capital flight easier (Clough, 2017).

A background study commissioned by the Tana High Level Forum on African Security in 2014 reported that illicit flows had grown by 12.1% annually since 1970. These figures did not include extra losses through drug smuggling and illegal fishing and logging. Sudan loses between $800 million and $1 billion a year through illegal fishing. It is estimated that between 2000 and 2009 South Africa lost $170 billion in IFF (Adow, 2014). The report published in 2015 estimated on average that IFFs from the continent were more than $50 billion per year and had been more than $1 trillion in the last 50 years. Multinational companies were the main culprits. The figures were probably underestimated as they excluded trading services and other forms of illegal flows, such as the trafficking of drugs, people and firearms. Nigeria had the highest losses, estimated at $217.7 billion, and 30.5% of the outflows from Africa between 1970 and 2008 (The African Union and Economic Commission for Africa, 2015). Reports from the NGO GFI show that since 2000 SSA has suffered the highest level of illicit financial flows as a percent of GDP in the world (Clough, 2017). Mark Curtis from the NGO Global Justice Now claims that in 2015 the countries in SSA were net creditors to the rest of the world to the tune of $41.3 billion (2017).

Corporations have been at the forefront of illegal financial flows out of the developing world since 2000. There are many ways to avoid tax: internal transfers of funds, transfer pricing, misinvoicing and trade mispricing. The most illegal financial flows are from the resource extracting sectors. Illegitimate funds are usually exported through tax havens (Oxfam International, 2018b). In the decade before 2009, illicit outflows from Africa increased faster than any other decade (22.3%), increasing from $10 billion in 2000 to $38 billion in 2006. In 2000, the balance of payment leakages (bribery, theft, kickbacks and tax evasion), estimated at $7.8 billion, was far greater than trade mispricing ($2.28 billion). By 2006, trade mispricing was the largest source of IIF, amounting to $20 billion compared to the balance of payment leakages of $18 billion. In 2008, IFF declined by 41%, assumed to be as a result of the GFC (reduced loans and FDI) rather than far-reaching economic reforms or improvements in governance in emerging markets (Kar & Freitas, 2011).

A more recent report from GFI confirmed that between 2005 and 2014, most global IFF (87%) were through the fraudulent misinvoicing of trade (Salomon & Spanjers, 2017). SSA led all other regions in the growth of illicit outflows during this period, averaging between 1.8% and 6.3% a year (between $36 billion and $69 billion) by 2014. The highest years for external flows were 2007 to 2009. Measured against the level of trade, SSA ranked the highest in illicit outflows in the world between 2005 and 2014. IFF in 2014 amounted to between 5.3% and 9.9% of SSA's total trade. The GFI uses data from the IMF and noted that because of difficulties in accessing information as well as changes in methodology, their estimates were conservative and misinvoicing of trade is likely to be underreported (Clough, 2017).

Nations in SSA also lose money through corruption, which contributes to indebtedness. Corrupt politicians have been sending money abroad since countries became independent. Misappropriated funds from loans, aid, profits and bribes are exported through tax havens (Oxfam International, 2018a and 2018b). Capital flight was made easier under financial deregulation. In the early 2000s, Africans had more money outside Africa than the total debt (Bond, 2006). Foreign companies and governments have been complicit in this corruption. Many brutal rulers were propped up by foreign loans and aid. Creditors often knew the money would be siphoned off by dictators and deposited in Western banks (Bond, 2006). Foreign companies have also considered bribery as a cost of doing business in Africa. There have been many incidents where foreign companies bribed local officials to get contracts or funds disappeared in development projects. Local officials have continued to expropriate funds and take bribes. There have been major corruption lawsuits in projects such as the Lesotho Highland Water Project, where more than $2 million flowed from a dozen multinational corporations to the Swiss accounts of the CEO of the project, Masupha Sole. He served nine years in jail but was then reinstated because he carried so much political influence. No charges were made in South Africa (Bond, 2017c).

In a region known for high levels of corruption, South Africa has one of the worst records. The 2014 and 2016 Economic Crimes surveys conducted by Price Waterhouse Coopers identified the South African corporate elite as the world's most corrupt. It has a poor record for taking punishment action (Price Waterhouse Coopers, 2014; 2016). The Johannesburg mining house Mvelaphanda was implicated during the prosecution of major New York financier Och-Ziff, found guilty of bribery related to mining or oil in six African countries. Leading ANC politician, Tokyo Sexwale, was one of the founders of Mvelaphanda. The South African government did not bother to prosecute the company (AmaBhungane, 2016, cited in Bond, 2018).

2.2.7. *Debt: Legitimate and illegitimate ('odious')*

During the 1960s and 1970s, loans were made freely to developing countries, often at very low interest rates. To borrowers at the time, it seemed that the Cold War would last forever and money would keep flowing. Lenders were not aggressive in demanding loan repayment. This early debt was partly the result of naivety on the part of borrowers and profligate lending. Borrowed money was also expropriated by corrupt officials. The oil crisis in the 1970s pushed up interest rates significantly. As debt increased, lenders began to impose more conditions before making further loans. By now, countries in SSA had become dependent on borrowing to keep functioning.

SSA's debt was $18 billion in 1975 (Ajayi & Khan, 2000). By 2000, SSA was the most indebted region in the world (Dembele, 2004). In response to mounting international pressure, in 1996, the BWIs launched the debt relief programme the Highly Indebted Poor Country Initiative (HIPCI). The HIPCI was conditional on compliance with the neoliberal structural adjustment conditions (IMF, 2017a). As the compliance period was initially seven years, there was no impact on SSA's total debt before 2002, when debt reached $210 billion (United Nations Commission on Trade and Development (UNCTAD), 2004). Countries kept borrowing to repay debt and to keep functioning. In the late 1990s, the WB classified Nigeria, Angola, Gabon, Equatorial Guinea, SãoTomé, Cameroon — and, after 2000, Chad and Sudan — as 'highly indebted nations' (Jerome *et al.*, 2005).

Even though growth rates in SSA after 2000 were among the highest in the world, many countries in SSA remained indebted. The HIPCI had little overall impact on SSA's debt which continued to increase until 2005. By 2003, the WB conceded that HIPCI goals had been too optimistic and rates of return unrealistic, as only eight of the original 21 countries who originally qualified for debt relief had met the conditions. Thus, instead of $34.7 billion in projected debt relief, only $11.8 billion had been granted (Jubilee Plus, 2003). By 2005, 34 countries in SSA qualified for the HIPCI, including 12 of the 25 most mineral dependent states. Ten of the most mineral dependent and six of the most oil dependent economies were classified by the WB as 'highly indebted nations' (Jerome *et al.*, 2005).

In 2005, at the request of the G8, $40 billion in debt to the WB, IMF and the African Development Bank was written off for 18 countries, 14 of these in Africa (Benin, Burkina Faso, Ethiopia, Ghana, Madagascar, Mali, Mauritania, Mozambique, Niger, Rwanda, Senegal, Tanzania, Uganda and Zambia). This initiative, the Multilateral Debt Relief Initiative (MDRI), commenced in 2006. It was not all the debt owed by these countries or all their creditors who provided relief. To be eligible, the countries had to be near completion point in complying with the neoliberal HIPCI conditions. Another nine countries were soon eligible — Cameroon, Chad, the Democratic Republic of the Congo, the Gambia, Guinea, Guinea-Bissau, Malawi, São Tomé e Príncipe and Sierra Leone (Mutume, 2005). Though not all debt relief under the MDRI went to SSA nations, the region's debt dropped to $200 billion between 2005 and 2007 (Bond, 2017f). This was only a temporary respite, however, and by 2007, SSA's debt levels were beginning to increase.

The region's debt remained relatively stable for the next two years. The global financial crisis (GFC) contributed to debt increase, and debt began to rise again around 2008. Low-interest rates also encouraged borrowing. Debt accelerated again after 2014 (Coulibaly *et al.*, 2019). Many countries in Africa that had reached completion point in the process of debt cancellation quickly re-accumulated debt (Jubilee Debt Campaign, 2015). After the phase of debt relief from 2005 to 2007, the pattern of borrowing in SSA changed. Previously, lenders had been mainly the BWIs and Paris Club members, but nations in SSA started taking out loans from private creditors. By 2016, multilateral debt accounted for 40% of debt, down from 53% in 2005. Rather than the Paris Club group of 22 lenders, more loans were being made from sovereign creditors including loans from China. Non Paris Club sovereign creditors accounted for 30% of debt in 2016, while Paris Club sovereign debt fell to 7% (Mustapha and Prisson, 2018). China's loans to SSA have grown rapidly since 2010, some for large infrastructure projects (Brautigam & Hwang, 2016). Another trend was that countries in SSA raised money by selling their debt as bonds to creditors (Sow, 2017). A number of states in SSA began issuing bonds after 2006 and concerns were raised that this might increase debt. Between 2006 and 2014, the cumulative total of money raised by issuing bonds was $25.8 billion. The countries issuing bonds were Zambia, Kenya, Côte d'Ivoire, South Africa, Senegal and Ghana (Adams, 2015). Debt accumulation was rapid after the collapse in commodity prices in 2011. Largely because of loans from China, SSA's debt had risen to $350 billion by 2014 (Bond, 2017f). Uganda, Malawi, Tanzania, Angola, Senegal, Equatorial Guinea, Burkina Faso, Zambia, Mali, Lesotho, Eritrea, Madagascar and Guinea-Bissau had the largest current account deficits (combined outflows of legal profits, interest payments and trade deficits) in 2015. It is interesting to note that only a few years previously a number of these nations had been celebrated during the 'Africa Rising' era (Bond, 2017f). In 2016, SSA's total external debt was $406 billion, 32% to other governments, 32% to the private sector and 36% to multilateral banks, including 16% to the WB (Jubilee Debt Campaign, 2018). According to the BWIs, in 2016, 16 nations in SSA were in debt distress or at high risk of debt distress: Burundi, Cabo Verde, Cameroon, Central African Republic, Chad, Djibouti, the Gambia, Ghana, Mauritania, Mozambique, SãoTomé and Principe, South Sudan, Sudan, Zambia and Zimbabwe (Jubilee Debt Campaign, 2018), and there was a growing alarm about Africa's debt sustainability (IMF, 2017c; Brautigam & Hwang, 2016). At this time, SSA's debt to China was only 20% of its overall debt (Jubilee Debt Campaign, 2018).

Regional and national debt figures are misleading because of the diversity and differences in the size of Africa's economies. A crucial figure is the debt to GDP ratio because it indicates the potential for economic growth. Developing nations can sustain or manage much lower debt to GDP ratios than larger more established markets because their economic potential is much less. When the debt to GDP ratio is 40% or less, debt can be managed without it becoming crippling (Africa and Middle East (AfricaME), 2017). In 1980, at the beginning of the neoliberal era, according to WB Global Development Finance, Africa's ratio of debt to gross domestic product (GDP) was 23.4%. This rose to 63% in 1990 and was 71% 10 years later. Most of that debt was to the BWIs (Dembele, 2004). In many countries, this ratio is much higher. In general, the region's debt has been on the rise, with the median debt to GDP ratio increasing from 31% in 2012 to 53% in 2017 (Coulibaly *et al.*, 2019).

2.2.7.1. *Cancellation of illegitimate debt*

SSA's debt burden has been one of the main reasons behind its lack of development. Debt servicing continues to be a major economic drain. Servicing debt from illegitimate loans is further injustice. There are major precedents for cancelling illegitimate debt. The US Congress in 1820 first established the principle against the perpetrators of the slave trade, that when money was lent to a violent regime, the loan was illegitimate and the creditor also complicit in the abuses. The Nuremberg Tribunal upheld the principle (Hertz, 2004). Foreign governments, multilateral organisations and multinational companies have a long history of collusion with repressive regimes in Africa, especially during the Cold War. Much of the debt SSA accumulated after the 1970s was borrowed by totalitarian leaders. The debt did not bring benefits to the population and was often used for repression, squandered or sent overseas to be hidden in tax havens. Loans were often made in the knowledge that they would be expropriated. Hertz uses three criteria for identifying illegitimate debt: the regime that borrowed the money lacked democratic consent, the funds were used in ways that were inimical to the interests of the population and the lender knew the funds would be used in this way. Blatant examples are the loans made to Mobutu in Zaire in the late 1970s and in the early 1980s to Sani Abacha in Nigeria and IMF loans to South Africa soon after the Soweto uprising in 1976. Commercial banks also loaned money to unelected leaders. The lenders had to have known the money would be used to oppress the people. Lawyers at the time called the loans 'odious' (Hertz, 2004). The BWIs, members of the Paris Club and aid donors were all complicit in lending to repressive leaders during the decades of independence when totalitarian rule dominated the region. This same group — the Washington Consensus — was demanding debt repayment and using debt to impose neoliberal policies. When countries were forced to make large debt servicing payments, it deprived them of funds for social and economic development.

2.2.7.1.1. Case study: Nigeria

The countries in SSA that suffered most from the overseas draining of their national wealth were Nigeria, Côte d'Ivoire, Angola, DRC and Zambia (Bond, 2006). Except for Côte d'Ivoire, all these countries are major resource exporters and share common profiles. Nigeria provides a classic example of the 'resource curse.' It is one of the most resource-rich countries in Africa. Nigeria has been burdened by the repayment of historical illegitimate loans, including the British government loans of £3 billion during the eras of Abachia and General Ibrhm (Hertz, 2004). The dictator Sani Abacha — in power between 1993 and 1998 — was rumoured to have stolen and transferred to a foreign bank account slightly less than $3.5 billion. Nigeria had also borrowed heavily from the WB, some years as much as $1 billion. It also received $3.5 billion in aid between 1980 and 2000, though was reduced in the 1990s because of Abacha's corruption. Nigeria remained indebted in 2005. It was estimated that the Nigerian government had earned $300 billion from oil and gas between 1975 and 2005 (LaFraniere, 2005). In 2002, Nigeria's debt stood at $34 billion. Debt servicing cost $2.9 billion that year compared to the $350 million spent on health (Hertz, 2004). Nigeria was not eligible for HIPCI because the debt was to the Paris Club of bilateral lenders, not the WB (International Finance Corporation) (Hertz, 2004). The Paris Club in 2005 still expected Nigeria to pay off interest and penalties incurred over 30 years of military rule (Bond, 2006). By 2005, Nigeria's external debt had reached $36 billion. An eventual debt resolution was conducted with the Paris Club the following year, which included $18 million debt relief and a discounted buyback, reducing Nigeria's debt stock by $30 billion (Moss, 2011; Birdsall & Moss, 2006).

Higher oil prices after 2000 resulted in larger IFFs from Nigeria. It is estimated that between 2000 and 2009 Nigeria lost $250 billion (Adow, 2014). During the same period, the average annual illicit flows out of Nigeria were estimated at $15.8 billion (Kar & Freitas, 2011). Balance of payments mechanisms were the major method for the unrecorded transfer of capital out of the country by major exporters (captured by the WB Residual or CED model) (Kar & Curcio, 2011). Between 2005 and 2014, Nigeria was listed as one of the 10 countries with the highest illegal outflows of capital in the world. Illegal financial transfers from the country were estimated at 13% of the total trade of $158 billion for that period. In 2014, Nigeria lost an estimated 9% of its trade ($12.5 billion) (GFI, 2017). Its debt in 2016 had reached $31.41 billion (31 December 2016 est.), but its debt to GDP ratio of 21.8% was healthier than that of many countries in the region (CIA, 2020a).

2.2.8. *Debt relief*

Apart from the argument of illegitimacy, an important reason for providing debt relief is adhering to the UN Declaration of Human Rights. A creditor's rights should not override human rights. This protection under the law is an underlying principle in most contemporary legal systems, protecting both debtors and larger municipalities. For the most part, this protection does not exist at a national level. There is a similar problem with the MDG. Many countries pledged to provide 0.7% of GDP in aid and failed to deliver it. Most notably, the US is continuing to spend 0.1% of its GDP on aid (Hertz, 2004).

African countries were some of the first in the world to get structural adjustment loans and the first to demonstrate their failure. During the 1980s and 1990s, there was widespread international criticism of the WB and IMF because of the hardship caused by structural adjustment programmes, even when they were not fully implemented. Debt continued to spiral in the developing world and there was a surge in calls for debt relief. Much of that debt was unpayable. In order to retain their credibility, the BWIs responded with a debt relief programme — the Highly Indebted Poor Country Initiative (HIPCI) — in 1996. After many years of not stimulating economic growth, the neoliberal prescriptions were not dropped but expanded. The same neoliberal policies became conditions for debt relief in the HIPCI. Conditionalities were expanded to include the privatisation of utilities, such as water (Bond, 2006). The way debt relief in the HIPCI was delivered deepened rather than lessened dependence. Terms of engagement were harsh and almost impossible to meet. The ratio of debt repayment set at 40% of export earnings was unpayable (Hertz, 2004; Halifax Initiative, 2004). The HIPCI debt relief programme had little impact on SSA in the 1990s because the qualifying period for governments to prove they were implementing the neoliberal conditions was seven years, reduced to six years in 2003. Only 10 countries had qualified for relief by 2003 (Isar, 2012). The HIPCI has been criticised for being politicised and more of a tool for larger economies to influence global governance and maintain smaller countries' dependence on biased decisions than a means for countries to reduce debt burdens and develop their economies. These criticisms were equally applicable to later debt relief programmes which introduced new initiatives for privatisation of resources (Isar, 2012). The programme was supplemented in 2005 with the Multilateral Debt Relief Initiative (MDRI), which rapidly provided relief of debt owed by low-income nations to the multilateral institutions. These countries had to have fulfilled the neoliberal conditions of the HIPCI.

Many of the SSA countries with high growth rates after 2000 were part of the HIPCI. The high growth rates had not enabled them to pay off their debt. By 2004, SSA's debt had gone up to $218 billion (Mutumi, 2005). Debt relief made little appreciable impact on the region until the Multilateral Debt Relief Initiative (MDRI) was introduced in 2005 as a means of enabling nations to meet the MDG. The G8 agreed to write off $40 billion in debt owed to the WB, the IMF and African Development Bank by 18 of the world's poorest countries. Fourteen of those nations were in SSA. This programme had a significant impact on SSA, and the region's debt fell from $240 billion in 2005 to $200 billion as a result (Bond, 2017f). For a short period, governments had money to spend on social services. The MDRI only applied to debt accrued before 2004 and was broadened to include nations who were indebted to the Paris Club but had annual per capita incomes lower than $380. This included Nigeria and Equatorial Guinea. To qualify for MDRI, countries had to have met the HIPCI conditions. Both programmes were ended in 2017. Of the 36 countries that qualified for debt relief under the HIPCI, 30 were in SSA. Debt relief to all eligible countries under HIPCI programmes was $76.2 billion (IMF, 2017a) and $43.3 billion under MDRI which ended in 2015 (IMF, 2017b).

2.2.8.1. *Case study: Uganda*

'One-size-fits-all monolithic neoliberalism' was not flexible enough to deal with the specific problems facing different nations. The HIPCI also ignored the possibility of economic shocks such as the impact of falling commodity prices (Isar, 2012). Uganda was the first country to meet HIPCI terms and qualify for $347 million in debt relief in 1998. It was promised further debt relief ('enhanced assistance') on producing a poverty reduction strategy (PRS). Total debt relief amounted to $2 billion. With this assistance, Uganda was expected to save $37 million a year in debt servicing for the next 10 years (IMF, 2000). That didn't happen. Over half of Uganda's export earnings came from coffee. After 1996, there was a decline in coffee revenues, equivalent to over half the debt relief it received under the HIPCI. A further steep drop in world coffee prices in 2000 was partly the result of BWIs' export-led policies, encouraging the growing of coffee in places like Vietnam. This lead to a glut in the world market (Charveriat, 2001). In 2000, Uganda's debt stock was $5.5 billion. In 2006, it received 100% debt forgiveness under the MDRI. Debt kept increasing, however, and reached $9.8 billion in 2017 (Ssempala *et al.*, 2020).

2.2.8.2 *Conclusion*

After 2000, the high growth rates in SSA that prompted the 'Africa Rising' cover stories in *The Economist* (2011) and *Time Magazine* (2012) illustrated how economic growth rates do not automatically spread into the wider economy, particularly when those growth rates are in the resource export sector. This sector operates in enclaves, usually owned by foreign corporations. Corporations were responsible for 87% of global illegal financial flows (IFFs) between 2005 and 2014, and these flows have been the highest in SSA (Salomon & Spanjers, 2017). The small percentage of profits corporations pay in taxes is all governments get from them, apart from bribes to individuals. Continuing poverty and lagging economic development in SSA are partly the product of the net transfer of wealth out of the region from debt servicing — both illegitimate and legitimate, foreign multinationals exporting profits from undervalued resources and powerful individuals expropriating their countries' wealth. Corruption occurs at national and international levels. Governments and the multinational organisations have played a central role in facilitating those outflows of wealth through imposing neoliberal policies on SSA for nearly 40 years.

2.3. Planet

SSA has many natural resources but suffers from political, economic and environmental disadvantages, which deprive the people of many of the benefits from those resources. The climate crisis is intensifying water scarcity and desertification. The major environmental problems in the region include land degradation and pollution from toxic chemicals used by corporations in mining, resource extraction and agribusiness. Other problems include damage from the building of infrastructure, soil erosion, deforestation and threats of species extinction. Expanding populations and the rapid unplanned growth of cities have created major waste issues. SSA also suffers from a $29 billion a year loss from illegal logging, fishing and trade in wildlife, according to NGO Global Justice Now (Curtis, 2017).

Africa has had pan-African environmental laws since 1963 and many African governments have good environmental policies. The establishment of the New Partnership for Africa's Development (NEPAD) in 2001 contained an environmental action plan. When the African Union replaced the Organisation for African Unity (OAU), it revised the earlier Algiers Convention on the environment, but governments have been slow to act on environmental issues. The revised Algiers Convention (2003) needed 15 countries to sign to become effective, but by 2016, only eight had signed. The weakness of state bureaucracies and low funding are some of the major obstacles in enforcing environmental policies. Policy implementation is low, environmental legislation at lower level institutions is inadequate, and there is poor legal enforcement and insufficient financial and human capacity to carry out the agreements (Shinn, 2016).

Widespread environmental injustices have occurred in SSA (Bond, 2018). Many of these injustices are perpetuated by foreign governments and corporations, although local governments are far from blameless. The main interest of many governments is exploiting their environmental resources for profit. Because nations in SSA are faced with so many challenges, such as poverty and corruption, protecting the environment is not a top priority. An international study of attitudes in 2014 by the Pew Research Center found people in Africa considered the greatest dangers in the world to be the spread of AIDS and other infectious diseases. Environmental concern was not seen as a major issue in eight out of the nine countries surveyed (2014).

For too long, the environment has been considered an infinite economic resource, and the economics of resource depletion have been ignored. Resources have been plundered without any consideration of the time or capacity required for the renewal of those resources. Ten African countries signed up to the Gaborone Declaration for Sustainability in Africa in 2012. The declaration agreed that GDP was not a reliable measure of well-being and sustainable growth. These nations agreed to incorporate natural capital accounting into their national accounting and corporate planning systems. The declaration was signed by Botswana, Gabon, Ghana, Kenya, Liberia, Mozambique, Namibia, Rwanda, South Africa and Tanzania (Bond, 2018). Though there are real dangers in quantifying nature using natural capital accounting (Monbiot, 2018), it does provide an estimate of the negative impact on the GDP of resource extraction, environmental exploitation, contributions to the climate crisis and production of greenhouse gases. The WB estimated that 88% of SSA had suffered a net negative capital accumulation in 2010, and the net loss of 12% of GDP once adjustment had been made for the loss of natural capital (The WB, 2014b; Bond, 2017d). A strong case was forming to justify keeping resources in the ground, especially if profits were mostly exported (Bond, 2017a). No progress had been made four years later (Bond, 2018). One response suggested was setting quotas that do not further deplete natural capital. 'We could recognise scarcity by setting quantitative limits on the resource flows at ecologically sustainable levels. The goal would be living sustainably from natural income rather than living unsustainably from the depletion of natural capital' (Daly, 2014). Natural capital accounting by placing a price on nature runs the danger of monetising natural phenomena and reinforces the idea that nature has no value unless value can be extracted. Confusing market values with intrinsic values diminishes the latter; 'this corrupts and degrades our intrinsic values and empties life of moral argument' (Monbiot, 2018). If SSA followed this path, it would lose not only its resources but also much of the value of profits from resource extraction through illegal and legal financial flows in the form of corporate repatriation of profits. As yet, there has been no attempt to 'fine and ban' or demand 'ecological debt' repayment from any corporations.

2.3.1. *Climate crisis*

The SSA region is at the forefront of the human impact of the climate crisis, though it continues to have the lowest levels of carbon emissions in the world (MDG Monitor, 2016). Within SSA, there is already a wide range of environments where it is difficult for people to sustain a livelihood. Climate changes intensify the frequency of extreme weather events including droughts, flooding, water scarcity and desertification. Though contributing little to the contemporary climate crisis, SSA is on the frontline in terms of its likely impacts. The accelerating climate crisis is the result of the accumulation of carbon emissions generated by high-income nations. Since the 1980s, emission levels have been rising rapidly as developing countries — particularly China and India — began to industrialise and produce more GHG emissions. These emissions contribute to the high levels produced in established industrialised countries. Much of this industrial production has been produced by multinational corporations. The fossil fuel sector is a major contributor to the GHG emissions that are accelerating the climate crisis. This sector has played an important role in international politics and policies and has been particularly successful at promoting climate scepticism in the US, which in turn has inhibited international action. The SSA region lacks power internationally. It is also particularly dependent on exploiting the resources that contribute to the climate crisis while already suffering from its effects, including global warming. The developed countries of the world owe the developing world a huge ecological debt in its role as a carbon sink for carbon emissions as well as the source of cheap resources (Bond, 2006). A WB study in 2015 estimated more than 100 million people will be pushed into poverty by the climate crisis, most of them in Africa (Schwartzstein, 2016).

2.3.1.1. *Carbon emissions*

The SSA region has the lowest levels of carbon emissions in the world. Its emissions increased in the decades after 1960 from 0.552 (in metric tonnes per capita) to a peak of 0.988 in 1980. In the following decades, structural adjustment-induced economic stagnation led to a decline in emissions to 0.84 metric tons per capita in 2000. Levels remained static between 2000 and 2014 when they were 0.84 metric tons per capita (WB, n.d.b2). The world's major CO^2 producers have an ecological debt to SSA and other developing nations for this low level of carbon emission and should be compensated by high emitters for their contribution to the contemporary climate crisis. More critically, the effects of those global climate changes will be felt intensely by Africa. The UNFCCC summit in Rio in 1992 acknowledged this ecological debt but the obligation was signed away at the UNFCCC Paris summit in 2015. South Africa, as the chair of the G77 developing nations, agreed not to hold developed nations into account for their historic role in creating the current climate crisis. Instead, they supported voluntarily determined national contributions which eliminated compensation for historic carbon emissions (Bond, 2018). Leading climate scientist James Hansen considered the agreements reached in Paris to be a travesty (Milman, 2015). Yet again, South Africa had played a comprador role, supporting the interests of the Washington Consensus. The appropriate response to this ecological debt owed to SSA should have been the provision of assistance in mitigating the effects of the climate crisis and embarking on a low carbon development model.

2.3.1.2. *Case study: South Africa*

South Africa is continuing to proceed with a fossil fuel-intensive development agenda. This country has the highest carbon output in SSA with much of its emissions from energy production. It remains highly dependent on coal as an energy supply. Its largest energy producer is the para-state energy producer Eskom which was 93% coal-fired in the early 21st century (Bond, 2018). In a deal valid until 2028, Eskom even sells energy to South Africa's largest consumer of energy, BHB Billiton, at heavily subsidised rates, one-fifth of what ordinary consumers pay and half of what it costs Eskom to produce the power. There is no incentive to reduce use (Bond, 2012). Since the UNFCCC summit in Paris, in 2015, South Africa has embarked on more fossil fuel-intensive projects that will increase carbon emissions and affect water management. It is building more coal-fired power plants, exporting coal, granting fracking contracts, expanding the petro-chemical complex in Durban, doubling the capacity of the Durban-Johannesburg pipeline and subsidising South African Airlines. Apart from greenhouse gas emissions, South Africa has other ecological problems, in minerals-related pollution, land and bulk water degradation, solid waste and maritime pollution (Bond, 2018).

2.3.2. *Food security and land acquisitions*

Africa's total land area is about 30 million hectares. The Sahara desert covers nine million hectares, and until recently, 6.4 million hectares were covered by forest. Only 8.7 million hectares are arable and suitable for farming. Africa is facing a food security crisis from a rapidly increasing population. The SSA region has the lowest level of food security in the world. It has the majority of the world's poorest and hungriest people, the majority of them being rural farmers (AusAid, 2012). Environmental conditions are particularly difficult and most of the soil is only marginally fertile. Much of the land is degraded. The population has the lowest global daily per capita calorie intake. Malnutrition levels are high. Agricultural productivity is low, irrigation is limited and methods of production are labour intensive. Because of the imposition of export-driven agricultural policies, SSA has to import a large amount of its food needs. The structural adjustment policies forbade agricultural subsidies or tariffs on imported food. Some countries are highly dependent on food aid (Ingwe *et al.*, 2010).

The chief priority for Africa is to provide enough food to feed its own population, by increasing agricultural productivity and ending the need to import food or rely on food aid.

The SSA region has very low levels of indigenous ownership of land. Foreign expropriation of land was one of the major tragedies inflicted in the region under colonialism and it is happening again. The largest amounts of land were expropriated by the British in Kenya and South Africa. Large areas were taken by force or with token payments to people who did not understand Western concepts of law and land ownership. Once acquired, the land was protected and maintained by force. In many countries, foreigners took the best land, the Kenyan highlands, the fertile coastal plain in South Africa, or the most valuable land in terms of resources. South Africa today has some of the lowest levels of indigenous land ownership in the world because of the 1913 Native Land Act. Ninety percent of the country was appropriated by the white settler population. Nelson Mandela promised land reform in South Africa in 1994, but land redistribution has not been easy to implement. SSA has become a battleground where competition for land is increasing. Many acquisitions are occurring in hunger-ridden, land-scarce countries leaving less area to produce food for the people who live there.

Though there is currently enough food in the world to feed every person, access to food is dependent on the ability to pay for it. Excess food is produced and stockpiled by subsidised agribusinesses in high-income nations. Fears about future food scarcity and access to food increased after 2000, particularly during the 2007 food crisis when extreme climate events reduced the size of the world's grain crops. When food prices rose and there were food riots, many governments became concerned about future food shortages and social unrest. They began searching for land in other countries. Contemporary land acquisitions are driven by countries wanting to import food. Food production is being outsourced, and land is now considered a profitable business investment (Ingwe *et al.*, 2010).

Land ownership in SSA is being threatened by foreign acquisitions. Much of what is happening today in Africa qualifies as 'land grabbing.' According to Oxfam, 'land grabbing' includes one or more of these features: violation of human rights and, particularly, the equal rights of women; flouting the principle of free, prior and informed consent of the affected land users, particularly indigenous peoples; ignoring the impacts on social, economic, and gender relations, and on the environment; avoidance of transparent contracts with clear and binding commitments on employment and benefit sharing; and eschewing democratic planning, independent oversight, and meaningful participation (2011). A report from the United Nations FAO, IFAD and the British think-tank, the International Institute for Environment and Development (IIED) (2015), described the recent unprecedented scale of land purchases and leasing in some of Africa's poorest nations as the 'new scramble for Africa.' The study examined land purchasing between 2004 and 2009 in Ethiopia, Ghana, Madagascar, Mali and Sudan. Qualitative studies were conducted in Mozambique and Tanzania. In these five countries, between 2004 and 2009, 2,492,684 hectares of land allocation were approved (excluding approvals for land under 1,000 ha) (Cotula *et al.*, 2009).

The Oakland Institute investigated over 50 land deals in seven countries in SSA in a 2009 report. It highlighted the role played by a wide range of international development agencies, multilateral institutions and so-called 'socially responsible' investment funds. These institutions use the language of aid organisations: 'helping Africa feed itself', 'improved food security', 'livelihood creation', and 'sustainable environmental policies.' However, a closer look at their agenda and policy prescriptions, and an investigation into actual transactions revealed a different picture. Despite growing evidence that the current African land grab is displacing small farmers and indigenous communities and threatening food and water security, the US and international development agencies continue to push for foreign agricultural land investment. This investment is as much about large-scale irrigation as it is about land (2009). The WB described the Guinea Savannah Zone, an area half the size of the US, as 'the world's largest reserves of underused land.' This land is home to 600 million small farmers and grazers (Pearce, 2012). Multinational companies from many countries are also playing a key role in the new wave of land purchases. These companies come from many countries: South Korea, Japan, Saudi Arabia, Kuwait, Libya, Egypt, China and India (GRAIN, 2009 cited in Ingwe *et al.*, 2010). China is not a big player in land acquisition compared to South Korea, the Gulf countries and Western multinational corporations (Smith, 2009).

There are many dimensions around land sales. Well-structured deals could guarantee employment, better infrastructure and improved crop yields. Badly handled deals could cause great harm, especially if local people were excluded from decisions about allocating land and if their land rights were not protected (Cotula, cited in Vidal, 2010b). In the worst cases, leaders sell their people's land without consultation. This is particularly problematic where people are itinerant and nomadic and do not have land ownership documentation. Individual land ownership is a Western concept; in Africa, land is often collectively owned. Land sales and leases are an area where there is significant potential for bribery and corruption (Pearce, 2012). Land ownership is also often communal or not bound by the same legal titles as in the West. The struggle for land often occurs between central governments and their own people. In Botswana, the San Bushmen of the Central Kalahari Game Reserve have been fighting their government for the right to remain on their traditional lands. The government began forcibly relocating them in 1997 because it wanted to search for diamonds, increase cattle ranching and expand conservation areas and provide access for WB and de Beers investments (The New Humanitarian (formerly IRIN), 2004). In Ethiopia, the government did not consult the people before selling land in the south-west Gambella Province. It tried to make nomadic people live in villages against their wishes. The people's lifestyle was simple, but they did have land. In some areas, people were brutally forced from their land or they were killed. Ethiopia is a country that frequently experiences famines and should not be leasing land to food exporters (Pearce, 2012).

2.3.3. *Desertification and erosion*

The layer of topsoil is very thin in many parts of Africa. Desertification and erosion are increasing. The rapid loss of that topsoil has been caused by overgrazing, overploughing and deforestation. Deserts are encroaching on cropland in Saharan

Africa, and the desert is moving both southward, engulfing Nigeria, and northward (Brown, 2009). Soil is frequently lost through wind erosion. The number of dust storms in the Sahara has increased ten-fold since the 1960s. The most affected nations are Niger, Chad, Mauritania, northern Nigeria and Burkina Faso. Mauritania in the early 1960s had two dust storms each year. After 2000, 80 dust storms were recorded in one year (Goudie cited in Brown, 2009). Wind-borne soil loss in the Bodélé Depression in Chad has increased hugely since 1947, the loss estimated at 1.3 billion tons annually. Africa loses nearly three billion tons of fine soil particles a year. This means a significant loss of fertility and productivity. Soil is also lost through water erosion. Ethiopia has major problems with water-borne erosion because it is mountainous and its soils are highly erodible. An estimated two billion tons of topsoil a year are washed away by rain. Overgrazing also causes soil erosion and desertification. Both population and livestock numbers have increased dramatically. Between 1950 and 2007, the human population grew from 227 to 965 million and livestock numbers increased from 273 million to 824 million. Grassland turns into desert when livestock numbers exceed grassland carrying capacity by half or more (Brown, 2009).

2.3.4. *Waste and pollution*

Since the 1960s, foreign companies have been responsible for the most toxic environmental pollution in SSA — from mining and oil extraction. SSA has increased its oil exports since 2000, producing 7% of the world's oil in 2012 (Environmental Investigation Agency (EIA), 2013). Oil spills pollute water and land and the burning of gases pollutes the air. The Niger Delta area has been devastated by oil activities. The livelihoods of local people have been destroyed and they suffer from serious health problems. In mining, the toxic chemicals used in the extraction of minerals from rock cause similar health problems and also destroy the land. Chemicals seep into the underground water table and pollute the water. Open-cast mining destroys large areas of land creating wastelands.

Changing land-use practises can also lead to environmental problems, including pollution from the chemicals used in agribusinesses. Cotton production is highly chemical intensive, while palm oil production leaves large pools of waste that produce high levels of methane. High levels of chemicals are used in the Kenyan flower industry. Both the lake water and the groundwater around Lake Naivasha in Kenya are severely polluted. People working with these chemicals suffer many health problems but few have been able to get compensation for health problems caused by pollution. Many chemicals that have been restricted elsewhere continued to be used in Africa. A World Health Organisation (WHO) study released in 2014 listed the harmful chemicals still in use in Africa as including heavy metals, fluoride, cyanide, air pollutants, benzene, asbestos, POPs and pesticides (WHO, 2014a).

Urban expansion in recent decades has created other problems because of the large amount of waste produced in cities that do not have adequate waste removal services. Waste is not collected in many shanty towns, and sewage disposal systems are inadequate. Many urban areas lack water and adequate housing.

Governments have not been able to deal with the rapid growth of cities even though vast wealth has been generated by resources, as in Nigeria. Health risks are increased when water services are inadequate or if they have been privatised and people cannot afford to pay for clean water. Millions of litres of untreated sewage and industrial waste from the surrounding cities in Kenya, Tanzania and Uganda have been dumped into Lake Victoria. The introduction of non-native fish to the lake has also threatened native species (Barlow, 2001).

The dumping of waste and e-waste from other countries is another problem in SSA that has emerged in recent decades. A series of incidents caused by the dumping of waste from high-income nations on poorer countries in the developing world prompted the OECD agreement, the Basel Convention on Hazardous Waste, which came into force in 1997. Though nations may sign these treaties, there is no means of enforcing the regulations (Basel Action Network (BAN), 2019). Major waste disasters have continued to occur since the signing of the Convention. In 2006, the British oil trading company Trafigura illegally dumped 400 tonnes of toxic waste from a chartered cargo ship in Côte d'Ivoire. At least 10 people died and thousands fell ill. It was the worst chemical exposure since the Union Carbide leak in Bhopal in 1984. The media exposure of these events prompted a public outcry and led to the initiation in 2007 of one of the largest class actions against the company ever taken in the UK (Vidal, 2007). In 2009, Trafigura was made to pay compensation to the 31,000 people harmed by the dumping of toxic waste (Monbiot, 2009).

There have even been suggestions — from both the West and SSA — for exporting polluting activities to SSA. In 1991, an internal memo from Larry Summers of the WB proposed that the Bank encourages dirty industries to move to Africa (1991, cited in Bosshard, 2008). Sometimes, local governments are complicit in these practises. In 2007, the Deputy President of South Africa, Phumzile Mlambo-Ngcuka, announced that her government was talking with China about moving polluting Chinese companies to South Africa. 'China needs to send some of its polluting industries elsewhere because it is choking on them', Mlambo-Ngcuka said. 'We have the capacity to manage emissions and want to regulate that agreement' (Mlambo-Ngcuka, quoted in Business Report, 2007, cited in Bosshard, 2008).

2.3.5. *Industrial agriculture*

Export-driven agriculture has been promoted by the BWIs as a means of reducing debt. Plantation agriculture and monocultural production lend themselves to increased use of pesticides and fertilisers which are sources of pollution. Plantation agriculture is expanding rapidly in SSA since land sales have increased. This expansion brings a number of problems. An environmental advocate, Vandana Shiva, claims that large-scale industrial agriculture has not only pushed people off the land but also increased the use of chemicals, pesticides, herbicides, fertilisers, intensive irrigation and large-scale transport, storage and distribution. Landscapes have been turned into enormous monocultural plantations (cited in Vidal, 2010b). Animals have no place in plantation agriculture systems, which means that the second largest animal migration in Africa is under threat. The migration crosses the Gambella National Park in Ethiopia and has the potential to be a major tourist attraction as important as the Serengeti. The park contains swamps, grasslands and woodlands, which could be destroyed to make way for agriculture. Already, some of its agricultural land is leased out. The main problem is that the Agriculture Ministry is more powerful than the Ethiopian Wildlife Conservation Authority (Pearce, 2012).

The Kenyan flower industry has frequently been cited as a successful local agribusiness. The global flower industry moved into the Lake Naivasha region of the Kenyan Rift Valley in the 1970s, driving out the local nomadic Maasai cattle herders. Since then, the population has increased significantly, from 29,000 in 1969 to 300,000 in 2007. Over the same period, Lake Naivasha, once 130 square km in area, contracted by 25%. Devastation of the lake is similar to that of the Aral Sea in Russia, which dried up in the 1970s. A combination of climate crisis and excessive draining is depleting it of water. Population pressure is increasing as more people come to work and to provide services for the workers. Trees are being cut down for fuel and the lake is being overfished. Waste and chemicals are being dumped into the lake and the ecological richness has been destroyed. Workers, as well as being paid very little, barely enough to live on, are also experiencing health effects from exposure to chemicals. There are high crime rates. Most of the workers are women, and there is a high level of child rape when mothers leave their children with elders when they go to work (Ogodo & Vidal, 2007). A study of the flower industry in Uganda found that practises were harmful to both the workers and the environment. Institutions responsible for regulating the industry were poorly funded and unable to work effectively. The firms in the sector do not uphold workers' rights or environmental and labour laws (The National Association of Professional Environmentalists (NAPE), 2012).

The expansion of palm oil production in SSA is another controversial issue. Demand for biofuels increased after 2003 when the EU introduced laws to increase the proportion of biofuels to 10% of its fuel consumption by 2015 (Vidal, 2010a). The law was intended to promote solar and wind power but instead led to a rapid increase in palm oil production, which itself produces high emission levels, for diesel. This production has accelerated deforestation, particularly in Indonesia and also in SSA (Transport and the Environment, 2018). The diversion of agricultural production from food to biofuels has increased the pressure on food availability (Brown, 2006). Palm oil production has significant environmental costs, including the cutting down of rainforests, producing carbon and rapidly depleting soils (Brown, 2011). The production process generates large ponds which contain the waste products from processed palm oil fruit. These ponds emit large amounts of methane into the atmosphere, accounting for more than a third of the carbon emissions created from palm oil production. Methane traps approximately 24 times the amount of heat that carbon dioxide does. The methane can be burned to create carbon dioxide which reduces its climate impact, but there are no incentives to make this happen (Milman, 2015). Palm oil production can lead to community development and provide labour intensive work for 25–30 years.

However, biofuel production is open to speculative plantation agriculture. Another problematic issue is the departure of investors if good profits are quickly achieved (Pearce, 2012).

Cotton is another product with a high environmental impact. In Mali, where cotton accounts for 50% of exports, the land is suffering from overuse. High levels of pesticide and fertiliser use reduce biodiversity, affect soil nutrient levels and have health risks for farmers. Efforts are being made to change land-use practises and use sustainable production methods to produce cotton. One German pilot project explored organic cotton production compared to customary production methods. They found yields were similar, and using fewer chemicals saved farmers' money (Settle *et al.*, 2014).

The majority of BWI policies and the activities of multinational companies have not promoted sustainable development in SSA, though some bilateral agencies and multinationals are investigating sustainable development options. In May 2007, Unilever became the first company to commit to sourcing all its tea in a sustainable manner. It formed a partnership with the Kenyan Tea Development Agency. More than 500,000 small-scale tea producers committed to the project, and by 2016, they met the certification requirements of the Sustainable Agricultural Network. Unilever was then able to sell its main brand Lipton Tea as 100% sustainable. Farmers also reported higher yields, better health and safety and improved livelihoods. Other tea companies began to follow suit (Cameron-Booth, 2017).

2.3.6. *Infrastructure*

Large infrastructure projects — in particular the building of dams — have had a major environmental impact in SSA. By 2013, there were 1,270 large dams in Africa (Hathaway & Pottinger, 2013), many built with WB funding. Social and environmental problems resulting from these projects prompted international public opposition and calls for the WB to cease building large dams. For nearly 20 years from the mid-1990s, it funded only medium-sized dams and renovated old dam projects. When China started supplying funding after 2000, the number of large infrastructure projects undertaken in SSA increased. China has a poor domestic environmental record and its projects in SSA have also ignored environmental impacts. Chinese competition eventually drove the WB to start funding mega-dams again in 2013 with more relaxed environmental regulations (Bosshard, 2013a).

2.3.7. *Deforestation*

Rising demand for timber from China, other Asian countries and Europe has increased rapid deforestation in some areas of SSA (World Wildlife Fund, 2018a). The clearing of forests both produces carbon and depletes the role forests play as carbon sinks. Biodiversity is threatened and the extinction of species accelerated. Traditional owners who practised shifting agriculture left the land uncultivated for periods of time to replenish. Many of the soils in African forests are thin and fragile and cannot support intensive agriculture. Land-use practises that replace forests have, therefore, damaged the ecosystem.

Major deforestation is occurring in Equatorial Guinea, the Democratic Republic of the Congo, Mozambique and Cameroon. The Congo Basin is the second largest tropical forest in the world and rapid deforestation occurred there in the 1990s. The rate of deforestation has slowed down since 2000, declining by as much as a third, according to a 2013 study by the European Commission Joint Research Centre. Between 2000 and 2010, the area of rainforest felled each year went down from 3,000 to 2,000 square kilometres (the size of Manhattan). This was partly because the main economic focus in the central African states has continued to be on oil and mining rather than on agriculture. This is good news for the region as trees in the Congo are higher than elsewhere and thus store more carbon. They play a vital role in addressing the climate crisis and biodiversity, as well as providing resources for the local communities (Morelle, 2013).

The pressure to cut down forests is intense when countries have high levels of debt. Cameroon's main exports are oil and timber. In 2016, its debt was 32.5% of GDP (CIA, 2020b). The Cameroon government initiated a number of large scale investment projects which, because the regulatory environment is weak, intensified illegal logging. Since signing the international climate agreement in 2015, increasing pressure from the EU and awareness of the climate impacts of depleting the Congo Basin forests, the Cameroon government has been taking more steps to control illegal logging. It is training the forest people to safeguard the forest by reporting illegal activity (Egalame *et al.*, 2017).

East Africa is the other major forested area in SSA, with a different variety of timbers and land covers: mangroves, savannahs and coastal forests. Mozambique, Tanzania and Zambia have experienced the most deforestation in East Africa. Coastal forests in Tanzania and Kenya, for instance, have been reduced to 10% of their original size. The main threats to forests are land conversion for commercial agriculture, slash and burn clearing, settlers wanting land, overharvesting of timber and firewood needs (World Wildlife Fund, 2018a). Unsustainable deforestation is also occurring in Mozambique, facilitated by cross-border trading between Mozambique and Cameroon. Approximately half of the logging in Mozambique was illegal, according to the British NGO EIA report Appetite for Destruction: China's Trade in Illegal Timber (2012). According to the environmental research organisation IIED, Chinese traders accounted for more than 90% of Mozambique's timber exports in 2013. Most of this trade is illegal as the value of logs entering China from Mozambique is much higher than the amount registered as leaving Mozambique. Because the trade is illegal, the government loses tens of millions in taxes. In 2012 it was estimated that 48% of China's timber imports from Mozambique were illegal (Environmental Investigation Agency (EIA), 2013). In 2014, the value of Mozambican wood entering China surpassed $400 million, a dramatic increase from the $90 million in 2009, according to the Africa Monitor. This situation is created by high demand from China converging with weak law enforcement and local corruption. Chinese demand has dropped since 2014 with the slowdown in the Chinese economy (Ning, 2016).

Other causes of deforestation are plantation agriculture, population growth and the production of charcoal. Prices for charcoal have risen in recent years which creates another incentive to cut down trees (Khadka, 2018). When roads are built to extract resources (oil, gas and minerals), forest access becomes easier and cutting of forests increases. Much of the deforestation that occurs has been illegal or unregulated. Roads built by logging companies open up forests for illegal logging and species poaching (World Wildlife Fund, 2018a). The United Nations programme Reducing Emissions from Deforestation and Forest Degradation in Developing Countries (REDD) provides incentives for countries to not cut their forests (Morelle, 2013). REDD Monitor and Friends of the Earth consider carbon trading not the answer. Friends of the Earth International (FOEI) believes the drivers of deforestation also need to be addressed: 'reduce excessive levels of consumption of food, timber and metals by wealthy countries and elites.' FOEI argues that an alternative to REDD is 'community forest management, based on customary traditional knowledge and led by communities.' An important first step is resolving outstanding land tenure issues (2014). One of the more well-known internationally led efforts has been the REDD+ scheme, which provides financial incentives for developing countries to promote sustainable forest management and thus reduce greenhouse gases. REDD+ refers to the conservation of forest carbon stocks, sustainable management of forests and enhancement of forest carbon stocks (FAO, n.d.).The effectiveness of REDD+ has been hampered by deforestation from competing for economic sectors: agriculture, mining, energy and forestry. Poor rural people often practise shifting cultivation. Sometimes, REDD+ activities have merely displaced deforestation to another location (Mbow *et al.*, 2012). The main problem with trading the carbon stored in forests is that the world needs to reduce greenhouse emissions and stop deforestation rather than trading one off against another. Another serious flaw in the carbon market is that when the price of carbon declines, as it did in the 2008 economic slowdown, then the investment incentive is reduced (Böhm & Dabhi, 2009).

2.3.8. *Endangered species*

Africa has many of the world's endangered species, which need protection (Brown, 2009). Some animals are at risk because of deforestation and habitat loss. Some animals are captured to supply the illegal trade in animals and birds. Others are at risk from poaching because they are valuable sources of products, like ivory. This has led to the massive slaughter of elephants. Most of the demand for ivory came from Europe before the Convention on International Trade in Endangered Species in 1989. Demand then declined. More recent demand has come from Asia. Ivory has always been valued in Chinese culture and economic development there has led to an expansion in the middle and wealthy classes with more disposable income. Increased demand for ivory led to a surge in the killing of elephants in Africa. The number of forest elephants has declined by 60% since 2002, while, according to The Great Elephant Census released in 2016, the population of savannah elephants declined by 30% between 2007 and 2014 (144,000 elephants). There are only about 400,000 savannah elephants remaining and the number is falling by 8% each year. In five years, Mozambique lost 53% of its elephants and Tanzania 60%. The DRC has lost almost all of its elephants and Central African Republic most of its savannah elephants. There is also widespread slaughter in Sudan, Zimbabwe and Gabon. Organisations such as Save the Elephants have helped stem the tide of killing (Sherwood, 2016). A study commissioned by a major Chinese conservation organisation explored different drivers behind the demand for ivory between 2002 and 2014 and placed the total number of elephants slaughtered at 362,940. The annual average number of elephants killed between 2002 and 2006 was well below 20,000 but increased to over 30,000 a year between 2007 and 2014 (Martin *et al.*, 2015).

Governments have done little to prevent the sale of ivory, and it is still openly for sale on the internet. China has been the destination for 70% of illegal ivory since the early 2000s. Prices for illegal ivory reached $2,200 per kilo between 2012 and 2014 (Sherwood, 2016). One of the reasons given for the recent decline in ivory demand and reduced prices in China was the crackdown on corruption since Xi Jinping took office in 2012. The giving of expensive gifts as 'guanxi' is going out of favour. Slower economic growth in China has also reduced demand for ivory and pushed down prices (Reuters, 2017). Trade in ivory generally has gone down in recent years due to trade restrictions, increased political pressure, more effective field conservation, improved intelligence grabbing and tougher penalties on criminals. The key variable is profitability, so the price drop in China plays a major role in reducing the slaughter of elephants (Bale, 2017). Another discovery by Martin, Moyle and Stiles was that the amount of ivory worked and on sale in China was far below figures for the number of elephants killed and poached. They considered it was possible ivory had been purchased as an item of speculation in the anticipation of increasing demand in future and its increasing scarcity (2015). Demand for ivory and rhino horn from other countries in Asia has grown recently as standards of living improved in those countries. A recent myth circulating in Vietnam that rhino horn cures cancer led to a rapid increase in rhino poaching in South Africa. The number poached from 2007 and 2014 increased from 13 to 1,004 (World Wildlife Fund. 2018b).

The world's largest primate, the eastern gorilla, is also critically endangered. Numbers have dropped by 70% in the last 20 years. The gorilla's habitat in central Africa has been destroyed by logging, mining and farming. The gorillas also continue to be eaten as a source of food (Monbiot, 2016). In countries like the Democratic Republic of the Congo, where government agencies have collapsed and hunger is widespread, the population of mountain gorillas has dropped precipitously. This story is repeated all over Africa where many of the world's remaining large mammal species are concentrated (Brown, 2009). Apart from the most famously traded animals, thousands of other species are also illegally sold for many uses (World Wildlife Fund, 2018b). Protecting endangered species is difficult and almost always requires close international cooperation. Poverty is another key driver of poaching but there is also a strong criminal component.

2.4. Conclusion

There are many challenges facing SSA in the 21st century, including feeding its population, increasing agricultural productivity, providing employment and dealing with the climate crisis. Also important are stemming the tide of land grabbing, making further progress toward democracy, combatting corruption, improving human rights and social justice. SSA leaders need to maintain a steady course of appraising and negotiating these competing interests. None of these things will happen without the reform of the international economic and political system. There is an urgent need to make international economic relations fair and equitable, curb the international inequitable balance of power and rein in corporate activity. Halting the IFFs out of SSA would be a major step towards dealing with the looming balance of payments crisis. SSA's debt burden — in particular illegitimate debt — needs to be addressed.

The colonial legacy in SSA left newly independent countries lacking the expertise and educated people to run autonomous economies. New international organisations, such as the WB and IMF, were established and they were part of the emerging development sector. When low interest loans (with floating interest rates) were offered to SSA governments, they borrowed freely. When interest rates dramatically increased, SSA became entrapped in debt and subject to the prescriptions of the lenders. There have been a multitude of development prescriptions identifying what is needed to promote economic development and to reduce poverty in SSA. Theories have changed almost every decade, but the main lenders of the 20th century, the BWIs, have been obsessed with economic growth and the belief that Western economists can provide all the solutions to developing world problems. All this finance and expertise had not eliminated poverty in SSA by 2000, which prompted the signing of the United Nations MDG, yet again identified and driven by the main lenders and donors and not by the participants. The failure to reach these goals prompted the Sustainable Development Goals in 2015, at last acknowledging the need for more consultation and engagement with participants, and that poverty is a multidimensional and not purely an economic issue. There is no acknowledgement at the policy level, especially by the main lenders of the BWIs, that their neoliberal policies contributed to the continuing high poverty levels and economic sluggishness.

Indebtedness to the BWIs and the Paris Club resulted in nations in SSA losing their political and economic sovereignty in the 1980s. Neoliberal policies were imposed and resulted in stagnation in economic and human development. Governments continued to be economically subservient to the neoliberal conditions of the Washington Consensus until China offered alternative sources of finance. SSA countries continued to dominate the Fragile States Index in 2016 (Fund for Peace, 2016). At one time, it seemed that SSA could benefit from playing China against the West, but China's promise of a win-win relationship with Africa might be offset by the predatory behaviour of the BRICS, including South Africa continuing in its comprador role as the location for further regional exploitation (Bond, 2018b). Loans from China have contributed to the rapid rise in

SSA's high debt levels (Brautigam & Hwang, 2016) but remain a small proportion of Africa's debt (Jubilee Debt Campaign, 2018).

Progress in human development in SSA after 2000 continued to be held back by cuts to subsidies and water privatisation. Government spending was constrained by high levels of debt servicing. Populations continued to increase. The role that debt played in human development was evident in the two years after 2005 when many countries had a portion of the debt to multilateral lenders removed under the MDRI. Governments could spend more on social services and education. However, within two years, debt repayments were back to former levels. It was a reflection of the ideological nature of such policies that the WB continued to press for privatisation despite repeated failures.

In contrast to the BWIs, the UNDP promotes a human-centred model of development, defining 'development' as meeting people's basic needs and providing the ability to fulfil their potential. A human-centred approach prioritises public expenditure, social allocation and social welfare, including the right to work (UNDP, 2016). Restoring the political sovereignty undermined by Western loan conditionalities would be a first step in achieving those goals. Allowing and supporting subsidies for health, education and agriculture along with stimulating employment provision would help relieve poverty. Cancelling any water privatisation agreements would be another important move. Curtailing illegal financial flows out of SSA would be a major step in providing governments with more funds to spend on social services (health and education) and economic development. It would immediately almost double the disposable incomes of governments. Economic development would be assisted if governments could make health and education services free. Poverty levels would be reduced if agriculture could be made more productive and food security improved.

Economic development in SSA has been held back by poor governance, corruption and, importantly, a net loss of capital from the region. SSA lost its economic sovereignty when neoliberal policies were imposed in the late 1970s and those same policies contributed to the loss of much of the value of its resources. The region has suffered from enormous financial outflows from trade liberalisation. The loss was estimated at $275 billion between 1985 and 2005, roughly the amount of its foreign debt. This amount is far less than the $40 billion offered in debt relief under the MDRI in 2005 (Christian Aid, 2005). As economic growth expanded in 2000, outflows of capital have steadily increased along with foreign acquisition of the region's natural resources. SSA is the region with the highest percentage of illegitimate financial flows (IFF) in the world. Between 2000 and 2014, the estimated IFF out of SSA was between $36 billion and $69 billion (Clough, 2017), and in 2015, financial outflows (legal and illegal financial transfers) were higher than inflows (aid, loans, remittances and FDI). Despite high economic growth, many countries remained trapped in debt and debt servicing repayments. Economic development has been stunted because the region does not benefit from the value of its resources. The resource boom after 2000 did not 'trickle down' to the majority of the population and there were only modest improvements in human development. The arrival of Chinese money brought benefits in the supply of infrastructure and jobs but not structural changes in the pattern of economic domination by the Washington Consensus. Economic growth flattened and exports contracted after 2011. By 2016, debt levels and the ratios of debt to GDP in many countries were alarmingly high.

Countries in SSA lack economic sovereignty and suffer from an unequal international regulatory environment. Neoliberal conditions favour Western lenders (bilateral, multilateral and commercial) and aid donors. WTO trade rules are biased against SSA. Allowing SSA subsidies and tariffs, or removing subsidies and tariffs in the EU and US would make market opportunities for SSA exports more equitable. Stopping illegal financial flows and ensuring legal tax obligations were met by companies would also enable governments to spend more on social and economic development and infrastructure. Auditing of debt obligations, cancelling illegitimate debt and providing compensation for past illegitimate debt repayments (debt cancellation) would also free up funds from debt servicing and enable the productive use of the money. Another significant change would be to audit and streamline international aid to SSA as proposed by the 2005 Paris Declaration. Aid would be more effective if it was rationalised between aid agencies, if aid recipients had more say in what aid they received and if waste and duplication were reduced. Greater transparency is needed in the aid sector (OECD, n.d.e). There is also an urgent need for transparent international and corporate agreements and public scrutiny. Loan conditions need to be made fairer. A global forum is needed, to avoid situations like the HIPCI conditions which included a rate of debt repayment, 40% of export earnings, that was impossible to meet (Hertz, 2004). Fairness is also needed in trade and in governments' ability to provide subsidies.

SSA nations need to diversify their economies as too many are vulnerable to price fluctuations because of a dependence on one or two main exports. Key priorities are employment-focused economic development, economic diversification (away from resource dependence) and to build up services and manufacturing. Higher government revenues from increased corporate taxes and higher export prices could be used to build infrastructure, particularly to improve regional trade links. Neoliberal policies were always justified as stimulating economic growth and enabling debt repayment and economic development. This was the rationale used for conditions for SAPs' loans and debt relief under HIPCI and MDRI, even though the WB in 1991 and an IMF audit in 2002 reported that both institutions had consistently overpromised on the results of loans (Easterley, 2007).

It is necessary to break the pattern of 400 years of rape and pillage in SSA. The way that resources are managed in the region will determine its trajectory in the 21st century. The major environmental challenge facing SSA is the climate crisis and the increasing scarcity of water. The exploitation of its resources has had major impacts on the quality of water, land and air. Mining and oil extraction have been extremely damaging to the environment. Deforestation and species extinction are other problems, as is the foreign acquisition of land. Countries in SSA need to regain control of their own resources, manage them sustainably and use them to contribute to raising the standards of living and human development. In the next decades, global demand for Africa's oil and minerals is likely to expand. Africa has 10% of the world's oil, 40% of its gold and 80–90% of its chromium and platinum. It is predicted that world liquid fuel consumption will increase by 25% (Leke *et al.*, 2010). There is a real need for change at an international level. Corporations need to pay the 'true cost of resources', both in terms of the loss from being non-renewable (natural capital accounting) and to pay workers higher wages that will lift them out of poverty as well as paying appropriate government taxes (stopping illegal cash flows). If real prices are paid for resources, governments will earn more from taxes which they can pass on to social services, health and education. Implementation of natural capital accounting could be monitored through the WTO in much the same way it monitors subsidies and tariffs. Governments need to have power to decide on their own subsidies and tariffs. Rather than focusing on neoliberal, export-oriented agriculture as mandated to earn money for loan repayment, African agriculture needs to produce more to meet local and regional needs (Pearce, 2012). Most of the population still work in agriculture, so improving productivity is a top priority and could be increased if countries could subsidise fertilisers and provide more education and training for farmers. Improving the local small-holder production model would also reduce the need for food imports and increase food security.

Chapter 3

China After 2000

This chapter examines China's internal evolution and changing international role in recent decades, advocating a more nuanced approach to understanding contemporary China, not as a monolithic entity but rather as a complex array of interests and agents that are reflected in a diversity of practices. According to one expert on China, Martin Jacques, there is no unified Chinese 'African policy' and no unified 'state' that Chinese companies represent (2012).

In the early decades after China embraced 'market socialism', the West greeted China's rapid growth with enthusiasm. China was seen as having a vast, potential, untapped market. Three decades later the global impact of the juggernaut of China's development had dissipated that enthusiasm. Until the 1990s China had been able to provide for its growth primarily with its own resources. After 1990 it began searching internationally for resources and export markets. When the Chinese government adopted its 'Go Global' strategy in 2000, many large Chinese companies began expanding overseas (Jacques, 2012), and the effects of China's rapid development began to be felt far beyond its borders. There were many dimensions to this expansion: competition for resources, food supplies and markets for goods. Rapid economic growth in China has also affected global pollution, carbon emissions and the environment.

3.1. People: Politics and Human Development

3.1.1. *Politics*

The contemporary political system in China continues to function as more of a system of 'fragmented authoritarianism' than the monolithic state portrayed in Western media (Lampton, 1987, cited in Taylor, 2009). China's policies and activities, both domestic and international, are not static and have been evolving since 1978 when the country began engaging more with the outside world.

Even though the Chinese Communist Party is determined to maintain control of power and to prevent the expansion of democracy, it is also aware of the need for change. One of the things it has done since 2000 is keep control of the core state-owned enterprises (SOEs) while continuing to allow private entrepreneurs to flourish. As the wealth and power of private entrepreneurs increased, the Party acknowledged their contribution by allowing a small number of them to become Communist Party deputies. The first seven were admitted at the 16th Party Congress in 2002, the number increasing to 17 at the 17th Party Congress in 2007 (statistics from the state-run *China Economic Weekly,* cited by He, 2012) and to 34 in 2012. All these new deputies were on the 2012 Forbes list of world billionaires. The Chinese scholar William Lam sees the Communist Party to be broadening its leadership base to help with the next stage of China's development. As China's GDP slowed and external markets contracted after the Global Financial Crisis (GFC), the government looked to these entrepreneurs to provide jobs and promote growth (cited by He, 2012).

3.1.1.1. *Democracy and human rights*

Since suppressing the 1989 Tiananmen Square democracy protests the Chinese Communist government has managed to stifle demands for greater democracy. As standards of living improved, some sections of the population voiced their dissatisfaction, particularly in relation to environmental issues. The government allowed some changes and loosening of regulations. Non-government organisations (NGOs) were permitted. The concessions were later revoked and restrictions imposed on NGOs, curtailing their activities. Any moves towards democracy in China still seem to be a long way off. Despite better standards of living problems persist, including the social impacts of legal and environmental policies, a lack of human rights and imprisonment of critics of the regime. China has a poor record on human rights and the persecution of minorities. There has been ongoing persecution of dissidents and dissent minorities, including the Falun Gong movement, and the Muslim Uighurs in the northwest region of Xinjiang. The invasion, suppression and colonisation of Tibet has been intermittent throughout the 20th century and into the 21st century.

3.1.1.2. *International role*

One of the missions of the Chinese government is to regain China's former position as a great power. It has expanded its multilateral linkages, joining the World Bank (WB) in 1980 and the World Trade Organisation (WTO) in 2001. In accordance with its policy of 'non-interference', China has made significant contributions to UN peacekeeping operations, its only form of foreign military intervention. In 2015, China increased its contribution of military personnel to 8,000, one-fifth of the 40,000 troops committed by 50 nations. It also committed \$100 million to the African Union Standby Force and \$1 billion to the establishment of the UN Peace and Development Fund (Fung, 2016). In 2016, China was the second largest contributor to UN peacekeeping funding (10.29%) after the US (28.57%) (United Nations, 2020).

China's voting power in the Bretton Woods Institutions (BWIs) does not reflect its position as the largest economy in the world. Its voting power at the WB was increased to 4.42% in 2010 (voting tables of IBRD, IFA, IFC). In the most recent voting reform at the IMF, China's share of votes increased from 3.81% to 6.16%, an increase of 2.35 percentage points. While this is a big proportional change, and represents a doubling of China's share since 2006, it still leaves China with a very small vote compared to its size in the world economy. On a purchasing-power-parity basis, it has 18.6% of the world economy — more than the United States — and its population is 4.3 times that of the US, yet the US has more than 2.6 times China's voting share at the IMF (Weisbrot & Johnson, 2016). China has also joined forces with other emerging powers as an alternative to the G7. The BRIC group (Brazil, Russia, India and China) became a formal institution in 2010. It was joined by South Africa and renamed the BRICS in 2011. In a move to provide an alternative lending mechanism to the BWIs, the BRICS established the New Development Bank in 2015.

3.1.2. *Human development*

China has roughly one-fifth of the global population (1.3 billion in 2016) (WB, n.d.g2). Since the 1980s the country has managed to lift the greatest number of people out of poverty in world history. Figures vary as China and the WB use different measures for poverty rates. In 2011, the Chinese reset their poverty level. By the end of 2016 Xinhua claimed there were only 43.35 million people living below the national poverty line of 2300 yuan (approximately US $334 a year (Xinhua, 2017)). The WB increased its measure for poverty in 2015 from $1.25 per day to $1.90 per day ($693.5 a year) (Jiao, 2015). According to its figures the poverty rate in China in 2016 was 4.5% or 58.5 million (WB, n.d.b). Unemployment levels have been comparatively low though there was a brief increase after the 2008 economic crisis. After dropping to 4.5% in 2010, rates increased slightly in the years up to 2015 and then declined (WB, n.d.c). China is still categorised as a middle-income country because its per capita gross national income (GNI) has remained comparatively low at $8,200 in 2016 (WB, n.d.a). Human development levels have improved from 0.7 in 2000 (ranked 99 in the world) to 0.738 in 2015, but China's ranking at 90 in the Human Development Index (HDI) is near the middle of the list (United Nations Development Programme (UNDP), n.d.).

3.1.2.1. *Social structure*

Social and economic differences began to emerge in China in the 1980s and have intensified since 2000. There are major contrasts between the eastern seaboard and the rural hinterland, as well as between cities and rural areas. A distinct Chinese middle class emerged after 1990, mainly in the larger urban areas. The actual size of this middle class is difficult to pin point and varies according to who measures it, but all indications are that it is larger than in any other country (Credit Suisse, 2015). Credit Suisse estimated this class to be 71.5 million people in 2000 (2010). It defines the middle class in China as those with an annual income of $28,000 in 2015, which is about 11% of the population (150 million). In comparison, the estimated size of the US middle class was 36% of the total population (Credit Suisse, 2015). Figures from the Pew Research Center show the middle classes numbered 29 million in 1999 but had increased to 421 million by 2013 (2017). A study by the Southwestern University of Finance and Economics in China has challenged the Credit Suisse figures. They estimated the size of the Chinese middle class to be 240 million (2016).

3.1.2.2. *Inequality*

Many of the benefits from economic changes in China have not been equally distributed. By 2000 the first generation of super wealthy people had emerged. The number of very wealthy people have continued to expand. In 2012, there were 1.4 million millionaire households (Boston Consulting Group, 2012). Three years later that number was 3.14 million, and there were 596 billionaires (Hurun Report China Rich List, in 2015, cited in Wildau & Mitchell, 2016). (These figures are measured in US dollars). Because there is so much unrecorded income in China, the figures for wealth are probably much higher (Wildau & Mitchell, 2016). Regardless, the Gini coefficient (the measure of wealth or income inequality) in the nation is rising. The WB considers 0.40 to be the benchmark for high inequality. In China the inequality of wealth moved beyond 0.40 in the mid-2000s (Tobin, 2011), reached 0.437 in 2010 and then contracted to 0.385 in 2016, according to the WB (n.d). In contrast, the Institute of Social Science Survey at Peking University reported China's Gini coefficient in 2012 as 0.49, higher than the US (0.41). Official Chinese figures are lower and show a decline from 0.477 in 2011 to 0.469 in 2014 (Wildau & Mitchell, 2016).

Though official statistics need to be treated with some caution, social information from China is positive. In 2015, the Premier announced that many of the social goals of the 12th Five Year Plan (2011–2015) had been met, including raising internal consumption and reducing poverty. He claimed that 100 million people had been lifted out of poverty, 300 million rural residents had gained access to safe drinking water, rural–urban income differences had narrowed and basic healthcare was now available to the whole population (Weibing, 2016). Social and economic changes have also had an impact on patterns of consumption. Standards of living have been improving since the 1980s and are reflected in product purchases, types of food consumed and lifestyle choices. The ageing population uses more energy (utilities, fuels, services and healthcare) while younger households spend more on education, clothing and vehicles (Dalton *et al.*, 2008). China's elderly have patterns of consumption similar to their counterparts in the US (O'Neill & Chen, 2002). Most significant in the pattern of food consumption is the rise in the eating of meat. Meat production has a much higher carbon footprint than grains.

3.1.2.3. *Urban/rural divide*

Urbanisation in China has accelerated rapidly. In 2000, the urban population was 35.8% of the total population (National Bureau of Statistics, 2006 and WB, 2006, cited in Nabeshima & Yusuf, 2008). This reached 49% in 2010 and 57% in 2016

(WB, n.d.e). Even though many city dwellers live in poverty, city incomes are still much higher than those in the countryside. In 2010, the average, rural, disposable income was 5,900 yuan ($898), while the urban average was three times higher at 19,000 yuan or $2,900 (Tobin, 2011). Far more of the rural population live in poverty and need to spend a much higher proportion of their income on food. Widening income disparities are reflected in the consumer products people own; the more affluent tend to own washing machines, fridges, colour television sets, computers and vehicles (Tobin, 2011).

3.1.2.4. *Employment, health and safety*

Health and safety regulations are poorly enforced in China. The number of industrial accidents is high and workplace conditions are often unsafe or unfair (BBC News, 2016). The Chinese mining industry has the highest per capita accident rate of any country in the world. A recent investigation of the statistics on mining accidents and deaths in China found that even though the country was cutting back its coal production, the rate of accidents and deaths was increasing. This is a result of both the age of mines and infrastructure and firms trying to maximise output because of high prices (Lelyveld, 2016). Workers are expected to work hard and for long hours, and labour conditions in factories can be problematic. One of the internationally most publicised cases was of the large number of suicides at the Foxconn factory in 2012. The Taiwanese-owned Foxconn is the subcontractor that produces the Apple iPhone and other common electronic products for external markets. When deadlines were urgent, workers were expected to work extremely long hours. They lived in compounds on the premises. There were also reports of poor treatment and wages that barely covered expenses. Suicides were not uncommon, to the extent that at one workplace Foxconn erected safety nets to prevent workers from taking their own lives (Greene, 2012). It could be said that consumers of Foxconn products were complicit in such questionable labour practices.

3.1.2.5. *Social issues*

Economic pressures that push people to migrate to find work are very disruptive for rural family life in China. Migrant workers are also discriminated against in the cities. The hukou household system, introduced in 1958, allocated people's social, welfare and educational entitlements to their place of birth. Migrant workers and their families are not registered in the cities and therefore not eligible for benefits, and neither are their children (Jacques, 2012). Millions of children left behind in the villages are brought up by grandparents, seeing their parents only once or twice a year. The results can create severe social dislocation and sometimes tragedy (China Labour Bulletin, n.d.). The annual migration of Chinese parents back to their homes in the countryside for Chinese New Year is the largest movement of people on the planet. The documentary *Last Train Home* tells the story of the hardships faced by parents living far from their children and able to see them only once a year (Fan, 2010).

The ageing population is another problematic social issue in China. Children are expected to look after their parents as they age. The proportion of older people in society has grown significantly. In 2000, 6.6% of the population was over 65, but by 2016 the figure had risen to 10% (WB, n.d.f). The age profile is younger in the cities, but because of migration there is often no one to look after the rural aged. As the population ages, the workforce is contracting. There is also a major gender imbalance in Chinese society as a result of the one child policy that came into effect in 1979. There was a preference for male children over female children and many female foetuses were aborted. The Chinese government relaxed this policy in 2015, allowing families to have two children (Lu, 2019). The rapid change has produced very different life experiences and worldviews among the various age cohorts. People born after 1975 (younger than 43) have completely different life experiences from earlier generations who lived through the tough decades of early Communism. It is this younger group that has enthusiastically embraced the consumer culture (Watts, 2010).

Another major problem facing China has been the growth in corruption as the Chinese government opened up to international markets and economic growth targets were delegated to the regional level. Corruption takes many forms, including graft, bribery, embezzlement, backdoor deals, nepotism, patronage and the falsifying of statistics (Lu, 2000). According to Yan, the Tiananmen Square demonstrations were more a protest against corruption than the desire for greater democracy (2004). Corruption continues to be a major problem in China. In 2012, when General Secretary Xi Jinping came to power, he embarked on an anti-corruption campaign. Since then there have been many thousands of arrests (GAN Anti-Corruption Business Portal, 2017). China's ranking on Transparency International's Corruption Perception Index has fluctuated: from 39 in 2012 to 40 in 2013, 36 in 2014 and 37 in 2015. The 2016 score of 40/100 remained poor (Transparency International, 2017). Bribery, kickbacks, theft and misplaced funds are estimated to amount to 3% of China's GDP (Pei, 2007).

Social unrest has increased in China since 2000. China's security minister, Zhou Yongkang, admitted that in 2004 there were 4,000 protests, involving more than 3.7 million people (Keidel, 2006, cited in Taylor, 2009). Reasons for growing unrest included widening income disparities, corruption and environmental pollution. One notorious case of corruption and neglect was the disaster in 2008 when many schools collapsed in the Sichuan earthquake. Large numbers of children were killed. Lack of regulatory oversight and corruption in the building of rural schools were cited as the main reasons for the tragedy. The buildings were inadequately reinforced and inferior materials used. Many families lost their only children (Yardley, 2008).

The large numbers of people relocated for infrastructure projects is another area of dissatisfaction. As China has industrialised, many people have been displaced and dispossessed of their land. The building of the Great Gorges Dam, for example, displaced 1.3 million people. The government is trying to remedy these issues, stimulate consumption and develop the rural hinterland (Weibing, 2016). Such initiatives are dependent on maintaining relatively high growth rates and keeping the economy buoyant. As the economy has slowed in recent years, improving standards of living and addressing issues of social unrest have been more difficult for the government.

China has not been without success in dealing with social issues. Lifting 800 million people out of poverty has been its greatest accomplishment since 1978, when 90% of the population lived below the 'extreme poverty line' set by the WB at $2 a day. Between 1981 and 2004 China raised more than half a billion people out of poverty, one of the greatest successes in world history (Allison, 2018). While this achievement is the largest single contribution to declining global poverty rates, the social transition of China's population has not been accompanied by an increase in human rights and democracy. Persecution of dissidents and ethnic minorities continues and there are indications that human rights are further eroding and the totalitarian system becoming harsher. The downturn in China's economy means that everyday life for millions of Chinese people is becoming more difficult, although not as difficult as it was in the past.

3.2. Profit

For decades China has had one of the fastest growing economies in the world. Between 1975 and 2000 the economy grew steadily at an annual average of 9% (Brown, 2006). The size of China's GDP is so large that since 1999 the country has been re-classified as a middle-income nation; at the same time it is still classed as a 'developing nation' because its GNI per capita remains low (WB, n.d.g2). By 2016 China's GDP had reached $11.2 trillion (WB, n.d.g2). The high growth rates of the late 20th century continued into the decade after 2000, reaching their highest level (14.2%) in 2007. Average growth between 2006 and 2010 was 10%, despite the economic crises elsewhere and a downturn in exports (*The Economist*, 2010a). Eventually growth rates dropped, due to the decrease in foreign demand for Chinese products after the GFC. In 2008, growth in China slowed to 9.6%. It increased to 10.6% in 2010 and thereafter declined annually, reaching 6.8% in 2016 (WB, n.d.h). The 2016 figure was the lowest since 1990 (Allen, 2017). After 2015 the Western media predicted the Chinese economy might fail (Woetzel, 2015) but growth rates have remained far higher than that of any Western nation.

3.2.1. *Economic development*

China's economic development has been partially dependent on foreign corporations which began moving to China in the 1980s when regulations were lifted. China's industrial transition followed strategies such as 'flying geese' (establishing special economic zones on the eastern seaboard to spearhead the first industries) and 'crossing the river by feeling the stones' (pioneering new forms of business) (Brautigam, 2009). The Japanese were the first foreign corporations to enter China, later followed by the Americans and Europeans. China insisted foreign companies set up joint ventures with local companies to ensure that they (the Chinese) learnt from foreign expertise. China was a challenging market for foreign companies. Coca Cola was one of the first American companies to enter the country, and it was 20 years before they made a profit (Weisert, 2001). The Chinese rapidly absorbed Western marketing concepts and strategies, and by the 1990s strong Chinese brands were beginning to emerge. Some of the largest Chinese consumer goods companies, including Haier and Lenovo, began expanding internationally. During the 1990s the government focused on improving the quality of Chinese goods. As consumer markets in China expanded and regulations on foreign entry loosened, many American auto manufacturers began production there. Foreign corporations continued to search for greater profits, with some companies moving into neighbouring SE Asian countries in search of cheaper labour (Shuman, 2016). That cheaper labour was not without problems, including lower levels of productivity and a less educated labour force. Within a few years, companies began to use what was termed a 'China+' strategy, keeping a base in China and setting up satellites in neighbouring countries (*The Economist*, 2012).

China also borrowed from the WB group to fund its economic development. By 1999 it had taken $9.9 billion in concessional loans from the International Development Association (IDA), the WB's low-income lending arm. Between 1999 and 2011, when China was reclassified as a middle-income nation, it borrowed $39.9 billion from the International Bank for Reconstruction and Development (IBRD), the WB's middle-income country lending arm. Borrowing from the commercial arm of the WB, the International Finance Corporation (IFC), was much lower, at $5.3 billion for 220 projects (Bretton Woods Project, 2011a). China continued to borrow from the IBRD for projects such as poverty reduction and air pollution control. In 2016, it passed the IBRD borrowing threshold, but loans have continued for projects that have benefits beyond its borders (Hue, 2019).

3.2.2. *Energy*

In 2014, China was responsible for 23% of global energy consumption. China's economic development has been based on coal as the main energy source. In 2014, China was the world's largest consumer of coal, responsible for over half the global consumption. In that year China accounted for 12% of global oil and 5.5% of natural gas (Fridley, Lu & Liu, 2017). In 2014, coal-fired power stations produced 66% of China's energy (International Energy Agency (IEA), 2017). In 2016, coal accounted for 62% of China's energy (Center for International and Strategic Studies, 2021). That year, though China announced plans to curb the building of 200 new coal-fired power stations, there were still many stations under construction (Forsyth, 2016). China's reliance on coal will persist for some time yet. China's second most important energy source is oil, and consumption has increased significantly since the late 1990s. By 2008 oil accounted for 20% of its energy (IEA, 2017). China has been a net importer of oil since 1993 (Taylor, 2006) and by 2004 was the third largest oil importer after the US and Japan (Downs, 2006). China's oil import dependence first reached 50% in 2008 (Lelyveld, 2017), amounting to 204 million tons annually, most from the Middle East, and a third from Africa (Zhao, 2011a). The growth in Chinese demand for oil has been the highest in the world since 2009. Supplies no longer come mainly from the OPEC countries; between 2012 and 2016 most of the oil was sourced from Russia, Oman and Brazil. Chinese domestic production declined in 2016, but demand and imports continued to increase (EIA, 2017). Demand grew 6.5% in 2016 (Jaganathan & Daly, 2017), and China overtook the US as the largest net importer of oil in 2014 (EIA, 2017). In 2016, 18.5% of China's energy came from oil (Center for International and Strategic Studies, 2021). Patterns of use also changed. As Chinese oil consumption levelled off, oil refining and the export of processed oil became more important. Oil imports have been stimulated by increased refining capacity rather than consumption. The Chinese oil company Unipec is now the world's largest trader in oil. China is now increasing its oil exports to Asia and Europe (Jaganathan & Daly, 2017). The nation is a world leader in the use of renewable energy, but these options continue to supply only a small amount of the country's total energy consumption. In 2014, biofuels and waste produced 7.1% of energy while natural gas supplied 5%. At the same time solar energy, along with wind and geothermal energy, produced 1.3% of total energy, and is increasing (*IEA*, 2017). China's commitment to renewable energy has transformed it into the world's largest supplier of solar panels.

3.2.3. *Economic changes*

The initial stage of development in China was founded on a huge supply of low-cost labour, considerable natural resources and large export markets. The benefits of its economic success have been unevenly distributed throughout the country and the government is keen to develop the interior regions, which represent a large potential market. The 12th Five Year Plan (2011–2015) focused on raising living standards and stimulating internal consumption, especially in rural China and the hinterland (Weibing, 2016). Raising standards of living and the economic development of the interior regions was given priority, to provide protection from the impacts of external economic fluctuations, especially after the 2008 GFC that hit Western economies and which lessened the demand for Chinese exports. Manufacturing intended for the internal market grew at this time. Stimulating consumption is not always easy in a culture that places a high value on savings. China's gross national savings rate was 46% in 2016 (Balding, 2018), much higher than in the West (Nabeshima & Yusuf, 2011).

The Chinese government's response to the 2008 GFC was an enormous $580 billion economic stimulus package. The package was investment-focused. Further stimulus packages in 2009 focused on infrastructure construction, in contrast to Western economies which provided incentives for consumption (Australian Treasury, 2018). An estimated 2% to 3% was added to the GDP in 2009 and 2010 (McKissack & Xu, 2011). This approach, using increased government spending to stimulate aggregate demand, is very Keynesian, according to Chinese economists Yi Wen and Jing Wu (cited in Matthews, 2016). The economic stimulus package generated a construction boom and high levels of non-productive investment, including the building of 'zombie' towns, built in anticipation of future needs that had not yet materialised (Gray, 2017). Nomi Prins is more positive about China's building programme, seeing it as more productive than the West's focus on financial bail outs (2018). The Chinese have significant economic interests in the US, including significant Treasury bonds, but in the future they want to reduce the risk of ownership and exposure to US federal policy (Prins, 2018).

The general contraction of the global economy since the GFC also slowed down growth in the Chinese economy, but China's economy continues to outperform the rest of the world, and in particular the US. The composition of its economy has changed from a focus on manufacturing and investment to one on services and consumption. There has also been an emphasis away from meeting external demand towards growing domestic demand. The Five Year Plan in 2016 predicted a 3% GDP government deficit, again much lower than other large economies (Breene, 2016).

3.2.4. *Trade*

In 2015, China was both the world's largest export economy, valued at $2.37 trillion, and the largest import economy, valued at $1.27 trillion. This left China with a balance of payments surplus of $1.1 trillion. The main exports are computers, broadcasting equipment, integrated circuits and machine parts while key imports are crude oil, gold, iron ore and cars (OECD, 2017). China's largest export market continues to be the US, valued at $475 billion in 2015. The US is China's second largest source of imports ($128 billion) behind Korea (OECD, 2017). The trade imbalance between the United States and China increased from $83 billion in 2000 to $347 billion in 2016 (US Census Bureau, 2017). Eliminating this imbalance was one of Donald Trump's major campaign promises in the 2016 presidential elections.

In the 1990s, when China could no longer meet its needs domestically, it began an international quest for resources. Resource imports increased significantly, including imports from Sub-Saharan Africa (SSA). In 2010, China overtook the US as the world's largest energy consumer, according to the IEA. The Chinese government disputed the figures (IEA, cited in Watts, 2010). China has become the world's largest importer of oil, with 22% coming from Africa. Angola was China's largest supplier of oil in SSA in 2016. Other suppliers included the Republic of Congo and South Sudan (Council on Foreign Relations, 2017).

3.2.5. *SOEs and Chinese MNCs*

The corporate profile in China has evolved as the country's economy developed and became liberalised. The Chinese government kept control of major state-owned entities (SOEs) but permitted private companies to operate. The SOEs retained control of the most significant sectors of the economy and continue to play an important economic role (Minto & Romei, 2012), especially in imports of essential raw materials. SOEs also play an important part in delivering infrastructure around the world. China dominates the global hydropower industry. By January 2012 International Rivers had identified China's involvement in 308 dam building projects in 70 countries, a 300% increase in active hydropower projects in the previous four years (2012a). After the government introduced the 'Going Global' strategy in 1999, Chinese foreign direct investment also expanded.

The exact amount of foreign investment and where that investment ultimately ended up are hard to determine from official government figures as much investment is channelled through tax havens (Salidjanova, 2011). Chinese companies operating overseas are extremely diverse and include product exporters, importers of resources and infrastructure companies.

After China joined the WTO in 2001, the number of foreign companies in China increased. These companies came from other Asian countries, the US and the EU. Foreign companies have been attracted by the potential of the huge internal Chinese market since the 1980s when Western markets were becoming saturated. They were initially compelled to form joint ventures with local companies, and even after the restriction to do so was lifted, many of these arrangements continued because of the complexity of the Chinese market. Foreign firms (including Sino-foreign contractual joint ventures, Sino-foreign equity joint ventures and foreign-owned enterprises) were responsible for 60% of China's exports in 2006, but by 2012 this had declined to 50% (Minto & Romei, 2012).

After 2000 China's internal market became even more important for both Chinese and foreign private companies. By 2010 the country was the world's largest market for automobiles and television sets, and the second largest market for personal computers. Automobiles, jewellery and cosmetics were the fastest growing sectors. Many foreign companies began to treat China as their primary market when sales began to flatten in the US at the turn of the century (Basulto, 2013). With costs rising in China, these foreign investors changed their focus from global production to producing for the Chinese market (Rabinovitch, the *Financial Times* Beijing correspondent, cited in Minto & Romei, 2012). This was the case particularly in the auto industry. Annual automobile market sales in China reached 11 million vehicles by 2010 and continued to increase, reaching 19 million in 2015. A consumer survey revealed people were becoming less status conscious and more practical in their attitudes to car ownership (Baan *et al.*, 2016).

3.2.6. *Conclusion*

The scale of economic development in China has had a global impact as well as transforming the lives of millions of Chinese. It was China that provided the world with cheap products, helping fuel consumer culture in the West and providing many people around the world access to products they could otherwise not afford. China has also challenged the economic dominance of Western industrialised countries. In the 21st century the path of economic development will need to change dramatically to deal with real issues of resource depletion and climate change, which are the consequence of the cumulative development of the industrialised economies, augmented by the recent rapid growth of newly industrialising economies. China will play a key role in that transition, being one of the largest consumers of resources and producing the second highest level of greenhouse gases (GHG), but also a country committed to finding solutions and embracing alternative energy sources.

3.3. Planet

Four decades of unregulated economic growth within China has had a toxic impact on its environment. In the process of economic development, the environment has been treated merely as a footnote (Jacques, 2012). China has a small *per capita* but huge *national* ecological footprint. The ecological footprint measures the ecological assets a population requires to produce the natural resources it consumes and to absorb its waste, while biocapacity represents the productivity of a population's ecological assets (Global Footprint Network, n.d.a). In 2008, China's per capita ecological footprint was 2.1 global hectares (ght), 80% of the global average of 2.7 ght, but its total ecological footprint was higher than anywhere in the world, at 9.4 billion ght, because of the size of its population. Carbon emissions, largely from the energy sector, had the fastest ecological footprint growth (WWF, 2012). By 2016 China's per capita ecological footprint had increased to 3.6 hectares. At this time its available per capita biocapacity was 1.0 hectares, which meant it had a biocapacity deficit of 2.6 hectares. The planet cannot sustain levels of resource consumption higher than 1.73 hectares per person (Global Footprint Network, 2019).

3.3.1. *Carbon dioxide (CO^2) emissions*

China's rapid economic development has been very carbon intensive, as its key energy source was coal-fired power. The country has continued to experience a rapid growth in emissions, which have contributed to the accelerating pace of global climate change. From 2002 to 2011, carbon emissions in China grew by 10% annually, but thereafter to 2015 annual growth slowed to 3% even though by 2014 66% of China's energy still came from coal (IEA, 2017). It did not help that the local coal is of poor quality and also causes air pollution (Netherlands Environmental Agency (PBL), 2016). In 2015, the government revised upwards, by 17% per year, its previous CO^2 emissions figures between 2005 and 2012 (Buckley, 2015). In 2007, China overtook the US as the world's largest carbon emitter (Vidal & Adam, 2007), and by 2013 was producing one quarter of total global carbon emissions — 150% of the amount produced in the US. Between 2010 and 2012, nearly three-quarters (73%) of the growth in global carbon emissions came from China. The role China plays in reducing its carbon emissions in the immediate future is central to the reduction of global carbon emissions and addressing climate change (Liu, 2016).

The slowing of China's economy after 2012 has meant a decrease in CO^2 emissions. The service sector was now expanding faster than manufacturing and was less energy intensive. There was also more emphasis on energy efficiency and a low-carbon energy mix. In 2015, emissions continued to drop as coal consumption declined and more non-fossil fuel power sources were used: nuclear, solar, water and wind. The reduction in China's carbon output has been the main reason behind the slowdown in global emissions. In 2015, national carbon emissions reduced by 0.7% and per capita emissions by 1.2%, although China is still the largest global carbon emitter (29%) compared to the US (14%)

and the EU-28 (10%). Coal-fired power stations at this time were responsible for 48% of China's emissions (down from 66% in 2014), compared to 31% for the US and 28% for the EU. The growing consumption of oil and cement production are key sources of rising emissions which have been stimulated by China's recent construction boom (PBL, 2016). Though China has the world's highest national CO^2 emissions, the US has the highest per capita emissions, nearly twice those of China, which is more on par with the EU. Because of the use of poor quality coal the carbon intensity of China's emissions is high, twice that of the United States economy and three times higher than in the EU-28 in 2014 (PBL, 2016).

As well as contributing to China's carbon emission levels, the burning of coal and oil for energy generates discharges that cause acid rain, produced by sulfuric and nitric acid released into the air and combining with water. Acid rain already falls on 30% of China, mainly in the south east, which has the largest concentration of people, power-plants and factories. Acid rain poisons land and water. It is harmful to human health and causes lung disease, heart attacks and asthma. Twenty-two cities in China are affected by acid rain. While the US had severe problems with acid rain in the 1970s and 1980s, China's initial problems began in the mid-1990s. The first attempts to cut emissions between 2000 and 2005 failed and instead they rose by 28%. Sulphur dioxide emissions have since been reduced by more than 13% even though more coal-fired power stations were built between 2006 and 2009. The nitric oxide problem received less attention (Larson, 2010).

3.3.2. *Industrialisation and construction*

Unregulated industrialisation has also had a major environmental impact in China. When industrialisation was devolved to the local level in the late 1980s, the main focus was on economic development, and rapid, unregulated industrial development caused significant environmental damage and pollution. In some areas the impact on the environment was devastating, particularly where industrial by-products were dumped in waterways, on the land or pumped into the air. Foreign companies have contributed to China's high level of carbon emissions and pollution. In the 1970s, when environmental regulations became stricter in Western nations, many corporations transferred their most polluting industries to China (Economy, 2004). The IPCC 2014 Report acknowledged that consumer goods and services production for export to the US and EU had contributed to the rise in carbon emissions in China and other developing countries. Carbon emissions rose twice as fast in the first decade of the 21st century than in the three previous decades (Goldenberg, 2014). If China enforced its environmental laws, the costs would flow on to Western consumers in higher prices and sales would be affected (Silk, 2013).

China's economic policies have evolved in recent years. China's economic growth between 2000 and 2013 was focused on heavy industry and was energy intensive, but by 2014 the government was signalling a change of direction towards a more sustainable and inclusive growth model. Green and Stern were predicting that China's emissions from industry would slow or possibly remain static and probably peak by 2025 (2016).

Rapid urbanisation has also had major environmental consequences in China. Between 1997 and 2006 12,800 square kilometres of land were converted into cities. Urban consumption generates higher carbon emissions (Liu, 2016). The number of Chinese cities with populations over one million grew from 34 in 2000 (China Population Yearbook, cited in Seto, 2000) to 102 in 2017 (Haas, 2017). The building of cities and infrastructure is very resource-intensive, requiring enormous amounts of cement, one of the most environmentally harmful products known. Construction also generates carbon emissions (Magnier, 2008), and the growth of cities encroaches on arable farmland. Large-scale infrastructure programmes — highways, waterways and dams — have been built throughout China, utilising large amounts of cement. Increased energy demand from such programmes has meant more dams have been built; more than 87,000 exist in China today, displacing an estimated 23 million people (International Rivers, 2017). The world's largest dam project — the Three Gorges Dam on the Yangtze River — was completed in 2012. Built in a storm of controversy, the dam seriously threatens the ecological balance of a large area and its construction displaced 1.3 million people. Beyond this dam are dozens of dams built on or planned for the upper reaches of the Yangtze, which seriously compromise the long-term viability of the river itself (Jiangtao, 2012). For the first time, in 2011, the Chinese government admitted there had been problems with the Three Gorges Dam. Despite these complications the Yangtze dam has been used as template for China's international dam building projects. The building of dams can cause issues other than displacing people. The building of a nearby dam in 2004 may have contributed to the 2008 earthquake in Sichuan in which 80,000 people were killed (Moore, 2009). Dams also affect the ecological balance of a region.

3.3.3. *Air, land and water*

China covers a huge land area and includes a wide range of climate zones and land use practices. Water scarcity is an important issue, and is predicted to be a major issue in the future (Watts, 2010), as changing climate conditions make water shortages even more acute. Large areas of northern China are prone to low levels of rainfall. Population growth has increased the demand for water, particularly in northern China where the water table is falling. To provide more water for Beijing there is a plan to divert 44 billion cubic metres of water a year from the Yangtze River to the Yellow River basin in the north, in the South–North Water Transfer Project (International Rivers, 2012b). The central route that diverts water from Hubei province to Beijing and Tianjin was completed in 2014, and the eastern route in 2013 (Baiyu, 2020).

The dumping of industrial waste into waterways and onto the land has created serious pollution issues. Over 42% of China's rivers are severely polluted and the water in 75% of its lakes and reservoirs is not suitable for human consumption or fishing (International Rivers, 2017). Water pollution in large cities is a major problem. According to official standards, in 2015, 85% of the water in Shanghai's major rivers was undrinkable and 56.4% unfit for any purpose. In Beijing 40% of the water was so polluted it was almost useless. Water pollution is also high in other cities (Deng, 2017). Air quality levels in China are some of the worst in the world, taking a major toll on public health. A study by the Health Effects Institute found that unhealthy levels of PM2.5 led to about 852,000 premature deaths in China in 2017. Household air pollution from burning solid fuels resulted in an additional 271,100 deaths that year. A joint 2016 study by the Health Effects Institute and Tsinghua University found that coal-generated pollution was the most important contributor to ambient PM2.5 pollution in China, with premature deaths resulting from coal burning totalling 366,000 in 2013 (Center for Strategic and International Studies, 2020). The rapid process of urbanisation has contributed to high pollution levels in the cities. According the World Health Organisation, by 2008 China had 16 of the world's 20 most polluted cities (Magnier, 2008). Later, WHO reported that over one million people in China had died from air pollution in 2012 (Vaughan, 2016). The government acted promptly and by 2016 there were only four Chinese cities listed among the world's 20 most polluted cities (CBS News, 2018).

Industrial pollution has impacted significantly on the health of people in China. Although it was officially denied for some time, the Chinese government finally acknowledged the existence of 'cancer villages', where rates of cancer are much higher than the national average due to contamination of land, water and air (Brown, 2009; Zhang, 2011). There are an estimated 400 of these villages in China (Watts, 2010). Death rates for Chinese farmers from liver cancer are four times the global average and China has twice the global average for stomach cancer (Hilton, 2010). As the health impacts of pollution increase, more people are dying of pollution-related illnesses. The government has also become concerned by the rising incidence of birth defects (Brown, 2006). Major industrial disasters, such as explosions and landslides, caused mainly by lax safety standards and criminal negligence, have resulted in many deaths. In 2016, 22,436 people died in work-related accidents (Lew, 2019).

Apart from the human costs, environmental pollution is economically costly. In 2007, the WB estimated that pollution was costing China 5.8% of its GDP. Other estimates were higher, 8% or 12% of GDP (Hilton, 2010). As a totalitarian state not bound by democratic accountability, the Chinese government has acted quickly and decisively on environmental issues and corruption in recent years. In 2014, a plan was introduced to improve air quality by banning cars that did not meet exhaust standards. Six million cars were taken off the road nationwide, 300,000 in Beijing (BBC World News, 2014). The government has also taken a firmer stand on waste issues. In 2014, the Chinese premier declared a 'war on pollution' (Branigan, 2014). That same year a landmark court case fined a number of Chinese companies a total of 160 million renminbi ($26 million) for dumping 25,000 tonnes of chemical waste into rivers, the highest penalty imposed in China to date. New environmental laws came into effect at the beginning of 2015 and NGOs have won a number of significant cases in the courts (Zhang, 2017). Though China signed the Basel Convention on Hazardous Waste, the importing and processing of toxic waste was permitted, and China processed vast amounts of waste, generated internally and imported from the developed world. Since the early 1990s China was the world dumping ground for plastics and handled nearly half of the world's recyclable waste, creating an enormous environmental problem there (Yale Environment 360, 2019). In 2017, China began banning the import of solid waste.

3.3.4. *Deforestation*

China has relatively few natural resources, and rapid economic growth has put enormous pressure on those resources, particularly forests. When the Communists came to power in 1949, only 8.6% of China was forested. Early Communist policies lifted the limits on grazing which increased deforestation and desertification. Deforestation contributes to erosion and flooding. Desertification has accelerated as population pressure has pushed people to farm marginal areas. China experienced severe floods in 1998 and the following year embarked on a massive re-forestation programme, spending $31 billion planting trees in the 10 years after 1999 (Caramel & Thibault, 2012). The government has undertaken further major re-afforestation programmes and by 2014 China's forests had increased to 22% of land area (Forest Legality Initiative, 2014).

China has become the leading importer, consumer and exporter of the world's timber. Its own forests provide less than 40% of its needs (Caramel & Thibault, 2012). Since 2000 China has tripled its output of paper, overtaking the US to become the world's largest source of paper and paper products in 2008. In 2009, China was producing 17% of the world's output (Haley, 2010). With growth in demand China increased its timber imports 300% between 2000 and 2011. According to the EIA, in 2011 one-third of all the timber sold worldwide was bought by China, with little regard to its origin (cited in Caramel & Thibault, 2012). In 2016, the largest wood exporters to China were the US, Russian Federation, Canada, Brazil and Japan (WB, n.d.i).

3.3.5. *Consumption*

Because the Chinese people make up nearly 20% of the world population, rising consumption in China has a global impact. The middle classes are the largest consumer group in contemporary societies and they are expanding rapidly in China. They live in cities and consume more products, food and energy than those in rural areas. This group is likely to expand if Chinese government policy to grow internal consumption is successful (Prasad, 2015). The growth of the Chinese middle classes already has a major impact on global GHG emissions and global resources. Increased meat consumption is an early indicator of rising standards of living, with meat consumption in China growing at twice the rate of population growth (Brown, 2006). The increased consumption of meat in China has a significant environmental impact. The ecological cost of producing one kilogram of meat is much higher than a kilogram of grain. Producing one calorie of meat requires 17 calories of feed, while an estimated 25,000 litres of water are needed to produce 0.2 kilograms of meat. Compared to this, in developing countries it takes only 550 litres of water to produce a loaf of bread (UN Commission on Sustainable Development, 2004, cited in Nierenberg, 2005).

The rising levels of automobile ownership, an important gauge of status, is another indicator of the growing affluence in China. Since 2000 more people have been able to afford to buy vehicles. Numbers increased from 20.14 million vehicles in 2002 (UN Statistics Division, 2008) to 279 million in 2015; 61% of these were automobiles. Nearly 24 million new cars were registered in China in 2015, though the rate of ownership at 31% remains comparatively low internationally (Xinhua, 2016a). After the GFC, foreign car manufacturers saw China as the place in which future growth would occur. China became the world leader in vehicle production and consumption after 2009 (Liu, 2016). The Chinese people have responded quickly to the need to cut carbon emissions, and there has been a rapid increase in electric vehicle and bicycle sales while sales of oil-powered automobiles has flattened (Jaganathan & Daly, 2017). The provision of subsidies for electric vehicles has accelerated uptake, enabling the Chinese government to almost reach the one million electric vehicle target set in 2010 (*The Economist* Intelligence Unit, 2017). Small-vehicle sales increased by 16% in 2016 in response to the government's tax cuts, but the fastest growing automobile segment in China is the large-engine sports utility vehicles, a similar consumer trend to the US and one which increases carbon emissions (Bloomberg News, 2017).

3.3.6. *Protests*

Since the 1990s a vigorous environmental movement has emerged in China in response to the social and environmental issues caused by rapid, unregulated economic development. People in China have little voice, representation or access to democratic processes. When pushed into extreme situations, often their only option is activism. Between 1995 and 2006 the number of environmental demonstrations increased roughly12 times, from 10,000 to 128,000 (Yan, 2006, cited in Xie, 2011). In 2004 there were 4,000 protests in China involving more than 3.7 million people, according to the Chinese security minister Zou Yongkang (Keidel, 2006, cited in Taylor, 2009). *Time* Magazine reported an advisor to the Chinese government, the economist Niu Wengyuan, telling an official forum that there were more than 500 large-scale protests a day in China (Ramzy, 2012). By 2013 the number of protests was estimated at between 30,000 and 50,000 (Bloomberg News, 2013).

Since 2000 there have been a number of foreign documentaries about environmental campaigns in China. The film *Voice of an Angry River* by Shi Lihong influenced a Canadian filmmaker, Gary Marcuse, to make *Waking the Green Tiger*, which covers the successful protest movement against the building of a dam in Yunnan and the growth of environmental campaigns since 2000. The Tiger Leaping Gorge campaign reflected a turning point in China's environmental movement, and Marcuse believes the film played a key role in changing government attitudes, one such change was the 2004 Environmental Impact Assessment Law, which allowed the public to speak out (Marcuse, 2013). The Dutch documentary *Rainmakers* profiled a series of local activists and their village level protests about water, land and air pollution in China (van Luyn, 2010). Jonathan Watts also described a series of environmental tragedies in his book *When 1 Billion Chinese Jump* (2010).

The expansion of the middle classes contributed to the rise of an environmental movement in China after 2008 (Jianqiang, 2013). Though the Chinese government is generally less responsive to public opinion, they were concerned about the high level of social activism. From the mid-1990s it permitted the establishment of non-government environmental organisations. According to *Economy*, in 2005 there were as many as 2,000 unregistered environmental NGOs in China (2005, cited in Xie, 2011), and by 2008 3,539 groups had registered with the Ministry of Civic Affairs. There was also a surge in the number of Internet-based NGOs after 2005 (Xie, 2011). The internet has become a platform for communication and mobilising participation in activities, according to Yang (2005a and 2005b, cited in Xie, 2011). Digital activism has been particularly empowering for Chinese activists. The government keeps a close check on what is available online in China, and Google, Facebook and Twitter are all banned (BBC World News, 2015). Activists have been able to circumvent this process by linking with activists in Hong Kong (Hook, 2013). When Xi Jinping became Communist Party Secretary in 2012, he began a clampdown on opposition, including NGOs, labour activists and human rights lawyers. This clampdown has extended beyond China. In 2017, a censorship row erupted when Cambridge University Press agreed to Chinese censorship demands to block access to more than 300 articles in *The China Quarterly* (Phillips, 2017).

3.3.7. *The climate crisis*

The Chinese government has realised the potential of taking a leadership role in the transition to a green economy. They want to become a world leader in addressing climate change. In 2014, China and the US signed a landmark agreement for the US to cut its emissions 26–28% from 2005 levels by 2025, and China agreed to limit peak greenhouse gas emissions by 2030 or before (Landler, 2014; McGarrity & Roberts, 2015). In 2015, China ratified the Paris Agreement – United Nations Framework Convention on Climate Change (UNFCCC), dealing with greenhouse-gas-emission mitigation, adaptation and finance (Phillips, 2016). China has a host of environmental problems arising from the rapid unregulated industrial development, but it is making advances in addressing these issues and tackling the major problem of the 21st century, the climate crisis.

3.4. Conclusion

Freedom of speech, democracy and human rights are still absent in contemporary China. Against this background China has, however, managed to achieve a major social transition under the umbrella of totalitarian rule, the 'China Model'. Over 400 million people have been lifted out of poverty since 1980. The Chinese have also achieved rapid economic development in a very short time. After the disasters of Mao's leadership when millions died in famines and the chaos of the Cultural Revolution, and since the introduction of 'market socialism' in 1979, progress has been measured, systematic and very successful. China's development has proceeded in stages and experimentally: disbanding agricultural communes and the 'iron rice-bowl' system; establishing special economic zones on the eastern seaboard, building infrastructure, industrialisation and market expansion in the 1990s. Other changes have included rapid improvements in product quality, the encouragement of China's major companies to expand outwards, combining a mix of SOEs for core industries and private company expansion. China has learnt from joint ventures with foreign companies, and has borrowed from the WB and other sources. It has also learned from foreign technology. China remains a society in transition and with millions of people still in rural areas who have been bypassed by development. Post 2000, China's spectacular growth continued for 10 years but slowed in 2011 as the country began to feel the effects of the GFC as US imports contracted. The major downside to China's spectacular economic achievements has been the havoc that unregulated development has wreaked on the environment. This has had significant human costs.

The recentness of China's transition means the memory of its experience of colonialism and political weakness is still fresh. After 2000 Chinese foreign policy became more outward looking with the 'Go Global' strategy, followed by the One Belt One Road project in 2013, renamed the Belt and Road Initiative in 2016. By 2016 the results of this policy were coming to fruition. Over 50% of GDP came from government investment, unheard of in recent economic history. This meant that rather than reacting to demand in the economy, the government encouraged businesses to create supply regardless of demand for the end product. Though growth rates have declined, China's growth rates remain much higher than in the US. Prins considers the Chinese response to the economic downturn, building infrastructure that will be used in the future, to be healthier than the US response which was to bail out banks, in effect rewarding their poor behaviour (2014a and 2014b). China has sought to regain its position as a major international power and this has been achieved remarkably rapidly, but it has not forgotten the lessons it learnt from its own economic development. This knowledge is valuable for contemporary economies in transition.

Chapter 4

The United States, World Bank and International Monetary Fund After 2000

This chapter discusses key characteristics of the US after 2000, based on its role as the leader of the capitalist world since 1945. The US was then the world's largest economy and had changed political direction from pre-World War II isolationism to the role of global policeman. Part of this global leadership role was implemented by dominating the two main financial institutions in the newly established 'development' sector, the World Bank (WB) and International Monetary Fund (IMF), collectively known as the Bretton Woods Institutions (BWIs) and named after the American location where they were established.

A number of potent myths have contributed to shaping the American identity, including the ideas of equality of opportunity and that success is possible through hard work and effort rather than inheritance (financial or educational opportunities, family networks, contacts and introductions) or the exploitation of others (Monbiot, 2012). Such ideas deflect attention from close analysis of the realities of the US political and economic system that works to benefit corporations and the wealthy. Because of the importance of the US international role economically and politically, these interests have a global impact.

4.1. People: Politics and Human Development

4.1.1. *Politics*

An imbalance between corporate and public interests lies at the core of developed nations (Hertz, 2004). This is particularly true in the United States, where the political and economic elites form an interlocking network of personal, family, business and political interests that have existed since the 19th century. The banking sector has played a key political role over that time, with particularly close personal links between Wall Street, the US government and US Treasury. Nomi Prins' research revealed that six major banks have controlled most of the financial interests in the US since 1900 (2014a). There is also a revolving door between the US government, Treasury and major corporations. Since the beginning of the neoliberal era in the 1980s, corporate influence over American politics has increased, largely as a result of a huge increase in the number of corporate lobbyists in Washington. The neoliberal policies which led to greater financial deregulation under President Clinton radically changed the US economy. The separation of commercial banking from lending services was removed. This was also a key act of deregulation that led to moral hazard in the banking sector — where banks misled clients about assets, liabilities and credit capacity. Banks began to speculate in financially unsound products, loans were sold to people who could not afford to repay them and lenders failed to do due diligence on lending. A sub-prime mortgage disaster resulted from large numbers of people defaulting on their loans, what was essentially a pyramid scheme culminated in the 2007–2008 financial crisis (Prins, 2018).

The economically powerful have always been influential in democratic politics. Since the 1980s, the corporate sector increased its influence over the US government. Under President Reagan, deregulation reduced limits on the size of corporations prompting a wave of mergers and acquisitions. The military, fossil fuel and motor vehicle sectors include some of the largest and most politically influential corporations in the US. In recent decades, corporations have gained more rights than those of citizens (Bissio, 2014). For most of the 20th century, US laws prevented corporate donations to elections, but in 2010, the Supreme Court 'Citizens United' vs Federal Electoral Commission ruling reversed campaign finance restrictions and enabled corporations and other groups to spend unlimited funds on elections (Lau, 2019). As manufacturing moved offshore, the financial sector — in particular international banks — became much more economically important. This is significant because of the long-time existence of a revolving door of financial leaders moving seamlessly between Wall Street, Washington and back to Wall Street (Stiglitz, 2009).

The evolution of US corporate and political interconnections is reflected in changes in terminology. More than 50 years ago, in 1961, the close allegiance between the US military and economic interests concerned President Dwight Eisenhower. He warned that the arms lobby, the 'military–industrial complex', had 'unwarranted influence' and needed to be kept in check. More recently, Senator McCain stressed issues with the power of the 'military–industrial–congressional complex' in his campaign for cancelling the F-22 fighter plane programme (Hartung, 2010). 'PRISM' was the code name for a US National Security Agency programme. Revelations from the PRISM programme showed the extent of the US and UK government surveillance of their populations with the cooperation of nine of the major digital companies (Gellman & Poitras, 2013). In 2013, Edward Snowden revealed the close connections between the major technology companies and the US State, and the vast extent of data mining for information conducted by the companies and the National Intelligence Service (Greenwald, 2013; Gidda, 2013). Christiane Amanpour broadened the definition to 'military, industrial, political and technological complex' to take into account the extent of the political use of digital technology and surveillance (CNN, 2018). The major military corporations Lockheed and Boeing, and service providers such as Haliburton, have major political influence through a network of politicians whose electorates they influence in the form of employment (Hartung, 2010). This influence is further reflected in the decisions of the WB and International Monetary Fund (IMF). These interconnections are facilitated by lobbyists and exchanges of personnel as people move back and forth from political to corporate positions. This power is reflected in the domestic and foreign policies that have supported corporate interests since the 1980s.

4.1.2. *US international influence*

The US continued to dominate the world stage politically and economically at the end of the 20th century. In 2000, the world order seemed unshakeable for the foreseeable future. The US had used its power to promote neoliberal free market economics since the late 1970s and was able to influence the decisions of the major international organisations of the UN, the WB and IMF (the BWIs) and the World Trade Organisation (WTO). The G7, the grouping of the largest Western economies plus Japan share many of the same interests as the US and tend to fall in line with US policies. In the BWIs, the US has both veto power and the largest number of votes. American policies promote US political and economic interests internationally, in particular the interests of corporations. One of the ways the US is influential internationally is through the network of powerful interests in the banking sector. Many of the prominent people in financial roles in European politics have close links with, and have worked for, Goldman Sachs (Fritel & Roche, 2011).

The US also exerts its influence through bilateral loans and aid. It is the largest donor of development assistance (aid) in the world. The USAID agency has always been clear that its primary motivation is self-interest. In 1961, President Kennedy announced to Congress that the provision of international aid was a means for the US to maintain its position of influence and control around the world, as well as providing a barrier against Communism (Hertz, 2004). The USAID website continues to state that one of its goals is to benefit the US economy (USAID, n.d.a) which it does by tying aid to American products, corporations and banks. The US includes military assistance as aid, which does not comply with the Organization for Economic Cooperation and Development (OECD) definition of aid (OECD, n.d.).

American international political influence has weakened since 2000, but the US remains the major international power because of its economic size. The US government lost international credibility when it embarked on a war in Iraq in 2003, and its justifications about the existence of weapons of mass destruction turned out to be lies. After 2000, emerging economies became politically and economically stronger, in particular China, and the balance of international relations began to change. One group of rising economies that began working together were Brazil, Russia, India and China, termed the 'BRIC' economies by

Jim O'Neal of Goldman Sachs (2001). They signalled the growing importance of developing world nations. When South Africa joined the 'Big Four' in 2010, the term was modified to the BRICS economies. This grouping weakened in the next decade.

As the US continues to dominate the global arms trade, the influence of the American military–industrial complex is far greater than just supplying arms to the American military. The arms trade peaked in the early 1980s when annual expenditures were well over $40 billion. Military expenditure declined after the end of the Cold War but has risen since 2000. The US is the largest arms exporter and sales continue to increase, while sales from Russia, the second largest exporter, are declining (Kuimova *et al.*, 2021). The US expanded its global military presence after the 2001 (9/11) attack on the World Trade Center and the Pentagon. Pro-war president George W Bush used the 2001 attack as justification for increasing defence spending. The 'War on Terror' became a propaganda tool to justify the militarisation of the American global presence. The military–industrial complex, which had been subdued since the end of the Cold War, expanded and became more powerful (Hartung, 2010). Military spending continued to increase under President Obama. The 2009 military budget was higher than Present Bush's last budget and higher than the total spending of the rest of the world (Defence Secretary Gates, cited in Hartung, 2010). In 2016, US military expenditure reached $612 billion, far more than the second largest military budget of China ($211 billion) (Fleurant *et al.*, 2017; SIPRI, 2019). The fight against terrorism has extended into cyberspace. American military hardware has been augmented by digital technology and surveillance. In particular, the US National Security Agency has expanded government surveillance. The surveillance programme, called PRISM, works with nine of the major digital companies, Microsoft, Yahoo, Facebook, Google, PalTalk, AOL, Skype, YouTube and Apple, who have handed over access to their data (Gellman & Poitras, 2013).

4.1.3. *US and the BWIs & WTO*

The economic power of the US is magnified because of its domination of the WB and the IMF (the BWIs), which have close ties with private, international, financial corporations (IFC). The WB was established to lend money for economic development; its first loans assisted the rebuild of Europe after 1945. The WB includes five organisations: the International Finance Corporation, which lends to middle-income and credit-worthy low-income nations; the International Bank for Reconstruction and Development (loans, guarantees, risk management products and advisory services to middle-income and creditworthy low-income countries, as well as coordinating responses to regional and global challenges); the International Development Association (interest-free loans to the poorest countries — 'credits'); the Multilateral Investment Guarantee Agency (insurance for investors) and the International Centre for Settlement of Investment Disputes (WB Group, n.d.a3). The original 1944 mandate of the IMF was to foster international economic stability. It was established to assist countries experiencing temporary balance of payment crises to ensure international financial stability (Hertz, 2004). The IMF only began lending to the developing world in the 1970s (*ibid*).

In the early decades, WB funding came from donors and interest on income. After the early 1970s under the leadership of Robert McNamara, borrowing was vastly increased. More funds came from the global bonds market as well as interest repayments from borrowers (Goldman, 2005). In 1968, the WB obtained $2 billion in capital from 20 Western countries and borrowed $3.5 billion from financial markets. Two decades later, the WB took in $4.7 billion in paid-in capital and borrowed $99 billion from global bond markets (Rotberg, 1994, cited in Goldman, 2005). This change in funding transformed the way the WB operated. As investors will pull out if profits are threatened, WB priorities changed from financing development to ensuring debt repayment (Goldman, 2005).

In 2000, the Meltzer Report — commissioned by the US Congress — concluded that the WB had been blatantly used by the US as a means of implementing US foreign policy and serving US interests (2000; Bello, 2006). As the US is the largest donor of aid, US priorities also dominate the 22 aid donors in the Development Assistance Committee of the OECD (the DAC group), as well as the Paris Club, the group of countries holding the bilateral debts from loans to individual nations. These groups are collectively known as 'The Washington Consensus', a term first used in 1989 by John Williamson to reflect the dominance of the US and Washington as the centre of power (Williamson, 2004).

The voting allocations of the WB and IMF are based on the size of the Western economies in 1944, thereby ensuring decision processes are undemocratic and unrepresentative. The size of the US contribution gave it the largest proportion of votes and thus the power of veto over BWI policies. The US remains the largest donor to the WB with 16.88% of total subscriptions, a $38.4 billion contribution and 16.57% of the voting power (WB, n.d.b3). The allocation of votes no longer represents the relative size of contemporary economies. OECD nations have much more voting power (63.09%) compared to their share of the world economy (45.06%) (Weisbrot & Johnson, 2016). Despite IMF changes to voting allocations in 2015, the US has continued to hold veto power and the largest number of votes. The US also selects the president of the WB, and the selection has been dominated by men from the US military or banking sectors (Touissant, 2014).

4.1.4. *People: Human development*

4.1.4.1. *Poverty and inequality*

In the US, the costs of providing domestic social services, health, education and the maintenance of infrastructure have been sacrificed to its vast military expenditure. Cutbacks in federal and state funding have occurred since the 1980s and accelerated after the global financial crisis (GFC). Though US gross national income (GNI) per capita was $56,180.00 in 2016, many people's incomes are significantly less than this average (WB, n.d.c3). In 2016, its HDI rate was 9.2 (One World Nations Online, 2016). Life is getting harder for more people in the US. Its human development index rating remained fairly static between 2010 and 2017 but dropped five places to 13th in the human development index ranking over that time (United Nations Development Programme (UNDP), n.d.).

Since 1945, life expectancy in the US has declined (WB, n.d.d1), and poverty levels are higher than for any other developed country in the OECD. The US has failed to institutionalise equality as a goal in US society. It has not provided social welfare policies or programmes that prevent or reduce poverty or reduce inequality (Brady, 2019). In 2010, 15.1% of the US population lived below the poverty line (Central intelligence Agency (CIA), 2020), an extraordinary statistic in a country that has so much wealth. Poverty there has increased since the 1980s, while in manufacturing unemployment has risen as companies have moved production offshore. Deregulation enabled corporations to crush unions, take away workers' rights, pay lower wages, casualise the workforce and cut back on safety regulations (Giridharadas, 2018). In the more relaxed regulatory environment, it was easier for corporations to avoid taxes, which reduced government, federal and civic expenditure. Lack of social infrastructure has contributed to a large number of homeless people on the streets. Many of these people have mental illnesses, but many mental institutions closed some time ago.

Neoliberal economic policies have continued to intensify inequality in the US since 2000. The WB considers 40 to be the benchmark for high inequality. The GINI co-efficient (a measure of inequality) for the US has increased from 40.3 in 2000 to 41.4 in 2016 (WB, n.d.e2). A study cited by Oxfam showed that the US government overwhelmingly supported the interests of the wealthy rather than the middle classes, while the interests of the poorest had no effect whatever on the votes of elected officials. The fortunes of the already wealthy became even larger. The Oxfam report *Working for the Few* estimated the combined wealth of 85 people in the world to be equivalent to that of 50% of the world's population. There is evidence that people were aware of the power grab by the wealthy that had enabled this inequality to happen, but the wealthy have been able to undermine democratic processes and promote policies that benefit themselves. In the US, inequality in 2014 was at its highest levels since the Depression (2014a). The global financial crisis also increased income disparities and caused unemployment to rise within the US. The growing dissatisfaction with traditional politicians prompted the rise of populist politics and a rejection of previous administrations, resulting in Donald Trump being voted into the White House in 2016. Prins sees that politicians got blamed for many of the problems created by the banking and financial sectors (2018).

4.1.4.2. *Health and education*

The version of capitalism that evolved in the US has been more brutal than in Europe where the welfare state has been more comprehensive, especially in the decades after 1945. Welfare provision in the US has been further eroded since the 1980s. The US has never had a national health service; private medical care has been promoted by the corporate sector. The lower and middle classes have to buy medical insurance or go without. The cost of US medical care is the highest per capita in the world but ranks much lower in terms of coverage. While quality is outstanding for those with private insurance, millions of people under 65 have not been able to afford healthcare. Free healthcare is available for people over 65.

In 2010, with great difficulty, President Obama introduced the 'Affordable Healthcare Act', and the number of people without healthcare dropped from 44 million in 2013 to under 27 million in 2016 (Henry & Kaiser Family Health Foundation, 2018). Though universal secondary education is provided, the funding has not kept pace with rising costs and the quality of public education has suffered. In the 2015 Program for International Student Assessment in maths and science, the US ranked around the middle and behind many other developed countries (Desilver, 2017).

4.1.4.3. *Unemployment, inequality and poverty*

When corporations moved offshore or to Mexico, the US manufacturing sector contracted dramatically. Unemployment rose. Many former industrial centres, such as Detroit, became ghost towns full of unemployed people. Standards of living have remained static — or declined — for most of the US population. Wages have not kept up with rates of inflation. Conditions of employment have become more difficult, the workforce has been increasingly casualised and zero-hour contracts have become common. Automation also has undermined job security and digital technologies have changed the nature of work. Unions have long been weakened. Guy Standing called the contemporary workforce in the US, and elsewhere, the 'precariat' (2014). For the first time since 1945, the standards of living and prospects for children of the current generation are lower than their parents. The latest figure for US poverty rates is 15.1% in 2010, and unemployment in 2017 was estimated at 4.4% (CIA, 2021).

4.1.4.4. *The penal state*

In contrast to declining public expenditure in other sectors, the US is expanding its prison system. The US is the world's largest penal state. But here, there is a disparity between extreme harshness against some groups in society (particularly black men) and dispensation for the powerful. The idea of the rule of law has been replaced by the concept of the rule of men, which protects the elite with the greatest power. Ordinary Americans are subjected to the world's largest and among its most merciless penal states. The US imprisons more of its citizens by far than any other country on the planet, and for longer periods, for more trivial transgressions and with less forgiveness than any country in the Western world. Criminal punishment is determined not by what you do but by who you are. The most clear-cut case of criminality during the Bush years was the NSA eavesdropping scandal, but no one was punished. In contrast, whistle-blowers were prosecuted to an extreme degree, with no accountability, which is a clear violation of the principle of the rule of law. The same applies to Wikileaks (Greenwald, 2011) and more recently Edward Snowdon's revelations in 2013. None of the major bankers were punished after the global financial crisis.

4.1.4.5. *Conclusion*

The American political system is an atypical democracy that has been distorted by the significant influence of the corporate and military–industrial sectors over politics. There is an absence of political will to address poverty and inequality, a product of a culture which blames the victim and celebrates individualism. These positions transfer responsibility away from government onto individuals. The US government has failed to support the interests of the American population. It has put corporate interests before the health and welfare of the total population. Though championing the ideas of democracy and freedom, it has failed to address poverty and equality. Repurposing government funding to the military and corporate subsidies could eliminate shortages of social housing and provide benefits to the poor and marginalised. The US is one of the most unequal nations in the OECD and has one of the highest poverty levels. It has continued to disempower American citizens and has given more rights to corporations both in the US and in international treaties (Bissio, 2014).

4.2. Profit

4.2.1. *Background*

The US was the world's largest economy after 1945. By 2000, the value of its GDP had risen to $10.29 trillion (WB, n.d.f2), an economic importance that has enabled it to influence international policies. In a global economy valued at $75.872 trillion in 2016 (WB, n.d.g1), the US with a GDP of $18.7 trillion (WB, n.d.f2) accounted for nearly 25% of world GDP. Between 2003 and 2007, the annual growth of the US economy was over five percent. In the first year of the GFC in 2008, growth rates were negative, only slightly improved in 2009 and then hovered around three to four percent for a few years (Standard & Poors, 2018). Economic growth slowed back to 2.9% in 2015 and dropped to 1.5% in 2016 (WB, n.d.h2).

4.2.1.1. *Neoliberalism*

The US experienced a long economic boom in the 1960s, which was accompanied by higher wages, increased government social spending and a highly productive economy. During the 1970s, the nation suffered an economic shock with fuel shortages, brought on by the OPEC countries cutting fuel supplies because the US supported Israel in the Arab-Israeli war in 1973. In response to growing inflation in the 1970s, the US took the dollar off the gold standard. The result was increased volatility in financial markets, higher interest rates and an economic slowdown. There was a rise in conservative neoliberal politics, and the Republican Ronald Reagan became president. Proponents of neoliberalism and deregulation such as Milton Friedman claimed neoliberalism would lead to financial stability. Instead, the era of deregulation has been characterised by a series of financial crises stimulated by financial speculation. Another turning point was the repeal of the Glass–Segal Act in the 1990s, instigated by Clinton-appointee Larry Summers. The Act had been passed in 1929 after financial speculation had led to a financial crash. It separated commercial banking from investor banking. After the repeal, the major banks became bigger, more powerful and consolidated their assets (Prins, 2014a). The lightly regulated financial sectors in New York and

London were particularly culpable of financial irregularities and speculation which culminated in the sub-prime market collapse and the 2008 financial crisis. The interconnectedness of the global economy meant the effects spread internationally and caused hardship for many around the world. Prins considers the Glass–Segal Act should be reinstated, but this was never mentioned by either President Bush or Obama (2014a).

Even though one of the core principles of neoliberalism is the light hand of government, the banks were only too happy to let the US government bail them out in 2008. Following the recommendations of financial advisors from the banking sector (in particular Goldman Sachs), the US government bailed out the major banks on Wall Street: Morgan Stanley Chase, CitiGroup, Goldman Sachs, Wells Fargo and Bank of America. Lehman Brothers, Goldman Sachs' main competitor, was allowed to go bankrupt (Fritel & Roche, 2011). Unlike defaulting nations, the banks responsible for the financial crisis did not have to comply with any conditions to qualify for bailout finance. These banks paid $110 billion in fines for fraud and other crimes before, during and after the crisis. They ended up buying hundreds of millions of their own stock with the money the Federal Reserve gave them. The human victims of the sub-prime market fraud were not compensated for their financial losses, let alone the human costs. These were often the most vulnerable people in society who were encouraged to take on unpayable loans (Prins, 2018).

The GFC hurt everyone except the banks and the wealthy. The banks were put in charge of their own recovery, and the massive bailouts were socialised and paid for by the American people through their taxes. The bank bailouts and subsidies amounted to $19 trillion. In order to stimulate the economy, the government implemented quantitative easing, expanding the cash flow and lowering the dollar. Debt was socialised onto the taxpayers, while more profits were returned to the private sector. Situations like this when money is created and does not get invested in economic production create a financial bubble. Quantitative easing and zero interest rates created a situation of increasing global inequality that enabled the wealthy to increase their wealth. One unintended consequence has been the rapid acquisition of American assets by the Chinese (Prins, 2018). Stiglitz says of the banking sector that during the GFC, 'We had become accustomed to the hypocrisy. The banks reject any suggestion they should face regulation, rebuff any move towards anti-trust measures — yet when trouble strikes, all of a sudden they demand state intervention, they must be bailed out, they are too big, too important to be allowed to fail' (2008). When the US government allowed the financial sector to write its own rules and allowed it to manage the recovery, it put the global economy at risk. The response of the US government and BWIs to the GFC was the opposite of the advice it gave to governments a decade earlier during the Asian financial crisis, which was to not bail out banks (Stiglitz, 2009).

The US response illustrated how the US operates a two-tier justice system. The major banks, which had committed large-scale financial fraud and brought on the financial crisis, were not penalised. The only bank to be charged and ruthlessly investigated was Abacus, a small private bank in Chinatown, New York (James, 2017). No major bank CEO during the GFC was punished, while at

Volkswagon in 2015 in a similar situation, the CEO was fired when emissions fraud was revealed. The fines imposed on banks were 0.8% of total assets and no CEO was imprisoned (Prins, 2014a). Apart from Lehman Brothers, all the major banks were bailed out rather than penalised. One law that President Obama did sign after the crisis was the Dodd–Frank Wall Street Reform and Consumer Protection Act. The law was designed to promote financial stability by protecting consumers from financial abuses, ending taxpayer bailouts of financial firms and dealing with troubled banks that are 'too big to fail'. The aim was also to improve accountability and transparency in the financial system, in particular, by requiring certain financial derivatives to be traded in markets that are subject to government regulation and oversight (Greenwald, 2011). Financial transparency for multinational companies on a country by country basis would also provide the US government with significant funding for much needed social spending and infrastructure (Eurodad, 2011).

The continued inadequacy of US banking regulations soon provoked the HSBC banking scandal in 2012. The bank was found to have facilitated terrorism by indirectly enabling the transfer of funds to al-Qaeda. It had also laundered money for Mexican drug cartels. The US justice system decided not to prosecute the bank and instead imposed a $1.9 billion fine, an amount the bank could have made in four weeks of profits. Prosecution would have meant that the HSBC would lose its US banking license, and its existence would be threatened. The reason given for not proceeding was that the closure of the HSBC would destabilise the US financial sector. This meant that whatever crimes that banks commit, they will not be prosecuted (Greenwald, 2012). Since 2008, the same leniency towards the banking sector has been shown to the CIA, NSA, senior officials in the administration and the telecoms industry. The nation's telecom giants, which independently broke laws written specifically to bar telecom–government cooperation in illegal spying, were retroactively immunised for their crimes by an act of Congress (Greenwald, 2011). Wholesale eavesdropping and surveillance have not been punished, while extreme punishment is exerted on others (Greenwald, 2014).

4.2.2. *US trade*

Because the US has been the largest economy in the world, it has long dominated international trade and trade policies. After 2000, the US share of world trade and world investment declined and China's economic importance increased. US exports were worth $780,000 million in 2000 and imports $1,258,080 million (WB, n.d.i1). By 2016, those export figures had gone up to $1,450,457 million ($1,450 billion) and imports were $2,248,209 million ($2,248 billion). The US had a trade deficit of -3.65% of GDP (WB, n.d.j1). In 2016, the US accounted for 14% of global exports and 18% of imports, compared to China which produced 17% of world exports and but only 12% of world imports (Eurostat, 2018). World trade declined in 2015 and 2016. The US now has one of the largest trade deficits, while China has one of the largest trade surpluses (United Nations Council on Trade and Development (UNCTAD), 2017a).

4.2.3. *US debt*

US debt has been on the rise, increasing from $5.629 trillion in 2000 to $8.2 trillion in 2005. The main cause was increased military expenditure after the invasion of Iraq in 2003. By 2016, debt had reached $19 trillion (Treasury Direct, n.d.). Though the US has high levels of debt, the ratio of debt servicing to GDP is low which softens the impact on the economy (Desilver, 2019). The US and China are heavily dependent on each other. The US currently owes China $1 trillion. China could jeopardise the US economy by sanctioning the dumping of US Treasury bonds; however, this would only harm China itself. Beijing's willingness to pump its own economy full of credit to finance unprofitable investment demonstrates its determination to avoid a sharp rise in unemployment. In 2016, nearly four percent of China's GDP came from the US, while only one percent of US GDP was dependent on China. At the same time, the US in turn had a $350 billion trade deficit with China. Another issue for the US was China's violations of WTO regulations (*The Guardian*, 2017).

4.2.4. *US corporations*

4.2.4.1. *Corporate political power*

In the neoliberal era, corporations increased their influence over political processes. Leverage could be exerted in a number of ways: by employing government officials, participating on national economic policymaking committees, contributing to political parties and sometimes bribery (Greer & Singh, 2000). Corporate donations to political campaigns meant that politicians were increasingly beholden to them. The number of lobbyists in Washington far outnumbers politicians. Lobbyists have even written legislation for politicians (Chang, 2013). Corporations have also been influencing public opinion through broadcast media for a long time (Chomsky & Herman, 1988). Conway and Oreskes demonstrated how historically corporations had manipulated public opinion about the dangers of tobacco use, the ozone layer and more recently had promoted climate change denial. The fossil fuel industry has had a significant influence over public opinion, in particular delaying the acceptance of the findings of the International Panel on Climate Change (IPCC) (2010).

Deregulation also led to the emergence of a large corporate lobby sector. The strongest sectors of the economy are energy and automobiles, the military–industrial–digital complex, agriculture and finance. There are a large number of lobbyists in Washington compared to the number of politicians in Congress and the Senate, and they reflect the power of corporate interests. In 2013, the number of lobbyists registered was estimated to be much higher than the relatively low 12,281 officially registered. This was the lowest number since 2002. James Thurber, who has studied lobby groups for 30 years, estimated the real numbers to be closer to 100,000. The reason is possibly that while lobbyists have been deregistering and official numbers declining, the unofficial number of lobbyists has exploded and the registration process does not cover many situations. Lobbyists can avoid scrutiny by working in 'faux grassroots organisations' or for private companies. The official spending on lobbying in 2013 was $3.2 billion, but Thurber estimates the industry earns more than $9 billion a year (Fang, 2014). In her book 'Dark Money' (2016), Mayer explores how such clandestine organisations operate. A study of the profiles of US lobby groups from 1998 to 2006 found an extreme concentration of lobby groups in law and public relations firms. The backgrounds of lobbyists tended to be in government and public relations. The most common characteristic of lobbyists was that they had previously worked in the White House or had worked for Treasury, Commerce or Defence, in descending order (Baumgartner *et al.*, 2008).

Corporate influence over politics is reflected in the regulatory environment, which includes government turning a blind eye to the operation of tax havens that enable corporations to launder money. Major multinational corporations (MNCs) make billions each year in profits. They also have many strategies for avoiding paying taxes in the countries in which their profits are earned, including in other Western industrialised countries. MNCs avoid paying tax in their countries of origin by relocating corporate head offices to tax havens. Major corporations, particularly the new technology companies, have been avoiding paying taxes in the US. Between 2005 and 2014, the NGO Global Financial Integrity reported that 87% of global illegal financial flows was between branches of corporations (2017).

4.2.4.2. *Service and financial sectors*

When consumer goods companies moved offshore, financial companies became more economically important. Since the 1980s, US banking and financial corporations have played a central role in the US political economy. Likewise, the service sector has contributed significantly to the economy, replacing manufacturing in terms of economic input, 80% in 2017. The rapid advances in technology have also made a major contribution to economic growth in recent decades (CIA, 2020), although production of that technology remains outside the US. The growth of the technology industry has changed the location of wealth production in the US from the traditional east coast urban centres to the west coast in California and Washington state. New technology centres are in Silicon Valley outside San Francisco and Seattle (Microsoft). These companies are adept at tax evasion. The financial sector continues to evolve its products and services. A new type of corporation — vulture corporations — emerged after 2000. These companies buy up debt in defaulting countries and try and exact payment from the defaulting country (Seager & Lewis, 2007).

4.2.4.3. *Commodities, energy and the automobile sectors*

The energy and automobile sectors have been very politically important in the US since the 19th century. The US government has subsidised the fossil fuel sector for over 100 years. It is estimated that the government pays $20 billion a year in subsidies to the fossil fuel industry (Greenpeace, n.d.). After 1945, the oil companies and auto manufacturers dominated the lists of top Forbes and Fortune 500 companies. Since the oil crisis in the 1970s, the government has made maintaining oil security a top priority. Deregulation in the oil markets in the 1990s led to practices similar to those in the financial markets. Unrestricted trading, price manipulation and illegal practices culminated in the Enron scandal which brought down the company. Energy traders moved to London's unregulated market and regrouped. The ICE commodity exchange attracted Glencore, Vitol and Trafigura, companies that controlled large amounts of the African and Dubai oil sectors (Sen, 2012). Resource security again became important after 2000 as Chinese demand for resources increased and international prices increased. After the attacks on the World Trade Center and Pentagon in 2001, the US sought to secure its oil supplies by diversifying its oil sources. Oil imports from SSA were increased at this time (Jerome *et al.*, 2005). The American invasion of Iraq in 2003 was primarily about oil security. The war greatly increased the budget deficit and led to disruptions in oil supplies from Iraq. At the same time, oil supplies from Venezuela were disrupted by attempts to nationalise oil resources. In the US, breakthroughs in technology enabled a major expansion of fracking to access natural gas resources after 2000. Though the social and environmental costs were high, these extra sources of energy made the US energy sector more secure. Energy demands levelled out with the economic slowdown after the GFC which also caused a decline in oil prices. Expansion of US production through fracking kept prices low throughout the decade. The US became a net oil exporter (Kolakowski, 2020). By 2015, the US Energy Information Agency (EIA) estimated that two-thirds of US gas production and about half its crude oil were derived from hydraulic fracturing (EIA, 2015). Apart from oil, the US economy is dependent on many minerals found in SSA, but China has been quicker to secure access to these minerals (Casey, 2019).

4.2.4.4. *Manufacturing and the military–industrial complex*

In the 1970s, the US was predominantly a manufacturing country, but after decades of deregulation, by 2017 industry accounted for only 19.1% of GDP (CIA, 2020). Commercial manufacturing moved offshore, but US military–industrial manufacturing remained within the US. The US military–industrial sector is economically and politically very important, with corporations locating production throughout states in areas of high unemployment. Local politicians are pressured into supporting laws that benefit these corporations (Boeing and Lockheed Martin in particular), in order to retain local employment. The influence of these corporations and the military establishment generally became more important when a pro-war president, George W Bush, was elected. After the declaration of the 'War on Terror', the vice president of Boeing is quoted as saying 'the purse is now open' (Hartung, 2011). US military spending increased after 2001 from $429 billion in 2000 to $612 billion in 2016 (Stockholm International Peace Research Institute (SIPRI), 2019). The US is the world's largest arms exporter. In 2016, the value of US arms exports was $9.9 billion. The bulk of military expenditure goes to supply the US military (SIPRI, n.d.a). The sector is heavily subsidised. Boeing is the largest export company in the US, and it relies heavily on taxpayer funding through the US Export–Import Bank (Exim). Before 2014, Boeing received about 40% of its financing from subsidies (government guarantees for private bank loans to government-owned foreign airlines). The close ties between government and Boeing are reflected in the appointment of a recent vice president at Exim, Kevin Varney, as the chief of staff for government operations at Boeing. A Goldman Sachs report revealed that Boeing, which has its own bank, does not need the government finance it loudly claims it does (Carney, 2017). That Boeing continued to function when the US Exim bank ceased operating between 2014 and 2019 was an indication it did not need government financing.

4.2.4.5. *Agriculture*

There has been increasing consolidation in the US agricultural sector and US agriculture is increasingly dominated by large corporations. In 1987, 15% of all cropland was held by farms of at least 2,000 acres; by 2012, that percentage had risen to 36% (Varinsky, 2018). US agriculture accounted for only 0.9% of GNP in 2017 (CIA, 2020) but remains politically important. Agricultural production is highly industrialised, relying on large quantities of chemicals, fertilisers and energy consumption. US agricultural products cost less because they are heavily subsidised. Such subsidies distort global markets, and overproduction lowers world prices and renders exports from developing countries uncompetitive. Despite the fact that the WTO was supposed to phase out all forms of subsidies, the US has instead increased them annually. From $367 billion in 1995, the first year of operations of the WTO, the total amount of agricultural subsidies provided by governments of developed countries rose to $388 billion in 2004. Of the 2.1 million farms in the United States, 39% receive subsidies (Edwards, 2018). Farm subsidies in 2002 were $16.5 billion (New York Times, 2002) increasing to $20 billion in 2016. Most of the subsidies go to the largest producers of corn, soybeans, wheat, cotton and rice (Edwards, 2018).

Apart from the high levels of productivity and subsidies to agriculture within the US, the neoliberal policies imposed throughout the developing world have hurt developing countries and benefitted US agriculture. The most subsidised Western agricultural products are sugar, cotton and grain, crops that are vital exports in some African countries. American subsidies on grain for the production of ethanol have also pushed up world grain prices, further impoverishing the poor (Brown, 2009).

4.2.4.6. *Corporate/private philanthropy*

Another particularly American phenomenon has been the rise of corporate and institutional philanthropy. When income taxes were introduced in 1913, a law was established that gave extremely wealthy people the ability to reduce their taxes through charitable works. This led to the establishment of charitable foundations by many of the most powerful families in the US — the Ford, Rockefeller, Mellon and Carnegie family foundations — as a means of avoiding tax. All profits from the first 20 years would go to non-profit charities and then the principal would pass to the trustees free of inheritance tax. The process through which these private charitable foundations operated turned many extremely wealthy US citizens into major players in the civic sector. The wealthy could get tax deductions (on the interest generated by trusts), control how the money was spent in their foundations and receive public kudos. There are few legal restrictions on private foundations and, from 200 in 1930, the number of private foundations in the US grew to 2,000 in 1950, 30,000 in 1985 and over 100,000 in 2013, with combined assets over $800 billion. Increasingly, these foundations have become the means for promoting particular political agendas of the very wealthy (Mayer, 2016).

The largest contemporary US foundation is the Gates Foundation, established in 2000. One of its missions is to improve the quality of US education, which it claims the government has failed to do. This claim is somewhat ironic as the aggressive way in which US companies such as Microsoft — the source of Bill Gates's billions — have expanded, and their ability to avoid taxes has contributed to the decline of social funding for education (Giridharadas, 2018). The Gates Foundation is very much a pillar of the US political and economic system. It is a strong supporter of the corporate sector, and with its focus outside the US on health issues, it works closely with US pharmaceutical companies. One of the major issues with its work is that the foundation is not accountable to anyone.

4.2.4.7. *Conclusion*

Because of the size of the economy, US policies and actions have a major impact internationally, especially through its influence in the WB, IMF and WTO. The impact of neoliberal policies and deregulation of the banking sector caused a worldwide recession. The US has continued to promote its own political and economic interests, particularly corporate interests. At the same time, the interests of the people, within the US and internationally, have been sacrificed to the interests of business, resulting in an increase in poverty, inequality and economic hardship.

4.3. Planet

4.3.1. *Introduction*

The US has a long history of environmental activism and awareness but this has never been part of mainstream culture. The environmental movement in the US traces its beginnings to the 19th century, while the modern environmental movement emerged in the 1960s (Rome, 2003). The Environmental Protection Agency (EPA) established under President Nixon in 1970 ushered in laws to protect the American people and the environment. In the 1980s, the ascent of neoliberalism led to a loosening of the regulatory environment and the dismantling of environmental regulations. One of the results of more relaxed regulation was the exemption of the oil and gas sectors from EPA requirements. This exclusion, called by critics 'The Halliburton Loophole' — it was the first company to use this process — also applied to the process of 'fracking', which expanded significantly after 2000 (Earthworks, 2007). By 2016, hydraulically fractured wells were supplying two-thirds of US natural gas production (EAI, 2016).

The US economy is extremely dependent on fossil fuels, and the US has one of the largest per capita energy consumptions in the world (WWF, 2012). In 2017, it was the world's second largest carbon emitter (4.8 GT), behind China (9.3 GT)

(Union of Concerned Scientists (UCS), 2020), yet China has three times the population (Sen, 2012). Contemporary global environmental problems are the result of the historical pattern of development and consumption in industrialised nations (Stern, 2007), and US society is characterised by overconsumption and rapid product obsolescence. The expansion of US industry — based on fossil fuels — over the last two centuries has caused major environmental damage. Coal, the main energy source in the 19th century, was augmented by oil in the 20th century. Until recently, the largest economy in the world, US economic development since the 1950s has made the biggest contribution to greenhouse gas accumulation and the current climate crisis. This fossil fuel-based model is unsustainable and no longer works for developed industrialised economies, or is it a feasible model for emerging economies. High levels of resource consumption in industrialised societies have depleted global resources, destroyed habitats and caused the extinction of species. By the 1990s, it was clear the earth's ecological limits were under threat, and that 'the dream that growth will raise world wages to the current rich country level and that all can consume resources at the US per capita rate is in total conflict with ecological limits that are already stressed beyond sustainability' (Daly & Goodland, 1993, cited in Greer & Singh, 2000). The US economy has been highly industrialised since the 19th century, and in the second half of the 20th century, it became increasingly consumer driven. After 1980, when US manufacturers moved offshore in pursuit of cheaper labour, retail prices fell and levels of consumption increased dramatically. The US also has one of the highest levels of per capita automobile ownership in the world (Highway Statistics, 2019). As a result, the US has one of the highest per capita ecological footprints in the world. It reached a peak of 11 hectares in 1973, declined to 9 hectares in 1982 and reached 8.1 hectares in 2016. Per capita biocapacity has also gone down from 4.4 hectares in 1980 to 3.6 hectares in 2016. The US per capita biocapacity deficit of −5.6 hectares in 1980 contracted to −4.5 hectares in 2016, but this level is completely unsustainable (Global Footprint Network, n.d.b).

4.3.2. *The climate crisis and carbon emissions*

Corporations have been the key engines of industrial development since the beginning of the 19th century. Evidence of accelerating climate change caused by human behaviour has been widely accepted by the scientific community since the first IPCC assessment report in 1990 provided evidence that accelerating climate change was the result of human activities. For decades, the scientific community has been aware of the impact of the rapid expansion of greenhouse gases (GHGs) on climate. The UN Conference on Environment and Development in Rio de Janiero in 1992 led to the United Nations Framework Convention on Climate Change, the Kyoto Protocol and the Paris Agreement (Leggett, 2020). The abstention of the US from signing the Kyoto Protocol (under President George W Bush) undermined international progress. The Stern Review in 2006 predicted an imminent major environmental crisis (2007). As the effects of an environmental crisis have evolved more slowly compared to the financial crisis in 2008–2009, they are more difficult to identify. Events that cause environmental damage and climate change have often occurred long before the results are evident. The world is only now experiencing the environmental impacts of activities occurring in the last 150 years. The accelerating pace of current climate change is the result of a cumulative build-up of carbon emissions, but even if carbon emissions levelled off today, temperatures would continue to increase for decades (Hansen & Sato, 2011). At the Conference of Parties (COP) in Copenhagen in 2009, the Green Climate Fund was established to supplement existing aid. It was agreed on in 2011 and became operational in 2014. That year, President Obama pledged $4 billion for the following four years. Before leaving office, he had contributed $1 million (Slezak, 2017). Developing nations believe they should not be penalised for greenhouse gases in the air produced by 150 years of industrialisation in developed countries before they have themselves have industrialised and developed their own economies. People in those countries aspire to the consumer lifestyles enjoyed in the West that have only recently been possible for them. They want to buy products, eat more meat and travel.

However, the possibility of concessions was lost in Paris in 2015 when developing world leaders succumbed to pressure from the US and Europe, signing a 'no liability' clause, through which they signed away the principle of common but differentiated responsibilities (CBDR) agreed to in 1992 (Bond, 2017a).

The rapid acceleration of major climate events in recent years and the current rise in global temperatures are evidence of the changes in climate the IPCC warned about in its first report in 1990. The US has a major global environmental impact through its continued reliance on fossil fuels and support of extractive industries, the auto sector and consumer lifestyles. The US government has prioritised energy security since the 1970s and continues to strongly support the interests of fossil fuel companies. Corporations in the sector have been at the forefront of the climate change deniers. American corporations ExxonMobil and Philip Morris have funded lobby groups denying climate change to give the appearance of a groundswell of public opposition (Monbiot, 2006; Conway & Oreskes, 2010). According to Greenpeace, between 2000 and 2016 fossil fuel interests spent nearly $2 billion to derail climate legislation (Greenpeace, n.d.). International competition for oil increased when China became an oil importer in the 1990s. In order to protect its energy supplies rather than exploring alternatives to fossil fuels, the US government encouraged a major expansion of 'fracking' — shale oil and gas extraction — after new extraction methods were introduced in 1999 (Krupnick & Wang, 2013).

Until recently overtaken by China, the US was the largest global source of carbon emissions. Two hundred years of industrialisation made the country a major contributor to today's high levels of carbon accumulation. In 2014, it was second in the world in carbon dioxide emissions from energy consumption (United States Environmental Protection Agency (EPA), n.d.). The US government has only recently begun to reduce its emissions. In 2015, the US was responsible for 15% of global carbon emissions, a drop of 2.6%, by burning more oil and gas and using less coal (Pidcock, 2016). In 2016, CO^2 emissions were reduced by 1.7%, largely because of reductions in the use of coal (Netherlands Environmental Assessment Agency (PBL), 2016).

It is important for governments to assess the economic consequences of climate change and develop responses to the challenges. In recent decades, various intergovernmental attempts to develop environmental sustainability action plans have been paralysed by Western politicians, in particular the Americans. These attempts include the World Commission on Environment and Development which released Our Common Future in 1987; the UN Conference on Environment and Development (Rio de Janeiro) 1992, which adopted 'Agenda 21, a blueprint for sustainable development'; the 1997 Kyoto Protocols, which strengthened the mandate of the 1992 Climate Change Convention where most industrialised countries pledged to reduce their CO^2 emissions by 6%–8% by 2008–2012 (Leggett, 2020). Under President George W Bush, the US government was slower than other countries to acknowledge climate change and President Obama was also hampered in his efforts to bring about a response.

In 2007, the UN Intergovernmental Panel on Climate Change (IPCC) declared that global warming was unequivocal, caused by human activity, and that greenhouse gases were a major cause of climate change. Since then, a major international political shift has occurred and governments began to acknowledge the gravity of greenhouse gases and commit to reducing them. The US government has been slow to respond to findings of the IPCC. Nearing the end of his term of office in 2014, President Obama signed an agreement with China to limit carbon emissions. The US was to make a 26–28% reduction below 2005 levels by 2025, while China would start lowering emissions after 2030 (Branigan & Taylor, 2014). After more than 25 years of discussion and disagreement, the IPCC Paris Agreement in 2015 finally succeeded in getting 195 nations to commit to keep global warming below two degrees Celsius. This agreement was not binding. Even if the goal was realised, the actual commitments made would still leave the planet with four degrees of warming. Leading environmental scientist James Hansen called the conference a fraud (Milman, 2015). One of Donald Trump's presidential campaign promises in 2016 was withdrawing from the US Paris Agreement, which he did in 2017 when he took office.

The sluggishness of the US to acknowledge the climate crisis is reflected in the WB and IMF. The WB approach to addressing climate change has been conservative and business friendly. The 1997 Kyoto Protocol recognised the Clean Development Mechanism (CDM) allowing the offset of emissions in developed countries by investing in emission reduction projects in developing countries. In 2000, the bank established the Prototype Carbon Fund, what Bond calls a 'dubious mitigation strategy'. The WB manages the funds from 17 corporations and six carbon-intensive Western governments and makes investments in emission reduction projects. There is reduced pressure on the high polluters who support the fund to reduce their emissions (Bond, 2007). There are other strategies for addressing global warming not involving commerce and not presupposing that big business already owns the world's carbon cycling capacity. These alternative options include 'regulation, taxation, support for existing low-fossil-carbon economies, energy efficiencies, development of renewables and non-fossil-fuelled technologies and responsible tree planting' (The Corner House, SinksWatch and Carbon Trade Watch, 2004).

4.3.3. *Pollution*

In the US, energy security and corporate interests have taken precedence over concern about the climate crisis and alternative sources of energy. Fossil fuel extraction increased in the US after 2000 with the rapid expansion of 'fracking', a hydraulic process where a toxic cocktail of chemicals is inserted into the ground to release natural gas. Technological advances enabled the expansion of this sector which was done by stealth without public disclosure of what the processes entailed or investigations of possible impacts on people or the environment. These chemicals seep into groundwater and contaminate the surrounding land. The exact chemical ingredients used in fracking are hidden behind patent laws but include gels, polymers, biocides, fluid loss agents, friction reducers, surfactants and breakers (enzyme, acid and oxidising) (Kosnik, 2007). Particularly notorious was the exemption of the fracking sector from the regulations of the Environmental Protection Agency. The agency was significantly undermined in 2005 when further exemptions from its regulations were granted to the fossil fuel sector (Earthworks, n.d.a). The documentary, *Gasland*, documented the impact of the fracking industry on the health of communities throughout the United States. It clearly demonstrates the extent of corporate power and government support for the fossil fuel sector (2010). By 2009, there were more than 493,000 active natural gas sites in the US, more than double the number in 1990 (Urbina, 2011). The percentage of US oil derived from fracking increased from two percent in 2000 to more than 50% in 2016 (Egan, 2014). By 2015, fracking was providing more than two-thirds of US natural gas production (United States Energy Information Administration (EIA), 2016). As long as these exemptions exist, the US government's commitment to sustainable energy cannot be taken seriously. In 2014, the US Government Accountability Office (GAO) reported that every day over two billion gallons of fluids were injected into more than 172,000 wells to enhance oil and gas production or to dispose of fluids brought to the surface during the extraction of oil and gas resources. The report concluded there was a need for greater regulation to enable better protection of groundwater (US GAO, 2014).

The oil and natural gas sector continue to keep looking for new sources of fossil fuels as most of the easily accessible sources have been tapped. As resource extraction has become more difficult, the risk of environmental disasters has increased. The widespread damage from BP's uncontrolled oil spill in the Gulf of Mexico Gulf in 2010 illustrated the hazards of offshore drilling.

The US continues to be reluctant to regulate corporations. The US oil industry is subject to many infrastructure problems which reflect the need for better regulatory oversight. A number of oil pipeline spills in the US in 2011 called into question the quality of oversight of the 167,000 miles of hazardous liquid pipelines crossing the country. In recent decades, there had been thousands of spills across the US, with more than 100 spills each year. The agency tasked with oversight is underresourced and understaffed and leaves much of the oversight to companies themselves, including reports from internal regulators. Federal data revealed that between 1990 and 2011 more than 5,600 incidents were reported involving land-based hazardous liquid pipelines, with more than 110 million gallons of mostly crude and petroleum products released (Frosch & Roberts, 2011).

As in the energy sector, a concentration of companies dominate the pharmaceutical sector. Some of these companies have been the main agents responsible for export and import of products and technologies that have been controlled or banned in some countries for health and safety reasons. Fifteen of the world's 25 largest drug and biotech companies in 2016 were American companies. The two largest were Johnson & Johnson and Pfizer (Jurney, 2016). Monsanto has been a leader in the production of genetically modified (GM) seeds. Monsanto is the world's leading producer of insecticide. The company introduced Roundup, the world's most popular insecticide, to the market in 1974. It was forced to retract early claims it was good for the environment and biodegradable. In 1996, it was found guilty of false advertising claiming that Roundup was 'safer than table salt' and 'practically non-toxic' to mammals, birds and fish (*The New York Times*, 1996). The key component of Roundup is gypsophate, which has been found to have strong links to cancer (International Agency for Research on Cancer, 2017). Since these findings, there has been a deluge of cases against Monsanto in the US. In 2016, Monsanto was bought out by Bayer, the 6th largest drug company (Jurney, 2016).

4.3.4. *Social and cultural change*

Attitudes are changing but changes in behaviour are slower to occur. The acceleration in extreme climate events has changed international political and public opinion about climate change since 2000. Global temperatures are rising steadily each decade and acceleration has been rapid since 2010. By 2020, the hottest year on record was 2016 (Climate Central, 2020). The Carbon Majors Report discovered that a small number of fossil fuel companies (100) has been the source of more than 70% of the world's greenhouse gas emissions since 1988. Most of the highest emitters in the world are non-Western, state-owned energy companies. Just 25 private and state-owned companies produced 51% of those emissions; these included four private American companies, ExxonMobil, Chevron, ConocoPhillips and Peabody (coal) and 17 Chinese companies. As one-fifth of global, industrial, greenhouse gas emissions are backed by public investment, investors need to 'put pressure on these public companies', according to Pedro Faria, technical director of the NGO Carbon Disclosure Project (Riley, 2017). Privately owned Western oil and gas companies have made policy statements and produced advertisements about introducing sustainable practices, adopting renewable energy policies and embarking on green investments. ExxonMobil, a company with a poor environmental record, has been exploring carbon capture and storage, while Chevron was investing in two of the world's largest carbon dioxide injection projects to capture and store carbon (*ibid*). Even though the companies extensively advertise these activities, most are merely 'Greenwash' as they amount to less than one percent of overall company activities.

Before the 2016 US election, the UCS conducted a review of eight fossil fuel companies, which have contributed nearly 15% of industrial carbon emissions since 1850. Each company was graded on several key factors, for example, its position on the validity of climate science and its internal targets for reducing carbon emissions. None of the companies has an internal, comprehensive plan 'to align its business model' with the goals set by the Paris Agreement. The efforts of fossil fuel producers to discredit climate research, along with the anti-science attitudes of many political leaders in the US, pose a grave threat to the legislation of future environmental policies, according to Kathy Mulvey, the lead author of the report. The ratings were ExxonMobil (poor), Arch Coal (poor/egregious), BP (fair), Chevron (poor), ConocoPhillips (fair), CONSOL Energy (poor), Peabody Energy (poor/egregious), and Royal Dutch Shell (fair/poor). Many other companies operate in totalitarian societies. The United Nations has a poor track record of enforcing policies, and the Paris Agreement itself was not binding. Most of the governments responsible for the state-owned companies in the list of the top 100 emitters had signed the Paris Agreement in 2015 (Riley, 2017).

4.3.5. *Risk assessment*

The environmental crisis is a threat to corporate profitability. The activities of multinational corporations contribute to the current environmental crisis, but they also have a key role in combating it (George, 2007). Two of the largest fossil fuel companies in the world are the American oil companies Chevron and ExxonMobil. These companies have a notorious record of refusing to acknowledge the climate crisis and funding media campaigns denying the validity of climate change. They have resisted changing their business models and diversifying away from oil and gas, and reducing their carbon footprints (Tabuchi, 2021). Most Western business models have rigorous planning and auditing procedures. In 2006, the 'Business and Ecosystems' report was published. It identified six environmental challenges of particular relevance to businesses: water scarcity, climate change, habitat change, biodiversity loss, overexploitation and nutrient overload. The report urged businesses to acknowledge this inextricable link and realise they have an impact as well as a reliance on these ecosystem resources, to establish policies to reduce adverse environmental impacts as well as to pursue new sustainable business opportunities (The Earthwatch Institute, the World Conservation Union, World Business Council for Sustainable Development and World Resources Institute, n.d.).

Corporations commonly use risk analysis as part of their business planning. They need to treat climate change and accelerating depletion of resources as realistic business risks. Corporate interests that favour the business-as-usual approach and ignore sustainable energy options are risking their long-term viability. Michael Brune, the executive director of US environmental NGO the Sierra Club, recommends that investors move out of fossil fuels; 'Not only is it morally risky, it's economically risky. The world is moving away from fossil fuels towards clean energy and is doing so at an accelerated pace. Those left holding investments in fossil fuel companies will find their investments becoming more and more risky over time' (cited in Riley, 2017). A study from Carbon Tracker in 2015 considered that fossil fuel companies risked wasting more than $2 trillion in the coming decade if they continued to pursue coal, oil and gas projects that could be worthless in the face of international action on climate change and advances in renewables. Losses could threaten future investor returns (Riley, 2017). Pressure on corporations needs to be made at every level of the consumption chain: international, national, institutional and individual. Investors have a role to play in pressuring these companies to adopt more sustainable practices.

Multinational corporations have been able to maximise profits because the environment has been treated as an infinite resource and not as a cost. Resource depletion was not treated as a net loss to a country. However, the looming crisis of scarcity of resources provides another risk to corporations. New assessment tools have been developed to assess accelerating resource depletion. The UN Statistical Commission established a System for Environmental and Economic Accounts (SEEA). This provided an internationally agreed method, similar to the System of National Accounts, to account for material natural resources like minerals, timber, and fisheries. Natural capital accounting is an analytic tool which places a price on resources, adjusted to factor in replacement cost, resource sustainability and the cost of the ecological impact of those resources. The WB started using natural capital accounting as an assessment tool in 2012 so that countries would be able to make better economic decisions if they took into account the value of natural capital. The next challenge was to build capacity in countries to implement the SEEA and to demonstrate its benefits to policymakers (WB, 2012a). Product prices also need to be adjusted to factor in resource sustainability and include an 'end of life' plan. With these variables factored into prices, they would increase and hopefully result in more sustainable patterns of resource consumption. Monbiot has criticised these efforts to monetise the environment because it is fanciful to prices on intangible benefits including those in the future, and thus, cost-benefit analysis tends to be biased in favour of business (Monbiot, 2014).

4.3.6. *Renewable energy*

The political influence of the fossil fuel sector has meant the US government has been slow to explore renewable energy options. A number of major companies in the US service sector have committed to 100% renewable power under RE100, a global corporate leadership initiative bringing together influential businesses committed to total renewable electricity. Led by the Climate Group in partnership with the Carbon Disclosure Project, RE100's purpose is to accelerate change towards zero carbon grids on a global scale. Nearly 100 companies, including Apple, Facebook, Google, as well as the Swedish company Ikea, have joined the initiative. Volvo recently announced that all its cars would be electric or hybrid from 2019 (Riley, 2017). It is easier for the service sector to make these changes, as it does not require a major shift in company practices nor do service companies have longstanding financial interests at stake.

4.4. Conclusion

The US has been the largest economy and the most politically powerful country in the world since 1945. US society is defined by a particular mix that celebrates individualism and personal achievement and neglects the poor and socially disadvantaged. As a result, it has some of the highest levels of poverty and inequality among OECD nations. Along with relatively low social expenditure, it has the highest military expenditure and is the largest arms exporter in the world. One of the reasons for low social spending is that corporate interests take precedence over social services. Since the era of neoliberalism began in the 1980s — accompanied by the loosening of corporate regulation — the corporate sector has gained enormous power over the political system. Also, the influence of the US over the WB and IMF means that this control has spread to the international financial system. The US also has international influence through its own aid as well as other aid donors and with commercial and bilateral lenders. The neoliberal policies imposed on the developing world have caused social and economic stagnation and economic crises (the Asian financial crisis in the 1990s), while speculation in the unregulated financial sector brought about the global financial crisis. The powerful influence and propaganda efforts of the fossil fuel sector has resulted in the US holding back international efforts to acknowledge and address the climate crisis for nearly two decades. The US has the second highest level of carbon dioxide emissions in the world and has been responsible for high levels of carbon emissions for the last two centuries. The US also has a high per capita ecological footprint because of its culture of consumption; that culture needs to transition to living within its ecological means. Change needs to happen at both the governmental, corporate and individual levels. How it responds to the climate crisis will be crucial in combatting global climate change. The expansion of China's economy, however, is changing the dynamics of US global domination and this Asian nation will possibly assume leadership of the efforts to address the looming climate crisis that will change life irrevocably in the 21st century.

Chapter 5

China in Sub-Saharan Africa Since 2000

China is a 'developmental state' and its political role on the world stage has been evolving since 2000. Chinese leaders are driven by the desire to play a prominent role in contemporary world politics as well as ensuring China's resource security (Taylor, 2009). The Chinese want to consolidate their global presence and regain their position as a great nation. China continues to see itself as the leader of the developing world, and its relationship to Africa has been part of its commitment to South–South (developing country to developing country) co-operation (Brautigam, 2011). It also wants to position itself as an option to the United States (Taylor, 2009). China's international operations can be better understood if the Chinese state is seen not as a consistent and unified whole but as a system of 'fragmented authoritarianism' (Lampton, 1987, cited in Taylor, 2009). There are many dimensions to China's foreign policy, and sometimes, those policies appear contradictory. Within China is a complex mix of political and economic interests that include central government, state-owned enterprises (SOEs), local officials representing provincial bureaucracies and private corporations. These various interest groups, with their different agendas, are all represented in the nation's international activities. According to Taylor (2009), SOEs in the key sectors remain in government hands and dominate resource procurement and construction in SSA, but the much more numerous provincial SOEs make up 90% of Chinese companies operating overseas. The key priority for SOEs at regional levels is to fill their mandate to make a profit (Taylor, 2009). The competing political interests of the Ministry of Foreign Affairs and the trade interests of the Ministry of Commerce are another dimension of China's overseas engagement (Sun, 2014a). All the while, private companies have continued to expand into Sub-Saharan Africa (SSA).

'China's foreign policy in Africa is similar to other countries, both self-serving and driven by economic and strategic considerations' (Guang Lei, cited by Taylor, 2009). Brautigam (2011) agrees that China's activities in Africa are motivated by both political and economic goals, adding that the balance has altered in recent decades. For most of the 20th century, China's main interests in SSA were political, but in the 1990s, political interests were superseded by procuring resources to meet development needs, ensure economic security and expand commercial interests. China built up a network of trade, aid and investment links with all countries in Africa that respected the One China Policy (Zafar, 2007) and engagement became increasingly pluralist (Taylor, 2009). By 2016, the only countries excluded, because they maintained ties with Taiwan, were Swaziland, Burkina Faso and São Tomé and Principe (Blenchard, 2018).

Two key themes characterise China's relations with SSA: 'non-interference' with domestic policies and mutual benefit ('win-win'). These were first articulated as part of the Five Principles of Peaceful Co-Existence signed at the Bandung Conference in 1955 (Stahl, 2016). The policy of 'non-interference' contrasts starkly with the conditionalities of much Western aid and investment. Much Chinese aid has been tied to Chinese products and contractors — in much the same way that aid from the US is tied — but not to economic policies. China has been criticised by Western powers for perpetuating the power of brutal leaders, harming peoples' lives and provoking civic unrest by engaging with dictators and military rulers, as in Sudan, the Democratic Republic of the Congo and Zimbabwe (Zafar, 2007). These criticisms have become muted as China's engagement has broadened to include most of the nations in the region. China in turn has used its permanent UN Security Council membership to protect African nations and the threat of its veto in the Security Council to counter or water down sanctions (Kobo, 2013).

China has been in Africa since the Communists came to power. It has always taken a long-term view in its relations with the continent and has been open about its 'win-win' focus to bring mutual benefits to both partners. In the 20th century, China viewed SSA as a 'developing' region, with many similarities to China in terms of having a low per capita income and millions of people living in poverty in the rural areas. China felt it had much to offer SSA nations from the experience of its own economic transition. It has provided little outright 'aid' in terms of grants or low-interest loans. Rather, the majority of its economic arrangements have been interest-bearing loans or resource-for-infrastructure exchanges. China has brought many benefits to SSA and its actions should not be judged on the narrow range of stereotypes that have appeared in Western media in recent decades. Chinese policies and practices overseas have since evolved. Expert on China Deborah Brautigam from the China–Africa Research Institute (CARI) has been challenging these stereotypes for over two decades (Ryder, 2021), and this has been picked up in the foreign media who, since 2010, have been more positive about the nation's activities in Africa (*The Economist*, 2011b; Kristof, 2012). In 2013, the International Monetary Fund (IMF) stated that China had brought positive benefits to SSA (2013), and financial analysts at McKinsey Global Institute concluded that the impact of Chinese activities in SSA in the 20 years since the mid-1990s had been largely beneficial to the region (Jayaram *et al.*, 2017).

The Western media were dismissive of SSA in the early 21st century. In 2000, *The Economist* ran a cover story entitled 'Hopeless Africa' (2000a) and, two days later, another article, 'The hopeless continent' (2000b). As late as 2009, Africa was still being described as the 'Lost continent' (Skidelsky, 2009). According to Brautigam, people in Africa had found these articles 'depressing', and China's offer of assistance and talk about 'win-win' after 2006 was seen as very positive and a source of optimism after the dismissal by the West (2009). China's rapid expansion into SSA since 2000 prompted a wave of criticism in the international media. A study of articles on China in Africa in six British newspapers between 2000 and 2007 found the steady increase in reporting to be increasingly negative. Western activities were sanitised, while the Chinese were demonised (Mawdsley, 2008). Brautigam has cited many incidents of unbalanced reporting about China's activities that ignore similar behaviour from the West at the same time, whether it be China's loans to Africa, its aid or its engagement with rogue states (2009; Brautigam & Hwang, 2016). Reports on China's activities in SSA continued to be predominantly negative until after 2010 when reporting on Africa became more positive. Criticisms of China decreased but did not go away. According to Yun Sun of the Brookings Institution, China's foreign activity in Africa gets a disproportionate amount of media attention (2014b).

5.1. People: Politics and Human Development

5.1.1. *Politics*

Early in the 21st century, China emphasised the similarities China and Africa shared as developing nations. China has signed very few international treaties on human rights (University of Minnesota, n.d.) and this stance is reflected in its attitude to development. China's development assistance prioritised 'economic rights' and the 'rights of subsistence' over Western concepts of democracy and freedom. The stance that economic rights and sovereignty should take precedence over human rights was welcomed by many African leaders (Brautigam, 2009a). Ties between China and Africa strengthened after the Forum on China–Africa Co-Operation (FOCAC) was established in 2000. Ministers were brought together every three years and there were regular summits between heads of state. China has since developed and revised its African policies as circumstances have evolved. The Chinese Ministry of Foreign Affairs produced its first White Paper on China's African Policy in 2006 (Stahl, 2016). Economic commitments increased after the 2006 summit. A second policy was released in 2015 (*China Daily*, 2015). China's relationships with individual nations in Africa can be very different, conducted through wide-ranging and multifaceted bi-lateral arrangements with individual countries. These arrangements include resource for infrastructure exchanges, the purchasing of resources, part ownership of resources, loans and aid (Taylor, 2009).

5.1.1.1. *Poor governance*

Early in the 2000s, critics pointed out that while China espoused the right of sovereignty, it was most active in countries where sovereignty was weak (Taylor, 2006). When China began searching for external resources, Western interests dominated many of the resources in Africa, and China was excluded from many of those markets. In the 1990s, China's early trade relations were, therefore, with nations in Africa shunned by the West for various reasons: brutal dictatorships, poor human rights records or the countries were engaged in civil wars. Following its policy of non-interference, its first trading partners were Sudan, Angola, DRC and Zimbabwe, all countries with strikingly poor governance (Chen *et al.*, 2015b). Today, China's presence remains proportionally higher in such countries (*ibid*). This is evident, for example, in Sudan where China bought up much of Chevron's oil interests when the company left in 1992 because of worsening relations between the US and Sudan (Shinn, 2016).

In the years after 2000, China was accused of supporting repressive regimes in SSA and criticised for arms sales to Sudan, Zimbabwe, Liberia and Nigeria (Zhao, 2011a). Zimbabwe, Nigeria and Sudan also had notorious human rights records and histories of repressing opposition and ethnic minorities (Taylor, 2009). In particular, China was criticised for dealing with Sudan after the West pulled out. China responded to criticisms of its supplying arms during the three years of the Darfur crisis by saying it was not the only country to export arms and equipment. By 2004, Sudan was China's third largest trading partner in SSA. Two years later, it was Sudan's largest investor, and the state-owned China National Petroleum Company (CNPC) owned 40% of Sudan's largest oil project, the Greater Nile Petroleum Operating Company. China's role in the Darfur conflict led to international criticism and protests and boycotts at the 2008 Beijing Olympics. In fact, initial Chinese involvement in Sudan reflected a 'complete package' approach, which included money, technical expertise and pressure in the UN Security Council to protect the country from sanctions. Military equipment was also supplied (Taylor, 2009).

China has been accused of undermining Western initiatives for good governance and transparency, but these concepts entered Western development discourse only relatively recently, in the 1990s. In 2004, when Angola was negotiating a loan with the IMF, the IMF insisted on greater transparency in the oil industry and the introduction of a Poverty Reduction Programme as part of their loan conditions. China provided an alternative source of finance, without those conditions (Taylor, 2006) and with a more generous repayment period. Brautigam cites as evidence of bias in Western media that only the Chinese loans made the headlines in the West. Within months of China's loan, banks from France, Germany and the US were showering Angola with loans. Angola later paid off the loans with oil revenues. Even though China did not impose conditions, Angola did introduce more transparency in the oil sector and paid off all its debts (Brautigam, 2009a).

The African Union and the economic development agency of the African Union, NEPAD, also expressed concerns about China's activities after 2000. These new organisations were strong advocates for democracy, human rights, good governance and environmental protection. In September 2006, an African Union task force identified that one of the challenges in Africa's new partnership with China was to ensure 'Chinese investment practices do not undermine Africa's efforts to promote financial transparency and combat corruption' (Wild & Mepham, 2006). A comment from a spokesperson for the Kenyan government reflected a common perception that 'The Chinese do not peg their economic activity or aid to political conditions. You never hear the Chinese saying that they will not finish a project because the government has not done enough to tackle corruption' (Alfred Mutua, USA Today, 2005, cited in Bosshard, 2007).

China's policy of non-interference ran into problems when states were not safe or stable. 'Quasi' or fragile states have a tendency to prioritise staying in power over development. There is also the risk of loss of assets with a change of government. Exporting resources becomes problematic in situations of political instability. According to Taylor, China's policy of 'non-interference' was selectively applied. China found it easier to deal with countries such as Sudan and Angola with poor governance (i.e., 'no government') than countries like Eritrea, which had a strong government concerned to retain its sovereignty, and also South Africa (2006). Operating in conflict environments has created supply problems for China and also endangered worker safety. In 2008, there were three incidents where Chinese workers were kidnapped, and in one incident, five workers were murdered in Sudan (*BBC News*, 2008). The unpredictability of events in Sudan affected the ongoing supply of resources — oil supplies were stopped in periods of unrest, and the Chinese began modifying their stance on non-interference in local politics when they began experiencing operational problems in these politically unstable countries (Taylor, 2009). Sudan, along with Nigeria and seven other African countries, was removed from the China Export–Import Bank (Exim Bank) list of countries eligible for concessional loans in 2007 (Bosshard, 2007). Attacks on Chinese workers in Africa have continued in the last decade (Sun, 2014b).

The Chinese have responded to such problems by becoming more socially responsible, engaging with civil society and responding to local concerns (Walker, 2014). The profile of China's trade partners has evolved, and by 2016, most of its economic engagement was with countries with much better governance. Recent studies have shown that contemporary loans and assistance are much broader than those provided in 2000. In 2017, CNBC compiled a map using data from the Brookings Institution and AidData, specifying the governance rating of China's top 20 borrowers between 2012 and 2014. In SSA, that number included Côte d'Ivoire and Sudan [rating: bad], Angola [bad], South Africa [good], Ethiopia [quite good], Kenya [less good] and Tanzania [quite good] (Chandran, 2017).

5.1.1.2. *Corrupt practices*

China does not have a Foreign Corrupt Practices Act like the United States or similar legislation as in other Western countries that criminalise bribes paid overseas in exchange for contracts (Madowo, 2018), but it ratified the UN Convention against Corruption in January 2006 earlier than most industrialised countries. The Convention commits signatory governments to take effective measures to prevent and prosecute corruption, including the bribery of foreign public officials. Transparency International's Bribe Payers Index — established in 1999 — assesses the propensity of companies to bribe abroad. It ranked Chinese companies 29th out of 30 countries in October 2006. According to Transparency International, 'In the case of China and other emerging export powers, efforts to strengthen domestic anti-corruption activities have failed to extend abroad' (cited in Bosshard, 2007). Many Chinese companies, especially private ones, have brought bad practices to SSA. Some individuals have been put under suspicion in cases of misappropriation of funds. The Chinese businessman Sam Pa was implicated in the $13 billion revenue missing from the Marange diamond fields in Zimbabwe. Fifteen billion dollars were expected, but only $2 billion materialised (Bond, 2018a).

The Chinese government is not able to monitor the behaviour of all Chinese corporations working overseas, especially private companies. Similar criticisms regarding lack of transparency apply to the operations of Western companies operating in SSA. Western governments, corporations and private banks have a long history of private deals with African governments. Foreign resource extraction corporations are the least transparent of all business sectors in both the West and in China. Little has been achieved to make these corporations more transparent because Western companies also benefit from the lack of transparency. The resource extraction sector remains opaque throughout SSA (Flynn & Liffey, 2015).

Problems have also occurred with the tendering processes of Chinese companies. By 2009, Chinese companies were winning about a quarter of all major World Bank (WB) construction contracts in Africa, with half of those funded by the African Development Bank (ADB) (Brautigam, 2009a). More Chinese companies working for multilateral institutions in SSA have had problems complying with oversight procedures than Western companies. A number of Chinese firms working in SSA have been blacklisted from tendering for WB and ADB projects. In 2014, the WB debarred the China Three Gorges Corporation subsidiary, China International Water and Electric Corporation (CWE) from WB projects for three years because of misconduct in Africa and South East Asia. The company misrepresented its experience for tendering on two WB projects. The sanctions involved getting the company to improve its compliance mechanisms (HanShih, 2014). In 2015, the WB Group debarred Gezhouba No. 1 Engineering Co. Ltd, Gezhouba No. 5 Engineering Co. Ltd and Gezhouba No. 6 Engineering Co. Ltd and their affiliates for a period of 18 months. In addition, China Gezhouba Three Gorges Engineering Co. Ltd and its affiliates were debarred for a period of six months. China Gezhouba Group Co. Ltd also received a letter of reprimand, valid for six months, during which the company was not eligible to participate in WB-financed activities (WB, 2015a). The China Harbour Engineering Company Ltd was banned from involvement in the Beitbridge-Chirundu highway project in Zimbabwe because of corruption (The Source, 2016). The WB and African Development Bank also blacklisted a number of Chinese firms, including Sinohydro and Gezhouba, from tendering in Kenya on the Thwake dam (Kisika, 2017).

China has been plagued with high levels of internal corruption. In 2016, its score on Transparency International's Corruption Perceptions Index was 40 (a number below 50 means the government is failing to deal with corruption) and it ranked 79 out of 175 nations (Transparency International, n.d.). There have been some changes. President Xi Jinping has introduced measures to reduce corruption since he came to power in 2012. The Chinese government has been accused of lack of transparency in its business interactions but is becoming more open about its lending practices. Before 2010, China did not reveal total figures for its concessional loans to Africa, although it published the amount of concessional funding for specific loans (Bosshard, 2007). Though not a member of the Organisation for Economic Cooperation and Development (OECD), China is a member of the United Nations, WTO and WB. After 2010, the Chinese government began to make more of its financial arrangements transparent, responding to OECD measures to improve transparency in its aid figures. One of the ways its 'win-win' approach has played out is in 'resource for infrastructure deals'. These are possible because of the important role the Chinese government plays in resource procurement. By paying out funds to Chinese companies in China, the local economy benefits, resources are procured and local misappropriation of project funding (a major problem in SSA) is avoided. China has dismissed Western criticism of its economic arrangements as jealous hypocrisy (Taylor, 2006).

5.1.2. *People: Human development*

China has provided support to SSA since the early years of Communist rule after 1949. It first provided assistance in health, education, agriculture and industry in the 1960s (Brautigam, 2009a). In 1980, the Chinese government provided 400 scholarships for African students to study in China. Assistance has increased since the China–Africa Cooperation Forum (CACF) was established in 2000 (Taylor, 2006). The training of African professionals, providing education in China and building training and research establishments in Africa were an important part of the Forum on China and Africa Cooperation (FOCAC) pledges (Brautigam, 2009a). Financial and political support for education both within Africa and in China has increased. By 2015, China was the second most popular destination for African students. Student numbers grew from just under 2,000 in 2003 to 50,000 in 2015, second to France where there were 95,000 African students (Breeze & Moore, 2017). China has also established more than 20 Chinese-run agricultural centres and over 40 Chinese language schools and education centres (Kuo, 2017a). China's extensive dam construction and the provision of infrastructure has been more of economic than social benefit and has only indirectly benefitted the poor. A study of the impact of the China-financed Bui Dam in Ghana revealed that electricity provided by the dam went largely to urban dwellers (14.5%) and to the wealthy and middle classes rather than the poor (4%) (Shen & Tang, 2019.)

5.1.2.1. *Health*

A healthy population is important to economic development, and China's medical assistance is a good example of its 'win-win' philosophy (Wang & Bateman, 2018). By 2005, there were already 500 Chinese doctors working in SSA (Lyman,

2005). At the 2006 FOCAC meeting, China agreed to broaden bilateral cooperation in medical care and public health. In that year, $35 million was spent on public health-related projects. By 2014, expenditure had increased to $150 million annually, providing funds, staff, supplies and building facilities. In providing medical assistance, China used a 'province to country' model, with each province supplying assistance to individual nations. Thus Yunnan helps Uganda while Shandong provides assistance to Tanzania. As a result, arrangements are spread unevenly and quality varies. China has also given a lot of health support to Zimbabwe. As with the Gates Foundation, the Chinese have specifically targeted malaria, a preventable disease. China has also provided humanitarian assistance by sending 1,000 medical professionals to West Africa and donating generic drugs and medical aid worth $125 million (Wang & Bateman, 2018). China benefits from this health assistance by using its domestic companies in health provision. One project has been the building of a privately funded hospital in Ethiopia. In Tanzania, a Chinese company has contracted to build a medical production facility. Capacity building initiatives such as these have not characterised Western private sector engagement, though hospitals have been built under bilateral aid programmes. China's low-cost generic drugs are also welcomed (Wang & Bateman, 2018).

5.1.2.2. *Labour and employment*

China has brought jobs and skills to SSA. Between 2005 and 2016, China created 130,750 jobs, three times more than the US (Xiang Bo, 2017). However, far more Chinese workers are brought in to work on projects than are jobs provided to local people. Within China, worker safety standards are low, international safety standards are disregarded and workers have few rights. These labour practices and low safety standards have caused problems in SSA where many countries have comparatively higher safety standards. Problems in Chinese enterprises have erupted over low pay and unsafe working conditions (Taylor, 2009). In Chinese-run mines in Zambia's copper belt, for example, labourers had to work for two years before they got safety helmets. Below ground ventilation was poor and fatal accidents occurred almost daily. Obstructionist shop stewards were sacked and workers who assembled in groups were violently dispersed. When cases ended up in court, witnesses were intimidated. The cost-cutting measures inflicted on workers and their poor treatment led to labour unrest, protests and increased anti-Chinese feeling in Africa (*The Economist*, 2011a). Most of the problems were in Zambia and Sudan where government oversight is poor. Six Zambians were shot dead in 2006 when they protested about wages and conditions in a Chinese-run mine (Taylor, 2009). In 2010, two Chinese managers fired at a crowd of miners protesting about poor conditions. At least 12 people were injured (*The Economist*, 2011a). In 2012, a Chinese manager in Zambia was killed during a mining strike over wages. Miners were being paid less than the monthly minimum payment of $220 granted to shop workers (*BBC*, 2012). Over the last decade, threats to the security of Chinese workers in Africa have persisted (Sun, 2014a). During the same period, far fewer incidents of Chinese bad behaviour have been reported.

Chinese construction companies have been accused of other unfair labour practices in Zambia and Namibia. The accusations included hiring contract workers to get around union conditions such as paid sick leave and annual leave, unfair bidding and low wages. In Namibia, Chinese firms were seen to be operating in the same way as local firms, while European-owned firms that complied with laws were disadvantaged (Brautigam, 2011). An investigation by Human Rights Watch in Zambia in 2011 reported that while the African workers appreciated the jobs, working conditions were abusive and failed to meet international standards or the conditions in other companies in Zambia. Chinese-run companies tended to treat health and safety issues as trivial. Workers were threatened with firing if they refused to work in unsafe places. Human Rights Watch did note, however, that pressure from the government resulted in Chinese companies providing more safety equipment, though replacing it when damaged was still a problem. Reports of physical abuse by Chinese supervisors also declined. Human Rights Watch urged the Zambian government to take a more active role in pressuring Chinese companies to comply with local laws on safety and union representation (2011). These problems with poor Chinese treatment of African people is inexcusable but is partly the result of poor regulatory oversight. Taylor sees that African governments need to take ownership of these matters (2009). Host nations need to ensure that Chinese companies comply with local laws (Taylor, 2009; Sun, 2015b). The Chinese government has also spoken out. In 2007, on a visit to Africa, President Hu Jintao repeatedly urged Chinese companies to comply with local laws (Bosshard, 2008). Other Chinese projects have been harmful to local people, especially large infrastructure projects such as dams. In the Merowe Dam project in Sudan, financed by the China Exim Bank, 55,000 people were forcibly removed from the fertile Nile Valley to dry desert locations. They lost their land and their livelihoods (Bosshard, 2008).

5.1.2.3. *Labour and immigration*

China's worldwide aid and development assistance is delivered, as is Western aid, by Chinese businesses and contractors. China is often criticised for importing its own staff rather than hiring local workers. In some countries, such as Angola where labour costs are high, the Chinese have brought in large numbers of labourers (Brautigam, 2011). Another criticism is that even when it does hire African labour, the management staff are Chinese. This profile varies in different countries, and in many countries, it does not happen. A lack of local technical and management expertise is cited as one of the reasons for bringing in labour (Taylor, 2009). Chinese workers brought in to Africa in 2016 numbered 227,407, thirty thousand fewer than in 2015. The majority of these workers (65%) were concentrated in five countries: Algeria, Angola, Ethiopia, Nigeria and Kenya. When the 40% working in Algeria (not an SSA country) is deducted, the number of Chinese workers to SSA was much less, at 136,400 (Xiang Bo, 2017).

Chinese immigration has also increased as the country's involvement in SSA expanded. By 2016, approximately one million Chinese were living in the 54 countries in Africa. According to Park, it is necessary to take a nuanced view of the types of migrants who enter SSA because they have very different levels of engagement

(2016). Apart from those working for state and private corporations, many private individuals have moved to SSA in pursuit of a better life. These migrants include private entrepreneurs and shopkeepers, labourers and farmers as well as people who came on contracts and stayed on. Other migrants came independently, including individual, small-scale Chinese farmers who began arriving after 2000. Chinese immigration has been seen as problematic in some countries, and in other countries, reactions have been more positive. A survey of attitudes to Chinese farmers in Ethiopia and Ghana found these farmers received no government help and were seen to be making a significant contribution (Cook *et al.*, 2016). Outside SSA, there is a view of a Chinese invasion of Africa, which has been building slowly since 2000. This perspective has been promoted in the international media, especially in the US, with books such as Howard French's 'China's Second Continent: How a Million Migrants are Building a new Empire in Africa' (2014).

5.1.2.4. *Peacekeeping and arms sales*

Because of China's 'non-interference' policy, it has not engaged in the internal domestic policies of nations, but its stance on non-interference has evolved. China is a member of the UN and has provided more soldiers than other members of the UN Security Council as part of the United Nations' role in peacekeeping in Africa. Other members supply more funding for peace operations rather than troops (Taylor, 2009). China also committed to expanding its security support as its own interests were threatened. Chinese peacekeepers have been killed in Mali and Sudan, workers were kidnapped in Cameroon and the spread of Islamic State in Africa has been problematic. In 2015, President Xi committed $100 million in military aid to the African Union. China also supports the defence and counter-terrorism capacity building of SSA nations (Albert, 2017). Before 2017, China had no troops in SSA (Kuo, 2017b).

China has also been criticised for arms sales to pariah states but is, in fact, a small player in the African arms trade and such accusations reflect an anti-Chinese bias. China has been criticised for its policy of exporting weapons to Sudan and its involvement in the civil war (Taylor 2006, 2009). According to the Stockholm International Peace Research Institute (SIPRI), China was the third largest supplier of arms to the war in Sudan between 1994 and 2004. Russia was by far the largest arms supplier (77.4%), compared to China which supplied only 9.3% (SIPRI, n.d.b cited in Bosshard, 2007). Finance generated from the sales of resources to China can also be used to buy arms from other sources, but this can be said of any sales of resources to any country. China has recently increased the supply of arms to SSA. Between 2008 and 2012, it supplied 16% of SSA's arms imports; this rose to 27% between 2013 and 2017. In comparison, the US supplied 11% between 2013 and 2017 (Tian *et al.*, 2018).

5.2. Profit

When China lifted millions out of poverty, it did so gradually and not by liberalising trade as pushed by the Washington Consensus. The Chinese model emphasises fiscal stability and macroeconomic balance, as well as learning and experimentation. This example is a good model for Africa (Brautigam, 2011). China's interaction with Africa is not altruistic but fulfils its 'win-win' philosophy of bringing benefits to African countries while also bringing benefits to China. Chinese projects in SSA which allow access to Africa's natural resources, local markets, business projects and infrastructure are of enormous economic benefit to Chinese companies. China's finance to Africa, including aid, creates business for Chinese companies and employment opportunities for Chinese labourers, a critical goal of Beijing's 'Going Out' strategy of 2001 (Sun, 2014a). Because of the size of China's economy and the extent of its international connections, China's interaction with Africa is far more important to Africa than to China. Africa's role in China's overall global policy is far less than the amount of foreign reporting would indicate (Sun, 2014b). China's approach to Africa is multifaceted. The Chinese government engages in SSA through complex forms of commercial diplomacy, which can be difficult to disentangle (Brautigam & Hwang, 2016). As a result, there is considerable misreporting in the figures for China's aid and investment in Africa, and this incorrect information often gets repeated (Brautigam, 2009a). The most accurate information would seem to be from Deborah Brautigam and the CARI, established in 2014 at the John Hopkins School of Advanced International Studies (SAIS), which tracks China's aid and loans. These are the sources of the figures on China's aid and finance used in this chapter. Deborah Brautigam is the director of the CARI.

China's involvement in SSA goes back to the 1950s, but its economic interests increased significantly in the 1990s. These interests were dominated by resource extraction but are much more diverse than just resources. The growth in political and economic importance of Africa was signalled with the establishment of the China–Africa Cooperation Forum (CACF) in 2000 (Taylor, 2006). The summit was renamed the Forum on China and Africa Cooperation (FOCAC) in 2006. These summits were repeated at three-yearly intervals, and after 2006, at each meeting, China increased its funding to Africa. China has been welcomed by many African leaders. It offers an alternative source of loans and aid to the WB, IMF and other Western lenders. China's loans are welcomed because they are condition-free and infrastructure-friendly (Zhao, 2011a). After 2004, China was using what has been called the Angola model, 'resources for infrastructure' exchanges or loans where resources are used as collateral. Western oil companies and private banks have provided loans to oil-producing countries, with oil used as collateral, but never tied to infrastructure. China has vastly extended the practice (Brautigam, 2009a). The Chinese government blurs the distinction between development finance and aid because they encourage agencies and commercial entities to 'closely mix and combine foreign aid, direct investment, service contracts, labour cooperation, foreign trade and export' (Piao Yingji, 2006, cited in Sun, 2014a). Most of China's finance is in the form of commercial loans and loans for commodity exchanges. China's aid is only a small proportion of its finance to Africa (Brautigam, 2009a).

5.2.1. *Trade*

As China's economy began expanding in the 1980s, its resources were steadily depleted. In 1993, it became a net importer of oil. The nation started to seek out resources in SSA but soon found that most resources were already tied up by the European nations, which had been in SSA for centuries, or the US. China's trade with Africa increased in the 1990s, part of a broad export policy aimed at expanding and diversifying its export markets. Between 1990 and 2010, Africa–China trade grew at approximately 20% annually (Mortished, 2010). While Africa supplied only a small percentage of China's total imports, by the middle of the 1990s, China had become Africa's second biggest trading partner behind the US (Taylor, 2009). China had a trade deficit with SSA until 2015. Trade between China and Africa grew 10 times between 2000 and 2008 (Brautigam & Tang, 2011). In 2000, trade between China and Africa was valued at $10 billion (Pilling, 2017; Dollar, 2016). In 2008, China's exports to Africa totalled $50.8 billion while imports from Africa stood at $56 billion, leaving China with a $5.2 billion deficit (Information Office of the State Council, 2010). Chinese trade with SSA hardly suffered after the 2008 global financial crisis (GFC) although SSA's exports to the West collapsed (Standard Bank of South Africa (Stanlib), cited in Mortished, 2010). By 2011, the value of trade between China and Africa had reached $166.3 billion, 16 times higher than in 2000. Sixty percent of the African products entering China had no tariffs imposed (Li, 2012). Since 2011, trade levels have fluctuated. In 2012, China's trade with Africa reached $198.5 billion. South Africa was China's largest trading partner in Africa at that time, and the value of trade between the two was $20.2 billion (Sun, 2014a). Chinese–African trade rose to over $220 billion by 2014 (Pilling, 2017; Dollar, 2016) and then declined to $188 billion in 2015 (Jayaram *et al.*, 2017) as the Chinese economy began to slow. Demand for commodities declined and prices contracted. That year, for the first time, Africa had a trade deficit with China of $510 million (China–Africa Research, 2018a). The deficit reached $28.6 billion in 2016 (Ernest & Young, cited in Dibie, 2017). In 2015, China was the destination for 15% to 16% of SSA's exports and the source of between 14% and 21% of the region's imports, according to estimates from Thomson Reuters and the WB (Albert, 2017). SSA's trade with China at this time was worth $188 billion but remained well short of the value of trade with the European Union (EU) of $305 billion. Africa accounts for less than 5% of China's trade, but 16% of Africa's trade is with China (The FOCAC Reporting Project, 2015). The Standard Bank considered SSA had a 'significant trade deficit with China' after 2014. Only five African countries had trade surplus with China (Madowo, 2018). In 2016, the value of Chinese–African trade was $143 billion and Chinese exports to Africa totalled $82.9 billion. Lower commodity prices resulted in a reduction in the value of Chinese imports from SSA to $54.3 billion in 2016 (Xiang Bo, 2017).

5.2.1.1. *Traded products*

In the years immediately after 2000, more than 80% of Chinese imports from SSA were crude oil, raw materials and resources. These included iron ore and platinum from South Africa, copper and cobalt from DRC and Zambia, and timber from Gabon, Cameroon, Congo-Brazzaville and Liberia (Taylor, 2009). From 2000 to 2010, China had relations with most African nations, but the bulk of its imports were oil, gas and minerals from four countries, Sudan, Angola, Nigeria and South Africa (Africa Research Institute, 2012). After 2002, China signed further contracts for oil exploration and extraction with the same suppliers Angola (2005 and 2006) and Nigeria (2006) along with other nations: Gabon in 2004 and Ivory Coast, Congo-Brazzaville, Ethiopia and Sudan in 2006 (Taylor, 2006). By 2005, China was importing 31% of its total oil from the African continent. Its main suppliers were Angola, Nigeria and South Sudan (Albert, 2017). In 2009, Angola was the second largest source of China's oil; other key suppliers were Sudan, the Republic of the Congo, Equatorial New Guinea and Nigeria (Zhao, 2011a). After 2010, Angola became China's largest supplier of oil in Africa, and bilateral trade between the countries exceeded $120 billion, although Chinese interests in Angola have remained much smaller than the large Western oil companies (Zhao, 2011b). Though the supplies are relatively small, they are strategically important. By 2016, SSA was supplying 22% of China's oil imports, second only to the Middle East. Other African suppliers included the Republic of the Congo and South Sudan. Angola was China's third largest oil supplier (Albert, 2017).

5.2.2. *Financial inflows to SSA*

5.2.2.1. *Commercial loans*

Most of China's loans to Africa have been commercial, interest-bearing loans and not concessional loans. These commercial loans came with far fewer requirements and conditions than loans from the West. Chinese loans come from China's main lender, the Export Credit Agency (China Exim Bank), China Development Bank and state-owned commercial banks. As interest-bearing loans, they have to be repaid (Brautigam & Hwang, 2016). Loans from the China Exim Bank may be part of larger cooperative arrangements. The bank has five types of loan instruments: export seller's credits to state-owned Chinese companies, export buyers' credits, preferential export buyers' credits, concessional foreign aid loans to governments and special state loans (Brautigam *et al.*, 2015). China has supplied more export credits to SSA than concessional loans (supplied at below commercial rates). Export credits have a maximum maturity of 15 years, and buyer must put up at least 15% of cost as down-payment (Brautigam, 2009a).

Brautigam and Hwang (2016) found that China's loans and aid have been consistently overestimated in Western reports. A common misconception in the West was that during the 2000s, China's loans to Africa exceeded those of the WB, but this was false (Brautigam & Hwang, 2016). The WB has continued to be the largest lender to Africa, despite the many articles claiming that China had overtaken the WB as Africa's largest lender. The tracking database at CARI estimated that between 2000 and 2014, Chinese banks, contractors and the government loaned $86.3 billion to Africa governments and SOEs. The database showed that between 2000 and 2014, 10% of Chinese loans went to oil and mining (much to Angola's state-owned mining company). Transport, power and telecoms made up 56% of loans and 33% went for commodities or natural resources. The research database also showed that two-thirds of the loans did not have resources as guarantees. The goal of the loans in places such as Angola seems to have been more to provide construction firms with business than acquiring equity in resources such as oil (Brautigam & Hwang, 2016). Between 2000 and 2017, the Chinese government, banks and contractors extended $143 billion in loans to African governments and their state-owned enterprises (CARI, 2019a). The pattern of lending dipped a little in 2014 and 2015 and increased to $30 billion in 2016 (CARI, cited in Madowo, 2018).

China was criticised for lending to rogue states in the 1990s, but since 2000, its lending profile has been very similar to that of the WB. Between 2000 and 2014, most loans were to Angola, then Ethiopia, Sudan, Kenya and DRC, a list much the same as the WB loans to Ethiopia, Nigeria, Tanzania, Kenya and the DRC (Brautigam & Hwang, 2016). Another financial venture that involved China was the New Development Bank (NDB) established in 2015 by the BRICS group (initially known as the BRICS Development Bank). The bank positioned itself as an alternative to the BWIs and offered nations in SSA the potential for more leverage with Western lenders. Concerns about integrity issues arose when early appointments to the bank included officials tainted with corruption (Bond, 2017c). Whether the bank is a better alternative is yet to be seen.

5.2.2.2. *Resources for infrastructure or commodity-backed loans*

The Chinese have a saying: 'to end poverty build a road' (Brautigam, 2009a), and one of China's most significant activities in SSA has been building infrastructure. In keeping with its 'win-win' policy and its own recent experience as a developing country, China has responded to African countries' requests for infrastructure. China's investment in Africa's inadequate infrastructure was desperately needed and welcomed by most recipients. Chinese companies have built hospitals, dams, government offices and stadiums, and refurbished facilities abandoned by Western companies throughout Africa (Taylor, 2007). It has also revitalised many of its former aid projects. Apart from the resource sector, the Chinese government has concentrated its financing in the infrastructure sector: in dams, roads, railways, ports, airports and schools. In other areas, state finance has partnered with private companies to invest in tobacco, sisal, rubber and sugar plantations (Brautigam & Hwang, 2016). China Exim Bank has been financing dams in Africa since 2000 (Brautigam, 2009a). Chinese firms make significant profits from infrastructure projects, but they also benefit the local economy and people.

Many of China's low-interest loans are made using commodities as collateral (Sun, 2015a). China's first 'oil for infrastructure' loan was to Angola in 2004. Between 2004 and 2011, China made similar arrangements worth nearly $14 billion with at least seven resource-rich African countries (Brautigam, 2011 cited in Sun 2014a). Hwang and Brautigam estimated that about a third of loans to Africa between 2000 and 2014 were secured to commodities (resource-backed loans) and tied to Chinese companies and services (2016). 'With China, you never see the money' (Brautigam, 2011). This way of doing business also directly benefits the African people. Resource-for-infrastructure arrangements avoid the misappropriation of funds. It is hard to embezzle funds that are deposited directly with the companies doing the work and in practical terms 'If the Chinese leave, the road remains' (Mortished, 2010).

5.2.2.2.1. Democratic Republic of the Congo (DRC) case study

China's resources for infrastructure exchanges have encountered problems. In countries such as the DRC where governance is weak and the state is fragile, there have been difficulties with loan repayments and resource deliveries. During the 1990s, Western lenders had denied aid and rejected loan applications from the Democratic Republic of the Congo (DRC) because it had defaulted on its loans. By 1999, DRC's outstanding debt was $14 billion. By 2001, the country was almost $500 million in arrears to the IMF and almost $50 million to the WB. Lack of aid and a series of wars had destroyed the country's infrastructure. In 2001, President Kabila agreed to restart peace talks and the country was stabilising. He was able to arrange $50 million in aid with the WB for roads, modernising schools and hospitals and helping with AIDS. It was the first aid it had received for 10 years (Stratfor, 2001). DRC was keen to increase investment. It joined the Extractive Industries Transparency Initiative (EITI) in 2007 (EITI, n.d.). In the same year, it made a loan agreement with China. The Chinese Exim Bank and other smaller Chinese banks arranged $3 billion funding for infrastructure and $3 billion to develop the Sicomines copper and cobalt mines. The Sinohydro Corporation and China Railway Group had another arrangement to build roads and hospitals for a 68% stake in the cobalt and copper mine in 2008 (Sun, 2014b). After Paris Club donors and the IMF raised concerns about the loan's negative impact on DRC's debt, the project was scaled back in 2009 to an estimated $6 billion: $3 billion for national infrastructure and $3 billion for the mining investment (Shinn, 2016). The project was hampered by severe power shortages, corruption and excessive bureaucracy (Ross, 2015). By 2014, $800 million had already been paid out in infrastructure investment and the mine was barely producing. Any returns in the form of resources were a long time coming, which was a wake-up call for the Chinese (Jaganathan & Daly, 2017). By 2016, it was still not clear which party was the clear beneficiary. The mines had been hampered by inadequate electricity supplies and higher costs of substitute fuels. The estimated scale of copper and cobalt resources was reduced as world prices had declined. Production was far below projected totals. The lack of transparency in the project — the closed nature of the contracts and fees agreed — meant it was not clear if profits had been lost from not selling on the open market. There were also supplier problems, including the appearance of major sinkholes in some of the roads constructed by the Chinese. Construction companies may have cut corners or not been subject to adequate local government scrutiny (Landry, 2018). This example demonstrates the problems of engagement with unstable governments. DRC remains highly dependent on resource exports for government revenue, and in 2018, extractive industries accounted for 98% of DRC's exports and 18% of GDP

(ITIE, 2018). Though there is significant demand for those resources, chronic instability makes it an unreliable partner.

5.2.2.3. *Aid and concessional loans*

China has been supplying development assistance to Africa for many decades. Before 2000, China's aid was predominantly through grants. Many of the aid projects, notably the Tanzam railway, fell into disrepair after the Chinese left. China's aid efforts in the 1990s went to reviving earlier aid projects that had fallen into disuse (Brautigam, 2009a). In the late 1990s, China's strategy changed and its focus became more commercial. There is considerable confusion surrounding the amount of China's aid to Africa, which is partly the result of the way China blurs aid and other types of finance. The fact that international definitions of aid do not match does not help (Brautigam, 2009a). The OECD/DAC definition of aid explicitly states that the money has to be used for social and economic development, it can go to countries or multilateral agencies, it must comprise 25% grant if it is a loan, and it specifically excludes military assistance (OECD, n.d.b). Neither China nor the US fits this definition. Both countries supply military assistance as aid. China does not consider debt relief to be aid, while the US and fellow members of the DAC group do (Brautigam, 2009a). Neither China nor the OECD considers export credits — below-market credits used to buy goods and services — as aid (Brautigam, 2009a). Chinese government institutions and banks play a prominent role in providing many types of development assistance in the form of loans and credits from the People's Bank of China, the China Development Bank, the Import–Export Bank of China and the China–Africa Development Fund (Albert, 2017). China does not make clear distinctions between development aid, and economic and commercial arrangements. China's financial arrangements are complex, and as they differ from the West, it has been difficult to establish actual aid figures. China did not release its first official aid figures for SSA until April 2011 (Brautigam, July 2011).

There has been considerable misreporting in the media about China's aid to Africa. Aid figures are often merged into 'investment and aid' (Brautigam, 2009a). A later CARI study of Chinese aid found enormous discrepancies in aid estimates. Most of these figures were based on reports in the media, and checking revealed that many of these projects had not been realised. A charted comparison between AidData findings and CARI figures for Chinese aid to SSA between 2000 and 2013 found totals were similar — $80.1 billion (AidData) versus $73.6 billion (CARI) — but the two sources of data differed in their interpretations of the distribution of that aid. Brautigam and Hwang quote Remi Bello, a political risk consultancy focused on Africa, claiming that only between 2% and 4% of memos of understanding are realised (2016).

According to Yun Sun, within the Chinese government, there are two different perspectives and priorities about the goals and management of Chinese aid to Africa. The bureaucrats at the Ministry of Foreign Affairs see foreign aid as a means of China strengthening its bilateral ties with African countries. Political priorities are the main criteria for decisions on aid projects, and economic benefits are of secondary importance. In direct contrast, the Ministry of Commerce prioritises economic growth and resource acquisitions along with economic benefits such as profitability, resource extraction or the acquisition of service contracts for Chinese vendors (2014a). China's aid is delivered through MOFCOM (China's Ministry of Commerce) and works mainly through grants, interest-free and concessional loans (Brautigam & Hwang, 2016). MOFCOM also supports Chinese businesses that assist China's resource diplomacy. Two main banks supply development finance. While the Chinese government provides some development aid in the form of outright grants through the China Development Bank, most of its aid takes the form of 'concessional' low-interest loans from the China Exim Bank (Brautigam, 2011). Early in the 2000s, the China Exim Bank did not disclose the conditions for the provision of concessional loans but published the terms for specific loans; that is, the interest rate for Benguela railway in Angola was 0.25%. China does specify that the loans be for projects that are technically feasible and will generate economic returns (Bosshard, 2007).

China gives more of its aid to Africa than to any other region. Between 2000 and 2003, 44% of China's aid went to Africa. By 2006, China's aid to Africa was approximately $300 million; this figure was around 50% of Exim Bank's concessional loans (Brautigam, 2009a). Between 2010 and 2012, 51.1% of China's $14.4 billion aid budget went to Africa (Areddy, 2014). Figures for China's global aid was similar in 2014 ($2.97 billion) and 2015 ($2.99 billion), but in 2016, it dropped significantly to $2.25 billion. Total foreign aid between 2003 and 2016 was $26.95 billion (China–Africa Research Initiative (CARI), 2019b). Between 2013 and 2018, 45% of China's foreign aid went to Africa (CARI, n.d.b). China has supplied aid to every country in SSA that followed the One China Policy, not just those with resources (Brautigam, 2009a). China's aid agenda in Africa is 'comprehensive, multidimensional and defies any simplistic categorization' (Sun, 2014a). The aid is made up of grants, interest-free loans, concessional loans, educational scholarships, food and medical assistance (The FOCAC Reporting Project, 2015).

Using its understanding of developing country needs and knowledge gained from its own experience, China has more recently focused on a wider range of development initiatives in its relations with SSA. This assistance has been delivered through a wide range of government providers, government departments and ministries, universities, think-tanks, policy banks, ministries of commerce and foreign affairs. It has been more willing to respond to African leaders' requests than the West has, especially requests to process raw materials. It has built roads in Liberia, established bauxite processing in Ghana and oil refining in Chad (Brautigam, 2011).

5.2.2.3.1. Tied aid

In 1991, the OECD member governments negotiated what became known as the Helsinki Package on tied aid. The Helsinki Package stipulates that export credit agencies can only provide tied aid (export credits that are at least 35% concessional) to projects that have genuine development characteristics and are not commercially viable. China does not abide by Helsinki Rules on tied aid; instead, it abides by the WTO Agreement on subsidies and countervailing measures, which specifies that interest rates of export credits must be market-based and adequate to cover long-term costs (Bosshard, 2007). Official concessional aid through the China Exim Bank is tied at 50% to purchasing Chinese goods and services. In response to the international effort to reduce tied aid, this figure reflects a reduction from the former level of 70%. Some countries, like Angola, specify that a certain proportion of concessional aid is allocated to local companies (Brautigam, 2009a). In 2011, China released its first public figures for aid. More than other countries, China ties aid to infrastructure delivered by Chinese companies. According to Chinese analyst Yang Fei, Africa is China's second-largest recipient of service contracts. China benefits from providing assistance as the value of service contracts is roughly equivalent to six times the amount of the assistance: 'when we give RMB 1 billion of assistance, we will get service contracts worth USD $1 billion (RMB 6 billion) from Africa' (Yang Fei, 2013 cited in Sun, 2014a).

After the first China–Africa Summit in 2000, China's Exim Bank had a '2-big development strategy', big companies and big ticket projects, usually expensive infrastructural projects (Bosshard, 2008). China's aid and development financing have filled gaps left by the West and promoted African development. Many projects taken on by the Chinese require large investments and allow long pay-back terms. Traditional Western donors are reluctant to provide these terms. China does not insist on the many conditions required by the West, including neoliberal structural adjustment policies, addressing poor governance or promoting fairness and sustainability. China's aid is largely 'tied' to the profitability of Chinese companies (Sun, 2014a).

5.2.2.3.2. Rogue Aid

China is often accused of delivering 'rogue aid', aid that avoids the scrutiny of the West. In 2017, Brad Parks of AidData in a *BBC* interview accused China of providing rogue aid. His example was Angola's rejection of IMF loans in 2004 — in favour of Chinese loans — because of conditions that included a poverty reduction strategy and more transparency in the oil industry (cited in Hatton, 2017). Angola soon paid off its debt with oil revenues and even introduced more transparency in the oil sector (Brautigam, 2009a). The media do not explore how humiliating or onerous those countries have found such conditions. Brautigam spent a chapter in her book, *Dragon's Gift*, discussing similar accusations (2009). Easterley's review of the IMF in 2007 found that even when countries agreed to conditions they did not necessarily fulfil them (2007).

5.2.2.4. *Chinese Foreign Direct Investment (FDI)*

In the early 2000s, China's FDI in SSA was less than its aid and loans. Chinese FDI into Africa increased after 2004 when the Chinese government began encouraging more overseas investment and made more investment funds available. Trade, investment and finance were closely linked (IMF, 2013). A key focus has been investment in infrastructure. These infrastructure arrangements were greatly beneficial to Chinese firms. In some countries, such as Angola, infrastructure and construction have been exchanged for oil, while other countries have more diverse trade, investment and financing arrangements (Madowo, 2018). China's FDI in SSA went up from $370 million in 2003 to $5.5 billion in 2008. China was able to provide large-scale finance at a time when African countries were being offered multilateral debt relief under the HIPCI programme (Paris Club and multilateral lenders), which brought with it the potential of future overwhelming debt burdens (Brautigam, 2011). According to the official Chinese figures, foreign direct investment in Africa between 2007 and 2010 averaged $1.5 billion per year (excluding 2008 when the Industrial and Commercial Bank of China (ICBC) purchased 20% of the Standard Bank South Africa for approximately $5.6 billion) (Brautigam, 2011). The 2017 Ernest & Young 'Africa Attractiveness Report' (AAR) estimated the value of China's investment between 2005 and 2016 to be $66.4 billion with 130,750 jobs created (Dibie, 2017).

Only a small proportion of China's global investment profile has been into SSA, and it has always been much lower than Western investment there. The United Nations Conference on Trade and Development (UNCTAD) reported that in 2011, China's FDI stock worldwide was $425 billion (2013), but, according to Yun Sun of the Brookings Institution, only 4.3% went to Africa. In 2012, less than 4% ($3 billion) of China's global FDI of $77.2 billion went to Africa (Sun, 2014b). By 2016, however, China's investment was 19.7% of its global FDI of $183 billion, which was 10.4% of world FDI (UNCTAD, 2017). Its investment in Africa until 2016 was always only a small proportion of foreign investment. After 2005, what China contributed was only 5% of total investment in the continent (Jafrani, 2012). In 2012, China accounted for 3% of investment in Africa (Chen *et al.*, 2015b), while, according to the World Investment Report 2015, its investment in 2013 and 2014 amounted to 4.4% of the total inward investment in the continent (Chen *et al.*, 2015b). China was the seventh largest financial investor in Africa in 2014, with the US the largest (Ernest & Young Attractiveness Survey Africa 2015, cited in The FOCAC Reporting Project, 2015). Chinese foreign investment in Africa increased to $36.1 billion in 2016, while investment from the US and UK dropped to $3.5 billion and $2.4 billion, respectively. That year, China became the largest foreign investor (Kazeem, 2017).

China's outward investment policies have not followed a unified strategy but have evolved in response to changing internal requirements and political priorities. Its investment and aid to Africa increased significantly after 2000 when political priorities were superseded by a focus on procuring resources for development needs, economic security and commercial interests (Zafar, 2007). The Chinese government has broader political and strategic goals in its investment and loans policies compared to private Western and Japanese investors who focus on short-term profits (Zhang *et al.*, 2013). It continues to control the main economic entities in core sectors. Of the approximately 150 very large corporations or state-owned enterprises (SOEs), a small number dominate China's resource procurement and large infrastructure project financing. Resource procurement has not always been profit driven because the government prioritises resource security. Chinese companies seeking access to resources and raw materials are state-owned and can, therefore, take a more long-term perspective. This is made easier by the low capital costs of these companies (Zhang *et al.*, 2013). Sometimes, the behaviour of SOEs has seemed to be inconsistent, as in the case of state-owned oil companies competing for contracts. This happened in Sudan when CNPC and Sinopec both tendered for one pipeline project (Taylor, 2009).

Most of China's FDI for resources comes from state-owned or partially state-owned firms with funding from Chinese government banks. The government offers integrated investment packages between state-owned companies and government institutions, mainly through the export credit agency, the China Exim Bank. Established in 1994, Exim was the largest lender for development in Africa in the first decade of the 21st century (Le Belzic, 2012). After 2000, Chinese FDI was focused on resource extraction, but by 2013, oil and gas made up only 50% of Chinese foreign direct investment, with manufacturing, financial services and construction comprising the other 50% (IMF, 2013). So, although China's state-to-state investment in resource sectors gets most publicity, the range of its investment is much more diverse. It has been able to fill a niche by focusing on transportation and power (Dollar, 2016). Engineering contracts make up a large part of China's investment (Brautigam, 2011). Engagement strategies in different sectors have varied. Dislocations occurred between the Chinese government and SOEs in the construction industry when companies came under pressure to deliver projects in Africa at a loss. While Western companies typically based their estimates on 15% profit — because of likely delays and cost overruns — the China Road and Bridge Corporation in Ethiopia has had to offer bids with a 3% profit margin. Chinese companies have found it very difficult to work with such low margins (Taylor, 2009), and in order to make a profit, these companies, especially those from poorer regions of China, would both compromise on worker safety and pay very low wages. Such decisions have prompted local worker retaliation (Brautigam, 2011).

Many Chinese profit-driven regional SOEs also invest in Africa. These companies are owned by provincial and municipal authorities and have different priorities from those of the central government (Chen *et al.*, 2015b). After 2000, thousands of private investors began investing in SSA, many of the smaller enterprises prominent in commerce and manufacturing. China's business interests in Africa have become increasingly diversified, and the types of investment are now more varied than American business interests (Taylor, 2006). As the Chinese economy evolved, smaller companies and private investors became more prominent in African services and manufacturing (Chen *et al.*, 2015b).

5.2.2.4.1. FDI destinations

By the time China started searching for resource imports, the West had sewn up most of Africa's resources, so early Chinese investment concentrated in resource-rich countries shunned by the West, where control was not already in foreign hands. Early investment was concentrated in Angola, Zimbabwe, Sudan and the Democratic Republic of the Congo, as well as in Nigeria which did, in fact, have a strong Western presence. China's presence today remains proportionally higher in those countries (Chen *et al.*, 2015b), but the destinations for China's FDI are now much broader. By 2007, South Africa was the leading recipient of Chinese FDI, followed by Sudan, Nigeria and Zambia (*The New York Times*, 2007). After the Industrial and Commercial Bank of China (ICBC) purchased part of the Standard Bank of South Africa in 2008, it offered renminbi accounts to foreign traders. This further increased investment in the region. South Africa became the base for China's expansion into the rest of SSA, similar to the role, the country played for Western companies. Patrick Bond sees South Africa as playing a comprador role for both China and the West (2018b). Other Chinese banks have since been established there (*The Economist*, 2011). By 2012, most Chinese investment was in Nigeria, South Africa, Zambia and Ethiopia, with more than 100 Chinese firms operating in each country. By 2015, Nigeria had become the largest recipient of Chinese FDI (Chen *et al.*, 2015a). Most of China's FDI between 2000 and 2017 went to Angola (30%); Ethiopia (10%); Kenya (7%); Congo Brazzaville (7%); Sudan (5%); Cameroon (4%) and Zambia (4%) (Dahir, 2018). Dollar points out that though China gets criticised for investing in countries with poor governance, Chinese investment is proportionately higher in those countries only because the West does not invest there, and its investment is in fact balanced by investment in countries with good governance. South Africa is the destination with the largest amount of Chinese FDI (2016). Sectors attracting Chinese investment have evolved over time. In 2009, about 39% of China's FDI to Africa went into mining and energy, 25% into manufacturing and 16% into construction. By the end of 2014 mining had declined (24.5%), and construction (24.7%), financial services (16.4%), manufacturing at (13.6%) and scientific research and technology services (4.2%) had all increased (Shinn, 2016).

5.2.3. *Transparency*

Since China's economic involvement in SSA increased it has attracted much criticism from the West, with some valid reasons for concern. Early concerns about China from African representatives, such as the African Union (AU) and NEPAD, were justified as both organisations were trying to expand transparency in the region (Taylor, 2006). The lack of transparency in China's resource procurements is similar to that of Western corporations. Early worries were offset by China's resource-for-infrastructure arrangements, which had tangible outcomes. The Chinese government has responded to criticism by becoming more open about its aid and financial arrangements. Since 2006 the Chinese Premier has announced much of this information at the three-yearly FOCAC meetings. The first White Paper on China's African Policy prepared by China's Ministry of Commerce (MFCOM) was published in 2011. It was broader in scope than earlier statements and indicated that China was encouraging more transparency in its aid to Africa. In 2014, MFCOM produced a draft publication on aid delivery entitled 'Measures for the Administration of Foreign Aid', specifying 51 articles defining the principles of development co-operation. This was incorporated into a state council white paper specifying regulations on foreign aid delivery. The later document was more explicit about previous Chinese aid between 2010 and 2012. It specified that areas of aid included infrastructure, goods and materials, the development of human resources (education), industry and agriculture, while its development role covered a wide range of sectors: infrastructure and natural resources, industry, health and agriculture. The figures were subsequently cross-checked by Brautigam and the China Dataset (Stahl, 2016).

5.2.4. *Rising African debt to China*

China began lending to Africa in 2002, and overall that lending has shown an upward trend. In 2005, many low-income nations in Africa received debt relief from multilateral agencies. When China began increasing its lending to SSA in the mid-2000s, African civil groups as well as development institutions feared the loans would result in a new round of indebtedness (Bosshard, 2007). Concerns increased in the next decade as China's loans to Africa expanded. The tracking database at CARI estimated that between 2000 and 2014 Chinese banks, contractors and the government had loaned \$86.3 billion to Africa governments and SOEs (Brautigam & Hwang, 2016). China's share of SSA's external debt rose from less than 2% before 2005 to 15% in 2012 (Chen & Nord, 2017). The size of some of these loans was enough to put countries at risk of rising debt. In 2012, the China Development Bank's loans to Ghana were equivalent to 10% of GDP (Sun, 2014b). Chinese–African foreign policy changed when President Xi Jinping took over the Chinese leadership in 2012. At the 6th China–Africa Forum in 2015, he increased China's financial pledges to \$60 billion, much higher than earlier pledges (\$5 billion in 2006, \$10 billion in 2009 and \$20 billion in 2012). Yun Sun also raised the issue of the large financial pledges made by President Xi Jinping in 2015, when he said there would be less emphasis on resources in future China–Africa relations and more emphasis on manufacturing. How would the loans be paid if not with resources? (2015b).

By 2014, there was still no debt crisis, but by this time, SSA had a trade deficit with China. A number of Chinese loan repayments fell due in the middle of 2015 (Bond, 2018b). That year, the CARI at John Hopkins University identified 17 countries with debt problems and potentially unable to repay their loans to China. Countries most at risk were Dijbouti, Zambia and the Democratic Republic of the Congo. In 2017, the total debt for the continent was estimated at \$417 billion (Jubilee Debt Campaign, 2018). The WB identified 18 countries in high debt distress, with debt-to-GDP ratios of over 50% of GDP. The IMF noted that the risk of debt in the region doubled in five years between 2013 and 2018. Critics say Chinese infrastructure is too expensive and burdening countries with debt, and that China is using this debt to expand its global influence. China claims that relations are mutually beneficial. Most of China's loans are for infrastructure. In 2016, Brautigam and Hwang expressed concern that debt levels were rising in many SSA countries and that governments might not be able to absorb the increased pledges Chinese leaders had made at FOCAC in December 2015. They also noted that debts to the Chinese are unlikely to be cancelled (Brautigam & Hwang, 2016). Though SSA's debt to China has grown and could cause problems in the future, in 2017, that debt was only 20% of SSA's overall debt (Jubilee Debt Campaign, 2018).

5.2.4.1. *Debt relief*

China has a history of cancelling the debts of low-income countries. In 2001, China cancelled all of SSA's outstanding debt that had gone into default by 1999. It realised this debt was unpayable (Brautigam, 2009a). Between 2000 and 2008, China had cancelled $3 billion in African debt, an average of $375 million a year (Brautigam, 2009a). Many overdue interest-free loans were also cancelled. Announcements to this effect are made at the three-yearly FOCAC meetings (2009, 2012, and 2015). Debt relief is limited to interest-free, concessional loans maturing at the end of the year. These loans are part of China's foreign aid programme and only a small part of Chinese lending in SSA (Brautigam, 2011). Debt relief programmes are confined to the 'least developed countries, heavily indebted and poor countries, landlocked developing countries and small island developing countries that have diplomatic relations with China', a similar profile to countries in the WB Highly Indebted Poor Country Initiative (HIPCI) (Brautigam, 2018). Chinese debt relief comes without the onerous liberalisation conditions stipulated by the Paris Club and debt relief programmes of the HIPCI and the 2005 Multilateral Debt Relief Initiative (MDRI). Between 2000 and 2018, China provided over $9.8 billion in debt relief, most to countries in Africa ($9.55 billion) (OCAC, 2019). The amount of debt relief provided by the BWIs and ADB to 36 nations (30 in Africa) under HIPCI and MDRI between 1996 and 2017 was much higher, at $78 billion (IMF, 2017a, 2017b).

5.2.5. *Impact of China on economic sectors in SSA*

China's involvement in SSA has been extensive. 'It mirrors what has been the dominant approach of Western governments and corporations to Africa's development for many decades' (Brautigam & Hwang, 2016). By 2006, the China Exim Bank was involved in 259 projects in 36 countries in Africa. Between 2005 and 2016, China invested $66.4 billion in 293 projects in Africa, diversified across resources, manufacturing and services. Investment destinations included resource exporters, such as South Africa, Angola and Nigeria, as well as agricultural exporters, such as Kenya (Ernst & Young, cited in Xiang Bo, 2017; Dibie, 2017). Chinese development assistance in SSA is less paternalist than Western providers. Based on its own development experience, China's assistance has covered a broad spectrum, from infrastructure to agriculture. It has been more willing to respond to African leaders' requests than has the West, to process resources and assist with agricultural training and the setting up of agricultural centres. In the decade after 2000, China undertook a wide range of projects, including building roads in Liberia, setting up bauxite processing in Ghana and oil refining in Chad (Brautigam, 2011). Attitudes towards non-interference and respecting the wishes of borrowers have meant China has also taken on symbolic projects, those which are not necessarily practical but designed to bring goodwill or prestige for the leader. No other country or institution has been as forthcoming as China (Jafrani, 2012).

5.2.5.1. *Resources*

China's increased demand for resources after 2000 stimulated a resource boom in SSA. This influx of money encouraged high-growth rates in the region for over a decade. Countries were still not able to pay off their debt to the BWIs, and many were recipients of debt relief packages through HIPCI and MDRI. Resource extraction tends to operate in isolated, self-contained enclaves. Though many governments received benefits in increased taxes, the bulk of the profits was exported as illegal financial flows because most of the commodities were under foreign ownership. Governments have often been complicit in these practices as resource-rich countries tend to have high levels of political corruption and repression as in Angola, China's largest oil supplier in the region. The reason for this collusion is that governments use the money they get from resources to arm and repress their populations. China has a joint venture with the government oil company in Angola. Angola has also benefitted from oil for infrastructure exchanges. Countries in SSA dependent on Chinese markets experienced a contraction after the GFC when the Chinese economy began to slow and demand for resources declined. The flow-on effect was particularly significant in the largest economies, Angola, Nigeria and South Africa, as well as in countries such as the Democratic Republic of the Congo (DRC).

5.2.5.2. *Infrastructure*

SSA's infrastructure throughout the region is still woefully inadequate and poorly integrated. Meeting this deficit has been consistent with China's 'win-win' philosophy of engagement, and China has offered unparalleled levels of low-cost financing and cheap labour to build infrastructure (Economy & Levi, 2014). Chinese companies and SOEs have built ports, railways, roads, airports, dams, telecom networks and power stations. Often, these projects are part of 'resource for infrastructure' bartering arrangements. In such exchanges, the Chinese do not specify or determine what infrastructure they will fund as do other Western nations and organisations. This gives more agency to local governments. An exchange of resources for infrastructure is preferable to loans, has tangible results and is less likely to incur unsustainable amounts of debt. SSA nations experienced the effect of debt when they were forced to comply with the SAPs' conditions of the Washington Consensus. Critics raised the issue that African countries might be locked into long-term supply deals or countries might lose 'opportunity costs' by not selling their goods on the open market (Eyal & Peh, 2010). Long-term supply contracts effectively keep resources out of the marketplace. After 2000, such contracts were seen as potentially disadvantageous for the suppliers if prices increased significantly, but they met the immediate needs of governments for funds. Such arrangements provide tangible results, compared to outright payment where there is more risk of corruption (Taylor, 2009). Given the downturn in commodity prices, countries in SSA might have benefitted from earlier long-term supply agreements.

There are acute electricity shortages throughout SSA and energy is vital for economic development. Many African leaders have been eager to build large dams, and the Chinese responded to their requests, especially when the West pulled out of this sector in the 1990s. China's international dam building programme is based on the Three Gorges Dam template. The companies involved in that project have since been leaders in global hydropower development. There has been considerable misreporting in the foreign media about the extent of China's hydropower and infrastructure projects in SSA. China has far fewer hydropower projects in Africa than commonly reported. The amount of resource-backed financing of hydropower has been quite low. China has not always been able to quickly finance and implement projects as previously thought. By 2013, China had provided finance for 17 dams in 22 countries in SSA though it had expressed interest in many more (53) large hydropower projects. Finance for these projects was around $13.3 billion with China supplying roughly half that amount. This total differs from other published accounts, including International Rivers and AidData. China was also providing construction work for six other dams (Brautigam *et al.*, 2015). Most of the large infrastructure projects that Chinese state-owned companies have been involved with in Africa are commercial deals with local governments or come from the winning of contracts from the WB (Shinn, 2016), and, therefore, it is not correct that social and environmental impact analyses were not carried out before projects commenced. China has been criticised for bringing in large number of workers, but the reality was more complex. Though Chinese companies brought in their own managers, engineers and skilled technicians, they also hired many African workers and worked with Western consulting engineers. Another misconception was that the China Exim Bank did not allow competitive tenders on its projects (Brautigam *et al.*, 2015).

China has been reliable in delivering on promises. At the 2015 Forum on China–Africa Cooperation, 10 'major programs' between China and Africa were proposed and launched soon after the forum. All 10 were under way, with some exceeding expectations, before the FOCAC meeting in 2018, according to Qian Keming, vice minister of commerce. After the programmes are completed, Africa will have 30 thousand kilometres of new roads and 85 million tons of harbour capacity a year, as well as more than nine million tons of clean water treatment capacity annually. The programmes will also create around 900,000 local jobs for African countries (Chen, 2018). In 2015, China was the largest financier of infrastructure in the region. The value of its investment was $21 billion, far higher than the second largest investor, France, at $3 billion (Jayaram *et al.*, 2017). In 2016, the Chinese completed the railway linking Addis Ababa in Ethiopia to the port of Djibouti, a $4 billion investment. Another large infrastructure loan was $476 million to Uganda to build a road from Entebbe to the airport, all part of a $3 billion package of loans (Madowo, 2018).

China has also contributed to skill development in infrastructure. A study from CARI explored how China and other foreign countries contributed to the development of skills in the construction industry in Ghana. China's businesses provided more short-term general training than other foreign enterprises, but the level and quality of technical training were low, employee retention rate was poor, project time frames were short and there were problems with communication and cultural barriers (Meng & Bempong, 2019).

5.2.5.3. *Manufacturing and trade*

Industry in SSA needs investment and structural transformation. Production and exports also need to be diversified (Sun, 2015a). Chinese foreign direct investment (FDI) has the potential to assist the regeneration of SSA manufacturing, which was decimated when neoliberal trade policies (SAPs) increased competition from foreign imports (Dollar, 2016). China also created a $1 billion fund for loans for African small and medium businesses provided through African development banks and established a $5 billion equity fund to help Chinese businesses who wanted to invest in public–private partnerships, joint ventures and manufacturing (Brautigam, 2011). David Dollar's review of the MOFCOM database of Chinese investment found that while most of the infrastructure investment was through SOEs, Chinese small- and medium-sized firms investing in Africa concentrated primarily on the service sector and manufacturing. This investment was welcomed by African leaders (2016).

China has made far more effort to help Africa expand its export-focused manufacturing than the West. Using its own history as a model, China helped establish special economic zones and industrial parks. After 2006, Chinese ministries, banks and enterprises supported the construction and management of six special economic zones (SEZs) in five African countries, and three Chinese private enterprises began the construction of private SEZs through direct negotiation and cooperation with local African governments. Fieldwork was conducted in the six official African zones: Mauritius-JinFei, Nigeria-Ogun, Nigeria-Lekki, Zambia-Chambishi/Lusaka, Egypt-Suez, and Ethiopia-Eastern, between 2007 and 2009 as part of the China–DAC study group (Brautigam & Tang, 2011). The report concluded that they formed a unique, experimental model of development cooperation in Africa. Market-based decisions and investment by Chinese companies were combined with support and subsidies. The study also identified serious political, economic and social challenges (Brautigam & Tang, 2011).

Following the establishment of the CARI at John Hopkins University in 2014, many field studies explored facets of the impact of China on Africa's industrial and agricultural sectors. The first study in Madagascar focused on the transfer of technology. Transfers were found to have been limited and constrained by the policy environment. Fieldwork investigations of both Chinese and Nigerian firms in three regions of Nigeria showed some evidence of positive but limited technology transfer. They also revealed negative perceptions towards Chinese investment. While Nigerian economic policies have served to promote Chinese investment and skills promotion in Nigeria, it was considered necessary to have a more coherent strategy to leverage this new, growing source of capital and the potential resources it brings (Brautigam *et al.*, 2018). A study of Chinese engagement in the Ethiopian leather industry found that China had made a strong contribution, but it was questionable whether that contribution would be sustainable and effective transfer of expertise had occurred. Though the Ethiopian government had been pro-active in supporting the sector, there was a clear disjunction between Chinese ability to respond to market demands and Ethiopian understanding of the subtleties of contemporary marketing which had led to mistakes (Xiaoyang, 2019b).

Other research from CARI explored the success of the special economic zones (SEZ) and Chinese private investment. In Ethiopia, a cross-sector and cross-company survey was conducted, along with interviews with Chinese expert managers and technicians in the enterprises. Similarities and differences in company management strategies and training provisions varied between industry sectors. Other significant variables were the scale of production and wider market conditions. Sixty percent of the local workers surveyed received training, but it was of varying quality and length. The workers were satisfied neither with the training provided nor the promotion opportunities in their current companies (Fei, 2018). A comparative study of SEZ in Vietnam and Ethiopia found that in both initiatives the governments were intent on reforming the domestic economy using industrial policies as catalysts of structural change. The issues arising out of the operating of SEZs made clear to local policymakers the sort of legal and institutional framework, infrastructure and administrative services needed to manage these zones (Tang, 2019). In Tanzania, Chinese investors successfully engaged in a local, plastic-recycling enterprise. Strong local linkages were forged because the undertaking operated mostly at the low end of recycling and manufacturing, relying on locally recycled waste plastics as raw materials. Chinese activities stimulated the local supply and growth of plastic recycling activities. Chinese investors provided suppliers with technological and financial support, supplied information about opportunities to participate in global value chains and facilitated knowledge transfer with local suppliers. The researcher noted that plastic recycling has potential health and environmental risks which need to be closely regulated and audited (Xia, 2019a).

Another study of Chinese manufacturing and agricultural investments in Tanzania found results had been significant and clear connections made with the local economy. Local supply networks had benefitted from the transfer of knowledge, and training opportunities had been provided through work with government and vocational training facilities. Again there was an issue with the ongoing sustainability of these achievements, because of the specific nature of the technological and financial cooperation with local firms, and the contribution to setting local standards was based on specifically personal relationships which were not transferable. Though Tanzania was politically secure and offered a large stable market, wider structural problems continued to hamper development, including poor infrastructure and energy supply, underdeveloped local supply chains, regulatory uncertainty and cultural differences (Xia, 2019b). The same author looked at Chinese manufacturing and agricultural investments in Kenya. China's investments in agriculture were recent and results could not be confirmed while investments in industry concentrated on building materials and light manufacturing. The sites where interviews were conducted had all provided onsite training. However, China's investment has demonstrated only low-level local linkages in recent years (Xia, 2019c).

Chinese exports to Africa are said to have undermined the products of local traders and manufacturers in Africa. The Chinese have also been accused of selling inferior products. As China is not a monolithic entity, and there are thousands of Chinese companies in SSA, Taylor asked 'which China are we talking about?' (2009). The whole export process is underregulated in China. Many companies producing goods exported to Africa are foreign companies in joint-venture arrangements with Chinese companies. Western multinationals are also complicit in these exports. The sellers of Chinese-made goods in Africa are usually African traders who have built up a strong trade network with China and have imported the products. There is also a large African expatriate commercial network living and working in Guangzhou. Many of the products imported from China are illegally produced, and the companies and the importers (often Africans) are beyond the control of the Chinese government. Though local traders in SSA are undermined by Chinese imports, manufacturing in Africa has been in decline for some time. The imposition of the SAPs by the Washington Consensus decimated fledgling industries in the region. African people also benefit from imports of cheaper goods. Sometimes, this is the first time poor people can afford consumer products, such as electrical goods. In comparison, products imported from the West were much more expensive and only the affluent could afford them (Taylor, 2009).

In particular, Chinese exports are said to have undermined African textile manufacturing. Textile production in cotton-producing countries, such as Malawi, Tanzania, Zimbabwe and Kenya, has contracted in size, but Chinese imports were only a small part of this scenario. The export of used clothes from US charities was another contributing factor (Brautigam, 2009a). African outdated production methods also contributed to the decline in local textile manufacturing (Brautigam, 2011). Cheap textiles came not only from China but also from South Africa and elsewhere in Asia (Assimwe, 2006, cited in Lee, 2007).

China's engagement with Africa has evolved and become more pluralist in recent years (Stahl, 2016). In 2013, UNCTAD predicted that as rapid industrial upgrading occurred in China, there would be more opportunity for SSA to attract Chinese FDI in manufacturing. Manufacturing could provide employment and training, and assist in diversifying economies that were historically held back by dependence on one or two primary resource exports (UNCTAD, 2013). At the 2015 FOCAC meeting, when President Xi Jinping made $60 billion in financial commitments, his speech focused less on resources and more on promoting 'industrial capacity cooperation' and 'strategic complementarity' as the goals of China's relationship with Africa. President Xi Jinping also said there would be more emphasis on industry and manufacturing. According to Yun Sun in 2015, as Africa aspired to industrialise, modernise and urbanise, China wanted to move labour-intensive industries to Africa. China had already assisted in helping Africa to industrialise, diversify its economies, build infrastructure and increase regional economic integration (Sun, 2015b). The recent economic downturn in China led to reduced investment in Africa and made future relations with Africa less easy to predict. A recent survey of 640 Chinese firms released by Peking University Center for Structural Economics and the Supporting Economic Transformation Programme at the Overseas Development Institute in London found that Chinese firms were not planning to move offshore prompted by rising wages in China. Though there had been a 9% to 11% increase in real wages between 2005 and 2014, the most common response of manufacturers was to turn to automation. Of the small percentage who said they would consider moving offshore (6%), Africa was not the preferred destination (Kuo, 2017c).

5.2.5.4. *Agriculture*

Transforming agriculture and providing food for the people is a major priority for African governments. There is an urgent and long overdue need to increase productivity and food security as well as ensuring development is inclusive (Sun, 2015a). In China, land reform preceded the development of agriculture and the creation of incomes for small farmers. Later, China opened up for foreign agribusiness. There were problems with many of China's agricultural investments and development projects in SSA in the 20th century, including economic inefficiency, shortage of funds and the difficulty of maintaining benefits achieved. Chinese techniques could have made land more productive, but they were not successfully introduced (Brautigam, 2009a). The Chinese also found African farmers less willing to introduce practices, such as levelling the land for growing rice and regular weeding. Most of the farming in Africa was done by women, and their pressing need was for draft animals, tools and finance to secure inputs so they could develop their farms beyond subsistence level (Brautigam, 2009a).

Since 2000, China has provided much assistance with agricultural development, an area neglected for decades. At the 2006 FOCAC meeting, China committed to establishing 14 new agricultural technology demonstration centres, using a public–private model that policymakers hoped would make the project sustainable (Brautigam, 2009a). These centres worked with Chinese institutes and agribusinesses. Development outreach services were cross-subsidised and opportunities for people to earn income explored. Twenty such centres had been established by 2011 (Brautigam, 2011).

Researchers at CARI investigating China's agricultural projects in SSA found that Chinese land acquisitions were grossly overstated in the foreign media. Of the more than six million hectares of land acquisitions allegedly acquired, less than 50% (252,901 hectares) had actually been procured. Most of this land is in Cameroon — 41% of the total — and largely comprised two purchases in 2008 and 2010 of existing rubber plantations, each over 40 thousand hectares. Chinese land acquisitions have since slowed down (CARI, 2019c).

5.2.5.4.1. Case studies in agriculture

In the last decade, the CARI has conducted many field studies investigating Chinese engagement in SSA. The research revealed a wide range of Chinese activities, from large, state-owned undertakings to small-scale private farms. There has been an increase in the number of small- and medium-scale farmers and entrepreneurs engaged in agriculture. These endeavours are independent of the Chinese government. The studies reveal some of the difficulties faced by external actors in bringing about economic development. Some larger scale undertakings have been successful and establish replicable partnership models for agricultural development. The China–Africa Cotton project provided out-grower farmers with seeds, fertilisers and assistance for cotton manufacture. The company plans to extend its production chain and install a cotton-processing plant. In Nigeria, the Chinese have a state-owned farm, Green Agricultural West Africa Ltd. (GAWA), a project established in 2002 by a SOE, China Geo-engineering Construction Overseas Corporation Nigeria (CGCOC), which is committed to long-term agricultural development. It has operations in 10 countries in SSA (Xiaoyang, 2019a).

5.2.5.4.2. Angola

Angola was a food importer before it became independent in 1973. Currently, 66% of the labour force works in agriculture, but the country is a net food importer. Less than 30% of the land is under cultivation and Angola has one of the lowest agriculture productivity levels in Africa. The annual food gap is around three million tons. The government has acknowledged that expanding agriculture is crucial to help diversify the economy away from oil and diamonds. Though it claimed it wanted to increase productivity from 2013 to 2017 by 90%, prior to that in 2009 it had cut the agriculture budget from 4.9% to 1.6% of GDP, far below the 10% goal of the African Union in the Maputo Declaration 2003 (Zhou, 2015).

China's relationship with Angola is wider than just resource procurement and infrastructure construction. As part of the oil for resources deal in 2004, China agreed to set up four agricultural projects, and more agricultural projects were established in 2008, supported by commercial loans from the China Development Bank. In 2015, China supported seven agricultural projects, only one funded through China Exim Bank (aid). The land still belongs to the Angolan government (state farms) and all production goes to the government. In 2014, the government detained many foreigners in Angola, which concerned the Chinese. China has worked to improve relations with the nation, and investment in agriculture is part of its 'soft-power' strategy to build trust and relations between the countries (Zhou, 2015). The main issue is sustainability of the projects after they are handed back at the end of five years. The companies involved were not able to make the investments profitable within five years but are seen as gateways to getting other construction work in Angola. The conclusion was that China's history of foreign agricultural aid and agricultural demonstration centres has been unsuccessful for long-term cooperation (Zhou, 2015).

5.2.5.4.3. Zambia

After Zambia became independent from Britain in 1964, it favoured socialist agricultural programmes, which failed to bring about economic development. In 1991, the one-party system was overturned and there was a change of political direction. Efforts were made to liberalise and develop agriculture. The Zambian government encouraged commercial agricultural investments from private and foreign investors. Chinese individual migrants, rather than the Chinese government, responded to these incentives. This group was different from the local, small-holder, subsistence farmers or historical, large-scale commercial investments. After 1995, foreigners were allowed to purchase land, and by 2015, there were two Chinese state-owned farms and 31 private farms in Zambia. Production was for the local market: crops, vegetables and livestock. Most of the Chinese private farms were medium-scale, between five and 200 hectares. Owners were 'emergent farmers', often with no farming experience but willing and keen to learn. These farmers were only a tiny proportion of the commercial farmers in the country. Most private farms are under 100 hectares. Life was hard and challenging. These farmers filled a gap between large-scale commercial farming with government support and small-scale farmers who have no support. Among the challenges they face is the complexity of local bureaucracy, especially over land sales. It is much easier to buy from the state than from individuals, and negotiations can last for years. There is some discrimination against them as local authorities try and protect local producers, especially in the sale of chickens. A group of entrepreneurs were identified who did not fit into the stereotypes of foreign enterprises. Learning from the successes and methods of these farmers has the potential to benefit local smallholder farmers (Chatelard *et al.*, 2015).

A comparative case study focused on technology transfer in Zambia and Malawi, comparing the cotton investments of China–Africa Cotton (CAC) with the US agribusiness Cargill. China already imports a lot of African cotton. China–Africa Cotton is the largest Chinese cotton producer in SSA and has been operating since 1993. It purchases only cotton. CAC operates in all levels of the production chain, provides employment for local people and has contracts with 100 thousand farmers in Southern Africa. Farmers are given seeds, fertilisers and pesticides. The American multinational corporation Cargill entered the Zambian market in 2006. Cargill purchases a number of products from producers: maize, soybeans, sunflower seeds and cotton. The three crucial aspects of cotton are seed, inputs and farm management, and Cargill is doing better than CAC in some aspects of its business, its buyer payments and its incentives as well as its staff training. CAC has the benefit of a Chinese government agricultural centre to assist with training. Its training and information manuals are not as good as that produced by Cargill, which recently established a farmers' training school. CAC needs to provide more training to local managers who could pass on more information to farmers. The strength of CAC is that it is vertically integrated into society and plans to extend its connections by establishing textile mills to stimulate local production. The positive aspects of CAC's operations include its openness to adopting existing African systems and practices, its willingness to take advice from local managers and its business model that is cautious about cost control and cost efficiency. It is also 'frugal' with its own investment. CAC is looking for finance from external partners to assist with business and technology transfer (Xiaoyang, 2019a).

5.2.5.4.4. Ghana and Nigeria

Chinese investment in agriculture in Ghana has been very limited. Between 2000 and 2008, Chinese investment in Ghanaian agriculture was 3% of Ghana's foreign investment and 2% of China's investment in Ghana. Chinese private investment in agriculture has grown since 2009. There are now four private farms owned by Chinese people in Ghana. They are small scale and produce largely for the local market. Private investors have great difficulty buying land. Chinese investment in agriculture has been more extensive in Nigeria where the Chinese have a state-owned farm, Green Agricultural West Africa Ltd. (GAWA), a large enterprise established in 2002 by the CGCOC. Its major shareholders are Sinopec and CGCOC. The project involves the governments of both countries as well as experienced Chinese engineering companies, and operates as a public–private partnership. CGCOC is already in 10 African countries. The company has been committed to agricultural development in Nigeria since 2005. Operations include seed research on hybrid rice, maize and millet; it sells seed to farmers and is involved in agricultural development. It has facilitated knowledge transfer which will be expanded when the proposed agricultural industrial park is built. It also markets Chinese agricultural equipment. The range and variety of undertakings provide a successful model for replication in other countries, which CGCOC has planned (Jiao, 2015a).

5.2.6. *Conclusion*

After 2010, the Western media began admitting that a considerable amount of criticism of China's engagement with Africa has merely disguised protectionism (*The Economist*, 2011a), or what Stiglitz has described as 'sour grapes' (cited in Madawo, 2018). The opacity of the nature of China's economic relations in Africa also generated attention and scrutiny (Sun, 2014b). Western analysts are finally conceding that Chinese engagement in SSA has been positive for the region. The provision of construction and infrastructure, as well as human resource development, are valuable contributions to the region's development. Investment advisers McKinsey Global Institute consider Chinese investment to have been largely beneficial (Jayaram *et al.*, 2017). In 2013, the IMF came to a similar conclusion (2013).

5.3. Planet

Until recently, China's own domestic environmental record has been poor. The country has environmental laws, but they have not been implemented effectively. When China promoted rapid economic development, little attention was paid to the environmental impacts of rapid industrialisation and urbanisation. Regulatory environmental oversight was minimal (Economy, 2004). In the context of widespread corruption and a desire to maximise profits, large-scale environmental destruction occurred. Pollution of land, air and water was widespread. There has been little regulatory oversight of company activities or respect for worker rights. Chinese industries and mines continue to have some of the world's worst labour conditions, and unions are still not permitted under China's totalitarian rule.

When the Chinese expanded internationally, they brought along the same environmental and social practices. China's activities have had a significant environmental impact in Africa through resource extraction and construction (dams, roads, rail and power transmission). Many projects have been undertaken with little regard for sustainability or suitability (Taylor, 2009). Changes began to occur within China after 2000 when the government realised that environmental damage was impacting domestic GDP. There were also many protests throughout the country. In January 2008, the Chinese Environmental Ministry SEPA signed a deal with the International Finance Corporation to introduce the Equator Principles, the environmental standards of international private banks, into China. The Bank of China and the China Banking Regulatory Commission jointly prepared a green credit policy, pressuring banks to comply more with government environmental policies, conducting environmental assessments and planning for resettlement and consultation with local communities. In October 2007, the Ministry of Environmental Protection and the Ministry of Commerce announced they would ban companies found seriously violating environmental rules from exporting for up to three years. For the first time, in November 2007, loans were withheld from 12 Chinese companies under the green credit policy (Bosshard, 2008).

In the early years of the Forum on China–Africa Cooperation (FOCAC), environmental concerns were not a top priority. China was often criticised for violations of environmental law in Africa (Bosshard, 2008). Such criticisms were equally applicable to Western companies. Environmentally damaging activities have been undertaken in remote areas and national parks, and most often in countries where governance is weak. The Chinese government's provision of assistance to SOEs involved in resource extraction is similar to the ways the US, French and South African governments have assisted private oil and mining companies in Africa with economic, political and military support. The China Exim Bank is the main source of finance for large budget SOE projects in Africa. In 2004, the bank issued its first environmental guidelines for overseas projects. These were publicly available in 2007. It also set company guidelines for social and environmental impacts in overseas operations and compliance with host country regulations. Bosshard pointed out that the Ministry of Environmental Protection (MEP) did not have much control over the 150 or so large corporations controlled by the Chinese government, and even less over the provincial, municipal and private Chinese companies operating overseas (2008). Around the time regulations were being tightened in China, the government became more sensitive to social and environmental issues in SSA. This was partly in response to local protests and riots provoked by human rights' abuses and environmental destruction. When President Hu Jintau visited Africa in 2007, he urged Chinese companies to obey the local laws (Bosshard, 2008). China may not be a member of the OECD and has not signed any OECD agreements on the environment, in particular the Common Approaches to the Environment first signed in 2003, but Chinese companies have started to use environmental impact assessments and have sought the expertise of Western companies that specialise in these studies (Shinn, 2016).

By 2014, nearly 50% of China's FDI into SSA was in construction and mining, equally spread between the two. These are both sectors with a large environmental footprint. The concentration of FDI and overseas engagement in the hands of SOEs and government-controlled banks means that if the Chinese government adopts and enforces strict environmental policies, it will have an important international impact (Shinn, 2016). In 2014, the government-affiliated China Chamber of Commerce for Minerals, Metals and Chemicals Importers and Exporters announced voluntary guidelines to regulate overseas mining investments and operations. The guidelines were developed in collaboration with the OECD, the German development agency GIZ, and Global Witness, an advocacy group that focuses on natural resource management. These guidelines encouraged Chinese companies investing overseas to pay careful attention to labour issues, environmental protection, supply chain due diligence and human rights concerns. More Chinese state-owned and privately owned companies are now demonstrating greater interest in protecting the environment. In 2000, one Chinese company had signed the United Nations Global Compact, a voluntary, corporate responsibility agreement that includes protecting social and environmental rights. This number had risen to 272 by 2015. However, this is still only a small proportion of the thousands of Chinese companies operating in SSA. While 79% of FDI in Africa is by state-owned companies with close ties to the Communist Party of China, it is not these companies but the rest, including small private companies and the medium-sized ones, affiliated with Chinese provincial and municipal administrations that are most resistant to improved environmental practices (Shinn, 2016).

One of the core environmental issues is that African governments also have not seen environmental protection as a priority. Economic interests tend to supersede environmental protection. Environmental agencies are underresourced and understaffed, and there is little government pressure on overseas investors to abide by national environmental regulations (Shinn, 2016).

5.3.1. *The climate crisis*

The rapid expansion of China's carbon emissions since the 1980s is part of the contemporary global climate crisis impacting on SSA. Though China participates in the G7, it does not consider itself a member. At the United Nations Framework Convention on Climate Change (UNFCCC) in Paris in 2015, the G7 pressured developing nations to sign away their rights to shared but differing responsibilities in addressing carbon emissions. Though the position of the US remains central, the power of the EU and China is seen to be increasing, and China has assumed more of a leadership role in international climate crisis discussions. It is hoped that China will take on the leadership role in the transition to clean technology and sustainable development. The most significant contribution China could make to the climate crisis is to drastically cut its own emissions, and cease operating, building and funding coal power energy both domestically and internationally. China first started funding power projects in SSA in 2001 (Streatfield, 2018).

China has led the world in expanding the global capacity of renewables (excluding hydropower) since 2009. It is the world's largest manufacturer and exporter of solar panels and is already a leader in wind energy technology and production (Shinn, 2016). It can bring enormous benefits to SSA by promoting alternative energy (both solar and wind power) as an option to hydropower. An International Energy Agency (IEA) report in 2014 concluded that African countries generally have abundant renewable energy potential to stimulate economic development. By 2040, renewables could provide more than 40% of all power generation capacity in the region, varying in scale from large hydropower dams to mini- and off-grid solutions in more remote areas. The provision of energy would be hampered if the population continues to grow rapidly (2014). Renewable energy technologies are essential for rural electrification in Africa, with solar energy the best option for people who live in remote thinly populated areas (Deshmukh & Wu, 2015).

China has started exporting this technology to SSA, predominantly to South Africa. Before South Africa suffered an economic downturn between 2012 and 2015, it attracted, on average, $4.1 billion of capacity investment annually. Wind power was also expanding (Frankfurt School and UN Environmental Program (UNEP) Collaborating Center, 2019). China began to produce solar panels in Capetown in 2014. The Hanergy Group has since announced it was investing $1 billion to construct a 400-megawatt solar power plant in Ghana, and Yingli Solar and Suntech Power Holdings are establishing joint ventures in South Africa, Benin, Sierra Leone and Mozambique (Shinn, 2016). The Chinese wind turbine manufacturer, China Longyuan Power Group, announced it would develop two wind farms in the Northern Cape province of South Africa (Shinn, 2016).

South Africa has been emerging as a regional leader in wind and solar technologies. A study by CARI researchers looked into the different ways Chinese companies have invested in renewable technologies in South Africa. Many characteristics of the energy sector were particular to South Africa; national energy policies, levels of energy access, infrastructure networks, technological capabilities and competition between investors. China's interest in South Africa was prompted by an energy policy introduced in 2011, the RE IPPPP, which allowed renewable energy to be sold to the state-owned energy supplier Eskom. Further incentives were provided by the Chinese government's policies 'Going Out' and 'Belt and Road Initiative'. Though wind energy is operated by SOEs in China and solar energy is conducted by private companies, both sectors were looking for overseas expansion because of domestic overcapacity and contraction in the local market. The RE IPPPP provided opportunities for expansion in South Africa but there were many hold ups and delays. Competition between Chinese, EU and US companies brought some complications, but the study revealed both competition and co-operation between Chinese and Western wind energy and solar panel producers. Chinese companies were more involved in equipment manufacture, technology supply, engineering procurement and construction than in project development (Baker & Wei, 2017). The large dams that China has built in SSA have provided a clean source of power that is usually more affordable than energy produced from sources with higher carbon emissions (Shinn, 2016). Hydropower, however, has its own environmental cost. It would be environmentally beneficial to cease the building of large-scale mega-dams and concentrate on smaller dam building projects.

5.3.2. *Infrastructure projects*

The social and environmental impacts of hydropower projects constructed by China in SSA have often been harmful and destructive. The Chinese government has gone into countries where the West has less involvement and has taken on projects Western institutions and companies have rejected, either because they were too risky or because of the social and environmental damage they would cause (Zhao, 2011a). The WB rejected the Grand Ethiopian Renaissance Dam on the Blue Nile and the Ethiopian proposal for Gilgel Gibe 111 Dam on the Omo River because of major environmental and social concerns. China then provided the funding (Rotberg, 2013). The Gibe dam site was granted World Heritage Status in 1980. Work started on the Gibe 111 Dam in 2003. It was the highest dam in Africa and construction had a major impact on downstream communities in the Lower Omo Valley and Lake Turkana in neighbouring Kenya. The damage has reduced the size of the annual flood and water levels will go down. The river supplies most of the water for Lake Turkana. An estimated 30% of the water is diverted to supporting large-scale conversion of land for agribusiness without consultation with local people. Many people face dispossession and loss of livelihoods (Avery, 2018; International Rivers, 2015). The Merowe Dam project on the Nile in North Sudan is another environmentally destructive dam, funded by China after other lenders rejected the project. The project authority for the dam had approached Malaysia, China, Canada and Arab and European countries for funding before getting finance from the China Exim Bank. The official export credit agency of France (COFACE) had rejected the request because of environmental impacts and the displacement of a large number of people. Construction began in 2004 (Bosshard, 2006). The China Exim Bank supplied most of the foreign finance ($520 million) with other funding supplied by the Middle East (Merowe Dam Project Implementation Unit, n.d.). The project had not been approved by Sudan's Ministry for the Environment (Bosshard, 2008).

The Chinese also funded the 660 MW Lower Kafue Gorge Project in Zambia, another project rejected by the WB and the European Investment Bank (Bosshard, 2008). A World Wildlife Fund (WWF) expert reported to International Rivers that the Chinese company Sinohydro had told the Zambian government that they should assess the project's economic return only and not bother with the environmental impacts (Bosshard, 2006). In Sudan, the Chinese-built Kaibar dam displaced many people and destroyed between 500 and 1,000 irreplaceable archaeological sites (Rotberg, 2013). The Bui Dam in Ghana, built by Sinohydro and funded by China's Exim Bank, flooded a quarter of the Bui National Park. Endangered species were put at risk, fish stocks were put in danger, and people were moved and lost homes, farms and livelihoods. There was also an increased risk of outbreaks of schistosomiasis (International Rivers, n.d.). China's lending for this dam was backed with cocoa revenue as security (Brautigam, 2009a). The Itezhi-Tezhi Power Company in Zambia contracted Sinohydro to build the 120 MW Itezhi-Tezhi Dam. The project was a joint venture between Zambia, China and India. The dam was built in a national park, home to a large variety of unique birds and wildlife (Zimba, 2016). In Ethiopia, Chinese companies built a dam taller than the Three Gorges dam, the 300 MW Tekeze hydroelectric dam, on a tributary of the Nile River. There have been environmental problems since completion. The canyon walls have collapsed and silted up the water flow, reducing energy production and water for irrigation. Further reinforcing was required. Energy from the dam was not intended for local people but for cities or export to neighbouring countries. This macro-level approach is possibly not the best strategy for economic development in Ethiopia. Certainly, local and international groups, such as *Bread for the World,* recommend an alternative development plan for this country, which includes small and medium dams, afforestation and hill terracing, and the development of alternative energy sources, to both sustainably tap the natural resources and equitably distribute its benefits. If future water flow decreased, the projected energy outputs would not be met (Bosshard, 2008). International Rivers evaluated the Mphanda Nkuwa Dam project on the Zambezi River in Mozambique before work commenced. The project did not meet any of the World Commission on Dams criteria. A needs assessment revealed it did not meet rural electrification needs. Local communities affected by the project were given little information and were not consulted. Other options such as solar, wind, geothermal, or natural gas were not considered. Problems already created by existing dams would be intensified if the Mphanda Nkuwa project proceeded, and the completed dam would cause further damage to ecologically sensitive areas in the lower Zambesi River and delta. The costs of the project were far too high compared to the projected benefits. The country-specific focus did not consider activities in other neighbouring countries. Among anticipated benefits was the sale of electricity to South Africa although, because of electricity produced by other dams in the region, notably the Inga dam in the Congo, there was no guarantee of demand from South Africa (Ribiero, 2004).

In keeping with its policies of 'non-interference', China does not specify conditions for its loans. African governments have asked the Chinese to build large dams and they have delivered them. African governments have prioritised national and industrial energy needs over the need for electricity for poor people and local people's land rights. This macro-level approach meets immediate energy needs but has ignored the future impacts of the climate crisis and potential changes in weather patterns, likely to bring more extreme and more frequent droughts and floods.

5.3.3. *Resource extraction*

5.3.3.1. *Oil and mining*

The oil sector is responsible for extensive environmental pollution in SSA. Western oil companies developed the oil sector in SSA long before China arrived in the 1990s, and China's practices have not been noticeably different from other foreign companies. There has been little foreign criticism of Chinese oil operations, possibly because similar criticisms are applicable to Western companies. China has responded to government requests or has joint arrangements with individual governments as it has with its two largest suppliers: Angola and Nigeria. In SSA, the energy ministries often overrule the environmental ministries, which are underfunded and underresourced. In Gabon, the SINOPEC oil company explored for oil in Loango National Park until the national park service ordered it to stop in September 2006. A second environmental impact study was conducted with the original Dutch company assisted by the World Wildlife Fund and a Gabonese organisation. The project then went ahead (Shinn, 2016).

Apart from Angola and Nigeria, Sudan, Chad and Gabon also supply China with oil. When China National Petroleum Corporation developed oilfields in South Sudan and Sudan, the social and environmental impacts were extensive. In conducting seismic surveying for oil, hundreds of kilometres of tracks were bulldozed, destroying farmland and increasing deforestation. The building of roads affected water flows and damaged irrigation systems. Communities were forced to evacuate. The most damaging impact has come from the discharge of contaminated wastewater from oil reservoirs and drilling mud. The issues have been ignored by the Sudan government. In 2012, in Chad, the government terminated a Chinese oil prospecting contract because of blatant disregard for the environmental damage it was causing. In 2014, five Chinese oil permits were withdrawn after a company refused to pay a $1.2 billion fine for oil spills around a drilling site (Shinn, 2016). Mineral extraction is another highly carbon-intensive process causing air, water and land pollution. Extremely toxic chemicals are used to extract metals from rock, and mining companies, including Chinese companies, have a poor record of dealing with waste created by resource extraction.

5.3.4. *Industry*

For decades, many Western companies exported their polluting industries and waste plastic to China, especially when domestic environmental regulations increased. There have been reports that one of the ways China is dealing with its own environmental crisis is to export its most polluting industries offshore, including to Africa. Some of China's heavily polluting companies are establishing plants in Africa, such as China's largest steelworks Hebei Iron & Steel. This giant producer of steel, cement and glass signed a contract in 2014 to build a five-million-ton steel firm in South Africa (Yap, 2014). It can be argued that China does not necessarily export polluting industries to Africa to get rid of them, as industrial development is closely related to such industries, and many of these industries meet local development requirements and produce mainly for the local market. Such industries include tanning, steel production, iron ore and cement. In 2015, Sinosteel announced plans to develop a plant in Kenya to meet the expanding demand for steel products, destined for sectors such as real estate and infrastructure construction including the Mombassa-Nairobi Standard Gauge Railway, the Lapsset corridor and the 10,000 km new road network project. The railway would connect Mombasa to Malaba and onward to Kampala, Kigali and Juba (Standard Digital, 2015). Sentuo Steel is already a leading steel manufacturer in Ghana and planned to expand its operations with a ceramics plant and a cement factory (Xinhua, 2016b). There have been complaints about Chinese polluting activities in other countries. Tanneries in Ethiopia and Somaliland have dumped waste that has affected the livestock industry. The government of Somaliland was too concerned about upsetting the Chinese to take action (Shinn, 2016).

5.3.5. *Deforestation*

In 1999, China embarked on a major domestic re-afforestation programme 'Grain for Green'. The goal was to increase the percentage of China covered in forests from 21.7% to 26% by 2035. This plan put pressure on China to increase its wood imports (Climate Action, 2018). A policy change in 2009 led to another increase in timber imports. China has been increasingly seen as a predator of the world's forests. The Environmental Investigation Agency (EIA) analysed trade data for 36 countries supplying timber to China, concluding that in 2011 approximately 10% of the logs and sawed timber used there were illegal. While Africa is not one of China's major timber suppliers, China is the destination of 75% of Africa's wood exports. Chinese demand for timber has a major impact in the countries in SSA where it operates and has been detrimental to tropical rainforests, especially in DRC, Sierra Leone and Cameroon (Weng, 2014). The British research organisation, Chatham House, estimated that each year between 2000 and 2008 China purchased between 16 and 24 million cubic metres of illegal timber (cited in Laurance, 2011). In 2013, it was estimated that 17% of wood products imported into China were illegal. Rosewood remains one of the most sought after woods. Rosewood is classified as an endangered species by the International Trade Convention and trade has been designated illegal. Trade in rosewood has continued to rise dramatically, triggered by demand from well-off Chinese households for reproductions of Qing and Ming dynasty furniture. Rosewood trafficking is especially lucrative. The main source of rosewood in SSA is Madagascar (EIA, 2012). In 2008, Sierra Leone banned timber exports because Chinese and other logging companies were plundering forests with no respect for the law (*BBC News*, 2008). Countries in SSA that ban the export of logs include Equatorial Guinea, Ghana, Côte d'Ivoire and Nigeria. Large quantities of logs from Nigeria were stopped by officials at the Chinese border in 2016, following investigation of a large-scale, illegal scheme involving Nigerian officials — who issued 4,000 retrospective permits — and members of the Chinese embassy (EIA, 2017).

Some of China's timber purchases are a result of FDI by Chinese logging and timber trading companies. Chinese companies have been buying concessions to ensure a steady supply of timber for the Chinese market. By 2010, Chinese companies owned about 25% of the timber concessions in Gabon. Seventy percent of Equatorial Guinea's wood products, more than 90% of Mozambique's timber exports and 50% of the Republic of the Congo's exports go to China. Gabon, Africa's largest timber exporter, sends 40% of its timber exports to China and, in 2009, provided almost 4% of China's total timber imports (Shinn, 2016). The Chinese government does not have regulations in place to ban the import of illegal timber. Concerns have also been raised about the impact of China's activities in terms of social equity and environmental sustainability. Putting roads in places like the Congo Basin opens the area to exploitation from wildlife poaching, illegal colonisation, mining and land speculation. By continuing to purchase illegal logs, China is encouraging these practices (Laurance, 2011).

A large proportion of Chinese timber imports are processed and then exported, mainly to Western markets. In 2014, 44% of China's timber exports went to the EU and the US (Richer, 2015). This suggests that Western consumers are complicit in the problems caused by deforestation. Boycott campaigns by environmental groups, such as World Wildlife Foundation (WWF) and Greenpeace, can have a major impact on what Western consumers purchase and thus can affect Chinese exports (Laurance, 2011).

5.3.6. *Endangered species*

Increased Chinese demand for ivory has also had a major impact on wildlife numbers in SSA. The market for ivory expanded in the 1990s when income levels in China began to rise. The Great Elephant Census Report, conducted by NGO 'Elephants Without Borders' and the Paul G. Allen Foundation, found that elephant populations declined by around 30% between 2007 and 2014, a loss of 144,000 elephants. Botswana has the largest percentage of elephants in Africa. Most live in protected areas like the Okavango Delta (Sullivan, 2018). According to the WWF, the poaching of elephants peaked at 30,000 a year in 2011 before easing to its present level of 20,000 annually. Elephants have almost been wiped out in Cameroon, DRC and parts of Zambia. Losses were also high in Angola, Mozambique and Tanzania (Dixon & Kaiman, 2016). The mass slaughter of elephants has led to international outrage. Ivory prices have begun to decline, dropping from $2,100 per kilo in 2014 to $730 in 2017. Increasing consumer awareness and a drop in demand are seen as the causes of this decline. The crackdown on corruption in China has reduced the need to pay for 'favours' from government officials. In 2017, the Chinese government announced its plan to end the domestic trade in ivory. Research by the conservation group 'Save the Elephants' has revealed that changes may already have had an impact on elephant numbers (Cruise, 2017). High returns are the key motivation for poaching, so the price drop in China plays a major role in reducing the slaughter of elephants (*China Daily*, 2017). However, there are other less positive trends. Prior to May 2018, Botswana had a shoot-to-kill policy with poachers, but the new president, elected in April 2018, disbanded the policy soon after coming into office. Since then, poaching has dramatically increased (Sullivan, 2018).

Another endangered species is rhino, also sought for its horns. In Namibia, rhino poaching has increased in recent years. As wildlife poaching became more difficult in the Kruger National Park in South Africa, criminal gangs moved into Namibia, home to a species of desert-adapted black rhino. The number of rhinos killed critically endangers the species; 61 were killed in 2014, 93 in 2015 and an estimated 63 in 2016. Other species, including elephants, are also poached in Namibia. Some accusations claim that wildlife poaching has increased since the arrival of Chinese immigrants. A number of Chinese people have been convicted on poaching offences in Namibia. Gangs of Namibians have since joined the poaching industry, along with foreign poachers. The illegal activity has become highly militarised and is expensive to monitor and regulate (Save the Rhino, 2017).

5.3.7. *Food security, land-grabbing and agribusiness*

There have been many reports in the foreign media that China plays a significant role in land acquisition in SSA, but, in fact, China has a very minor role (Pearce, 2012) compared to Western acquisitions. A CARI investigation into an alleged six million hectares of Chinese land acquisitions found the actual figure was only 252,901 hectares. Of these acquisitions, 41% were in Cameroon where China had purchased two existing rubber plantations (over 40,000 hectares each) in 2008 and 2010. Researchers investigating Chinese farming investments in SSA found them 'surprisingly modest'. China actually exports more food to Africa than it imports. Acquisitions have slowed in recent years (Brautigam, 2016).

5.3.8. *Planet: Conclusion*

China's footprint in SSA has grown significantly since 2000 and environmental impacts have been significant in the resource extraction sectors and construction. China's footprint is, however, much smaller than that of the West. China has had a high profile in SSA for less than 20 years. In comparison, the US and multilateral organisations have been active in the continent since the mid-20th century. The Chinese have built fewer dams and provided much less funding in the way of loans, aid and investment. There is also the issue of a power imbalance between China and governments in SSA. According to Yun Sun, if African governments do not like the way these companies, the Chinese and other countries, operate, they need to regulate them themselves (2015b), echoing Taylor's comments a decade earlier (2006, 2009). However, African governments have become reliant on Chinese finance. The countries where environmental impact is most devastating are those with the poorest governance records. African regional organisations, such as the African Union, need to put pressure on both China and African countries to sign agreements such as the Extractive Industries Transparency Initiative (EITI) (n.d.). African leaders need to consolidate their position and coordinate their goals in relation to China and employ collective bargaining (Sun, 2015b). But China has evolved and modified its policies in keeping with international agreements. It has addressed issues of tied aid, lack of aid transparency and adhering to local environmental regulations and labour laws. Also, the Chinese government is not able to monitor the activities of all the Chinese companies working in Africa, especially private companies.

5.4. Conclusion

In terms of foreign policy, Africa ranks the lowest on the US international political agenda and second lowest on China's. China's level of engagement in Africa gets far more attention than it warrants. Earlier, Africa played a prominent role in China's 'prestige diplomacy' and helped consolidate China's position as a 'developing country' and its goal of bringing about a 'new international order' (Sun, 2014b). Early on China stressed the similarities between itself and Africa both being developing countries. As it assumes more of a leadership role on the international stage, however, China no longer portrays itself as a developing nation with problems similar to those of African nations. Though China has financially contributed to, and given political support to, the G77 — the coalition of developing countries — it no longer considers itself a member.

China's role in Africa is motivated by political as well as economic goals, and central to its policies is the concept of 'win-win'. There is little evidence of negative repercussions of China's commitments in Africa compared to the impact of Western neoliberal policies since the 1980s, which possibly have caused the most damage to the region. China's engagement is multifaceted, encompassing trade, foreign direct investment, materials, engineering contracts, development assistance, development finance and humanitarian assistance (Brautigam, 2011). There are many ways China has brought benefits to SSA, including trade, finance, infrastructure, education and employment. China's relationship with SSA has evolved since 2000 and its economic ties have become stronger. Even the principle of 'non-interference' has been modified, and China has very recently increased its military presence.

Though China still delivers most of its aid to Africa, it is not an advocate for SSA's interests in opposition to the West. As China's role on the world stage has become more prominent, it has formed other alliances, including those with fellow members of the BRICS group and the G20. Its role in SSA has also changed. The recently established BRICS development bank, the NDB, seems to be following the same formula as the BWIs. Chinese investment (and that of other BRIC countries) in Africa at times does not differ from the historic exploitative role of the West that continues to this day (Bond, 2017a). China has used South Africa as a base to conduct business elsewhere in the region.

China has brought many benefits to SSA but its activities have also caused harm, displaced people and damaged the environment. Its biggest contribution has been the provision of infrastructure. After 2000, China provided many countries with resources for infrastructure exchanges which lessened the opportunities for corruption and the accumulation of debt. Since 2010, China's loans have increased while resources for infrastructure exchanges have declined and debt levels have increased. In the 21st century, China's interest in Africa has become more economic than political. It has been seeking resources and export markets.

The strength of China's position in Africa lies in the fact it was never a colonial power in the region. Because of the wide range of actors and the diversity of Chinese interests, operations in Africa are not always consistent with government policies. The Chinese government cannot control all its citizens working and living in SSA. Chinese engagement has not been without problems, particularly in the oil and mining sectors, where safety and labour laws have been disregarded. Dams have been built in environmentally sensitive areas, but China is as guilty as the West on these issues. Western governments will become more credible in expressing concerns regarding China's impact on the environment and good governance in Africa if they uphold and strengthen the standards ruling their own overseas investments (Bosshard, 2008). Where China could play a crucial role in the next decades is in assisting sustainable energy development in SSA. The most important action China could undertake to assist SSA is to drastically cut its own national carbon emissions and thereby reduce its contribution to the climate crisis.

Chapter 6

The Impact of the US, the World Bank and IMF on Sub-Saharan Africa Since 2000

The impact of the US, the World Bank (WB) and International Monetary Fund (the Bretton Woods Institutions (BWIs)) on Sub-Saharan Africa (SSA) since 1945 has been dominated by politics and economics. The recent addition to the mix has been the US contribution to the current climate crisis through its accumulated carbon emissions. The size of the US economy has translated into global political influence. The US is one of the world's largest markets, the world's largest aid donor, one of the largest military weapons exporters and — until recently — US corporations dominated the international economy. The US government has always been open about the fact that its priority is to serve US interests, in particular corporate interests. US influence extends to its dominance of the international development sector through the BWIs, the aid donors (the Development Assistance Committee) and the western lenders that meet as the Paris Club. This group is collectively known as 'the Washington Consensus' (Williamson, 2004). The BWIs have been the main source of loans, aid and policies for international development and the main source of SSA's funding since the early decades of independence. At the time when nations became indebted to the BWIs in the late 1970s, neoliberal political and economic ideology was adopted by the US, the BWIs and other members of the Washington Consensus. All further loans and aid from the BWIs and the US became conditional on adopting neoliberal policies. These included market deregulation, cuts to tariffs and subsidies, privatisation of state assets and reducing the size of government. The policies were promoted as a means of stimulating economic growth and enabling debt repayment. The policies have favoured Western interests, in particular the expansion and profits of foreign companies. Market deregulation has enabled the transfer of vast amounts of funds and resources out of Africa. These policies were reinforced by unequal trade policies, where local subsidies were cut and producers had to compete with Western agricultural products that were subsidised. These neoliberal policies undermined the political and economic sovereignty of governments in the region, and social and economic development stagnated for over two decades after their introduction. Though the policies failed to achieve their objectives — stimulating economic growth and enabling debt repayment — they have remained after 2000 as part of loan, aid and debt relief programmes in SSA and elsewhere. Neoliberal policies were economically beneficial to lenders and foreign corporations. Deregulation increased foreign ownership of African resources, enabled higher profits and facilitated the illegal flow of finance out of the region. These flows increased in the economic boom after 2000, further depleting the region of much-needed finance. SSA has remained burdened with debt and debt servicing despite a decade of strong economic growth. The global financial crisis was another event brought on by neoliberal policies, the deregulation of the US financial sector. It too led to social and economic stagnation in SSA when its export markets contracted. The policies and practices of the US/BWIs have also had an environmental impact in SSA, particularly in the failure to uphold environmental policies. The most significant regional impact of the US in the contemporary era is its contribution to climate change. The WB has funded dam projects that have destroyed large areas and displaced populations, encouraged resource extraction which has caused widespread pollution and devastation, and promoted policies that accelerated deforestation.

6.1. People: Politics and Human Development

6.1.1. *Politics*

6.1.1.1. *Political sovereignty*

In the second half of the 20th century, the US priority in SSA was preventing the spread of communism. During the decades of the Cold War from 1947 to 1991, the US and the BWIs provided loans and aid to a long list of non-communist totalitarian rulers in SSA, no matter how corrupt or repressive, and this support enabled these rulers to remain in power. As the US has dominated the policies and practices of the BWIs, this triad dominated financing supplied to SSA in the 20th century. Driven by American political and economic ideology, foreign aid and loans have been tied to neoliberal policy conditions since the late 1970s when nations became indebted. Neoliberal policies were imposed on 38 countries in SSA, the highest number in any region (Halifax Initiative, 2004). Governments wanting funds had to relinquish political sovereignty and follow policies imposed by lenders. Not until China rapidly expanded its engagement in the region after 2000 was this hegemony challenged.

Nations in SSA have been relatively powerless in bilateral relationships with foreign governments and international organisations. Power in the BWIs is closely tied to economic importance and SSA's economy has always been comparatively small. In 2016, the GDP of SSA was only one per cent of global GDP, $1.516 billion (WB, n.d.a1), compared to global GDP of $75.872 trillion (WB, n.d.b1). The voting structure of BWIs was established in the 1940s — before African countries became independent — with votes allocated based on economic size. The US made the largest financial contribution and was allocated the majority of votes. The imbalance in the allocation structure has remained despite major political and economic shifts in the intervening years. Decision-making remains undemocratic and effectively ensures that countries in SSA have little political influence. When votes were reshuffled at the IMF in 2015, the countries in SSA lost more votes (Nigeria (–41%), Namibia (–26%), Gabon (–26%) and South Africa (–21%) (Bond, 2017d). Only two board directors represent the 46 nations in SSA and IMF policy and decisions require board approval. Underrepresentation in the BWIs has meant that SSA is unable to influence decision-making (Bradlow, 2019). The voting structure of the WB is equally biased, with the US continuing to hold the majority of votes and having veto power. Over half the voting power in the WB is held by the financial institutions of the G8 (Bosshard, 2002).

6.1.1.1.1. Collusion, corruption and transparency

The financial support the US and BWIs provided to totalitarian leaders in SSA during the Cold War contributed to the stalling of political and human development in the 20th century. These countries include Nigeria, apartheid South Africa, Zaire, Sudan, Ethiopia, Kenya, Congo, Mali, Somalia, Malawi, Togo, Rwanda, Uganda and Zimbabwe. Financial support made lenders and donors complicit in the poor governance of those leaders, the suppression of the population and human rights abuses (Bond, 2006). Lenders were also complicit in the theft of funds. Boyce and Ndikumana identified capital flight as one of the key impediments to development in SSA. The theft of money has been occurring since loans and aid were supplied to independent nations and corporations were extracting resources (2012). More than half the money borrowed by African governments in any one year departed in the same year and often ended up in the same banks that loaned it (Boyce & Ndikumana, 2011).

Capital flight increased during the economic boom after 2000 when oil prices increased (Boyce & Ndikumana, 2012). Capital flight is associated with power relationships and a failure of national institutions. That capital flight continues to undermine those institutions. Most capital flight occurs in the oil producing countries, many of them being fragile states (Boyce & Ndikumana, 2011). The US and the WB have continued to provide funds to poorly governed, repressive 'fragile states' after 2000 despite the high risk of theft. The US government and the WB are either the largest donors or among the top three donors to many fragile states in SSA, including Ethiopia, Sudan, South Sudan, Somalia, the Democratic Republic of the Congo (DRC), Zimbabwe, Nigeria Burkina Faso, Cameroon, Central African Republic, Chad, Mali, Mauritania and Niger. The results of US efforts at providing development assistance to address 'fragility' have been 'mixed at best' (D'Alelio, 2018). In countries where civil society is weak, there is little evidence of greater transparency (Lujala *et al.*, 2017) or efforts to prevent the expropriation of funds.

Corporations are also involved in the theft of funds. For decades, many Western governments condoned bribery as an acceptable operating cost in developing countries. The cost of paying a bribe to win a contract was eligible for a tax deduction (Bolton, 2008). Even after the US government passed the Foreign Corrupt Practices Act in 1977 companies continued to pay bribes. In the next two decades, prosecutions were rare (Salbu, 1997). The governments in the Organization for Economic Cooperation and Development (OECD) signed further agreements to combat bribery in 1996 and 2009 (OECD, n.d.a). The US also ratified the UN Convention Against Corruption (CAC) in 2006. The Convention covered a broad spectrum including 'bribery, trading in influence, abuse of functions, and various acts of corruption in the private sector' (United Nations Treaty Collection, 2021). The US and BWIs have put in place regulations that attempted to curb corruption. In the 1990s, the WB expanded its lending conditionalities to include dealing with corruption and promoting good governance (Brautigam, 2009). After 2001, the WB tried to introduce transparency into DRC's extractive sector. In 2010, it had to cancel new programme loans because state-owned companies had continued to secretly sell assets. Loans were resumed in 2011 and then put on hold again in 2012 for the same reason. The Bank was also criticised for failures in its restructuring programme for the state-owned mining company Gecamines. The restructuring involved cutting 10,000 jobs. Subsequently, these workers filed court cases because promised severance programmes and rehabilitation programmes had failed to materialise (Bretton Woods Project, 2012b). Later audits of the BWIs revealed that the organisations were continuing to ignore their transparency and good governance policies (Easterley, 2007).

The countries with the highest levels of capital flight have poor national institutions and a corrosive institutional environment. Because there is an international system of enablers involved with lending and capital flight, greater transparency in lending, payments and export of finance would assist in curbing those flows (Boyce & Ndikumana, 2011; Eurodad, 2011). These enablers include the US and BWIs, because of a lack of due diligence in lending practices and their failure to actively support efforts to promote transparency and major international anti-corruption initiatives. The 2003 Extractive Industry Transparency Initiative (EITI) has been the most important initiative to introduce transparency into the resource extraction sector (n.d.). Implementing this initiative would have helped prevent capital flight from SSA. The WB failed to come up with a response, while the US signed the EITI in 2014, only to withdraw soon after. In 2011, the Bank's Vice President for Sustainable Development admitted the sector had been characterised by 'corruption, rent-seeking, environmental damage, disregard for the rights of local communities, [and] conflict and fragility'. In response to criticism that it was failing to prevent corruption in its funding for mining extraction, the WB introduced the E4D Extractives For Development policy in 2012 (Bretton Woods Project, 2012a).

The WB has continued to lend to governments with poor human rights records but where corporations have had financial interests. The Chad–Cameroon pipeline project was a $4.2 billion, 1070 km pipeline to take oil from landlocked Chad to the ocean, crossing Chad and Cameroon (Rice, 2008). The Bank ignored many warnings that the pipeline would empower and entrench the brutal dictatorship in Chad without benefitting the health, education and rural development of its people or benefit future generations (Bond, 2007). Amnesty International criticised the WB for ignoring human rights to further the profits of export credit agencies, private banks and three oil companies — Chevron, ExxonMobil and Petrobras (Wroughton, 2008). The Bank finally withdrew from the project in 2008. The government in Chad had repeatedly broken its social commitments and used the oil funds to buy weapons (Gulali, 2018).

Large foreign companies have considerable power in SSA where most countries are single or dual export economies. After the sale of state assets under neoliberalism, company taxes became important sources of government revenue. Many of these companies are worth more than the GDP of the countries in which they operate. The foreign corporations dominating resource extraction in SSA have a long history of keeping their activities opaque. They have played a central role in the 'resource curse' plaguing resource-rich nations in SSA. They have been complicit in supporting governments that are corrupt, authoritarian and repressive. Vast government income from resources coexists with extremely low standards of living, high levels of poverty, corruption and inequality. Foreign corporations have also been also complicit in perpetuating cultures of corruption and repression through the payment of taxes and bribes to officials and rulers, enabling them to expropriate wealth from the sale of resources, what is known as 'balance of payments leakages'. These funds have been transferred to foreign bank accounts or used to repress the population. US oil companies in Equatorial Guinea have ignored the appalling human rights record of the ruling dictator President Mbasogo Obiang, and the US government has also turned a blind eye. He was even hosted by the Obamas in Washington (Kenyon, 2018).

The largest US companies operating in SSA include ExxonMobil, Chevron and Halliburton (provider of products and services to the energy industry). In many countries, including Angola, Nigeria and Equatorial Guinea, the governments earn billions in oil revenues as do their foreign partners. In both Angola and Nigeria, ExxonMobil and Chevron are closely tied to governments through joint venture partnerships. As a result of the lack of transparency in transactions between oil companies and governments, vast sums of money are open to corruption. The worlds' largest company until 2013 — ExxonMobil — came under scrutiny for its transactions with the Nigerian government in 2009. The government accepted a bid for oil concessions that were substantially lower than an offer from a Chinese–Nigerian consortium (Thielman, 2016). In Equatorial Guinea, the US oil company Exxon has paid millions to the royal family, empowering a dictatorship which deprives the people of any benefits from its wealth (Maddow, 2019). The activities of Chevron in Angola and Nigeria have also come under international scrutiny. Chevron endorsed dos Santos, the notoriously corrupt and nepotist former dictator of Angola. The company claims to have donated millions to improve the lives of local people, but evidence is scant (dos Santos, 2016). Most of the oil wells in Angola are offshore in the Cabinda Bay and Chevron has been able to ignore the consequences of repeated oil spills in its offshore wells. Because any criticisms apply equally to its partner Sonangol, the state-owned oil company, the government turned a blind eye (Corpwatch, 2011).

The close ties between US corporations and the US government have played out in legal cases in SSA. The Republican politician Dick Cheney was hired as CEO of oil service provider Halliburton in 1995 on the strength of his government contacts. He had no experience in the oil industry. Over the five years of his tenure, Halliburton increased its government-backed loans from the US Exim Bank from $100 million to $1.5 billion and the company's government contracts also grew from $1.2 billion to $2.3 billion. Halliburton also profited from contracts from loan recipients. After Angola won a $86 million loan from US Exim Bank in 1998, it rewarded Halliburton with a $200 million contract to upgrade its Cabinda oil facilities, part of a larger $316 million investment from the same bank to improve Angola's hydrocarbon sector (Briody, 2004). In 2010, Dick Cheney and Halliburton were charged with bribery by the Nigerian government. Halliburton had paid $180 million in bribes to Nigerian officials between 1998 and 2006 to secure $6 billion in contracts for natural gas projects in the Niger Delta. The company reached a settlement with the Nigerian government, choosing to pay fines of $579 million to have the charges dropped. Most likely the company acquiesced to the settlement in order to maintain the US access to oil in the Niger delta. It was reported that former US President George H Bush and former US Secretary of State James Baker were involved in the settlement (Smith, 2010).

Another successful prosecution was lodged in 2016 by the US Securities and Exchange (SEC) in New York against the financier Och-Ziff Capital Management (valued at $39 billion). The company had advanced risk capital at high rates. It also pleaded guilty to supplying bribes in DRC. The company paid $412 million in company fines and the CEO paid a further $2.17 million. The company was also charged for bribery of state officials from Libya, Chad, Niger and Congo but entered into a deferred prosecution agreement (Raymond, 2016).

Neoliberal policies benefitted corporations and increased their profits by enabling them to buy state assets cheaply, keep wages low and avoid paying taxes. The deregulation of markets facilitated illegal financial transfers. These transfers increased significantly after 2000. A number of US corporations have been implicated in illicit transfers and money laundering for politicians. When the International Consortium of Investigative Journalists (ICIJ) investigated the financial affairs of the daughter of the former president of Angola and head of the state-owned oil company Sonangol, they discovered that Price Waterhouse Cooper and Boston Consulting Group had ignored 'red flags' and helped her transfer money and invest it around the world. Documents published in 2020 showed how consultants at Boston Consulting had set up a complex money-laundering scheme for Sonangol and sought ways of opening non-transparent bank accounts (TRT World, 2020). An investigation revealed the American-owned Riggs Bank was involved in extensive money laundering for clients in Equatorial Guinea. Between 1995 and 2004, the bank opened over 60 accounts for the President of Equatorial Guinea, his family and officials. Over $13 million was deposited in various family accounts between 2000 and 2002. The bank had deposited funds from oil companies into the presidents' bank accounts and created shell — anonymous — accounts for the president and his family. Other deposits had been made without due diligence. Oil companies had entered into joint ventures with businesses partly or wholly owned by members of the regime and made 'substantial payments' to government officials, family members or entities controlled by them. ExxonMobil, for example, established an oil distribution business in Equatorial Guinea which is 85% owned by ExxonMobil and 15% by a company controlled by President Obiang. This investigation led to prosecution in the US (AfricaFocus, 2004). Corporate bribery in Equatorial Guinea extended to one American oil company funding the education of President Obiang's son in the US (Kenyon, 2018).

6.1.1.1.2. Military assistance

US foreign policies in SSA have prioritised political interests over human rights and democracy. Early in the independence era, the CIA engaged in covert operations to topple leaders they feared were too left-wing, such as Patrick Lumumba in DRC in 1961 and Kwame Nkrumah in Ghana in 1965 (*BBC*, 2016). Using the covert activities of the CIA, the US also engaged in proxy wars against democratically elected communist regimes in Mozambique and Angola, supplying the South African military with arms and training. These interventions prolonged conflict in those civil wars. The US military presence expanded after 2000 as part of US President Bush's 'War on Terror'. Even local terrorist attacks and insurgencies were treated as potential threats to the US. The US established its first base in SSA, Camp Lemonier in Dijbouti, in 2001. After 2003, the Pentagon and CIA slowly spread throughout the continent, and that expansion accelerated under President Obama. In 2007, the US government set up the United States Africa Command (AFRICOM), based in Stuttgart. Funding was also provided for Trans-Saharan Counterterrorism Initiative (TSCTI) to support countries involved in counterterrorism against threats of al Qaeda in Africa. The main recipients were Chad, Mali, Mauritania, Niger, Senegal and Nigeria (Lobe, 2007). US interventions in the region also increased. By 2014, the US had troops in 13 SSA countries: Burkina Faso, Congo, Central African Republic, Chad, Dijbouti, Ethiopia, Kenya, Mali, Niger, Nigeria, Somalia, South Sudan and Uganda. Again, the line between US military operations and the CIA in Africa became increasingly blurred (Taylor, 2014). That year, the US carried out 674 military missions across the whole continent (including North Africa) (Turse, 2015a). In 2015, the NGO Tom Dispatch identified 60 outposts in 34 countries. There were varying levels of activity at these bases, camps and compounds. Many of these nations are known to be corrupt and have repressive rulers and poor human rights records (Turse, 2015b). There have been instances of 'blow back' from the US military presence in the region. In 2013, US-trained troops using weapons that had been discarded in Libya instituted a military coup in Mali and toppled the democratically elected leader. They were soon overthrown by other 'rebels' (Turse, 2015b) and the weapons were then used against them. The US sells weapons to many African governments as well as providing military training, but it is not the major arms supplier to the region. The US supplied 11% of the total arms imported into Africa between 2013 and 2017. The arms sold to Africa were only 2.2% of total US arms exports (Fleurant *et al.*, 2018). The US supplies arms to poor countries as aid or by selling off obsolete weapons cheaply (Rich, 1999). US arms assistance to fragile states in SSA is concentrated in Somalia and South Sudan (D'Alelio, 2018).

6.1.2. *Human development*

Human development is a complex issue closely tied to health, education, employment and the reduction of poverty. Human development in SSA lags behind other regions. The UN Development Programme created the Human Development Index in the 1990s to focus attention on the key role people and their capabilities contribute to the development of a country. The central aspiration is that people have a long and healthy life, are educated and have a 'decent standard of living' (UNDP, n.d.).

Human development in SSA stagnated for two decades after 1980 until economic development stimulated by China's resource purchases led to modest improvements in standards of living in the decade after 2000. Neoliberalism dominated policy thinking in the US and BWIs in those decades and was imposed on SSA as structural adjustment loan conditions. By 2000 there was a broad consensus — that did not include the BWIs and the US — that neoliberal structural adjustment policies were harmful to human development and increased poverty (SAPRIN, 2004). There has been no acknowledgement of the role these policies played in undermining human development and increasing poverty in SSA. The devastating impacts of these policies have been enduring and persist to this day (Bretton Woods Project, 2019). Most harm came from cuts to subsidies for health, education and the agricultural sector and the introduction of fees for services. Incomes also suffered when markets were deregulated and producers had to compete with imported products. Deregulation facilitated large scale capital flight which could have been used to repay debts. Instead, debt repayments absorbed large amounts of government income leaving little over for social services. By 2002, Nigeria was spending $2.9 billion annually servicing debt. In 2004, its debt was $34 billion and only $350 million was spent on health services (Hertz, 2004). Even debt relief programmes were accompanied by long periods of compliance with neoliberal conditions. The 1996 Highly Indebted Poor Country Initiative (HIPCI) required seven years of compliance with neoliberal conditions — later reduced to six years. The HIPCI was ineffective until 2003. Countries had to have met the same requirements before being eligible for the later Multilateral Debt Relief Initiative in 2005. During the compliance period, countries had to continue making debt repayments set at high ratios to GDP. This debt sustainability framework (DSF) was operationally flawed (Easterley, 2007).

Governments were left with little finance to stimulate economic or social development and soon became indebted again (Hertz, 2004). The improvements in human development in the brief period after 2005 when nations were able to spend more on social services demonstrated the debilitating consequences of debt servicing. Foreign corporations have brought few benefits to local people in SSA in terms of employment, health or welfare. These corporations were concentrated in the resource extraction sectors where employment levels were low. Neoliberal policies enabled companies to kept wages low and minimise workplace safety. The health impacts of pollution from resource extraction were ignored.

Another flaw in the BWIs approach was their focus on economic growth, assuming that economic growth would lead to improvements in standards of living. For the two decades after 1980, this assumption was not tested as the neoliberal policies failed to stimulate economic growth. After 2000, with 10 years of high economic growth, improvements in standards of living and human development were only modest. Not until 2017 did a Bank study confirm what had been known for decades, that high growth rates did not translate into improvements in human development (Chuhan-Pole *et al.*, 2017).

6.1.2.1. *Poverty*

By 2000, the first 50 years of loans and development assistance had clearly failed to eliminate poverty in SSA. The United Nations established the Millennium Development Goals (MDG) that year, but instead of a change in strategy, the proposed solution was to supply more aid. Donor countries were urged to actually deliver the 0.07% of GDP in aid that they had agreed to in the 1970s. The US has been the most prominent country to have failed to meet this target. United States Agency for International Development (USAID) has not focused on poverty reduction but on health initiatives. When the US has addressed poverty its approach was to come up with economic solutions rather than social spending and redistributive tax policies.

In 2004, President Bush established the Millennium Challenge Corporation as a separate entity in the US aid programme. Its motto was 'Reducing poverty through growth' and the aim was to promote good governance and human rights through economic growth (Millennium Challenge Corporation, n.d.). Another aid project established in 2015 was Power Africa set up by President Obama. The aim was to supply energy to 60 million homes in Africa through corporate partnerships (USAID, n.d.b). The BWIs have also prioritised economic growth, even though the WB's motto is 'Working for a World Free of Poverty', and after 1999 the IMF required countries to have a poverty reduction strategy before they would be considered for debt relief or aid. Because the BWIs institutions are partly funded by private sector finance, commercial priorities, notably debt servicing, have taken priority over social needs (Hertz, 2004).

In 2000, the Melzer Report to US Congress concluded that the IMF and the WB were irrelevant to eliminating poverty. It concluded that their priorities were driven by bureaucratic expansion. Both institutions serve the interests of the G7, and in particular the IMF serves the interests of the US government and financial interests. The BWIs have continued to endorse conservative policies towards poverty since that report (Bello, 2000). Neoliberal policies have focused on economic growth and the assumption that wealth will 'trickle down'. In 2011, the Independent Evaluation Group (IEG) of the WB assessed the degree to which the poverty focus of the commercial lending arm of the WB — the International Finance Corporation (IFC) — was reflected in the projects it funded. It found 'fewer than half the projects reviewed included evidence of poverty and distributional aspects in project objectives. Only '13 per cent of projects had objectives with an explicit focus on poor people' (IEG, 2011; Bretton Woods Project, 2012b). The auditing offices of both the WB (the Independent Evaluation Group) and the Independent Evaluation Unit of the IMF concluded that the BWIs are locked into bureaucratic procedures and practices that make them unwilling to accept criticism or modify their behaviour despite evidence confirming these practices are not producing the desired outcomes (Bretton Woods Project, 2019; Bossoni, 2011). The 2016 WB report Poverty in a Rising Africa concluded that rising population was the reason poverty levels remained high (2016a).

6.1.2.2. *Health and education*

According to Boyce and Ndikumana, there is an international system of enablers involved with lending and capital flight. They estimated that over 50% of loans to SSA between 1970 and 2004 were exported illegally. They explored the human costs of this capital flight through the loss of funding for social spending. Capital flight had two aspects, the inflow of money was much reduced but the full amount of debt had to be repaid, and repaid with interest. Their correlations between debt servicing and public health estimated that for every dollar of debt servicing there were 29 fewer cents to be spent on health. In economic terms, debt servicing crowded out health expenditure. They found that each $40,000 in reduction of health expenditure translated into an infant's life and calculated that the debt servicing of loans that were lost to capital flight was equal to 75,000 extra infant deaths per year (2011).

Neoliberal policies had other negative impacts on health and education in SSA apart from enabling capital flight. In order to reduce government spending, there was an insistence on cuts to health and education subsidies. Privatisation led to the introduction of fees. The poor were excluded from access to health services and education. The largest group excluded from education were girls. Governments have lacked funding to spend on social services because of the size of their debt repayments, the illegal outflow of funds and government corruption.

The USAID has focused on health initiatives favouring a corporate-driven approach. It works in liaison with US pharmaceutical companies to provide patented medicines which are more expensive but benefit corporations. Cheaper generic drugs would make drugs available to more people. The USAID programme in Africa has concentrated on the reduction of HIV, malaria and tuberculosis, with some success. However, the US government is also one of the worst countries in the OECD for tying its aid to delivery by US corporations and supporting corporate interests. It attempted to impose drug restrictions in 1999 when pharmaceutical companies took the South African government to the WTO to protect their patents and prevent the introduction of cheaper generic drugs to treat AIDs. After a wave of international criticism, President Clinton was forced to modify US trade policies to enable poor countries — including South Africa — to gain access to essential medicines. The decision to waive patent rights and allow the poorest nations to buy parallel imports was adopted by the WTO at Doha in 2001 (Fisher & Rigamonti, 2005). The US continued to promote the interests of the pharmaceutical sector and after the Doha agreement wanted to narrowly restrict the list of drugs to HIV, malaria and TB and a number of diseases only found in Africa (Denny & Elliot, 2002). President Bush's Emergency Aids Plan for Africa (PEPFAR) was launched in 2003. The programme has contributed to reducing the numbers dying from AIDS but has been criticised for its conservative approach in its initial 'ABC model' that promoted Abstinence, Be faithful, and correct and consistent Condom use. There has been an evolution in prevention programming, broadened to include specifying certain groups that are at higher risk of transmission (sex workers, homosexuals and intravenous drug users). The actual success rate has not been quantified (The National Center for Biotechnology Information, n.d.).

The programme has continued to receive the bulk of US health funding. The US also contributes to the Global Fund (an independent, international multilateral financing institution that provides grants to countries to address HIV, TB, and malaria) and provides bilateral assistance for TB and malaria programmes (Kaiser Family Foundation, 2020).

The privatisation of water is another WB neoliberal policy that has been harmful to health and which has also discriminated against the poor in SSA. The Bank was the largest global lender for water privatisation between 1993 and 2003. In 2002, the WB president stated that water and sanitation loans to Africa would be 'out of the question' unless they included private sector participation (Alexander, 2002, cited in the Halifax Initiative, 2004). Millions of people in SSA were left without access to clean water. Contaminated water transmits diseases, such as diarrhoea, cholera, dysentery, typhoid and polio, and also carries worms. The health-related costs of these diseases can amount to one-third of the income of poor households in SSA (Schlein, n.d.). Water privatisation contributed to the cholera epidemic in KwaZulu Natal South Africa in 2004. When their water was disconnected local people lost access to clean water (Bond, 2014b). Poor water is the cause of most child deaths from diarrhoea in SSA, and these deaths are preventable. The BWIs continued to insist on water privatisation despite the poor performance of private water companies both in Europe and the developing world. Private water companies had increased the price of water, made huge profits, cut off water supplies for those who could not pay, reduced water quality and indulged in bribery and corruption (Barlow & Clarke, 2004a).

Water privatisation policies also contravene the 2010 United Nations General Assembly resolution that access to safe and clean drinking water and sanitation is a human right. The resolution urged 'states and international organisations to provide resources and to foster the transfer of technology to developing countries, with a view to providing access to water and sanitation' (Dwivedi, 2011). In 2012, the World Health Organization (WHO) estimated that 52% of the population in SSA drank contaminated water and 229,300 people died (WHO, 2014b). The impact of water privatisation in Zambia after 1990 was extreme. Apart from the spread of AIDs, water privatisation and reduced access to clean water contributed to the decline in life expectancy from 54 years in 1990 to 34 years in 2000. Infant mortality doubled between 1992 and 1997 (Grant, 2009). After 2000, Zambia proceeded with full-scale water commercialisation in major cities and towns. By 2010 there had been little improvement in affordability or access for the poor. Huge disparities existed between urban and rural communities and for the rural, urban and semi-urban poor (Chitonge, 2011). The Lesotho Highlands Water Project led to price increases in Johannesburg. There was a surge of protest against the Paris-based water company Suez which was the municipal supplier to Soweto (Bond, 2017c).

The activities of US corporations in SSA have also adversely affected peoples' health and welfare. Corporations that have paid hundreds of millions of dollars to governments in taxes, royalties, license fees and bribes have influenced governments that depend on them for revenue. The oil companies are particularly powerful. Oil pollution has seriously harmed the health and welfare of local populations, particularly in the Niger Delta region. Between 2006 and 2010, there were over 2,400 oil spills in Nigeria, most of them in the Niger Delta region. ExxonMobil has been responsible for some of these offshore oil spills (Eboh, 2010). Both Chevron and ExxonMobil are in partnership with the Nigerian government which has turned a blind eye to any transgressions in the Niger Delta. Coastal land and wetlands have been contaminated by oil spills and the air polluted by gas flaring. Life expectancy in the delta area has dropped and incidences of birth defects and miscarriages have increased. Fishing and farming livelihoods have been severely affected by pollution from oil. Gas flaring causes asthma, respiratory illnesses and cancer. Even though gas flaring is illegal in Nigeria the government does little to stop it. It imposes small fines which companies pay and continue their activities. Local people would like the gas to be used for electrification, but their requests have been ignored because it is cheaper for companies to burn off the gas than process it (Corpwatch, 2011). Harm caused by oil companies has led to local violence and destruction. In 2016, a wave of sabotage against the Nigerian government and international oil companies reduced Nigerian oil outputs. A new group 'The Niger Delta Avengers' were prominent in this surge. Their demands were similar to past demands including Niger Delta autonomy, greater participation in the oil wealth, and cessation of environmental destruction (Steffen, 2016). Both companies are also active in Angola. In Angola, most of the oil wells are offshore in the Cabinda region. Land pollution is not extensive though there are concerns about oil spills harming fishing stocks. Most of the gas produced by the Cabinda wells is left to flare and pollute the air (Corpwatch, 2011).

The mining sector is also dominated by foreign companies. The health impacts of mining are severe. Working conditions in mines are dangerous and safety conditions are poor. There are high rates of injury and accidents because of hazards from machinery and explosions. Air, land and water pollution from the toxic chemicals used to extract minerals affect workers and local communities. Many health effects are not immediate but present many years later. The pollution from dusts, gases and chemicals can persist for a long time. Mine dumps can continue to pollute the land long after the mines are closed. Chemicals, such as arsenic and cyanide, are used to extract gold from rock and they leach into local groundwater (Regional Network for Equity in Health in East and Southern Africa, 2018). Often, iron ore is embedded in rocks that contain lead, which is increasingly recognised as a global threat to health and child development as it is highly toxic. High levels of lead exposure in children can cause brain, liver, kidney, nerve, and stomach damage, as well as permanent intellectual and developmental disabilities (WHO, 2019). A study of the gold and platinum sectors in South Africa after the 2012 Marikana strike found significant social and health problems. There were high rates of occupational injury and disease including silicosis and related illnesses. Unemployment was high, conditions of work in the mines were dangerous and exploitative and workers had few basic rights and no social security. Rural and agricultural communities had been disrupted (Cairncross & Kisting, 2016).

The US has the highest number of philanthropic organisations in the world. Some of these foundations are active in SSA. Through the sheer size of their grants, personal networking and active advocacy, large global foundations have played an increasingly active role in shaping the agendas and funding priorities of international organisations and governments (Vidal, 2016). With assets of over $60 billion, the Gates Foundation is the largest private foundation in the world. The Gates Foundation has a high profile in the health sector in SSA. In 2006, Bill Gates presented his 'creative capitalism' philosophy at the World Economic Forum. Gates blamed 'market failure' as the reason the poor could not afford medicines and proposed harnessing the forces of 'self-interest' and 'caring for others' by using donor funds to overcome these failures. He has ignored the persistence of structural economic and political relationships — Microsoft's own business model — that result in the profits being extracted from the developing world at a rate ten times the size of any form of aid (*BBC Four*, 2012). In applying this business model, the Foundation favours corporate-driven technical solutions, in particular, the development of vaccines to directly save lives. It spent $9 billion in Africa from 2000 to 2015, in efforts to reduce child mortality, eradicate polio, and fight malaria and the HIV/AIDS epidemic (Philanthropy News, 2016). The Gates Foundation works closely with USAID and NGOs and is also a major funder of the World Health Organisation (WHO). It specifies what projects it funds which undermines WHO sovereignty. It focuses on media attractive issues like finding a cure for malaria rather than the provision of clean water which would address the issues of water-borne diseases, one of the main causes of death in SSA. The Foundation has a large marketing budget. The achievements of the Foundation should not be underrated, but with an organisation of this size, there needs to be ongoing monitoring, ensuring due diligence and transparency (Ogden, 2011).

6.1.2.3. *Employment*

Neoliberal privatisation and deregulation policies undermined wages and eroded labour rights and conditions of employment in SSA. The policies benefitted foreign corporations by reducing their operational costs (Bretton Woods Project, 2019). Low wages have been upheld by international agreements. When Mandela's government tried to raise wages in South Africa after independence, they were taken to the WTO and forced to retract (Klein, 2006). The reduction in state bureaucracies resulted in job losses. Incomes in the agricultural sector also suffered from the elimination of rural assistance programmes and subsidies. The removal of tariffs opened markets to foreign competition and also hurt the incomes of agricultural producers, especially those competing against subsidised agricultural products from the EU and US. Rural unemployment increased and many people were forced off the land, moving to cities and nearby countries in search of work. US aid and investment created only a small number of jobs in SSA. Most US investment has been into the extraction of resources where employment levels are low. The US provided approximately 44,000 jobs in SSA between 2005 and 2016, one-third of the number provided by China (*China Daily*, 2017), but neither country has dented the high levels of unemployment and underemployment in the region.

The BWIs have also funded many projects that have been detrimental to peoples' health, working conditions and human rights. Capital-intensive development projects have forced large numbers of people off the land, out of the forests and fishing areas. Due diligence in project management and compliance with their own policies has been weak. They have not been held accountable for the harm caused by their projects. Many major projects have resulted in large numbers of people being displaced from their land without adequate compensation (Bretton Woods Project, 2019). Resettlement has often increased poverty. Most dam projects involve resettling inhabitants of the land, and often project planning and costings have only given cursory consideration to the social impacts of relocating people. In some dam projects, there has been simply no land available for farmers. In the WB funded Kandadji Dam project on the Niger River, the first group of the projected 60,000 people resettled did not have access to basic necessities including drinking water. There was insufficient land to resettle all the people. This was also the situation in Guinea when the WB funded the Fomi dam and 50,000 people needed to be relocated. Over a million people downstream in Mali were also impacted by the dam (International Rivers, 2016; Bosshard, 2016). In the Bujagali hydropower project in Uganda, resettlement and compensation for displaced people were superficial. There was no resettlement plan for this project. No consideration was given to the destruction of the famous Bujagali falls or the loss of income from associated tourism, which previously earned around $4 million annually (Pottinger, 2000).

One of the WB's most notorious failures was at the Marikana platinum mine in South Africa, owned by Lonmin (formerly Lonrho). Soon after the company was bought in 2007 by Lonmin, the IFC provided a $150 million debt and equity package as a public–private partnership initiative. It was IFCs largest investment to date in SSA. The project required the introduction of IFC 'best case' practices, ranging from economic development to racially progressive procurement, community involvement and gender work relations. One of the goals was to 'empower 350,000 local people by providing business opportunities' (IFC, 2007). Early on the WB often cited the Lonmin mine at Marikana as a success story. The company even won a green mining award in 2008. The project later revealed major operational flaws and a lack of due diligence in relation to project deliverables and project compliance (Davies, 2015). Part of the IFC loan to Lonmin was an agreement to build housing for the workers at the mine. Lonmin committed to building 3,200 houses and convert 70 hostels by 2011. Only three houses were actually built (as show homes) and 29 hostels were converted (Dasnois, 2014). The project goals were never met. The work was dangerous and workers' living conditions and wages were poor. Five years later the workers went on strike for better working and housing conditions and a living wage. The company called in the police and 34 miners were shot. An investigation revealed the IFC had done little to ensure compliance with its environment and social policies. The promised housing was not delivered. The IFC sold its stake in Lonmin in 2016. A commission set up after the massacre found that the IFC contract had not required compliance with IFC performance standards and did not engage with worker security or industrial relations issues (Coalition for Human Rights in Development, 2019).

6.1.2.4. *Human rights*

The foreign-dominated resource extraction sectors have a poor human rights record in SSA. A report to the US Senate Judiciary in 2008 revealed that Chevron had an ongoing history of collusion with the Nigerian government and was implicated in human rights and environmental abuses. The Nigerian military has at times intervened on the behalf of Chevron. This company has been complicit in military abuses by providing air and water transport to military personnel to launch attacks on protesting villagers. ExxonMobil also has close connections with the Nigerian military. Military police shot 11 people who were protesting over compensation from an oil spill in 1998 (The US Senate Judiciary Committee on Human Rights and the Law, 2008). Companies have continued to ignore local community protests and claims for compensation. In over 44 years operating in Nigeria, ExxonMobil has only once paid compensation to local communities for oil spills (Isine, 2014). Chevron failed to uphold the promises it made in 2005 to supply local people with jobs and social welfare programmes. Most of the money from the oil industry has accrued to the Nigerian elite, the 1% of the population that holds the power (Corpwatch, 2011).

There have been few attempts to redress historical wrongs in SSA, but in 2002, in the Khulumani case, a group of South Africans sued 20 US banks and corporations in the US Federal Court for complicity in crimes committed under the apartheid government. These crimes included extrajudicial killings, torture and rape, and among companies involved were Chevron, ExxonMobil, IBM, Ford and General Motors. Litigation continued in the US until 2016. A settlement was reached with General Motors in 2012, but the other cases were eventually dismissed on the grounds that the plaintiffs had not shown sufficient connection with the United States to warrant the case being heard in a US court (Business and Human Rights Centre, n.d.).

Foreign corporations are also complicit in the use of child labour and child slavery by purchasing the products of that labour. The export crops tobacco, cacao and rubber sectors have high levels of child labour. Malawi has the highest number of child workers in SSA. They work in tobacco production, Malawi being one of the main tobacco producers in SSA. Tobacco provides 70% of its GDP and 90% of that production is for export. Children as young as five years old work to meet family quotas for the tobacco purchasers. Universal Corporation and Alliance One International are the two main tobacco buyers in the region and their largest clients are Phillip Morris (Marlboro) and British American Tobacco (Lucky Strike). By purchasing this tobacco, the companies are complicit in the use of child labour and violation of International Labour Organization regulations on child labour. Child labour contributes to enormous corporate profits (Palitza, 2011). Using children to work is also common in rubber production. Firestone rubber plantations in Liberia have been subject to litigation in US courts for use of child labour and incidences of semi-slavery (Rizvi, 2005). Child labour is also common in cacao production in Côte D'Ivoire and Ghana. Often, these children are sold by their parents in poor countries to the north, such as Burkina Faso, and brought south to work as slaves on cacao plantations. The large cacao purchasers — and chocolate consumers — become complicit in those practices (Kenyon, 2018).

Human rights and ownership rights have been violated in many of the large-scale projects funded by the WB in SSA. The IFC has provided loans to corporations that have violated human rights. In 2006, the WB (Multilateral Investment Guarantee Agency) supplied a $13.3 political risk insurance investment to the Australian firm Anvil Mining for the Dikulushi Copper-Silver Mining Project in Katanga province in the DRC. At the time, there was ample evidence that the region was politically unstable. Soon after the insurance was granted in 2004, a massacre occurred and DRC armed forces killed 100 people. The Australian Broadcasting Corporation reported that the Dikulushi company had collaborated with the army and had supplied the trucks that moved the troops to the site of the massacre and then moved corpses out (cited in Bond, 2007). Land ownership rights have been violated in projects including the Chad–Cameroon Pipeline and many of the large-scale dam projects. The WB is also encouraging land sales and the commercialisation of agriculture by foreign agribusinesses.

6.1.3. *Conclusion*

The US, other Western nations and the BWIs have supplied loans, financial aid and policy assistance to SSA for nearly 60 years but have not been able to significantly reduce poverty or improve standards of living for the majority of the population. The neoliberal development policies (SAPs) imposed on most SSA governments since the 1980s deprived nations of political and economic sovereignty and contributed to the lack of progress in human development and standards of living compared to other regions. The ideological and self-interested dimensions of neoliberalism meant the policies have persisted despite evidence that they were not working. Countries have been forced to open their economies to foreign trade at the same time they have had to compete with subsidised products from the US and EU in international markets which undermined rural incomes. Asset sales meant governments lost workers and income. Foreign ownership kept wages low and liberal regulations enabled enormous illegal financial outflows of Africa's untaxed wealth, wealth that could have been used for social services. Privatisation of health and education has excluded the poor and suppressed human development. Neoliberal policies have benefitted foreign corporations who have continued to exploit resources and labour and export profits and vast untaxed wealth out of the region.

6.2. Profit

The economic impact of the US/BWIs on SSA has been significant. The WB has been the largest lender to SSA since countries gained their independence. African countries were some of the first countries to become indebted in the late 1970s. They lost their economic sovereignty when their creditors the BWIs, the US and other members of the Washington Consensus imposed neoliberal policies (structural adjustment programmes) as conditions for further loans. Countries in SSA were among the first countries to get structural adjustment loans and the first to demonstrate the failures of those policies (Easterley, 2007). The WB reinforced its dominant position in the development sector by becoming the repository of development data, the 'knowledge bank'. Leaders were co-opted by funds (aid and loans), training and foreign technical advice. The deregulation of the market under these policies increased foreign corporate ownership of state assets, increased their profits and facilitated illegal capital flight that — along with servicing debt — has deprived countries of finance that could have been used for social and economic development. Aid, loans, development policies and programmes have benefitted foreign lenders and corporations more than recipients. Many projects have failed, economic predictions have not been fulfilled and debt has increased. Foreign interests have continued to exploit SSA's resources and since 2000 have begun to acquire land and expand industrialised agriculture that benefits few local people. African economist Moyo considers that aid has been problematic and has contributed to low development and poverty in Africa. She argued it should either be cut by half or done away with entirely (2009). Her solution that African governments raise money by selling bonds was adopted in the next decade, but this approach led to rising debt rather than economic development.

6.2.1. *Trade*

Trade relations between the US and SSA have always been unequal. The US was Africa's largest trading partner until 2009, when it was supplanted by China.

Trade with Africa was, however, a tiny percentage of US trade — only 0.93% in 2016 (US Department of Commerce, 2018). Neoliberal trade policies imposed on SSA have been disadvantageous. Free trade and the removal of tariffs meant producers had to compete with subsidised foreign products. The US has subsidised its agriculture sector since the 1930s, and these subsidies are a direct government handout to agribusinesses. They make it hard for poorer countries to sell their agricultural products. US agricultural multinationals are able to swamp markets with subsidised products but agricultural products were not included in the 2000 US African Growth and Opportunity Act (AGOA). The food and agriculture sectors in SSA need export markets, especially for sugar, tobacco and cotton, but the US has been intransigent about access because they would compete with American products (Njiraini, 2014). Another condition of the AGOA was compliance with US foreign policy (US Department of Commerce, 2018).

Oil exports have always dominated trade between the US and SSA. The main purpose of the AGOA was to allow oil and a few other products' tariff-free entry to the United States. Between 2001 and 2011, 90% of AGOA imports were oil (Schneidman & Lewis, 2012). Because of this narrow emphasis, only a small number of countries, and American oil consumers, benefitted from AGOA (Amusa *et al.*, 2018). Three oil exporters dominated the AGOA in 2011 — Nigeria (47%), Angola (19%) and South Africa (13%). They earned 68% of the $20.3 billion that came into Africa from the US. The value of non-oil products exported to the US was comparatively small, only $1.4 billion in 2000 and $5 billion in 2013. Apparel made up 17% of non-oil exports in 2012 (Njiraini, 2014). US global oil imports began to decline when shale oil production expanded in the US (The Economist Intelligence Unit, 2014a). Oil exports to the US from Nigeria, Angola — and Algeria — went down from 520 million barrels in 2000 to less than 120 million barrels a year in 2015 (Woody, 2016). There was a further 48% drop in oil exports between 2015 and 2016. Other exports to the US included diamonds, platinum, cocoa and vehicles. The top AGOA partners in 2017 were South Africa, Nigeria, Angola, Chad, and Kenya (US Department of Commerce, 2018). The US trade deficit with Africa declined from $-17.5 billion in 2000 to $-6.6 billion in 2016 (US Census, 2019) and US trade with SSA declined 8.5% between 2015 and 2016 (from $36.9 billion down to $33.7 billion). While exports to the US fell, imports from the US rose (US Department of Commerce, n.d.).

6.2.2. *Financial inflows to SSA*

6.2.2.1. *Loans and aid*

The US has been providing loans to nations in SSA since they became independent, mainly in the form of aid (grants and low-interest concessional loans), bilateral loans and commercial interest-bearing loans. Concessional loans are provided through USAID. The US is the largest aid donor in the world but one of the lowest as a percentage of GDP (0.18 %). It ranks 22 out of 28 countries in the OECD. This is far below the 0.7% agreed on by members of the Development Assistance Committee in the 1970s (McBride, 2018). From its inception in 1960 USAID has been justified as a means of serving US strategic interests both political and corporate (USAID, 2019). As the aid donor rather than the recipient decides what type of aid will be delivered, sometimes there is a fine line between aid and bribery (Hertz, 2004). USAID during the 1960s and 1970s was motivated by Cold War political priorities. Behind France, the US was the second largest aid donor to SSA but by 2000 had fallen to fourth largest donor (Copson, 2000). Strategically important nations got the most aid rather than those that had the greatest need. The US provided aid and loans to many totalitarian governments in SSA in order to combat the spread of communism and keep the region open for American business. After the 11 September 2001 attacks in the US, as part of the government's 'War on Terror' President Bush broadened the remit of US foreign aid to include global development as a pillar of US national security (USAID, n.d.a). Aid to Africa tripled between 2000 and 2005. The new aid came with conditions for improving governance and combatting corruption (cited in Lafraniere, 2005). By 2008, the US was delivering 28% of its aid to Africa. During the Obama administration, aid plateaued, varying between $7 billion and $8 billion (US Congressional Research Service, 2020). Three countries in SSA, Nigeria, Tanzania and Ethiopia, were among the 10 largest USAID recipients (Shendruk, 2019). The US is the major contributor to the multilateral aid distributors the WB and IMF.

The types of assistance the US includes as aid compromise its aid expenditure figures. The OECD Development Assistance Committee (DAC) defines aid as serving economic or social development. Aid can take the form of an outright grant but loans with up to a 25% grant component still meet the DAC definition. This definition does not include debt relief, humanitarian aid or military assistance (OECD, 2003, n.d.b), but the US government includes these as aid (USAID, n.d.a). Humanitarian aid does not meet the OECD criteria of promoting development. The US is the largest supplier of humanitarian aid. Some years the value of food aid dwarfs other expenditures. One million tons of US food aid to Ethiopia in 2003 was valued at $475 million, a sum larger than the $354 million in agricultural aid the US provided to all developing countries in 2001 (Eicher, 2003). Critics of food aid point to government subsidies to US agribusinesses that lead to overproduction and huge stockpiles of food. These stockpiles are used to supply countries in crisis as part of 'humanitarian aid'. Apart from saving lives in emergencies and improving nutrition food aid can have negative consequences. External supplies of food can push down local prices, displace products, or can increase prices if bought locally. Dietary preferences can also change in favour of imported products (Barrett, 2006).

Both the WB and IMF encouraged governments in SSA to borrow to stimulate economic development and promote economic growth. The WB has been one of the largest suppliers of aid and loans to SSA since nations won their independence. WB aid to low-income nations in the region included low-interest loans (concessional), zero to low-interest credits and grants provided through the International Development Association (IDA). The amount of WB lending increased dramatically during the 1970s. It was the main lender to SSA. In addition to member contributions when the Bank began raising funds from the commercial banking sector, it started operating more like a commercial bank.

Ensuring that debts were serviced became a priority. Lending was a mix of project lending and allocation of funds to subsidiary banks to finance projects. Over time as nations' debt grew the WB advanced loans to service debt (Hertz, 2004). The IMF broadened its mandate beyond assistance for short term crises in the 1970s and began providing loans for development. The IMF added poverty reduction to its loan conditionalities in the late 1990s (Dawson, 2003). The purpose of many IMF loans was to assist the implementation of structural adjustment policies.

The US also supplies American goods and services through commercial loans to buyers in SSA. These are secured through the US Export–Import Bank (Exim). Any defaults on these loans get picked up by the US government and added to the nation's debt to the US. This government security encouraged profligate lending by commercial banks; the interest on commercial loans was higher than the concessional rates of bilateral and multilateral loans and disadvantaged borrowers (Hertz, 2004).

6.2.2.1.1. Tied aid and export credits

The US government has a long history of acting to protect the interests of US corporations and used its influence in the WB, IMF and WTO (Meltzer, 2000a). The USAID programme has been used to promote American interests by tying its aid to US products and services. The US is one of the worst offenders for 'tied' aid, defined by OECD as including official grants or loans that limit procurement to companies in the donor country. Aid becomes compromised as recipient countries do not receive good value for services or goods. Tied aid can increase the costs of development projects by 15% to 30% (OECD, n.d.c). USAID is handled through the US Export Credit Agency (ECA) and funding is provided by the US Exim Bank. The Bank's mission is to promote the sale of American products (Doyle, 2019; Hochberg, 2015). The purchases are effectively a subsidy to corporations (Hertz, 2004). Tied aid provides major financial benefits to lenders and donors (OECD, n.d.c; Meeks, n.d.). In 2005, ActionAid estimated that 80% of US aid was 'phantom' — non-existent — because it was so heavily tied to US goods and services and so badly targeted at poor countries (ActionAid International, 2005). Another form of phantom aid is debt relief. It is essentially an accounting exercise rather than any form of actual assistance. A significant proportion of aid is tied to technical assistance as well as neoliberal conditions like privatisation (Bond, 2006). Technical assistance, administrative costs and fees of highly paid consultants on large expense accounts and 'hardship allowances' are all deducted from aid payments.

In 1992, the OECD tried to minimise the problem of tied aid by introducing the 'Helsinki Package', stipulating that export credit agencies could only provide tied aid — export credits that are at least 35% concessional — to projects with genuine development characteristics and not commercially viable. It was a voluntary non-binding agreement (OECD, n.d.d) and US did not sign. In 2007, the US ceased to disclose the extent of its tied aid (Easterley, 2007). By 2014, the US fell

80% short in reducing the amount of tied aid (OECD, 2014). In 2011, major international development donors agreed to be more transparent about their aid spending. Again the US failed to comply and the USAID Transparency Review conducted by Publish What You Pay in 2015 found the US was unlikely to meet the transparency requirement by the end of 2015 (2017). In an effort to make aid more effective, the OECD put in place the Accra Agenda for Action, followed by the 2005 Paris Declaration establishing five core principles: ownership, alignment, harmonisation, results and mutual accountability. The US did not sign the agreement (OECD, n.d.e).

There are other imbalances and contradictions in aid relationships. President Touré of Mali commented that his nation's bilateral aid from the United States in 2002 — $37.5 million — was less than the $55 million Mali lost through the drop in cotton prices resulting from subsidised US cotton flooding the market (Eicher, 2003). Another issue is that the donor decides what aid it will deliver and how it will be delivered. USAID programmes directly support the pharmaceutical, agricultural and military–industrial sectors. USAID is concentrated in the delivery of health programmes, the Food Aid programme uses surpluses from heavily subsidised agribusinesses and the military–industrial complex supplies the hardware for military assistance. Recent presidents have established signature programmes. In 2003, President Bush launched the President's Emergency Plan For AIDS Relief (PEPFAR). ActionAid considered Bush's AIDs programme a means of supporting corporations by promoting expensive drugs and avoiding cheaper generic drugs (2005).

6.2.2.1.2. Public–private partnerships

By the end of the 20th century, Cold War political pressures had diminished and international criticism was mounting concerning the failure of aid programmes to produce results. Aid delivery began to change in the 1990s and more aid was delegated to NGOs and corporations. US aid to SSA declined in the 1990s, reaching its lowest point in 1997 (US Congressional Research Service, 2020). Instead of providing aid through grants and low-interest loans, the US and BWIs began promoting public–private partnerships (PPP) (Lafraniere, 2005). The WB was one of the strongest advocates for these partnerships which were funded through its corporate arm the IFC. The IFC became the largest global development institution providing finance to the private sector and for private–public partnerships. The BWIs shifted their earlier focus on the market and reducing the size of the state and began talking about reframing the role of the state to enable the private sector to pursue its objectives, described as 'leveraging the resources of the private sector' (Bretton Woods Project, 2019). Corporations were seen as embodying the skills needed in developing economies.

Water privatisation was one of the first areas where the public–private model was implemented. Privatisation had been a Bank priority in the 1980s and in the 1990s water privatisation policies were added to lending conditions. After 1993, the IFC was the leading funder of water projects in developing countries. Though water and sanitation were among its worst-performing portfolios the WB persisted with privatisation, even providing subsidies when major water corporations considered the projects too risky. In such incidences, the WB donor countries were subsidising the Bank's ideologically driven pet projects. These projects often disadvantaged the poor. In Ghana, water management was eventually returned to public ownership in 2011 after the private company Aqua Vitens Rand failed to fulfil its contract. WB conditions led to a 95% increase in water tariffs (Amanthis, 2012a, 2012b). In South Africa, the terms of the Lesotho Highlands Water Project included a 100% increase in water prices in Johannesburg (Bond, 2018). In 2008, the WB made a further attempt to engage the corporate sector. The IFC established the 2030 Water Resources Group bringing together financial investments from multinational corporations — including Nestlé and Coca-Cola — to transform water and sanitation sectors. Concerns were raised that water governance would transfer public ownership and control of water commons to private ownership and consolidate the power of large companies (Barlow, 2011). Nestlé and Coca-Cola are two of the largest suppliers of bottled water in the world so there are definite conflicts of interest in giving these companies more power over public water provision.

The application of the PPP model in the water sector began to lose momentum. In 2015, the WB admitted that it had lent $75 billion for water projects around the world in the previous 20 years. The overall project failure rate in that period had been 28%, while the failure rate for the past five years was even higher at 34%. Many water utilities had been re-municipalised. Common problems with private water management were lack of infrastructure investments, tariff hikes and environmental hazards. In 2015, the Bank admitted it had no ongoing water concession projects in Africa. Cities, such as Lagos, began exploring alternatives including the public–public model (Vidal, 2015). The WB Group eventually moved the 2030 Water Resources Group from the IFC to the WB where it would be part of Global Water Practice (Water GP). Here too there is talk of an evolving model, public–private–civil society collaboration in the water space (Jenkins *et al.*, 2017).

Agriculture was the next sector in which the PPP model was introduced. By 2010 — three years after the international food crisis — the UN Food and Agriculture Organisation (FAO) estimated that 239 million people were suffering from hunger in SSA. The FAO and G7 — including the US — considered that the PPP model would increase food security in Africa. They promoted agriculture-oriented investments as part of development aid (Sasson, 2012). The FAO intention was to create a 'favourable investment climate' for private agricultural investment (Miyazako & Syed, 2013; FAO, 2012). Part of this programme was the launching of The New Alliance for Food Security and Nutrition (NAFSN) at the G7 Summit in 2012. The goal was to lift 50 million people out of poverty by 2022 through increasing private investment and stimulating agriculture-led growth in nine African countries. A year later Oxfam produced a critical evaluation of the initiative in Ghana, Tanzania and Mozambique. The emphasis on private investment had been directed at governments and companies. It had not focused on small-scale producers or inclusive agricultural development that engaged with small-scale producer organisations, civil society and local communities. Oxfam recommended the projects have social and environmental impact assessments. They identified the need for greater transparency by making more information available at global and local levels (2013).

President Obama's 2013 Power Africa project was another PPP initiative co-ordinated by USAID and partially funded by the WB (The Economist Intelligence Unit, 2014b). The goal was to double access to electricity in Africa in five years. Little progress was made during Obama's term as unforeseen obstacles emerged. After 2018, the project was reworked into the Power Africa 2030 Roadmap (USAID, 2018). The Africa Compact — a similar initiative to the Power Africa project — was established by the G20 in 2015. Its goal was to provide SSA with infrastructure using the private–public partnership model. Patrick Bond saw these initiatives as efforts to assist multinational companies to extract more resources to compensate for recent declines in profits (2017a).

Elsewhere the PPP model continued to fall out of favour. In 2018, the EU report on the performance of PPPs in Europe recommended that no further PPPs be initiated until the many problems identified had been worked out. These problems included cost, transparency and value for money (European Public Service Union, 2018). If PPPs caused so many problems in developed countries, with high technical and regulatory capacity, they were likely to be even more problematic in developing countries (Seery & Seghers, 2019). The WB has persisted in promoting the PPP model across many sectors: agribusiness, education, health, ICT, municipal, power, tourism, transport and water and sanitation (2019). The fact that the WB has been slow to dismiss this model is in keeping with the findings of the independent auditors of both institutions. The BWIs have been reluctant to respond to criticism or admit failures in their policies. The PPP also has benefitted the corporate sector, an ongoing bias of both institutions (Bretton Woods Project, 2019; (IMF) Independent Evaluation Office (IEO), 2007).

6.2.2.2. *US Foreign direct investment (FDI)*

The SSA region has not attracted significant amounts of foreign investment. US investors continue to view the region as a risky destination and US FDI is lower here than elsewhere. The small proportion of US total investment in Africa is concentrated in resource extraction. Only foreign companies had the financial and technical ability to extract resources and they dominate the sector. US total investment stock in 2016 was $28.9 billion, with the largest concentration in the tax haven of Mauritius ($6.9 billion), South Africa ($5 billion) and Nigeria ($3.8 billion) (US International Trade Commission, 2018). The US's largest trading partners are Nigeria and South Africa which are the two largest economies in SSA.

6.2.2.2.1. Corporate regulation

Large corporations have often acted illegally, causing social and environmental harm both within their countries of origin and internationally. Corporate power increased in the US during the 1980s as deregulation prompted mergers and acquisitions that enabled corporations to vastly increase in size. Their political power also increased that power internationally. The United Nations Conference on Trade and Development (UNCTAD) confirmed that corporations actively enlist the help of their home country governments to further or protect their interests in developing countries (2001) and the US is no exception. Regulating corporations has proved difficult to implement as most initiatives have remained voluntary. These efforts include the 2000 UN Global Compact, a 'voluntary corporate responsibility initiative committing businesses to align their operations and strategies with ten universally accepted principles in the areas of human rights, labour, environment, and anti-corruption'. The agreement was signed by the WB, IMF and African Development Bank but not the major US corporations Chevron and ExxonMobil (United Nations, n.d.). The OECD Guidelines for Multinational Enterprises in 2005 were another set of recommendations rather than binding regulations (n.d.f). Cases have been brought to the OECD regulatory body, including the illegal exploitation of resources in DRC by US companies. Case numbers have been relatively low. Acceptance that the guidelines were not fulfilling their purpose led to two years of investigation and a report in 2021 (OECD Watch, 2021).

Lack of transparency is a major problem with international corporations, particularly in the oil and mining sectors. These are the sectors with high levels of corruption, bribery, 'balance of payments leakages' (theft) and collusion with repressive leaders. The first major attempt to bring about change was the 2002 Extractive Industries Transparency Initiative (EITI). Governments and corporations agreed upon 12 EITI principles the following year. The US oil companies Chevron and ExxonMobil signed the agreement but have since been accused of non-compliance (Gardiner, 2021). The G8 subsequently called on the IMF and the WB to provide technical support to governments wishing to adopt transparency policies. The Multi-Donor Trust Fund (MDTF) for the EITI was established in 2004 administered by the WB (WB Independent Evaluation Group, 2009). The US signed the agreement in 2014 and then withdrew soon after in 2018. The US Congress established its own corporate transparency standards, the 'Lugar-Cardin' Provision in the Dodd–Frank Act of 2010, which required all international oil, gas and mining companies listed on the New York Stock Exchange to disclose payments to governments. Chevron and ExxonMobil were part of the 'Big Oil Lobby' that fought against both the implementation of the EITI and the Lugar-Cardin Provision. Both companies refused to submit their tax payments to the US government (Publish What You Pay, 2017; Human Rights Centre, n.d.; Landau & Eisen, 2018). The EITI remains voluntary, which has led to a crisis of relevance and legitimacy (Oxfam, 2016).

6.3. Debt

The BWIs promoted borrowing as a path towards accelerated development ('the influx of finance' model) in the early days of independence but nations in SSA soon became indebted. This debt has contributed to the lack of development in SSA since the late 1970s.

6.3.1. *Profligate lending*

The debt crisis that occurred in SSA in the 1980s was partly attributable to bad governance in borrowing countries but also to errors on part of the lenders. Some of that debt falls into a grey area. The main lenders to SSA in the 1970s were the WB, the IMF and US commercial banks. Recipients were often given more than they requested and loans were advanced without due diligence in checking whether countries had the ability to repay the loans. Hertz described these loans as 'profligate' and accused lenders of being complicit in entrapping countries in debt (Hertz, 2004). Former financial advisor John Perkins in his book *Confessions of a Financial Hitman* described how staff were encouraged with bonuses to supply large loans (Perkins, 2004b). The original purpose of debt was to earn income to repay debt but those loans did not generate the projected economic growth and debt levels rose. The focus of the BWIs became the servicing of debt. Though the IMF was established to supply loans to help countries through economic crises, many countries consistently needed debt rescheduling and entered long periods of debt service borrowing (Easterley, 2007). Interest repayments contribute to the funding of the BWIs.

6.3.2. *Odious debt*

During the Cold War many totalitarian dictators were provided financial support in return for political allegiance. These loans were described as 'odious' at the time, as it was acknowledged they would not be repaid and that they would be appropriated and probably transferred out of the country or used to repress the population. Debts from such loans qualify as 'odious or illegitimate' (Hertz, 2004). The US and BWIs compounded this injustice by mandating the repayment of the debts of these leaders after they were no longer in power (Bond, 2006).

One of the most notorious cases involved the funds supplied to prop up the dictator Mobutu in Zaire during the 1970s and 1980s. Funds were supplied to repress a possible socialist backlash in response to his behaviour. He also protected Western interests (Bolton, 2008). Soon after the Soweto uprising in 1976 when the IMF and commercial banks lent money to South Africa they became complicit in the repression. They had to know that the money would be used to oppress the people. Lawyers at the time called the loans 'odious' (Hertz, 2004). At the end of apartheid in 1994, the new South African government was forced to repay the debts of the apartheid government before further loans were advanced (Klein, 2006). After 30 years of military rule, in 2005, Nigeria owed $12.4 billion in debt, accrued interest and penalties to the Paris Club creditors. During those years Nigeria had already paid $11.6 billion in debt servicing. At the end of military rule, the victims of that oppression were made to take on the debt. Because the IMF wanted to keep Nigeria from repudiating its debts it took over debt repayment supervision. It was then able to impose neoliberal policies on Nigeria under the 'Policy Support Instrument' (Bond, 2006). In 2005, Nigeria's debt had reached $36 billion. As this debt was to the Paris Club export agencies rather than the BWIs, it was not eligible for HIPCI or MDRI. In 2005, the Paris Club cancelled $18 billion of that debt and debt stock worth $30 billion (Birdsall & Moss,

2006). The director of UK NGO the Jubilee Debt Campaign Nick Dearden said, "The experience of DRC goes to show that debt relief schemes are still operating in the interests of the 'creditors'. DRC has spent years shelling out tens of millions of dollars in debt 'repayments' while also implementing economic conditions which make its economy more attractive and 'safe' for foreign investors." Civil society groups are calling for audits to establish whether countries' debts are legitimate, or a legacy of irresponsible lending and undemocratic governance, in which case such debts should be repudiated (cited Bretton Woods Project, 2010).

Repayment of odious and illegitimate debt is part of the greater problem of illegitimate financial outflows from SSA. Over 50% of SSA's crippling debt in the early 2000s was odious debt (Bond, 2006). An investigation of capital flight from 33 countries in SSA between 1970 and 2010 concluded that $814 billion (in 2010 US$) had been lost to the continent. If compound interest was factored in, the amount would have been much higher. This amount far exceeded the aid received ($659 billion) as well as the $309 billion in foreign investment. In real terms, for every dollar in external loans to SSA over 50 cents flowed back out in the same year. SSA's liabilities in 2010 only amounted to $189 billion. Most (72%) of the capital flight was from oil-rich countries ($591 billion). Capital flight increased after 2000 because of increased oil prices. Thus SSA is actually a net creditor to the rest of the world (Boyce & Ndikumana, 2012).

6.3.3. *Operational failure and project lending*

The poor performance record of WB projects was one of the most significant revelations of the 2000 Meltzer Report. The Bank's own assessment showed an outstanding 65% to 70% failure rate in the very poorest countries — which included most countries in SSA — and a 55–60% failure rate elsewhere (Meltzer, 2000a; Bello, 2000). The loans funding these projects still had to be repaid. The ongoing overestimation of benefits from BWIs structural adjustment policies and loans played a key role in indebtedness. According to the IEO review in 2007, the IMF had overestimated growth projections in 76% of the 29 cases it evaluated. The review concluded that excessive loans resulting in debt should be erased rather than used as political and economic leverage (Easterley, 2007).

6.4. Financial Outflows: Legitimate and Illegitimate

6.4.1. *Legitimate outflows: Loan repayments and export of corporate profits*

The many forms of legitimate financial outflows include debt servicing, payment of interest on loans, patents and fees as well as corporate profits and dividends (Bond, 2017b). Outflows may be legal yet not necessarily fair. Asset sales enforced by neoliberal policies resulted in high levels of foreign ownership, particularly in the resource extraction sectors. Large profits enabled by tax holidays and government incentives were also legitimate, even if they brought few local benefits. Foreign corporations have made enormous profits from SSA's resources and labour. Most of these profits have been transferred out of Africa rather than reinvested in the region.

6.4.2. *Illegitimate outflows*

The NGO Global Financial Integrity identified tax avoidance by multinational companies and balance of payment leakages by governments (theft) as the two main forms of illegal financial flows after 2000. Trade mispricing accounted for an average of 54.7% of cumulative illicit flows from developing countries between 2000 and 2008 and 45.3% for unrecorded payments through the balance of payment leakages by governments. The illegal financial flows in oil-exporting countries like Nigeria are much higher (Kar & Curcio, 2011). A GFI study covering 2005 to 2014 estimated an average of 87% of illicit financial outflows was from corporate fraudulent misinvoicing of trade (Global Financial Integrity (GFI), 2017). Estimates for SSA are even higher. Measured against the level of trade, SSA ranked highest in illicit outflows in the world between 2000 and 2008. The estimated annual average IFF as a percentage of trade was between 7.5% (annual average $7.5 billion) and 11.6% (annual average $9.5 billion). There was a slight contraction in those flows by 2014 when IFF amounted to between 5.3% and 9.9% of SSA's total trade. The GFI noted these estimates were conservative and that misinvoicing of trade was likely to be underreported (Clough, 2017a).

6.4.2.1. *Corporate tax avoidance*

Neoliberal policies imposed by the Washington Consensus benefitted multinational corporations. Lighter regulatory frameworks enabled companies to keep wages low, undermine safety regulations and make higher profits (Bond, 2017b). Companies also increased profits by reducing their taxes and by expanding intra-company trade between corporate subsidiaries. Such trade accounted for 33% of world trade between 1960 and 2000 (Greer & Singh, 2000) but then increased dramatically. While individual country operations may be insignificant to the global operations of a company, in lesser developed countries the impact of large corporations is enormous and the loss of revenue to corporations is significant to the economy (Romero & Ruiz, 2011).

Companies have used a range of complex intra-company financial transactions to avoid tax, including internal transfers of funds, transfer pricing, misinvoicing and trade mispricing (Ismi, 2004). Other practices include the misinvoicing of inputs, evasion of royalties, bribery, 'round-tripping' investment through tax havens and outright theft of profits (Bond, 2017b). Internal transfers between branches of corporations use price manipulation to take full advantage of differing laws and tax rates in different locations. Transfer pricing involves invoicing at low prices in countries where taxes are high and rising prices where tax rates are low, resulting in a loss of tax revenues for the host country. Prices charged in these transfers bear no relation to the real market prices for these goods (Romero & Ruiz, 2011). Misinvoicing or mispricing also happens with trade. Imports can be overpriced in some countries (which results in an export of capital) and underpriced on entering other countries, which maximises profits (Greer & Singh, 2000).

Some of the largest companies operating in SSA have used these tax avoidance strategies. A *BBC* Four documentary in 2011 titled 'Why Poverty: Stealing Africa' explored the ways mining giant Glencore — a former US company — avoided paying taxes in Zambia (Guldbrandsen, 2011) through misinvoicing of trade. In recent years, some US companies have been brought to court for tax evasion in SSA, both in the US and in SSA. Chevron was accused of tax evasion amounting to $10.8 billion in Nigeria. When the US House of Representatives investigated they could only substantiate $492 million (Lee, 2006). In 2011, a Nigerian court ordered ExxonMobil to pay $83 billion in education tax to Nigerian Inland Revenue (Sahara Reporters, 2013). One of the largest US mining companies operating in Africa, Angloplats, was found guilty of tax avoidance, while its subsidiary de Beers was found guilty of misinvoicing of trade (Bond, 2018). These convictions are only a small percentage of illegal activities that occur. The WB has also been compromised by links to companies that avoid paying taxes. In 2016, an investigation by Oxfam revealed that 51 of the 68 companies to which IFC lent finance to fund projects in SSA in 2015 used tax havens (Oxfam, 2016).

6.4.2.2. *'Balance of payment leakages' by governments (theft)*

Corruption is a major factor inhibiting economic development in SSA. The term 'balance of payment leakages' refers to the differences between funds paid and funds recorded in government records. Corrupt politicians have expropriated billions of dollars and transferred these funds offshore through tax havens. Many parties are complicit in these processes. Politicians have expropriated foreign aid and loans as well as wealth from corporations extracting natural resources. Many corporations have paid bribes to politicians to secure contracts. Bilateral and multinational agreements have a history of secrecy. There is a tradition of developing countries and their counterparts in Western countries to cut secret political and economic deals (Holzner & Holzner, 2006).

Balance of payment leakages by governments were estimated to be 45.3% of illegal financial flows after 2000 (Kar & Curcio, 2011). Expropriation of revenues is most prevalent in oil and mineral exporting countries. Angola and Equatorial Guinea are prime examples where leaders and their families have expropriated vast sums of oil wealth and transferred it offshore (Maddow, 2019; Kenyon, 2018). Tax havens play a central role in assisting companies and individuals to avoid taxes and illegally transfer funds (Romero & Ruiz, 2011). Tax havens are part of the complex networks of enablers involved in capital flight (Boyce & Ndikumana, 2011).

6.5. Failures in Policy and Operations

6.5.1. *Neoliberal policies*

The most significant policy failure in SSA since the 1980s has been the imposition of neoliberal structural adjustment policies (SAPs) by the BWIs, the US and other members of the Washington Consensus. These programmes failed to meet their goals — stimulating economic growth, generating income to repay debt and reduce poverty (Easterley, 2007). Neoliberal policies persisted into the 21st century in various forms, despite evidence that they had failed (Hertz, 2004). The US and the BWIs have remained ideologically committed to neoliberalism as a means of opening economies to foreign business. The policies benefitted international corporations by allowing them to purchase state assets, and the lighter regulatory environment enabled higher profits. Tax avoidance and illegal transfers of funds out of host countries via tax havens became easier. Companies gained access to cheap labour and resources for export.

Late in the 1990s, the Structural Adjustment Participatory Review International Network (SAPRIN) conducted a review of these policies. The WB was a contributing partner. The final report was highly critical of the WB, claiming that the imposition of structural adjustment policies made it responsible for decades of economic stagnation and impoverishment (SAPRIN, 2004). Structural adjustment had caused many economies to implode. The combination of low investment, reduced social spending, reduced consumption and low output interacted to create a vicious cycle of decline and stagnation rather than a virtuous circle of growth, rising employment and rising investment, as originally envisaged by WB–IMF theory. Minor alterations were made to policies introduced but nothing much changed. Modifications to policy after 2000 amounted to 'the old approach of deregulation, privatization, and liberalization but with safety nets' (Bello, 2005). The WB withdrew from the project and continued to reject the conclusions. In 2004, the WB publication 'Adjustment in Africa' evaluated 29 countries that had installed SAPs in the 1980s and claimed 'in African countries that have undertaken and maintained policy reforms, adjustment is working'. It admitted that no country had implemented the full programme (WB, 2004). Because the IMF persisted in making loans to enable debt servicing even when its conditions (policies) were not implemented, Easterley queried the nature of its commitment to neoliberalism and whether the priority of the IMF was 'defensive lending' (2007). The IMF has persevered in promoting neoliberal policies. A review of the 41 countries with IMF agreements in 2009 found that most (31) of the loan agreements contained pro-cyclical fiscal policy, monetary policy, or both. Pro-cyclical policies were seen as more likely to intensify economic slowdowns (Cordero *et al.*, 2009).

Occasionally reports from the WB and IMF admitted failures or flaws in policy, but these admissions did not result in any change of direction. In 2003, the chief economist at the WB conceded that severe damage had been inflicted by two decades of financial liberalisation (Rogoff *et al.*, 2003, cited in Bond, 2006). In the World Development Report (2001), the WB admitted that the first round of SAPs did not result in either a reduction in poverty or improved growth (WB, 2001 cited in Easterley, 2007). This conclusion was confirmed in 2003 when it conceded that projections about future export earnings and about countries' ability to pay back debts had been 'unrealistic' (Bond, 2006). In that year, only 10 countries reached the HIPCI completion point (Isar, 2012). The projected income generated from WB projects, the BWIs growth projections and countries' ability to repay loans all failed to occur yet the BWIs did not contemplate dropping neoliberal policies.

An IEO review of the operational performance of the IMF in SSA between 1999 and 2005 identified ongoing operational problems with the BWIs policy-driven approach. The way the IMF disbursed aid was conservative and lacked understanding of the practicalities of delivering aid. The IMF relied too much on overconservative macro-economic programmes and did too little to address the reduction of poverty. Growth predictions had been overestimated in 76% of cases. 'IMF staff tended to focus narrowly on macroeconomic stability, in line with the institution's core mandate and their deeply ingrained professional culture' (IEO of the IMF, 2007). The WB was also reluctant to accept criticism or to acknowledge failure and subsequently modify its behaviour (Independent Evaluation Group (IEG) of the WB, 2009). The most prominent failures of the BWIs have been the structural adjustment programmes (SAPRIN, 2004; Easterley, 2007).

Mounting debt was one of most damaging outcomes of neoliberal structural adjustment policies and loans. SSA's debt doubled quickly from 1979 to 1985 and doubled again in the early 1990s, rising from 25% of GDP to 80% of GDP between 1980 and 1994 (Woods, 2008). International outrage and protests about debt in developing countries led to demands for debt relief. The BWIs were compelled to respond and introduced the Highly Indebted Poor Country Initiative (HIPCI) in 1996 (IMF, 2021). Nine years later in 2005 the BWIs offered the Multilateral Debt Relief Initiative (MDRI) (IMF, 2017). The long compliance period attached to the HIPCI meant the programme did not come into effect until 2003, and its impact was underwhelming. The tenacity of the neoliberal proponents meant neoliberal conditions were attached to both programmes, and countries continued to struggle economically. Countries were still expected to service their debt while meeting the HIPCI conditions. The method of assessing the level of debt a country could service — the debt sustainability framework (DSF) — was operationally flawed (Easterley, 2007). Levels of payment were set so high there was no excess money to stimulate economic development so future debt accumulation was inevitable (Hertz, 2004). Before countries were eligible for debt relief under the 2005 Multilateral Debt Relief Initiative (MDRI), they had to have fulfilled the HIPCI conditions. Most countries in the programmes were accumulating debt as they strove to meet those neoliberal conditions. Eurodad has described the BWIs' conditions as a 'development injustice' (2006).

6.5.2. *Transparency and corporate responsibility*

Since 2000 a number international agreements have attempted to address global problems, work for global good and bring about more fairness and equity in international relationships. Since 2000 transparency in domestic US affairs has been eroded. Edward Snowdon revealed how an era of mass digital surveillance of the American population — and beyond — began when G W Bush embarked on the 'War on Terror' in 2001 (2019). Because the US has not been a strong advocate for transparency it has held back international progress. The 2003 EITI was an important step towards addressing international financial corruption. The US did not sign the EITI until 2014 and then withdrew in 2017 (EITI, 2021a). The US corporations ExxonMobil and Chevron signed the agreement and then disregarded the policy in countries that had not signed the EITI (Gardner, 2021). There are other examples of the US government prioritising corporate interests in SSA. The US ambassador in Equatorial Guinea was censored after oil companies complained that he had jeopardised their interests by criticising the dictatorship for its extreme human rights abuses (Maddow, 2019). The BWIs have also been subject to criticism. Though the WB has provided support to countries implementing the EITI (EITI, 2021b) the BWIs' own lending practices and project oversight have been flawed. The BWIs began including greater transparency and addressing corruption as part of their loan conditions in the 1990s, but later reviews of BWIs practices found those policies had made little operational difference (Easterley, 2007). A review of the BWIs by the US government in 2007 concluded that the WB did not make the extractive industry transparency a condition of its loans or part of its country's assistance strategy. It failed to use its leverage to bring transparency to projects it financed through the IFC, as in the Chad–Cameroon Pipeline. The same report revealed that regional banks, such as the African Development Bank, were even worse in using public money to contribute to secrecy in the extractive industries. Likewise, though the IMF promoted greater transparency in its Guide on Resource Review Transparency in 2005, these guidelines remained voluntary and transparency was not actively promoted (United States House of Representatives Committee on Financial Services, 2007).

6.5.3. *Failure to address goals*

The WB's motto is 'Working for a world without poverty' and its twin development goals are reducing poverty and inequality. As well as its main goal — financial stabilisation — the IMF is also committed to poverty reduction. The conclusion of the 2000 Meltzer Report to Congress was that in the poorest countries — most nations in SSA — the WB had been irrelevant to the achievement of its avowed mission of alleviating global poverty. A survey of aid recipients revealed that middle income nations got the most aid, not the poorest nations (Meltzer, 2000a; Bello & Guttal, 2006). The Independent Evaluation Review of WB projects in 2011 reported that only a small number of projects addressed poverty or economic development, considered to be the fundamental goals of the institution (Bretton Woods Project, 2012b). WB policies were infused with economic determinism and a fixation with economic growth. Despite all the rhetoric about poverty reduction their policies have increased poverty (Bello, 2000). Operational criticisms included: structural underrepresentation of the global South, an undermining of democratic ownership, an inability to learn from past mistakes and a lack of impunity from the harm projects caused. Decision-making was biased and inconsistent, there was a lack of evidence of positive impacts and no measuring of harmful impacts (Bretton Woods Project, 2019). Similar criticisms have been made about the IMF, 'IMF staff tended to focus narrowly on macroeconomic stability, in line with the institution's core mandate and their deeply ingrained professional culture' (IEO, 2007).

6.5.4. *Lack of due diligence*

One of the most glaring faults in WB procedures is the lack of due diligence in both its pre-approval processes and project oversight. There continue to be instances where the WB has not effectively dealt with corruption in its own projects and contracts (Rich, 2019). Many of the loans to SSA have been fraught with problems, including corruption, bribery, lack of transparency and insufficient diligence in project oversight. Problems occur on both sides of the lender and recipient relationship. Before the 1990s, WB lending decisions in borrowing nations were not constrained by corruption and tyranny. Loans were advanced to many corrupt and brutal dictators. WB audits have revealed 60–70% of loans disappeared through 'leakage', the term for misappropriated funds (Hertz, 2004). Though the WB added good governance and addressing corruption into its loan and aid conditions in the 1990s, a later investigation revealed there had been no change in their operational behaviour since the end of the Cold War (Easterley, 2007). Project failure has often been blamed on local 'corruption' but the WB's track record reveals its own poor standards (Bond, 2017f). The bank has supplied loans despite ample prior evidence that countries were politically unstable and that loans were risky and should not have been made. In 2005, loans to Kenya were cancelled after the publication of a report revealed the government had ignored massive corruption. A loan to Ethiopia was cancelled after a massacre of civilians (Bond, 2007). In Chad, the WB set up a poverty reduction plan in which 85% of oil funds would be put into a poverty reduction programme. The government repeatedly diverted funds to the military, and profits were used to oppress the population. The WB finally withdrew from the project in 2008 (Gulali, 2008).

6.6. Flagship Projects

A number of the largest WB projects in Africa reflect operational flaws in project planning, approval and implementation. The WB's funding mechanisms are tailored to the supply of large-scale projects delivered by large corporations (IEO, 2007; Bond, 2018). The Bank continues to be driven by pressure to lend. It has approved projects where potential problems have been flagged early on and the projects only partially meet their goals. The Bank has been particularly lax about social dislocation and environmental impacts. It has used false rationales to push through enormous loans for environmentally destructive projects (Rich, 2019).

6.6.1. *Eskom power project*

The Eskom project displayed many characteristic flaws in WB project funding and project oversight. The South African parastate company Eskom is the largest energy supplier in SSA. The Eskom Power Project was an ambitious project designed to meet South Africa's energy requirements. The project involved building two coal fired power stations. Loans were advanced even though the company had a history of debt, mismanagement and corruption. The project was spectacularly unsuccessful in meeting energy targets or completion dates (*The Economist*, 2019). The WB supplied a loan of $3.75 billion for the Medupi power plant, its largest energy loan in its history. The project had been justified as providing cheaper energy but to repay the loan the company had to increase the price of energy by 100%. The South African government estimated that the price increase would push 37% of poor people back to using dirty forms of energy. The Bank failed to restructure Eskom's agreement with BHB Billiton which was paying only 10% of rates paid by other consumers and far below the market price. To increase income it raised prices (Bond, 2014b). Eskom's debt ballooned in the next decade and the company came close to bankruptcy (Rich, 2019).

6.6.2. *The Bujagali Dam project*

The Bujagali dam project on the Victoria Nile was a WB flagship project for its new private–public sector engagement model in the 1990s. The objective of the dam was to provide Uganda with low-cost energy. It was the largest foreign investment in West Africa at the time. Though critics raised many concerns about the destructiveness of the project the WB approved it. It provides another example of the institutional culture of loan approval and pressure to lend (Rich, 2019). The WB has a history of working with a small group of favoured compliant companies, including the Canadian firm AES, one of the largest independent power construction companies in the world. The company claimed to be the largest recipient of IFC contracts at the time. There were close connections between AES, the US government and the WB. One AES director was a senior advisor to the WB and another was the former US Secretary of Energy. Such conflicts of interest made the approval a foregone conclusion (Pottinger, 2000). AES was used to evaluate the Bujagali project, and later the Ugandan government awarded AES Nile Power (AESNP) the contract without putting it out to tender. Controversy arose immediately over the lack of competitive bidding on the project (Environmental News Service, 2003). AES also received a $70 million partial-risk guarantee from the WB and $85 million from the IFC. Other funds came from various export credit agencies ($225 million), commercial loans, the African Development Bank and the company itself. Many problems emerged during and after construction. AESNP was found by a WB audit in 2001 to have a severe shortfall in expertise, poor performance in social, economic and environmental aspects, evidence of corruption and a failure of financial disclosure. AES pulled out in 2002 and the project stalled for five years (Irigoyen, 2017). The Ugandan government had committed to utmost transparency in its procurements, but the Ugandan energy minister stepped down after being accused of receiving bribes from AES in 1999. He was then appointed Alternate Executive Director of the WB. The Bank claimed that while the alleged corruption may have occurred it did not 'directly affect the merits of the project'. The WB inspection panel found that the risks had not been adequately assessed. Apart from habitat and environmental destruction and the need for the resettlement of people, the project had economic risks. The project also undermined Uganda's debt policies as well as being unfavourable to, and not complying with, its own transparency and good governance policies (Bosshard, 2002). The project was finally completed in 2012, 18 years after it commenced. Projections proved to be false, electricity prices increased and only half the projected energy capacity was realised. Project costs far exceeded original projections (Irigoyen, 2017).

6.6.3. *The Lesotho Highlands Water Project (LHWP)*

The Lesotho Highlands Water Project (LHWP) was another major project partially funded by the WB where the project goals — supplying water for Johannesburg and earning income for the Lesotho Government — were prioritised while social and environmental problems were neglected. The resettlement programmes in Lesotho were inadequate, living standards declined and cultural traditions were disrupted (Gulali, 2018). The people who were displaced were impoverished, compensation plans were inadequate and the resettlement and development plans were flawed (Hoover, 2001). Again increases in water prices disadvantaged the poor in South Africa. There was also a lack of due diligence in project oversight resulting in a series of high-profile bribery cases. A dozen multinational corporations, including construction companies with close ties to South Africa's ruling party, paid more than $2 million in bribes to the project's CEO to obtain contracts. He served nine years in jail but was then reinstated in his former position on the strength of his political connections (Bond, 2017c). Those same companies later admitted to large-scale price collusion in building the 2010 Soccer World Cup stadiums (Bond, 2014b). The Bank promoted the LWTP as an example of best practice. There was an extensive resettlement programme and compensation for people displaced by the project. The project was monitored regularly by environmental experts. It failed to realise its goals.

6.6.4. *Rift Valley Railway*

The Rift Valley Railway — running between Kenya and Uganda — was another WB project that ran into problems with corruption. In 2016, the NGO 'Finance Uncovered' revealed that the WB had opened an inquiry into potential embezzlement of $144 million of IFC funds invested in the Rift Valley Railway for modernisation, buying new trains and upgrading lines. The amount was half the total project budget of $287 million. Trains were still breaking down and services had not improved. Second-hand trains had been bought rather than the new trains specified. There was no explanation for the missing funds. The company running the project was owned by a shell company fronting for an extensive network of offshore companies. Though the WB eventually debarred the company from bidding on WB projects, the main holding company — Qalaa Holdings, an Egyptian-based private equity fund — continued to get WB funding. Finance Uncovered found that the WB had effectively whitewashed the project (Turner, 2018).

6.7. The Impact of the US and BWIs on Economic Sectors

The impact of the US and BWIs on the economic sectors in SSA has been uneven, but all sectors have been affected by the neoliberal policies and governments' financial constraints because of debt repayments. The focus of the WB and IMF has been on large-scale, macro-economic projects. Such projects suit their funding and administrative processes (IEO, 2007). US corporate investment in SSA has been concentrated in the extraction of resources, particularly oil extraction. USAID focused on health initiatives. The WB provided loans for large infrastructure projects, primarily providing dams for irrigation and energy. The BWIs also encouraged export-oriented activities to enable countries to service their debt obligations. There has been little foreign interest in manufacturing in the region and African agriculture was also neglected before 2000. Rising population, pressure on resources and concerns about food shortages have raised the profile of agriculture and land in SSA since 2000, and the region has experienced an onslaught of foreign land acquisition.

6.7.1. *Resources*

US foreign investment in SSA is concentrated in resource extraction, and US oil companies have a long history in SSA. Chevron began working in Angola in 1930. SSA has been an important source of US oil supplies though US imports have been steadily dropping since 2000. American oil companies have played an important role in the countries in which they operate. These oil-producing nations of Africa display typical 'resource curse' profiles and foreign companies have worked with, and supported, repressive governments and supplied the revenues that have kept those governments in power. ExxonMobil and Chevron have partnerships with state-owned oil companies in both Angola and Nigeria. ExxonMobil is the world's largest publicly traded oil and gas extraction company and it has significant African holdings. Its earnings from Africa in 2008 accounted for 17% of its net oil and gas production (Institute of Development Economies Japan External Trade Organization, n.d.). The resource extraction sector has brought few benefits to the people in SSA. Angola and Nigeria are among the most resource-rich countries in SSA but their governments are corrupt; they repress the people who have some of the lowest standards of living and human development rankings in the region.

Both the US and BWIs have assisted the oil sector in SSA. The US continued to promote fossil fuel extraction and supported the sector through the African Growth and Opportunity Act which allows exemption from taxes for oil imports into the US. The neoliberal policies promoted by the US and BWIs benefited foreign multinationals, increased profits, and made it easier for corporations to avoid taxes and illegally export finances. The US government assisted corporations through Exim Bank loans and IFC loans. BWIs aid, development funding and policies have encouraged governments to earn income from resource extraction. The US government and the BWIs have not been strong advocates of corporate transparency. The American companies Chevron and ExxonMobil continue to operate in secrecy and even refused to submit their tax payments to the US government (Publish What You Pay, 2017; Landau & Eisen, 2018).

6.7.2. *Manufacturing*

Manufacturing was never strong in SSA and the sector has largely been ignored by the aid donors and lenders. There had been some early efforts at import-substitution manufacturing in SSA but market liberalisation policies undermined local manufacturing and wages while local manufacturers could not compete with imported goods. External corporate investors, lenders and donors were not interested in strengthening manufacturing in SSA. Many African countries had a modest textile industry in the 1990s, though few exported their products. After the textile trade was liberalised and tariffs lifted, many local factories were forced to close because of competition. The US is one of the biggest exporters of used clothing to Africa which further undermines local textile production (Brautigam, 2009).

6.7.3. *Agriculture*

An evaluation of the previous 50 years of aid to African agriculture concluded that these efforts were unsuccessful in transforming African agriculture and making it more productive. A wide range of agricultural approaches were tried, with donor priorities and policies changing almost every decade after the 1950s. Developing agriculture was not a high priority for governments in SSA in the 20th century. Donors had little interest in agriculture and allocated only small amounts of aid which was unevenly distributed (Eicher, 2003). Donor aid for agriculture fell from 17 % in 1980 to a low of 3.8 % in 2006 with a slight increase to 5% in 2008 (Sasson, 2012). The WB's lending for agriculture also declined from 30% to 7% between 1980 and 2000 (Peck, 2012). The neoliberal policies imposed by the US and BWIs also undermined African agriculture. The removal of subsidies for tools, seeds and farm credit lowered productivity and food security (Bretton Woods Project, 2019; McAfee & Murphy, 2005). The region already had the lowest level of fertiliser use in the world and the removal of fertiliser subsidies further reduced the already low rates of productivity. The loss of subsidies for rural infrastructure reduced farmers' access to markets (Njiraini, 2014).

Structural adjustment policies imposed by the US and BWIs pressured African producers to focus on export-driven agriculture to earn income for loan repayment rather than production for local markets (McAfee & Murphy, 2005). Countries in SSA previously self-sufficient in food eventually had to import food (Njiraini, 2014) and though the region has ample land available for agriculture it has been a net food importer since 1980 (Burch *et al.*, 2012). Net food imports increased by 3.4% annually between 1980 and 2007 (Rakotoarisoa *et al.*, 2007). The dependence on food imports meant countries were particularly vulnerable to fluctuations in food prices. Falls in export prices put people at risk. Shortages in some commodities led to the 2008 international food crisis and steep price increases for food imports. Food purchases further depleted government balances of payment (Burch *et al.*, 2012).

Some USAID practices have been detrimental to African agriculture, including the practice of donating goods as aid to NGOs who could sell the products to fund their own projects. In Uganda, the US exported cooking oil and auctioned it off, with the profits going to fund specific development programmes. This seriously undermined local producers. The same process occurred with wheat (Lee, 2007). Private American foundations also reinforce American corporate interests. The largest private foundation in the world, the Gates Foundation (GF), is actively involved in many agricultural projects in SSA. The GF has close links with agribusiness giant Cargill. Because of the amount of money at its disposal the GF has a lot of power in influencing government decisions. The GF has also been closely allied to the promotion of genetically modified (GM) seeds. The foundation bought shares worth $23 million in the chemical company Monsanto in 2010 (Vidal, 2010) and has worked with it to promote GM seeds in SSA, using South Africa as the gateway into the region (Bond, 2017c).

Market concentration has pushed up international food prices. Oxfam reported in 2011 that four companies — Cargill, Archer Daniels Midland, Bunge and the Louis Dreyfus Company — dominated international markets in staple foods. Three of the companies are American. These companies control 75% to 90% of the global grain trade and are also dominant in key commodities of rice, palm oil and sugar. As the companies controlled the entire commodity supply chain they could extract value at every stage along the chain (Lawrence, 2011). The US food aid programme has been criticised as 'corporate welfare' for grain giants (Lawrence & Provost, 2012). These corporate food giants have been accused of making huge profits while passing on the risks to small farmers (Peck, 2012). Market concentration also disadvantages African producers because they have to compete with American agribusinesses which are heavily subsidised by the US government. The focus on agricultural exports had other negative impacts. Overproduction in crops like coffee — promoted by the BWIs in Vietnam — led to downturns in international prices. The economies of Ethiopia and Uganda, the main coffee producers in SSA, were badly hit when coffee prices dramatically declined in 1998 and continued to drop. In 2001, real prices plummeted to the lowest ever recorded (Hallam, 2003).

From 2002, the Bank began promoting a 'small-holder first' approach to agriculture in SSA. In 2009, another change in policy and agriculture — along with forestry and fisheries — was promoted as a means of ending poverty and hunger. Between 2007 and 2011, Africa got 26% of agriculture funds for low-income nations (IBRD and IDA) and 9% of IFC funds. The Bank has been criticised for advocating land reforms that enable land acquisitions by agribusinesses (Peck, 2012). In 2002, the WB introduced a Doing Business ranking system, scoring countries on the ease of doing business, and 10 years later the bank developed a similar system for agriculture: Enabling the Business of Agriculture. Both systems have been adopted by donors and investors, but the recommendations are potentially harmful. The WB provided a framework for governments to improve their agriculture policies to facilitate the emergence of a 'more modern and more productive commercial agriculture and agribusiness sector'. The promotion of agribusiness facilitated a trend of large-scale land grabs in developing countries. The Bank continues to promote the interests of agribusiness over farmers. A number of countries in SSA have adopted these reforms including Liberia and Sierra Leone. They have attracted foreign agribusinesses — sugar cane, palm oil and rubber planters — who acquired large tracts of land (Martin-Prével, 2014). Foreign acquisition of land does not benefit local, small-scale and subsistence farmers. Rural workers and landless people lack secure access to sufficient food, land, water and the means of production. They also have the most marginal and insecure employment (International Assessment of Agricultural Knowledge, Science and Technology for Development (IAASTD), 1 June 2016). These people do not have the resources to defend their land against foreign purchases.

6.7.4. *Infrastructure*

The SSA region has suffered from a deficit of infrastructure since the era of independence. Lending for infrastructure has not been a US or WB priority (Brautigam, 2009), though the WB has always funded the building of dams. Hydropower projects in SSA have been criticised on environmental, social and economic grounds. Hydropower projects have been an enormous drain on budgets and countries were left highly indebted. Returns rarely measured up to financial projections. The Bujagali dam is a classic example where the financial feasibility of project was inadequate (Center for Public Impact, 2017). The WB has a macro-level focus. Hydropower projects were built to provide power for corporations, earn revenue for governments and stimulate economic growth. Providing electricity for the poor has not been a priority. Some of these projects were intended to produce surplus electricity that could be sold to neighbouring countries. Often, projects like the Lesotho Highland Water Project and the Bujagali dam in Uganda raised the costs of water (Bond, 2018; Center for Public Impact, 2017).

When the Chinese began building infrastructure throughout the region after 2000 it stimulated the US and BWIs' interest in infrastructure. In 2010, the WB report, 'African Infrastructure: A Time for Transformation', calculated that Africa's power sector required an annual investment of $41 billion. It continued to focus on hydropower as a cheap, clean, renewable and indigenous power source (Hattaway, 2010). The Power Africa project established by the US President Obama in 2013 was another attempt to provide African nations with electricity using the private–public partnership model (The White House Office of the Press Secretary, 2015). The project achieved little in its first few years. The WB and IMF have also promoted the private financing of infrastructure, rather than increasing and supporting the public funding of infrastructure which happened in developed countries. Infrastructure has particular characteristics that do not suit private investors. It tends towards natural monopolies, is long term, has high initial costs and its social benefits are often more significant than its financial benefits. The BWIs share an institutional bias against public spending, particularly the IMF with its macro-economic focus. A Eurodad study found they often do not give countries the option of public finance. In 2017, the WB Group introduced its Cascade Approach, a 'private-finance-first' model that prioritised private financing options over public financing (Ghosh & Sial, 2021). Private investors have been unwilling to invest in infrastructure as they do not like the risk-reward ratio. Public funding for infrastructure would be more available for governments if wealthy countries address issues of multinational tax evasion.

6.8. Planet

6.8.1. *Policies*

The activities of the US and BWIs have had an environmental impact on SSA both at the global level and within the continent. There have also been environmental consequences resulting from SSA's dependence on the US and the BWIs for finance, aid, development assistance and policy advice. At the time SSA nations gained their independence, environmental protection was not a central issue; the BWIs and governments in SSA prioritised economic development over environmental protection. Environment regulation by local governments has been weak. When neoliberal policies insisted that governments reduce the size of the state, environmental agencies were further weakened by staff losses.

The US has held back international progress on environmental regulation by not signing international agreements and recommendations on climate and the environment (Kyoto Protocols, the Extractive Industry Review, the World Commission on Dams, Basel Convention on Hazardous Waste). Or it has been a signatory but has ignored the policy in practice (OECD Export Credit Agencies (ECA) voluntary agreement 'Common Approaches to the Environment', n.d.g). Though the US established an Environmental Protection Agency in the 1970s, its integrity was later undermined with the fossil fuel sector exemption from regulation in the 1990s. The fossil fuel sector has disregarded the environmental impact of its operations within the US and internationally. US corporations in the resource extraction sectors have been able to act with impunity in SSA, although they are no worse than companies from other countries.

The WB is the major funder for development in SSA, and its environmental impact there has been significant. Though the Bank introduced environmental policies into project guidelines and loan conditions in the 1980s, nearly 40 years later these policies are still ineffective. The BWIs has continued to promote an export-led capitalist growth model that emphasises fossil fuel investments and mega-projects (Bretton Woods Project, 2019). The BWIs funded these projects and resource extraction so that governments could earn foreign currency for debt repayments rather than funding small-scale projects that provide for local needs. Large projects suit their administrative operations and also provide contracts for foreign corporations. The prioritising of profit over social and environmental concerns was demonstrated in 2003 when the WB introduced its 'high-risk/high-reward' strategy in the water, forestry and extractive industries. The reforms of a decade earlier were reversed. It re-engaged with oil, mining and gas projects in poorly governed and unstable countries (Environmental Defence, Friends of the Earth and International Rivers Network, 2003). The IFC also increased its investment in 'high risk' projects by 300% between 2013 and 2015 (Bretton Woods Project, 2017). Another WB strategy has been the promotion of the commercialisation of nature: 'Green growth is about good growth policies — addressing market failures and "getting the price right" by introducing environmental taxation, pricing environmental externalities (such as carbon pricing), creating tradable property rights and reducing inappropriate subsidies' (The WB, 2012b). Natural capital accounting was incorporated into its economic-growth framework and used to assess the economic value of resource depletion and environmental impacts (Izvorski, 2018). Environmental policies have been ignored in favour of continuing with 'business as usual'. Audits by the independent evaluation units of both institutions concluded that neither followed their own policy guidelines (Bretton Woods Project, 2019). The institutions merely pay lip service to their own environmental policies and have continued to fund projects that cause significant damages. The private financial sector is similarly duplicitous (Mackay, 2004).

The BWI's record on environmental regulation and oversight has been poor throughout their history and they have been responsible for widespread environmental damage. They have consistently failed to meet their own policy guidelines. The potential for disaster increased after 2000 when the WB increased its promotion of engagement with, and lending to the private sector — the Private–Public Partnership model. Two early flagship projects in SSA were the Marikana Mine in South Africa and the Chad–Cameroon Pipeline Project. The lending arm of the IFC allocates approximately 40% of its development loans to third-party lending institutions, other banks or micro-finance institutions (private companies). These financial intermediaries were expected to comply with IFC environmental and social requirements, protecting people and the environment from harm. An internal audit in 2013 of IFC lending revealed that though sub-clients were expected to keep records there were no oversight mechanisms in place. As 60% of IMF projects funded through sub-clients failed to meet environmental and social standards, the impact of this negligence on development projects is significant and the sums involved are large. In 2013, IFC lending amounted to approximately $20 billion. There was no sound reason for such lack of oversight as other lending institutions — such as the Asia Development Bank and the US Overseas Private Investment Corporation (OPIC) — have managed to implement effective working models of due diligence (Biron, 2013). In his review of 75 years of the Bank's achievement, Bruce Rich concluded that the Bank's 'environmental legacy is one of cumulative, avoidable ecological and social harm'. Any reforms have been half hearted (2019).

6.8.2. *The climate crisis*

SSA's contribution to the contemporary climate crisis is minimal. SSA has the lowest level of carbon emissions in the world but is experiencing the extreme effects of this crisis: severe weather events, food scarcity, water shortages, crop failures and increasing desertification. The climate crisis has the most serious impacts on those who are already poor and without resources to mitigate the effects of severe climate events. The crisis increases poverty and SSA already contains many of the poorest people in the world. They do not have the resources to withstand climate challenges and the accompanying economic shocks. The region needs help to deal with the effects of climate change and introduce mitigation efforts as well as future-proofing the economic security of the people. It is only fair that those who created the high levels of carbon emissions should do the most to mitigate the impacts and assist those affected by dramatic climatic events. There are two key issues for SSA related to this crisis. All countries in SSA need access to energy for economic development and the region needs help in adopting a low carbon development path. According to a study commissioned by International Rivers, two-thirds of the countries studied in SSA could cover all their projected power needs by wind and solar energy alone, and local communities there are better served by wind, solar and micro-hydropower projects which do not depend on a central grid (Bosshard, 2016). The other key issue is that governments are dependent on income from the sale of fossil fuels. Both these governments and the foreign companies that dominate the sector are unlikely to support alternative energy models.

The most intangible environmental impact of the US on SSA is its carbon emissions. The US is historically responsible for 20% of the current global accumulation of carbon and is currently the world's second largest producer of carbon emissions. The slowness of the US government to acknowledge the climate crisis and other environmental issues has held back international efforts to address problems that include global warming, species extinction, pollution and depletion of resources. The fossil fuel sector is extremely politically powerful in the US and has funded large-scale climate change denial campaigns (Orestes & Conway, 2010). The WB has also contributed to the crisis as the largest lender for fossil fuel extraction. It has also been slow to acknowledge the severity of the climate crisis (Bond, 2014b). The WB's first response to carbon emissions was the conservative and business-friendly Prototype Carbon Fund, a carbon trading scheme which became operational in 2000 (European Environmental Agency, 2018). The scheme enabled high carbon producers to buy out their emissions and continue producing rather than lowering total emissions. Unsurprisingly, finance for the fund came from 17 corporations and several carbon-intensive Western governments (Bond, 2007). The fund was judged unlikely to generate a measurable change in greenhouse gas concentrations. It also largely bypassed SSA in terms of projects for offsetting emissions according to the Operations Evaluation Department of the Bank (Kelly & Jordan, 2004). There is an ongoing fundamental contradiction in the roles played by the Bank as a climate trustee, firstly administering the investment projects of the Global Environmental Facility for climate mitigation and, after 2008 administering the Climate Investment Funds and as a major funder of fossil fuel projects (Rich, 2019). Since 2000 the WB has continued to concentrate its energy funding on coal and oil extraction, along with hydropower. It ignored the 2003 Extractive Industry Review (EIR) recommendation that the WB cease lending for oil, gas and coal projects (Bond, 2007). WB's investment in fossil fuels in Africa expanded in the decade up to 2010 and was greater than its investment in mining (Bretton Woods Project, 2010).

One of the main achievements of the United Nations Framework Convention on Climate Change in 1992 was the agreement on Common But Differentiated Responsibilities (CBDR) for dealing with climate change. Wealthy nations would take most responsibility for action on climate as they created the problem and had better resources to respond (United Nations, 1992). However, at the UNCCC in Paris in 2015, Western governments pressured the G77 nations to sign away these obligations (Bond, 2018). Wealthy nations were not required to specify what they would provide for remediation in their nationally determined contributions (NDCs). This reversal was particularly harmful to SSA where an estimated 506 million (61%) can be defined as 'multi-dimensionally poor', or by the poverty measure of $1.90 per day 391 million people were considered poor in 2016 (Multidimensional Poverty Index, 2016) and lacked the resources to deal with the effects of the climate crisis.

The WB has also been slow to embrace alternative energies in SSA. In 2006, it promoted nuclear power and mega-dam hydropower as potential 'clean energy' sources along with carbon sequestration (Bond, 2007). In a later report published in 2012, 'Turn down the heat: Why a 4°C warmer world must be avoided', the WB pledged to increase lending for renewable energy. An audit by the Bank's own Independent Evaluation Group found the Bank tended to emphasise contemporary climate variability but lacked the policy to guide future adaptation efforts and systematic procedures for screening projects for climate risks (Bretton Woods Project, 2012c). BWI strategies for ending the use of fossil fuels have continued to be limited and conventional. The Bank introduced the Scaling Up for Renewable Energy Program in 2013 but implementation was slow (Bretton Woods Project, 2014). In 2014, 56% of the Bank's power sector lending was allocated to large hydropower projects, while 30% was used for wind, solar and geothermal projects and 14% for oil and gas. The WB has started lending for alternative energy projects in South Africa but such projects are dwarfed by the coal-based Eskom Power Investment Support Project (Bretton Woods Project, 2019a). Only in 2015 did the IMF acknowledge climate change to be an emerging issue closely related to macro-economic stability and how economies performed. More reporting and policies have emerged but the IMF has yet to develop clear and consistent policies (Bretton Woods Project, 2019a).

6.8.3. *Environmental impacts of resource extraction*

The SSA region is very rich in a wide range of minerals including asbestos, antimony, bauxite, chromium, cobalt, copper, diamonds, manganese, nickel, gold, lead, phosphate, platinum, titanium and uranium. The minerals are unevenly spread throughout the region. South Africa has the largest mining sector, while the DRC has the world's largest supply of coltan, an essential component in mobile phones. The extraction of minerals has created large-scale environmental destruction. Foreign companies dominate mineral extraction in SSA and have a lot of power. They have the support of their own governments while local governments are often too weak, dependent on the company taxes or working in collusion with these companies, to enforce environmental regulations.

Since the 1980s, the US and BWIs have promoted resource extraction as a way for countries in SSA to service their debt. After 2000, the WB increased its funding for mineral extraction and announced its plans to expand extraction in Africa (Bretton Woods Project, 2010). In 2011, the IFC announced it would invest $300 billion in mining projects in Africa (Bretton Woods Project, 2011b). After 2000, there was a boom in resource extraction in SSA driven by demand from China. Between 2000 and 2014, mineral resources made up 66% of the region's exports and resource extraction continues to be promoted by the WB (Izvorski, 2018). Foreign companies dominate the sector.

Foreign companies have acted with impunity, ignored environmental regulations and have created widespread devastation. Mineral extraction processes produce toxic waste and pollute air, water and soil. Mines destroy large areas of land. In gold mining, over 99% of the extracted material is left as waste contaminated with heavy metals. Many metals are extracted with cyanide. The heavy metals in gold mine tailings include arsenic, cadmium, nickel, lead, copper, zinc, cobalt and mercury. The level of mercury emissions in South Africa is second only to those in China (Babalola *et al.*, 2016). The process of extracting minerals from rock is also very carbon intensive, one of the reasons BHB Billiton secured the advantageous electricity deal with Eskom in South Africa.

In 2003, the Bank began considering new oil, mining and gas projects in unstable and poorly governed countries. This went against the advice of its own evaluation unit. The WB's own poor track record provides ample evidence of the risks in such projects. WB projects in 'fragile states' including the Chad–Cameroon Oil and Pipeline Project, mining projects in DRC, forestry in Cameroon and the Bujagali dam in Uganda have all been plagued with environmental problems (Environmental Defense, Friends of the Earth and International Rivers Network, 2003). In 2003, the Extractive Industry Review (EIR) recommended that the WB introduce better social and environmental policies. It also recommended the mandatory sharing of environmental and social impact assessments with local communities, identification of environmentally sensitive areas where mining or drilling was forbidden, that new projects include bans on the dumping of mining tailings in rivers, making environmental restructuring obligatory and investing in renewable energy. In 2004, the WB Board rejected these recommendations (Bond, 2007).

Many WB-funded projects in SSA violated the Bank's own environmental policies. In Ghana, in 2006, the IFC persisted in financing Newmont Mining's Ahafa project in the face of protests by NGOs because of unresolved issues concerning the protection of groundwater, forests and land near where tailings would be deposited (Bretton Woods Project, 2006; Wroughton, 2006). The IFC also supplied funds to Lonmin for the Marikana platinum mine in 2007. The Marikana dispute in 2012 prompted a multifaceted study of the effects of gold and platinum mining in South Africa. A wide range of environmental damage and health problems were revealed, including vast quantities of tailings, dumps, waste rock and lakes of polluted water. The physical and social environment was devastated (Cairncross & Kisting, 2016).

Within the WB, resource conservation has not been a priority, but it has acknowledged the significance of resource depletion in SSA. Using natural capital accounting, economists at the WB estimated that the average decline in per capita African net wealth due to the extraction of 'natural capital' — minerals, energy and forest products — was 12% in 2010 (WB, 2014a). The introduction of natural capital accounting has been used to support the long-standing WB focus on economic growth. Countries in SSA have been categorised as 'resource rich' and 'resource poor', with oil and minerals being the dominant feature of the resource-rich countries and land the main characteristic of the resource-poor nations. In 2018, a leading WB economist was advocating the increase in Africa's natural wealth by the expansion of resource extraction (Izvorski, 2018).

6.8.3.1. *Oil*

Only a relatively small number of nations in SSA — around 10 — are dependent on oil revenues, but in those countries, the extraction of oil has created widespread environmental destruction. US oil corporations have done little to address the environmental impacts of their activities. Chevron and ExxonMobil are the largest American oil companies operating in SSA. They are among the largest companies in Angola and Nigeria but also have interests in Equatorial Guinea, Ghana, Benin, Cameroon, the Republic of the Congo and Togo. The most damaged region in SSA is the Niger Delta, which is one of the most polluted regions in the world. One thousand oil spills were reported in Nigeria between 1970 and 2006 (Aroh *et al*., 2010). Oil spills have contaminated coastal land and wetlands. Life expectancy in the delta area has gone down and there is a high incidence of birth defects and miscarriages. Fishing and farming have been severely affected by oil spills. Gas flaring is another aspect of oil extraction which creates air pollution as well as generating carbon emissions. Gas flaring causes asthma, respiratory illnesses and cancer. Though gas flaring is illegal in Nigeria the government does little to stop it. The small fines imposed are paid by companies who then continue their activities. Local people would like the gas to be used for local electrification but their requests have been ignored because it is cheaper for companies to burn off the gas that process it. Oil companies are compelled to form partnerships with the Nigerian government which is complicit in polluting the region. Similar behaviour occurs in Angola another large oil-producing state. Chevron and ExxonMobil are in joint venture partnerships with the state-owned oil company Sonangol. Most Angolan oil wells are offshore in Cabinda Bay. Oil spills have polluted the water. Local fishing has been destroyed by such spills, and by shipping traffic, underwater explosions and noise. Most of the gas produced by the Cabinda wells are left to flare. Oil companies and the government have ignored the oil spills. The first time the Angolan government instructed Chevron to clean up an oil spill was in 2011, which was attributed to diplomatic tensions between the US and Angola (Corpwatch, 2011).

The Chad–Cameroon Pipeline was a large project partially funded by the IFC and initiated by a consortium of oil companies — Exxon (40%), Petronas (35%)

and Chevron (25%) (ExxonMobil, 2019). The project was launched in 2000 and finished in 2003. Most funding came from the IFC and private lenders coordinated by the IFC along with the US Exim bank and the French export credit agency (Inkpen & Moffat, 2011; Joseph, 2001). The justification for the development of Chad's oil reserves was to finance social and economic development. A number of NGOs, including Amnesty International, raised concerns about Chad's record on human rights. They also identified a lack of proper legal and technical environmental safeguards in Chad which would exonerate the oil consortium from any future liability or accountability with respect to its operations. A two-year moratorium on approving the project was requested. Critics were also concerned that oil revenues would be used to purchase weapons rather than implement poverty reduction programmes that were part of the loan conditions. From November 2000, the military repeatedly diverted funds to purchase weapons (Hatthaway, 2010). In 2008, the WB finally withdrew from the project. Over 30% of oil revenues were used to fund weapons (Gulali, 2018). The pipeline caused hardship, splitting properties and disrupting farming, creating construction-generated pools of water that bred mosquitoes, and there were oil spills that polluted the land causing many farmers to give up their land.

The pipeline also caused problems in neighbouring Cameroon, crossing 900 kilometres of land and impacting on 248 villages. There were no compensation agreements for displaced villagers or budget allocations for those affected by the pipeline (Gulali, 2018). Also, contractors took advantage of inexperienced negotiators in Cameroon and arranged a very low rate of payment — 0.45c cents per barrel — for rights to cross its territory. The price was not linked to inflation, the price of oil or any review. After seven years of operation, Cameroon had reportedly earned $277 million from the pipeline, nearly 50% of Cameroon's GDP for that period. In comparison in 2006 the consortium — Exxon, Petronas and Chevron — that owns 90% of the Cameroon State Petroleum Company COTCO, made back their initial investment of $3.66 billion plus $5.05 billion in profits (Badgley, 2010). Ten years later, in 2013, Cameroon managed to renegotiate the fees to $1.30 per barrel, with a five-yearly review, adjusted for inflation (Badgley, 2013).

6.8.3.2. *Coal*

The WB has been criticised for urging the reduction of carbon emissions while simultaneously funding coal mines and coal-fired power stations. The Bank argued that sometimes coal was the cheapest resource countries had for energy supply. Their argument was that each country had the right to determine its own strategy for its energy aspirations (Volcovici & Yukhananov, 2013). One of the WB's largest development projects in SSA was the Eskom Power Investment Support Project in South Africa. Approved in 2010 the project involved the construction of two coal-based power plants, intended to address the acute energy shortage in South Africa which was hampering economic development. The $3.75 billion loan was the Bank's largest loan in South Africa. The total cost of the project was $10.75 billion (WB, 2016b). South Africa is the seventh largest coal producer in the world and accounts for 94% of the region's coal production

(Infrastructure Consortium for Africa, 2016). At the start of the project, South Africa already had the highest carbon emissions in the region. The two power plants in the project — Kusile and Medupi — were projected to be the third and fourth largest coal-fired power plants in the world (Khumalo, 2018). In 2013, when the president of the WB travelled to South Africa he praised the project as a clean coal initiative, ignoring the fact it would emit 25 to 35 million tonnes of CO^2 per year, more than the emissions of 115 countries. The project had been justified as providing cheaper energy but loan conditions included 100% energy price increases, increases that would drive poorer people to use cheaper, dirtier alternatives, such as wood, coal and paraffin (Bond, 2014b). Corporate interests were prioritised over those of the poor. Approximately 44% of the energy production was consumed by 28 corporations in South Africa's Energy Intensive Users Group (Bond, 2018). The project suffered long delays, price overruns and failed to deliver projected quantities of energy. Oversight of the project did not require due diligence regarding management and ensuring a reliable supply of energy. Energy supplies have continued to be erratic.

Both the IFC and President Obama pledged to end all funding for coal-burning power plants in 2013 (Volcovici & Yukhananov, 2013). In 2016, four NGOs conducted a three-month investigation and found that since 2013 IFC had financed 41 coal projects in Africa, South Asia and Bangladesh, causing environmental damage and human rights abuses as well as contributing to climate change (Turner, 2016).

6.8.4. *Infrastructure: Hydropower*

SSA has always had a serious energy deficit and many dams were built to supply electricity as well as irrigation. The WB has been one of the main sources of finance for these dams since 1959 when it supplied funds for a hydroelectric power project in Uganda (WB, n.d.c2). The BWIs energy policies prioritised the provision of energy for industry or to generate funds (through the sale of energy) rather than to supply the wider population. The US Exim Bank has also provided loans at commercial rates for infrastructure projects delivered by US companies (EXIM Bank, 2000).

During the 1980s, dam projects funded by the WB caused so much environmental destruction and social dislocation that they prompted a wave of international protests. In an effort to retain its credibility, the WB pledged to identify new priorities and set new standards in environmental and social impact in the next decade (Rich, 2019). However, in 2003, another policy change saw the WB announce its new 'high-risk/high-reward' strategy, a plan to take on projects in unstable environments. This policy change increased the possibilities of further social and environmental destruction. One of the defining characteristics of fragile states was the lack of institutional capacity (Environmental Defence, Friends of the Earth and International Rivers Network, 2003). An audit by the World Commission on Dams in 2003 was highly critical of WB practices. The auditors offered a number of recommendations including mandatory revenue sharing with communities, extensive environmental and social impact assessments and increased renewable energy investments. The WB undermined its credibility by ignoring the recommendations (Bond, 2007). The Bank also lobbied governments in the developing world not to accept the recommendations. Despite all the environmental guidelines, policies and agreements, the BWIs have continued to ignore the environment in planning and implementing projects (Bosshard, 2016).

Problems with the Lesotho Highlands Water Project (LHWP) highlight the risks with large-scale projects, even those not in 'fragile states'. The LHWP was a WB flagship project in the late 1990s. It was promoted as a way for the Lesotho government to earn revenue for social and economic development. Water and electricity were be sold to meet the water shortage in South Africa's largest industrial and commercial area between Johannesburg and Pretoria. The project entailed building five dams and bringing water across the mountains from Lesotho into South Africa (Bond, 2019). International Rivers concluded that if the WB had followed the guidelines of the World Commission on Dams 2000 report on managing demand and correcting the massive waste (up to 70%) in the current system, the dams might not have needed to be built. The downstream effects of the project were not adequately assessed nor were the harmful effects of the diversion of so much water from the river systems of Lesotho. These rivers were sometimes reduced almost to 'wastewater drains' (Hoover, 2001). The building of the Katse Dam in Lesotho caused seismic activity and earthquakes, known as 'reservoir-induced seismicity (RIS)'. The earthquakes began when the reservoir was filled in 1995, five months after the project was completed (International Rivers, 2010). Lack of adequate project oversight resulted in a series of corruption cases involving international corporations. Water prices also increased, disadvantaging the poor and increasing health risks (Bond, 2018).

The Bujagali dam in Uganda was another problematic WB project. Twenty NGOs lobbied the WB in 2001 to halt the project as it did not meet a core mandate of the WB — meeting the local development needs of the population, in this case for energy. The dam also failed to meet the World Commission on Dams guidelines. The Bank ignored the fact that wood was the largest source of fuel in Uganda, so sustainable forestry would be a feasible option. There were many flaws and omissions in the analysis of the impact on the Nile river system and fisheries. Community participation and feedback was also severely flawed (International Rivers, 2001). A WB external review panel found the project did not comply with many of the Bank's own social and environmental policies (Independent Review Panel, 2008). The company that won the contract — AES Nile Power — withdrew in 2002 because it lacked the expertise and work was halted between 2002 and 2007. The dam was finally completed in 2012 after years of controversy. There was a large cost overrun; the initial estimate was $580 million and the final cost was $902 million, but other estimates put the cost at $1.3 billion. This amount could have been far better used to explore alternative power options, especially as 87% of Ugandans are not on the grid and have not benefitted. Electricity prices also increased. The amount of energy produced was lower than projected. Social and environmental impacts were severe. The level of Lake Victoria was lowered, which affected fishing. About 8,700 people were relocated and entitled to compensation equivalent to what they had lost. The implementation of the programme was delayed and inadequate for many people who lost livelihoods (Irigoyen, 2017).

In 2013, the WB announced a return to building large dams, starting with the Inga 3 on the Congo River in DRC and the Batoka Gorge and Mphanda Nkuwa dams on the Zambezi River. The purpose of these projects was to supply energy for industry and resource extraction (Bosshard, 2013a, 2013b). All three prioritised the electricity demands of the mining sector at the expense of poor Africans. The WB has still not addressed resettlement issues and people displaced by its dams continue to be impoverished. (Bosshard, 2016; Sanyanga, 2014). The Grand Inga dam proposed for the Democratic Republic of the Congo was intended to be the world's biggest dam project. The goal of the project was to generate energy for export and earn revenue for the government. Large infrastructure projects are notorious for cost overruns and are notoriously prone to corruption. Initial costs were estimated at $80 billion but would almost certainly be much higher. The project would not deliver power to the poor (Asanzi, 2016). As the DRC is one of the most unstable countries in the world, there is a high probability that problems will occur, outcomes will not be realised and the project will enlarge government debt.

The WB continues to promote large scale projects even though its own project record has been poor. Significant benefits of these large dams accrue to foreign companies and suppliers of finance, rather than the local people who suffer through resettlement, inadequate compensation, loss of livelihoods and environmental destruction. Large scale infrastructure projects also burden governments with unpayable debt.

The International Energy Agency recommends that more than 60% of the funds required to bring about universal access to electricity is invested in distributed renewable energy projects, such as wind, solar and small hydropower plants (Bosshard, 2013a, 2013b). This raises the question as to who are the intended beneficiaries of these projects.

6.8.5. *Agriculture*

The agriculture sector in SSA was neglected by governments, foreign donors and lenders during the 20th century even though over 50% of the population worked in agriculture. Agricultural workers were the poorest people in the region. According to environmentalist Fred Pearce, industrial agriculture is not a suitable model for the African smallholder farmer because of the nature of the climate and soil quality. The focus of African agriculture should be on improving the productivity of small holdings to both feed the local population and for export (Pearce, 2012). This approach has never been adopted by aid donors or the BWIs.

USAID has been involved in agricultural development projects in SSA for over 50 years but only as a minor part of its programme (USAID, 2013). After the late 1970s, neoliberal policies imposed by the US and the BWIs required governments to concentrate on export-driven agriculture to stimulate economic development and earn capital for debt repayment. Farmers were diverted away from production for local consumption. Most large-scale agriculture was under foreign ownership and poorly paid jobs were the only benefits to local people (Goldman, 2005; WB, 2013). In the 20th century, African agriculture did not attract foreign investment but after 2000 there was growing interest from US corporations and private foundations. Corporate expansion has been accompanied by large-scale foreign land acquisition. The food produced is exported and there are few benefits for local communities. The WB has continued to advocate policies that promote the expansion of the agribusiness model in agriculture (WB, 2013; Forest People's Programme, 2013).

The largest foundation in the world — the Gates Foundation (GF) — has also become prominent in the agriculture and health sectors in SSA. Bill Gates' approach has been to target what he identified as the main problems with African agriculture: the lack of technology and functioning markets. In 2006, the Rockefeller and Gates foundations launched the Alliance for a Green Revolution in Africa (AGRA). This Foundation has since distributed more than $3 billion in assistance and funded 660 agricultural projects. The approach has focused on bio-technological farming methods and corporate farming. Critics claimed that under the guise of eliminating hunger in Africa, AGRA was being used to open Africa for American agribusiness (Vidal, 2016). A subsequent review of AGRA by Timothy Wise of Tufts University found it was not meeting its own goals. It failed to reach small-scale producers, when it did reach them the promoted methods failed to raise incomes and it did not reduce poverty or increase food security. It was recommended that donor and African governments switch their funding from AGRA to programmes that politically and financially supported small-scale food producers, particularly women and youth, and develop climate-resilient ecologically sustainable farming practices, such as agroecology, which has been increasingly recognised and supported by the Committee on World Food Security (Wise, 2020; False Promises, 2020). Another US initiative was the Feed the Future programme established by President Obama. Led by USAID it again stresses collaborative partnerships between private and public sectors (11 US departments). The programme supports agricultural development assistance in eight African countries: Ethiopia, Ghana, Kenya, Mali, Niger, Nigeria and Senegal (Feed the Future, 2021).

Genetically modified (GM) seeds are a key component of US industrial agriculture and the US has been the main advocate for GM seeds in SSA. Advocates claimed there were no proven risks and that GM seeds provided an opportunity to feed the world's poor (Specter, 2014). GM seeds have also been promoted as reducing the need for pesticides and increasing food security. The US used its Food Aid programme to promote its GM agenda. In the early 2000s, Zambia, Zimbabwe and Angola rejected the World Food Programme and US food relief because of the risk of future US GM threats (Bond, 2006). Producers were also concerned that they would lose their export markets in the EU. Monsanto and the GF have been key drivers of the GM lobby in SSA. South Africa was used as the entry point as it had a willing government and an existing industrial agricultural system (Bond, 2018). The GF's corporate links have raised issues concerning conflicts of interest. In 2010, the Gates Foundation bought a large number of shares in seed giant Monsanto; it was also closely linked to the multinational company Cargill, one of the agribusinesses that dominate the international food chain (Vidal, 2010). Monsanto has become infamous because of its 'terminator seeds', which could not be used in subsequent years. These seeds tie farmers to annual seed purchases often leading to debt. Large numbers of indebted cotton farmers in India committed suicide (de Tavernier & Thomas, 2017). By 2016 the expansion of GM seeds in SSA remained limited. The only countries in Africa to have approved local production and sale of GM food were South Africa, Burkina Faso and Sudan. The only country where GM use was widespread was South Africa (Thomson, 2015; World Politics Review, 2019).

6.8.6. *Land grabbing*

The recent expansion of the foreign acquisition of land is another major threat facing SSA. Foreign land acquisition increased after 2000 and then rose precipitously after the 2007–2008 food crisis. The people of Africa need that land to feed themselves and to achieve food sovereignty, especially as the climate crisis worsens (GRAIN, 2019). Africa has large areas of uncultivated arable land — the World Economic Forum estimates 60% of the world's uncultivated land is in that region (Plazier, 2016). Another estimate was that SSA had 45% of the world's land area suitable for the expansion of sustainable production. Africa also has abundant but significantly underutilised water resources. Only 2–3% of renewable water resources are being used (Li & Wang, 2016). This apparent abundance, combined with food shortages, prompted the increase in foreign land purchases and leasing.

Research by the Oakland Institute revealed that the WB is the most significant driver of land sales in Africa. It has encouraged the expansion of land sales as a major opportunity for agricultural development. The WB facilitates this agenda by encouraging African countries to reform their land laws and fiscal regimes to make them attractive to foreign investors. An investigation of a series of land deals across Africa found that the purchases of land, often by large institutional investors and wealthy nations are mostly unregulated, deliver few of the benefits to local people, are driving people off the land, threatening food security and causing environmental harm (Bretton Woods Project, 2011c). The IFC finances investment in land purchases through intermediaries. Because the IFC's arrangements are not transparent, it leverages funds without revealing the final destination of those funds (Bretton Woods Project, 2017). Land acquisition was also promoted by the 2013 New Alliance for Food Security and Nutrition (NAFFN), a G8 project supported by USAID. The programme goal of the New Alliance was to lift 50 million people in SSA out of poverty, through 'inclusive and sustained agricultural growth'. The initiative was more an exercise in self-interest — land acquisition and corporate expansion — than altruism. African countries were offered public and private funds for signing agreements and forming partnerships with G8 countries and the private sector (usually multinational companies). The corporate partners of the alliance included Monsanto, Cargill, Dupont, Syngenta, Nestlé, Unilever, Itochu and Yara International. The agreements included the standard neoliberal conditions, removing subsidies and any market barriers that disadvantage their own farmers. Companies were allowed to acquire land, patent their seeds and monopolise food markets. Most important were the land agreements which had binding requirements for African governments and no requirements — such as removing domestic subsidies and biofuel quotas — for G8 countries. Countries that already had given up a lot of land agreed to relinquish more. Mozambique evicted local farmers from a large area of land and wrote new laws agreeing to form 'partnerships'. Côte d'Ivoire agreed to 'facilitate access to land for smallholder farmers and private enterprises', usually corporations. By 2013, it had made deals with French, Algerian, Swiss and Singaporean companies covering 600,000 acres of prime arable land, displacing thousands of farmers. Ethiopia already had a poor record of human rights abuses over land and agreed to provide more private investors access to land (Monbiot, 2013). In 2014, Oxfam asked for greater transparency from the New Alliance in the 10 countries in which it operated. Oxfam saw a serious risk that the initiative would marginalise small-scale agriculture, undermine land tenure security and endanger the right to food of the most vulnerable people (Oxfam, 2014a). The past record of foreign corporate engagement, promoted as encouraging development and the transfer of expertise since the 1980s has had a very poor track record, and there is no reason to expect any difference with the recent expansion of agribusinesses.

The Land Matrix, a joint, independent, land-monitoring initiative of civil society, intergovernmental organisations and research institutes, has collected key information regarding land grabbing. It found that almost 9% of Africa's total arable land has changed ownership since 2000 (International Assessment of Agricultural Knowledge, Science and Technology for Development (IAASTD), 1 June 2016). An investigation by Global Land Project — based on media reports — showed that from 2008 to 2010 between 53 million and 61 million hectares of land in Africa were assigned in land deals or under negotiation in 27 African countries. The investigation discovered that most of the land transactions were for biofuel production by private businesses, and by Gulf and East Asian countries for food and fuel production. Actual confirmation of this information was lacking (Bretton Woods Project, 2017). A 2011 report from the Oakland Institute, *Understanding Land Investment Deals in Africa*, revealed that hedge funds were buying land in Africa to boost profits in food, biofuel sectors and cut flowers. By 2009 hedge funds and other speculators had bought or leased 60 million hectares of land in Africa, an area the size of France. The study investigated land deals in Ethiopia, Tanzania, South Sudan, Sierra Leone, Mali and Mozambique. Often, land was acquired without proper contracts or made with gullible or corrupt leaders. Companies also offered incentives but did not deliver on their promises (*BBC News*, 2011). An Oxfam study in 2013 confirmed that US investors — mainly private equity and hedge funds — for the previous 10 years had played a major role in financing agribusiness companies employing monoculture production in low-income countries at the expense of biodiversity and greater food security. Nearly half of the reported large-scale land deals involving US investors had taken place in SSA (Humphreys *et al.*, 2013).

6.8.7. *Deforestation*

The impact of the WB on the forestry sector has been significant even though lending for forestry has been only a small part of its total portfolio. Export-oriented agricultural policies promoted by the WB increased deforestation and intensified the extinction of species dependent on the forest habitat (Goldman, 2005). The Ivory Coast lost two-thirds of its forests after it increased growing cocoa for export (Burnett & Games, 2007). Many of the large-scale projects in Africa funded by the WB also increased deforestation. The building of hydroelectric dams flooded large areas and destroyed the land, while road building opened up large areas to logging, cattle-raising, agriculture and mining (Goldman, 2005). Widespread criticism of the impact of its projects in the 1980s led the Bank to introduce a Forestry Protocol in 1991. The Bank's Operations Evaluation Department (OED) Forestry Review in 1999 found that staff and management had ignored the policy. There was no effective implementation plan, new trees were not planted and forest destruction in the tropical regions was not reduced, particularly in Cameroon. Deforestation in Cameroon was driven by the need to generate income. Deregulation policies had enabled foreign logging companies to expand their operations. The building of roads for the Chad–Cameroon pipeline also opened up the frontier forests of the eastern provinces. The WB World Development Report in 2001 continued to claim that market mechanisms or marketing would be used to protect forests. Criticisms and recommendations of the OED Forestry Review were also ignored (Carrere, 2002; Lele *et al.*, 2000; WB Independent Operations Evaluation Department, 2000). In 2003, the Bank introduced its 'high-risk/high-reward' policy, considering forestry projects in unstable and poorly governed countries against the advice of its own evaluation unit (Environmental Defence, Friends of the Earth, and International Rivers Network, 2003).

The expansion of industrial palm oil production also increased deforestation. A report from Greenpeace France announced that Africa had become the new frontier for palm oil and rubber (Greenpeace International, 2012). European-owned (Belgian) Socfin is one of the largest owners of palm and rubber plantations in Africa. It controls vast tracts of tropical land in Nigeria, Sierra Leone, Liberia and Cameroon (Greenpeace Africa, 2016). Socfin has been the recipient of IFC funding, including a $10 million loan to Socfin in 2008 to expand its rubber plantations in Liberia. The company has been embroiled in a number of controversies, including a complaint to IFC citing human rights violations from the Liberian NGO Green Advocates on behalf of 22 villages (Bread for All, 2020). In 2016, Greenpeace urged Socfin to join other multinational companies in adopting a 'zero deforestation' policy. These multinationals included GAR, Cargill, Agropalma, Unilever, Nestlé and L'Oréal. Socfin refused to commit to a zero deforestation policy (Greenpeace Africa, 2016).

6.9. Conclusion

Many of the problems currently experienced in SSA are the result of a complex legacy of colonialism, unequal development policies and corrupt leaders who have exploited and repressed their people. The US and BWIs have contributed to this trajectory through their policies and their control of finance, both loans and aid. The US has driven the agenda of the Washington Consensus — the other developed nations, the BWIs and multinational corporations. After most SSA countries fell into debt in the late 1970s, they lost their political and economic sovereignty and were forced to implement neoliberal structural adjustment policies. The result was more than two decades of social and economic stagnation where only lenders, donors and corporations benefitted. Repressive governments continued to be supported with loans and aid and corporations colluded with the same despotic and corrupt leaders. These leaders held back economic and human development in the region and committed theft on a grand scale. This capital flight deprived the region of funds for development. The neoliberal policies imposed, which included the privatisation of health, education, and water, cuts in social spending and the dismantling of labour protection, stifled improvements in standards of living. The activities of corporations were also detrimental to human development. The processes of resource extraction were harmful to health, employment conditions were poor and wages were kept low. Some policies — the privatisation of water — contravene the United Nations Declaration of Human Rights. Neoliberal economic policies led to decades of economic stagnation. Debt and the servicing of that debt also deprived the region of funds for development. Some debt was the result of systematic failures by lenders, in particular the WB. Failures included a lack of due diligence, profligate lending, loans to repressive and corrupt leaders (illegitimate debt) and project failure. The WB was culpable of many of these financial outflows from SSA — including corporate profits and illegal transfers of funds — which were facilitated by market deregulation and a complex system of enablers. These illegal transfers have been estimated as being equivalent to the development finance that entrapped borrowers in debt. Loans for failed and compromised projects still had to be repaid and contributed to debt burdens. Since 2000 the US and BWIs have promoted the private–public model for aid and development, yet again promoting corporate interests.

The US is responsible for a large proportion of the carbon emissions producing the current climate crisis. Climate change has already caused major social and environmental problems in SSA. Neoliberal policies have also had an impact on the environment. Large dam projects caused destruction and social dislocation, while corporations extracting resources caused widespread environmental damage and pollution. The latest travesty imposed on SSA has been foreign land acquisitions. The WB has played a dominant role in facilitating land sales and the expansion of corporate agriculture in SSA.

The neoliberal policies and programmes imposed by the US and the BWIs have been ideologically driven. The policies have remained in place without acknowledgement of flaws or failures. Policy changes and modifications have tended to occur in response to external pressures. The central question in assessing the impact of the US and BWIs on SSA is: who has benefitted? Foreign corporations, foreign lenders and aid donors, corrupt leaders and small numbers of the elite surrounding those leaders. The BWIs were first informed about the shortcomings of their neoliberal structural adjustment policies in a G24 working group report in 1987. The group — including executive members of the BWIs — concluded that 'IMF-supported adjustment programs had led to a decline in both levels of output and rates of growth, and had increased unemployment and had adversely affected income distribution in developing countries' (Hertz, 2004). The Meltzer Report to Congress and the SAPRIN reviews reconfirmed previous criticisms of neoliberal policies and conditions. Despite the term 'structural adjustment' disappearing from policy titles, the policies have persisted in loan and aid conditions as well as in debt relief programmes. Since 2000, the promotion of corporate interests through the PPP model has persisted even though flaws have emerged in that approach. Corporate interests continue to prevail and expand into land acquisition and corporate expansion in agriculture.

Chapter 7

Conclusion

This book has investigated the activities of China and the main Western powerholders — the US, World Bank (WB) and International Monetary Fund (IMF) — in Sub-Saharan Africa (SSA) since 2000. The focus of the investigation has been their contribution to 'development', in three specific categories: people and politics, economics and environment (the 'triple bottom line'). I have taken a human-centred approach that prioritises the wellbeing of the population and their ability to meet their basic needs in terms of health, housing, employment, education and freedom from political repression. Meeting these needs requires a willingness and commitment by governments to spend money on these sectors, and having the money to spend. Improving human development also necessitates economic development and safeguarding of the environment. One of the notable effects of providing health services and education is the lowering of population growth (Rosling, 2018), which also has economic and environmental benefits.

Since countries in SSA became independent, there were brief periods when more money was spent on health and education: in the early years of independence and after the debt relief programmes, the Highly Indebted Poor Country Initiative and the Multilateral Debt Relief Initiative, which provided short periods of relief from debt servicing. A key measure of human wellbeing is the Human Development Index published annually by the UN Development Program (UNDP) since 1990. The index was broadened to include inequality in 2010, and renamed the Multidimensional Human Development Index. It showed that in the 1960s and 1970s, standards of living improved briefly. Once countries became indebted, this spending ceased. The neoliberal policies imposed by Western creditors required cuts to health, education and agricultural subsidies. Both social services and employment suffered. Most of the population worked in agriculture at this time. Human development levels stagnated for the next two decades. The human development rating for the region increased from 0.421 to 0.523 between 2000 and 2015, but SSA continued to lag behind the rest of the world. Between

1990 and 2015, countries in SSA dominated the lowest rankings in the Index (UNDP, 2016). Inequality across the subcontinent also increased between 2000 and 2016 as wealth was funnelled upwards to the elite while the numbers of people living in poverty increased (Bond, 2017e).

Improvements in standards of living necessitate a government willing to invest in people and having the funds to do so. In many countries in SSA, government priorities have been to retain power and repress the population. These governments have no interest in human development. There are two overlapping categories of countries with this profile: fragile states and 'resource curse' countries. The 12 fragile states are (Very High Alert) South Somalia, South Sudan, Central African Republic, Sudan, Chad, and the Democratic Republic of the Congo (DRC), and (High Alert) Guinea, Nigeria, Côte d'Ivoire, Burundi, Zimbabwe, Guinea Bissau (Fund for Peace, 2016). These countries account for 41% of the region's population (United States Census Bureau, 2019). The other category — the 'resource curse' countries — generate great wealth but have the lowest levels of human development. Oil exporting countries dominate this category. Of the oil exporters, Chad, Sudan and Nigeria are also 'fragile states', the others being Angola, Gabon, Equatorial Guinea, São Tomé and Cameroon (Fund for Peace, 2016). Fragile states and those suffering from the 'resource curse' share many characteristics: political repression, high levels of corruption, very low levels of human development and high levels of inequality. Governments in these countries tend to be totalitarian dictatorships. Income generated from resources is used to buy arms and repress the population or is stolen and transferred offshore into private accounts. These 17 countries rank among the lowest in the human development index and changes are unlikely to occur if current conditions persist. Most of the 31 other countries in SSA also suffer from low levels of human development. Even the most successful, South Africa, has major problems with corruption, has the highest level of inequality in the world and extremely has high unemployment and poverty.

The ongoing legacy of neoliberal policies and lack of funds for development has contributed to these low levels of economic development. Most of the governments borrowed from the BWIs in the 1960s and 1970s and have been indebted ever since. These countries have been trapped in an ongoing cycle of borrowing, debt servicing and implementing neoliberal policies. Market deregulation reinforced unequal trade policies, where unsubsidised African products had to compete with subsidised products from American and EU agribusinesses. Farmers' incomes were undermined at a time when the majority of the population in SSA earned their living from agriculture. Enforced privatisation of state assets transferred ownership to foreign companies and deregulation facilitated both legal (profits and debt servicing) and illegal financial outflows of capital. This capital flight was higher than the incoming aid and loans provided. Between 1970 and 2010, SSA was a net creditor to the rest of the world (Boyce & Ndikumana, 2012). There was a brief economic boom between 2000 and 2011 driven by Chinese demand for resources. High growth rates reflected 'catch up growth' as real GDP per capita had been falling for a long time before 2000 (*The Economist*, 2011). SSA continued to be the poorest region in the world. Capital flight also increased. According to Global Financial Integrity, between 2000 and 2014, SSA had the highest level of illicit financial flows as a percentage of GDP in the world (Clough, 2017). After the global financial crisis — primarily the consequence of deregulation of the US banking sector — demand from China contracted and SSA again experienced an economic downturn. The three largest economies, South Africa, Angola and Nigeria were hit the hardest. Current account deficits rose quickly along with foreign debt (Bond, 2017e).

SSA is experiencing the effects of rapidly changing climate even though its contribution to global carbon emissions has been negligible. SSA also suffers from a net loss of resources. Using the method of natural capital accounting, the WB estimated that SSA lost 12% of its natural capital in 2010 (WB, 2014a). Large scale environmental destruction occurred when dams were built and resources were extracted for export. Resource extraction physically destroys large areas. Mining pollutes the environment with toxic chemicals used to separate minerals from rock. Oil extraction is usually accompanied by oil spills that pollute the earth and waterways, and gas flaring that causes carbon emissions and air pollution. Another environmental hazard has been widespread deforestation. Forests are pulled down for the export of trees or for agribusinesses such as palm oil production. Wood from Africa is often illegally exported to China by private entrepreneurs. Deforestation also contributes to species extinction and produces carbon emissions. As the forests of Cameroon and DRC play a global role as carbon sinks their destruction has implications for the whole planet. The most recent environmental challenge for SSA has been the acceleration of foreign land acquisition since 2000, accompanied by the expansion of agribusinesses.

China, the US, the WB and the IMF have all been engaged in SSA since the 1950s. Both China and the US/BWIs supported and colluded with repressive leaders in the 20th century. Until recently, the influence of China was far less extensive than of the West. In the 20th century, China's interests were predominantly political, assisting communist movements, contributing to the civil wars in Angola and Mozambique and supporting socialist states with aid and loans. China in turn sought the support of African states to get a seat at the United Nations. After the Chinese departed, their aid programmes fell into disrepair. In the 1990s, China began acquiring resources and this demand stimulated an economic boom that lasted until 2011. After 2000, China rapidly expanded its economic interests in the region. It also began supplying more aid, but its lending far exceeded its aid. China's development assistance to SSA has been based on the principles of 'win-win' and 'non-interference'. China has allowed countries to retain their political sovereignty and has not imposed conditions for aid and loans. It has treated leaders with more respect than the West, it has allowed leaders to make their own decisions in the use of loans and aid, and also demonstrated this respect in repeated visits by leaders to the region. Chinese aid and development projects were based on knowledge gained from its own experience as a developing nation. China is more willing to listen to recipients and provide them with what they want, particularly infrastructure and agricultural assistance. It has established training and education programmes as well as sending large numbers of people to China for education. According to *China Daily*, China provided approximately 132,000 jobs in SSA between 2005 and 2016, three times the 44,000 provided by the US (Xiang Bo, 2017). Given the population of SSA is over a billion, both figures are insignificant. Projects investigated by the China–Africa Research Initiative (CARI) at John Hopkins concluded that though many projects had positive outcomes, as yet they have not been transformational or likely to provide templates for future successful projects (CARI, n.d.a). China has been criticised for bringing in Chinese labour to work on projects, but this is not the case everywhere. China's rationale is the lack of local expertise in some countries. China has a poor domestic record in labour rights, and the way the Chinese have treated African workers has led to occasional incidents of violence.

The US also became more interested in SSA during the Cold War as nations became independent. American interests were also political. The US wanted to prevent the spread of communism, keep countries within the capitalist system and protect American business interests. After 1945, American corporations, particularly the oil companies, increased their activities in the region. The WB began lending to SSA in the late 1950s and encouraged newly independent nations to borrow funds to stimulate economic development. The lenders and donors decided what projects they would fund. The US also provided aid and supported commercial lending SSA through US Exim Bank guarantees. Many loans were to totalitarian rulers who used the money to repress the population or stole it and sent it offshore. Such loans are 'odious' or illegitimate. Corporations also colluded with these leaders, providing much of the funds that were stolen either as taxes or bribes. The period of profligate lending ended in the 1970s with the global economic downturn and governments in SSA were left with large debt burdens that included the repayment of odious debt. The US/BWIs made any further finance (aid and loans) conditional on the implementation of structural adjustment programmes. These same conditions were adopted by the other members of the 'Washington Consensus': the Paris Club, the aid donors and private lenders. Countries had no alternative source of funds and were forced to comply. Countries that borrowed were forced to relinquish their political sovereignty and submit to onerous monitoring programmes. Neoliberal conditions were imposed on 38 nations in the region. For the 20 years after 1980 human development in the region stagnated. The privatisation of health, education, and later water were all detrimental to human development in SSA.

The WB and IMF are both undemocratic institutions where the US has the power of veto and the region of SSA is underrepresented. The fact that these institutions represent US interests was confirmed in the Meltzer report to the US Congress (2000). The relationships between the US, the BWIs and SSA have always been unequal and paternalistic. The economists at BWIs have always considered they knew what Africa needed in order to develop. Though the definition of those needs was modified each decade, once the US/BWIs embraced neoliberalism, this became their defining agenda. Neoliberal policies have held back human development and poverty reduction in SSA. The BWIs have also caused further harm by ignoring their own policies on good governance, worker rights and transparency (Easterley, 2007). Neoliberal policies have served western corporate and financial interests. The West gained access to cheap labour and resources, corporations purchased state assets cheaply and deregulation enabled tax avoidance and capital flight on a grand scale.

The most significant difference between China and the West has been the absence of conditions in China's aid and lending. Also, China does not have a military presence in the region, except as part of the UN forces. It has respected the wishes and priorities of the recipient governments. In 2001, China cancelled all of SSA's outstanding debt that had gone into default by 1999. It realised this debt was unpayable. China did not impose conditions (Brautigam, 2009). China has supplied more than $3 billion in debt relief since 2000, negotiating debt on a case-by-case basis rather than applying blanket conditions (Acker *et al.*, 2021). However, SSA's debt to China has steadily increased since 2010. By 2017, that debt to China ($83 billion) was 20% of its overall debt (Jubilee Debt Campaign, 2018). There has been little reporting of capital flight through tax avoidance and transfer pricing by Chinese companies; however, many transactions conducted through Hong Kong are not transparent and China's financial arrangements with governments are opaque. Chinese companies also benefit from the light regulatory environment that was imposed under structural adjustment programmes.

Since the 1990s, China's economic relations with SSA have been dominated by resource extraction. In the 1990s, China was criticised for its ties with rogue states, but in the next decade, it developed political and economic relationships with most nations in SSA. The acquisition of resources by China stimulated an economic boom and high growth rates in the resource rich countries in the period up until 2011. Local markets in Africa have been flooded with cheap Chinese goods, which has in some cases undermined local producers. Often these goods are all the local people can afford. China's policies have not created the economic stagnation caused by neoliberal policies. China also allows more products tariff-free entry than the US. China has also undertaken development projects to stimulate manufacturing and agricultural development. China allows more processing to take place within Africa, which brings benefits to the local economy. Resource purchasing has stimulated economic growth but did not raise standards of living because governments in resource-rich countries did not put the income from resources into social services. In some cases, China exchanged resources for infrastructure. This strategy avoided corruption and theft on the part of recipients. Resource exchanges became less common as China expanded its operations beyond the resource-rich countries. In recent years, more financial assistance has been supplied through aid and commercial loans. Chinese aid to SSA has been significantly less than its commercial loans. Until 2016, nations in SSA had not fallen heavily into debt to China but there were indications that debt would soon be a problem. China's contribution to capital flight is unknown. There have been no accusations in the international media of complicity with capital flight (assisting theft by corrupt politicians) or corporate tax avoidance but light regulations do make it easier to transfer money out of the region. There have been problems with Chinese projects: some projects have failed, work has sometimes been shoddy and corners have been cut. These problems are more prominent where local oversight is poor, as in the Democratic Republic of the Congo (Taylor, 2009). There have also been incidents of corporate corruption. More Chinese companies have been temporarily disbarred from tendering for WB projects than companies from elsewhere. China has brought economic benefits to SSA, but there is the prospect of future indebtedness and it is yet to be seen whether the Chinese loans and aid supplied without conditions have translated into economic and social development.

The relationship between the US/BWIs and SSA in the 20th century has been more of a 'win-lose' situation, with most of the benefits going to the US/BWIs and other members of the Washington Consensus while nations in SSA experienced two decades of social and economic stagnation (Structural Adjustment Participatory Review International Network (SAPRIN), 2004). Most of the benefits of the economic boom after 2000 were also lost to capital flight, and SSA has lost out in trading relations with the US. US trade with SSA has been dominated by oil. Oil is exempt from tariffs under the African Growth and Opportunity Act, bringing cheaper oil to US consumers, while agriculture products — the main exports of many SSA economies — are not exempt from tariffs, which protects US agribusinesses. The US is allowed to subsidise its agricultural products, which compete with African products where subsidies and tariffs have been removed. Many of the financial relationships between US/BWIs and SSA have been unequal. The WB has been the largest lender to SSA since the 20th century. SSA has been indebted since the late 1970s. Some of this debt was odious (made to repressive leaders), the result of profligate lending or aid projects that failed to meet projected goals. By the early 2000s, over 50% of SSA's debt was odious debt (Bond, 2006). SSA has been subject to neoliberal structural adjustment programmes since the late 1970s. The rationale for these programmes was that economic growth and development would generate surpluses for debt repayment. These surpluses failed to materialise and 38 nations in SSA became entrenched in servicing debt, borrowing and implementing neoliberal policies which continued to fail to produce results. Deregulation also enabled capital flight from the region equivalent to the incoming finance. An investigation of capital flight from 33 countries in SSA between 1970 and 2010 concluded that $814 billion (in US$ 2010) was lost to the continent. If compound interest was factored in, the amount would have been much higher. This amount far exceeded the $659 billion in aid plus the $309 billion in foreign investment ($968 billion in total) that entered the region. In real terms, for every dollar in external loans to SSA more than 50 cents flowed back out the same year. Most (72%) of the capital flight was from oil-rich countries ($591 billion). Capital flight increased after 2000 when oil prices increased. SSA is actually a net creditor to the rest of the world (Boyce & Ndikumana, 2012). A later investigation by Curtis concluded that in 2015 the 48 countries in SSA were net creditors to the rest of the world to the value of $41.3 billion. Africa countries received $161.6 billion that year (loans, personal remittances and aid in the form of grants) and $203 billion was taken from Africa (legal and illicit cash flows and debt repayment), while a further $29 billion was stolen in the traffic in illegal logs, fishing and wildlife (Curtis, 2017).

The key beneficiaries of these policies were the corporations and the multilateral and private lenders who earn interest from ongoing loans. Corporations bought state assets cheaply, avoided paying local taxes and bribed politicians, while light regulations increased profits and made it easier to transfer money (both legally and illegally) out of the region. Theft from loans, aid and money from resources, described as 'balance of payments deficits' enabled politicians to transfer vast amounts of money offshore through tax havens. Capital flight was dependent on an international system of 'enablers' (tax havens, banks and lawyers) to facilitate the process (Boyce & Ndikumana, 2011). Apart from capital flight, countries had little disposable income to spend on economic development as levels of debt servicing were so high. The WB complemented its lending role and extended its influence by becoming the 'knowledge bank' for development. It performed a dual role, both imposing policies and providing training to recipient country economists to enable them to implement those neoliberal policies. The policies included the emphasis on resource extraction, export-focused agriculture to earn revenue to service debt and borrowing for large-scale energy projects which also increased debt. Agricultural producers became more vulnerable to international prices, and because they were not producing for local consumption, food insecurity was increased.

From the 1980s onwards, the BWIs were subject to widespread international criticism because of the rising indebtedness in the developing world. The BWIs were pressured into establishing a debt relief programme, the Highly Indebted Poor Country Initiative (HIPCI), in 1996. Most of the countries in SSA qualified. The HIPCI had a long compliance period and had no impact until 2003. Debt relief was conditional on the implementation of neoliberal policies for seven years (later reduced to six years) and continued debt servicing during the compliance period. The amount of this servicing was worked out at such a high debt-to-GDP ratio there was little finance left to generate economic development, and economic stagnation was more likely to result. It was soon obvious that more debt relief was needed if countries were to achieve any of the MDGs. The Multilateral Debt Relief Initiative was established in 2005 to provide debt relief to countries indebted to the BWIs. To be eligible countries had to have met the HIPCI conditions. These programmes only provided temporary relief and the accompanying terms and conditions meant countries very soon accumulated more debt.

Donors' enthusiasm for aid programmes diminished in the 1990s after the end of the Cold War. The political motivation had gone and aid projects had a high rate of failure. The BWIs and US began promoting the private–public partnership as their latest development model. This fitted the neoliberal privatisation agenda. Corporations were seen as providing expertise and an entrepreneurial model. Possible contradictions between the profit agenda and provision of social services were not considered. The model was introduced into the energy and water sectors. These contradictions soon became apparent in the water sector where it was difficult to generate profits. The model also was applied to agriculture. After neglecting agriculture in the 20th century the public–private partnership (PPP) model was seen to be the key to transforming agriculture through the expansion of agribusinesses. This ushered in an era of accelerating land sales or 'land-grabbing'. Neoliberal policies remained on the agenda. They were included as conditions in the 2013 New Alliance for Food Security and Nutrition. African countries were offered public and private funds for signing agreements and forming partnerships with G8 countries and the private sector (usually multinational companies) (Monbiot, 2013).

Economic priorities and development have taken precedence over the environment in SSA in the past. By the 21st century, environmental issues have become a major concern. The carbon emissions behind the escalating climate crisis were generated outside of SSA but the effects there are already extreme. Though China is not responsible for the historical accumulation of emissions it is currently the largest producer of carbon emissions, and those emissions will continue to rise as long as China persists in building coal-fired power stations. The most recent position taken by China is that it will reach peak emissions in 2030 and it plans to carbon neutral before 2060. These pledges are insufficient to meet the Paris goal of 1.50° and is more likely to result in 3° degrees of warming. This alone will have a disastrous effect on SSA. In contrast, the US has contributed 20% of historical emissions and is currently the second largest producer of carbon emissions. It has pledged to be carbon neutral by 2050. Its proposed 2030 target is to reduce domestic emissions by 50–52%. This goal is considered 'almost sufficient' by Climate Action Tracker but will still not enable the Paris target of 1.5° to be reached. If all countries followed the US lead, the result will reach up to 3° of warming (Climate Action Tracker, n.d.).

Within SSA, China has played a central role in supplying the technology for solar energy. As SSA's emissions are relatively minor, this change will have little impact on global emissions but has the potential to solve many of the energy needs of a large percentage of the population who are currently without power. China has also been a funder of large dams which are a source of clean energy but these have come at a high environmental cost. China has a weak domestic record on environmental protection and has a similar record in SSA. Chinese contractors have built dams with no regard for environmental protection. China has also continued to fund coal-burning power stations. Chinese private entrepreneurs have a major impact on the forestry sector and are responsible for much of the deforestation occurring in SSA. Deforestation is a major problem where governments are weak, particularly in Cameroon and DRC. Deforestation is accompanied by rapid species extinction. China is making positive contributions in other areas. Banning the sale of ivory has reduced the slaughter of elephants for ivory and China is not prominent in the current surge of land grabbing in SSA.

The US/BWIs have extensive environmental policies but there have been many instances where environmental and social policies have been ignored. The WB has also continued funding fossil fuel projects. One of its notorious projects was the Eskom power project in South Africa. The project's two coal-fired power stations were anticipated as being the 3rd and 4th largest coal-fired power plants in the world (Khumalo, 2018). South Africa was already the largest producer of carbon emissions on the continent. Both the US and the International Finance Corporation have continued to fund coal-burning plants. Both President Obama and the WB pledged to end funding for coal-burning plants in 2013, but an investigation three years later found that these investments were continuing in SSA (Turner, 2016). The WB also has been the major lender for dams in SSA. Both the WB and IMF have good environmental and social protection policies but have ignored them for decades. Though the WB established the independent high-level World Commission on Dams to investigate the development impact of dams, it has steadfastly refused to implement the recommendations of its 2000 report. The Commission identified that the WB lacked the necessary tools to even address the social and environmental legacies of its projects. In SSA the World Bank's Lesotho Highlands Water Project and the Bujagali dam have been identified as seriously flawed (International Rivers, 2007). The WB announced in 2003 that 'high-risk, high-reward' projects would be undertaken and it would resume funding large dam projects. This was a declaration and further confirmation that profits were being prioritized over policy. Another recent trend in Africa has been the acceleration of foreign land grabbing. The US and the WB are also encouraging land sales and the commercialisation of agriculture by foreign agribusinesses which fits well with their PPP model.

The US/BWIs have had more impact on the people of SSA than China. The US continues to dominate the international organizations the WB and IMF and the triad have undermined the political sovereignty of most of the nations in SSA by imposing neoliberal policies as loan and aid conditions. The privatisation of health and education and the removal of agricultural subsidies has held back human development. The US has expanded its military presence throughout the region. Both the US/BWIs and China can be accused of propping up repressive governments in states categorized as 'fragile' or defined as being 'resource cursed'. China has offered more development assistance in education and training and the health sector while US aid has been concentrated in the health sector and works through partnerships with pharmaceutical companies. The US has provided little education and training. The US is also accused of supplying high levels of 'phantom aid', aid in the form of debt relief that is merely an accounting exercise, or aid that benefits US corporations more than the recipients.

China has been economically active in SSA only since the 1990s when it began importing raw materials. That engagement expanded after 2000 and by 2010 China had a presence in most countries in the region. In a very short space of time, China seemed to be 'everywhere' in Africa. China has used a variety of approaches in SSA including exchanges of resources for infrastructure, aid and loans. After 2010, there was an increase in lending as countries felt the effects of the economic downturn. China's loans continued to be without the stringent conditions of the West. By 2017, SSA's debt to China was only 20% of that of the West (Jubilee Debt Campaign, 2018). China is also willing to process materials and supply more jobs. The IMF judged the impact of China on SSA as being mostly beneficial (2013). The economic impact of the US/BWIs on SSA has been much longer than China's and has been more far-reaching. Trade policies have disadvantaged nations in SSA and they have been also burdened by debt and debt servicing for the last 40 years. Neoliberal economic policies have been imposed and they have not stimulated economic development. Instead, the main impact of deregulation has been to facilitate illegal flight of capital either through corporate tax avoidance or 'balance of payments leakages', enabling theft by politicians. Capital flight (including legal capital in the form of debt servicing and corporate profits) was equivalent to total aid and loans to the region between 1970 and

2010. Countries have lacked the finance to fund their own development. Another issue is the very high failure rate in development projects funded by the WB, thus burdening countries with more debt and not contributing to economic development. The environmental impact of the activities of both China and the US/BWIs has been damaging to SSA. The contributions of both China and the US to contemporary carbon emissions and the climate crisis have far-reaching impacts in SSA. Both China and the WB have funded coal projects in SSA. China has a poor domestic track record of environmental protection and environmental considerations have been ignored in many of its large infrastructure projects. The WB has many environmental and social protection policies in place, but external reviews have repeatedly found the policies have been ignored. Both Chinese and the US companies engaged in resource extraction have caused widespread devastation and pollution. Neither has received much criticism in international media. It is still too soon to say whether China's condition-free loans and assistance have made a better contribution to development in SSA than the loans, aid and assistance from the US and BWIs.

References

Acemoglu, D., Naidu, S., Robinson, J. A. & Restrepo, P. (2014) Democracy causes economic development. *VOX, CEPR*. [Online] Available from: http://www.voxeu.org/article/democracy-and-growth-new-evidence [Accessed 12th August 2018].

Acker, K., Brautigam, D. & Yufang, H. (2021) Debt relief with Chinese characteristics. *China-Africa Research Initiative*. [Online] Available from: https://mronline.org/2021/03/03/debt-relief-with-chinese-characteristics/ [Accessed 27th December 2021].

ActionAid International. (2005) *Real Aid: An Agenda for Making Aid Work*. [Online] Available from: https://actionaid.org/publications/2005/real-aid-agenda-making-aid-work [Accessed 21st June 2020].

Adams, P. (2015) Africa debt rising. *Africa Research Institute*. [Online] Available from: https://www.africaresearchinstitute.org/publications/africa-debt-rising-2/ [Accessed 8th January 2022].

Adow, M. (2014) Out of Africa: The great money migration. *Aljazeera*. [Online] Available from: https://www.aljazeera.com/indepth/features/2014/04/africa-hobbled-capital-flight-20144296537621865.html [Accessed 28th May 2019].

Africa and Middle East (AfricaME). (2017) *Sub-Saharan Africa's Most Ddebt-Laden Nations*. [Online] Available from: http://africa-me.com/sub-saharan-africas-debt-laden-nations [Accessed 19th May 2017].

Africa Research Institute. (2012) Between extremes: China and Africa. *Briefing Note 1202*. [Online] Available from: www.africaresearchinstitute.org [Accessed 24th January 2013].

AfricaFocus. (2004) *USA/Africa: Oil and Transparency*. [Online] Available from: http://www.africafocus.org/docs04/eq0407.php [Accessed 23rd November 2020].

AidWatch. (2013) *A Brief History of AID*. [Online] Available from: http://aidwatch.org.au/where-is-your-aid-money-going/what-is-aid/a-brief-history-of-aid [Accessed 4th June 2013].

Ajayi, S. I. & Khan, M. S. (Eds.). (2000) External debt and capital flight in Sub-Saharan Africa. *IMF*. Online] Available from: https://www.imf.org/external/pubs/nft/2000/extdebt/index.htm [Accessed 16th July 2019].

Albert, E. (2017) China in Africa: Backgrounder. *Council on Foreign Relations*. [Online] Available from: https://www.cfr.org/backgrounder/china-africa [Accessed 7th August 2017].

Allen, K. (2017) China's growth slips to slowest pace for 26 years. *The Guardian*. [Online] Available from: https://www.theguardian.com/business/2017/jan/20/chinese-economic-growth-dips-to-67-the-slowest-for-26-years [Accessed 8th August 2017].

Allison, G. (2018) Beijing's anti-poverty drive has lessons for all. *China Daily*. [Online] Available from: https://www.telegraph.co.uk/china-watch/society/decreasing-chinas-poverty/ [Accessed 14th July 2019].

Amanthis, J. (2012a) Ghana rejects water privatization. *Pambazuka News*. [Online] Available from: http://www.onthecommons.org/magazine/ghana-rejects-water-privatization#sthash.SCrkgPBt.dpbs [Accessed 25th February 2019].

Amanthis, J. (2012b) *How the Private Sector Didn't Solve Ghana's Water Problems*. [Online] Available from: https://towardfreedom.org/story/archives/africa-archives/how-the-private-sector-didnt-solve-ghanas-water-crisis/ [Accessed 18th June 2020].

Amoding, M. & Wass, G. (2015) Thorns among the roses. A Cross-country analysis of human rights issues in flower farms in East Africa. *IPIS*. [Online] Available from: https://ipisresearch.be/publication/thorns-amongst-the-roses-a-cross-country-analysis-of-human-rights-issues-in-flower-farms-in-east-africa/ [Accessed 3rd June 2020].

Amusa, K., Monkam, N. & Viegi, N. (2017) How US aid to Africa has changed in the wake of China's growing influence. *The Conversation*. [Online] Available from: https://www.huffpost.com/entry/how-us-aid-to-africa-has_b_9803626 [Accessed 17th June 2020].

Anyinam, C. (1994) *Spatial Implications of Structural Adjustment Programmes in Ghana*. [Online] Available from: doi:10.1111/j.1467-9663.1994.tb00703.x [Accessed 3rd June 2020].

Areddy, J. T. (2014) China touts $14.4 billion in foreign aid, half of which went to Africa. *Wall Street Journal*. [Online] Available from: https://blogs.wsj.com/chinarealtime/2014/07/10/china-touts-14-4-billion-in-foreign-aid-half-of-which-went-to-africa/ [Accessed 29th May 2020].

Aroh, K. N., Eze, C. L., Gobo, A. E., Harry, I. M., Ubong, I. U. & Umo-Otong, J. C. (2010) Oil spill incidents and pipeline vandalization in Nigeria: Impact on public health and negation to attainment of Millennium Development Goal: The Ishiagu example. *Disaster Prevention and Management*. 19 (1). [Online] Available from: https://www.emerald.com/insight/content/doi/10.1108/09653561011022153/full/html [Accessed 28th June 2020].

Asanzi, A. (2016) The Grand Inga — A false solution to energy poverty. *International Rivers*. [Online] Available from: https://archive.internationalrivers.org/blogs/337/the-grand-inga-a-false-solution-to-energy-poverty [Accessed 11th October 2021].

AusAID (Australian Government Aid Programme). (2012) *Sub-Saharan Africa*. [Online] Available from: http://www.ausaid.gov.au/country/africa/sub-saharan-africa.cfm [Accessed 23rd April 2012].

Australian Treasury. (2018) *China's Stimulus Package.* [Online] Available from: https://treasury.gov.au/publication/chinese-macroeconomic-management-through-the-crisis-and-beyond/2011-01-chinese-macroeconomic-management-through-the-crisis-and-beyond/4-chinas-stimulus-package/ [Accessed 5th November 2018].

AVERT. (2018) *HIV and AIDs in East and Southern Africa: Regional Overview.* [Online] Available from: https://www.avert.org/professionals/hiv-around-world/sub-saharan-africa/overview [Accessed 1st July 2017].

Avery, S. (2018) How Ethiopia and Kenya have put a world heritage site in danger. *The Conversation.* [Online] Available from: https://theconversation.com/how-ethiopia-and-kenya-have-put-a-world-heritage-site-in-danger-99458 [Accessed 29th May 2020].

Ayittey, G. (1994) *Africa Betrayed.* London, Palgrave Macmillan.

Baan, W., Gao, P., Sha, S. & Zipser, D. (2016) *Finding the Fast Lane: Emerging Trends in China's Auto Market.* McKinsey and Company. [Online] Available from: https://www.mckinsey.com/industries/automotive-and-assembly/our-insights/finding-the-fast-lane-emerging-trends-in-chinas-auto-market [Accessed 22nd May 2020].

Babalola, O. O., Fashola, M. O. & Ngole-Jeme, V. M. (2016) Heavy metal pollution from gold mines: Environmental effects and bacterial strategies for resistance, *International Journal of Environment Research Public Health.* 13 (11), 1047. [Online] Available from: doi:10.3390/ijerph13111047 [Accessed 23rd June 2020].

Badgley, C. (2010) *Pipeline: Cameroon Earns 277.6 Million U.S. Dollars in Seven Years.* [Online] Available from: http://www.pipelinedreams.org/2010/12/pipeline-cameroon-earns-277-6-million-u-s-dollars-in-seven-years/ [Accessed 16th June 2020].

Badgley, C. (2013) *Better Late than Never: Cameroon Renegotiates Pipeline Transit Fees.* [Online] Available from: https://www.pipelinedreams.org/tag/cnpc/ [Accessed 2nd July 2020].

Baiyu, G. (2020) Vast river diversion plan afoot in western China. *China Dialogue.* [Online] Available from: https://chinadialogue.net/en/nature/11762-vast-river-diversion-plan-afoot-in-western-china-2/ [Accessed 17th March 2020].

Baker, L. & Wei, S. (2017) *China's Involvement in South Africa's Wind and Solar PV Industries.* Working Paper No. 2017/15. China-Africa Research Initiative, School of Advanced International Studies, Johns Hopkins University, Washington, DC. [Online] Available from: http://www.sais-cari.org/publications [Accessed 29th May 2020].

Balding, C. (2018) Chinese savers won't save China, Households have less money to spend than many think. *Bloomberg Opinion.* [Online] Available from: https://www.bloomberg.com/opinion/articles/2018-07-08/chinese-savers-won-t-save-the-chinese-economy [Accessed 5th June 2020].

Bandow, D. (2012) Shut down the World Bank: Jim Yong Kim should be its last President. *Forbes.* [Online] Available from: https://www.forbes.com/sites/dougbandow/2012/07/23/shut-down-the-world-bank-jin-yong-kim-should-be-its-last-president/#6aff1e7026a6 [Accessed 6th August 2020].

Barlow, M. (2001) *Blue Gold: The Global Water Crisis and the Commodification of the World's Water Supply.* [Online] Available from: https://www.ircwash.org/sites/default/files/Barlow-2001-Blue.pdf [Accessed 25th July 2020].

Barlow, M. (2011) *Blue Future*. New York, New Press.

Barlow, M. & Clarke, T. (2004a) Water privatization. *Polaris Institute*. [Online] Available from: https://www.globalpolicy.org/component/content/article/209/43398.html [Accessed 30th July 2018].

Barlow, M. & Clarke, T. (2004b) Water privatization: The World Bank's latest market fantasy. *CADTM*. [Online] Available from: http://www.cadtm.org/spip.php?page=imprimer&id_article=391 [Accessed 16th June 2020].

Barr, C. (2017) Inequality index: Where are the world's most unequal countries? *The Guardian*. [Online] Available from: https://www.theguardian.com/inequality/datablog/2017/apr/26/inequality-index-where-are-the-worlds-most-unequal-countries [Accessed 30th June 2017].

Barrett, C. B. (2006) Food aid's intended and unintended consequences. *Background Paper for FAO State of Food and Agriculture* (2006) [Online] Available from: http://barrett.dyson.cornell.edu/files/papers/MixedEffectsv2Mar2006.pdf [Accessed 21st June 2020].

Basel Action Network (BAN). (2019) *Global Ban on Exporting Hazardous Waste to Developing Countries Becomes Law*. [Online] Available from: https://www.ban.org/news/2019/9/8/global-ban-on-exporting-hazardous-waste-to-developing-countries-becomes-law [Accessed 16th June 2020].

Basulto, D. (2013) Apple: Designed in California, made in China? *Washington Post*. [Online] Available from: http://www.washingtonpost.com/blogs/innovations/post/apple-designed-in-california-made-in-china/2013/01/25/7f5318c4-66fb-11e2-85f5-a8a9228e55e7_blog.html [Accessed 14th January 2015].

Baumgartner, F., La Pira, T. & Herschel, T. (2008) *The Structure of Washington Lobbying Networks: Mapping the Ties that Bind*. [Online] Available from: https://www.unc.edu/~fbaum/papers/MPSA08_Baum_LaPira_Thomas.pdf [Accessed 17th September 2018].

BBC. (2012) *Zambian Miners Kill Chinese Manager After Pay Protest*. [Online] Available from: http://www.bbc.com/news/world-africa-19135435 [Accessed 11th August 2017].

BBC. (2016) *Four More Ways the CIA has Meddled in Africa*. [Online] Available from: https://www.bbc.com/news/world-africa-36303327 [Accessed 16th June 2020].

BBC News. (2008) *China Hostages Killed in Sudan*. [Online] Available from: http://news.bbc.co.uk/2/hi/7694106.stm [Accessed 19th August 2017].

BBC News. (2011) *Hedge Funds 'Grabbing Land' in Africa*. [Online] Available from: http://www.bbc.co.uk/news/world-africa-13688683?print=true [Accessed 23rd July 2013].

BBC News. (2016) *China's Grim History of Industrial Accidents*. [Online] Available from: http://www.bbc.com/news/world-asia-china-35149263 [Accessed 12th October 2017].

BBC World News. (2006) *Zambia Overwhelmed by Free Health Care*. [Online] Available from: http://news.bbc.co.uk/2/hi/africa/4883062.stm [Accessed 23rd July 2020].

BBC World News. (2012) *The World Debate*. [Online] Available from: http://www.bbc.co.uk/programmes/p00j2pq1 [Accessed 3rd December 2012].

BBC World News. (2014) *China to Scrap Millions of Cars to Improve Air Quality*. [Online] Available from: http://www.bbc.com/news/business-27583404 [Accessed 8th August 2017].

BBC World News. (2015) *The Travel Show: China Travel Show Special with Benjamin Zand*. [Online] Available from: http://www.bbc.co.uk/programmes/n3csy4df [Accessed 16th February 2016].

Beegle, K., Christianensen, L., Dabalen, A. & Gaddis, I. (2016) Poverty in a rising Africa. *World Bank Group*. [Online] Available from: https://openknowledge.worldbank.org/handle/10986/22575 [Accessed 26th August 2018].

Bello, W. (2000) *Meltzer Report on Bretton Woods Twins Builds Case for Abolition But Hesitates*, *Focus on Trade*, 48. [Online] Available from: https://www.tni.org/en/article/meltzer-report-on-bretton-woods-twins. [Accessed 17th January 2022].

Bello, W. (2005) Jurassic Fund: Should developing countries push to decommission the IMF? *Transnational Institute*. [Online] Available from: https://www.tni.org/my/node/5707 [Accessed 5th December 2021].

Bello, W. (2008) *Destroying African Agriculture*. [Online] Available from: http://fpif.org/destroying_african_agriculture/ [Accessed 1st February 2017].

Bello, W. & Guttal, S. (2006) The limits of reform: The Wolfensohn era at the World Bank. *Race & Class*. 47 (3), 68–81. [Online] Available from: doi:10.1177/0306396806061087 [Accessed 20th June 2020].

Birdsall, N. & Moss, T. (2006) Nigerian debt relief. *Center for Global Development*. [Online] Available from: https://www.cgdev.org/topics/nigerian-debt-relief [Accessed 20th June 2020].

Biron, C. L. (2013) *IFC Under Fire on Environmental, Social Safeguards*. [Online] Available from: https://www.globalpolicy.org/globalization/globalization-of-the-eco…fc-under-fire-on-environment-social-safeguards.html?itemid=id#43499 [Accessed 6th November 2018].

Bissio, R. (2014) *Hold the Powerful to Account*. [Online] Available from: http://www.globalpolicy.org/component/content/article/252-the-milleni...-monitoring-and-accountability-framework-for-development-agenda.html [Accessed 10th May 2014].

Blenchard, B. (2018) China wins back Burkina Faso and urges Taiwan's last ally to follow. *Reuters*. [Online] Available from: https://www.reuters.com/article/us-china-burkina/china-wins-back-burkina-faso-urges-taiwans-last-african-ally-to-follow-idUSKCN1IR09W [Accessed 20th November 2018].

Bloomberg News. (2013) *Chinese Anger Over Pollution Becomes Main Cause of Social Unrest*. [Online] Available from: http://www.bloomberg.com/news/articles/2013-03-06/pollution-passes-land-grievances-as-main-spark-of-china-protests [Accessed 8th September 2020].

Bloomberg News. (2017) *China Car Sales Climb at Fast Pace in 3 Years on Tax Cut*. [Online] Available from: https://www.bloomberg.com/news/articles/2017-01-10/china-car-sales-rise-16-in-2016-on-tax-cut-for-smaller-autos [Accessed 9th September 2017].

Böhm, S. & Dabhi, S. (Eds.). (2009) Upsetting the offset: The political economy of carbon markets. *Mayfly Books*. [Online] Available from: http://mayflybooks.org/?p=206 [Accessed 8th January 2022].

Bolton, G. (2008) *Aid and Other Dirty Business*. London, Edbury Press.

Bond, P. (2006) *Looting Africa: The Economics of Exploitation*. Pietermaritzburg, University of KwaZulu-Natal Press and London, Zed Books.

Bond, P. (2007) *Civil Society and Wolfowitz's World Bank: Reform or Rejection Revisited?* [Online] Available from: http://www.cadtm.org/Civil-society-and-Wolfowitz-s [Accessed 13th June 2020].

Bond, P. (2012) The poor pay the electricity bill of the world's largest mining company. *Ejolt*. [Online] Available from: http://www.ejolt.org/2012/10/in-south-africa-the-poor-pay-the-electricity-bill-of-the-worlds-largest-mining-company/ [Accessed 25th July 2025].

Bond, P. (2014a) The 'World Versus Bank' seen from South Africa. *Counterpunch*. [Online] Available from: https://www.counterpunch.org/2014/10/10/the-world-versus-bank-seen-from-south-africa/ [Accessed 18th March 2019].

Bond, P. (2014b) The 'World Versus Bank' seen from South Africa. *Pambazuka*. [Online] Available from: https://www.pambazuka.org/global-south/world-versus-bank-seen-south-africa [Accessed 12th October 2021].

Bond, P. (2017a) Commons victories in South Africa. In: Westra, R., Albritton, R. & Jeong, S. (eds.) *Varieties of Alternative Economic Systems: Practical Utopias for an Age of Global Crisis and Austerity*. London, Routledge.

Bond, P. (2017b) 'Africa Rising' in retreat. *Committee for the Abolition of Illegitimate Debt (CADTM)*. [Online] Available from: http://www.cadtm.org/Africa-Rising-in-retreat-Signs-of3 [Accessed 2nd December 2021].

Bond, P. (2017c) The BRICS re-scramble Africa. In: Westra, R. (ed.) *The Political Economy of Emerging Markets: Varieties of BRICS in the Age of Global Crises and Austerity*, London, Routledge.

Bond, P. (2017d) Uneven development and resource extractivism in Africa. In: C. Spash (ed.) *Ecological Economics: Nature and Society*. New York, Palgrave Macmillan.

Bond, P. (2017e) 'Africa Rising' in retreat: Signs of new resistances. *Pambazuka*. [Online] Available from: https://www.pambazuka.org/global-south/'africa-rising'-retreat-signs-new-resistances [Accessed 3rd January 2022].

Bond, P. (2017f) Obsolete economic ideas and personal corruption are closely linked in Africa. *American Herald Tribune*. (Interview by Mohsen Abdelmoumen).

Bond, P. (2018) Sub-imperial ecosystem management in Africa: Continental implications of South African environmental injustices. In: Holifield, R., Chakraborty, J. & Walker, G. (eds.) *Handbook of Environmental Justice*. New York, Routledge. [Online] Available from: https://www.routledge.com/The-Routledge-Handbook-of-Environmental-Justice/Holifield-Chakraborty-Walker/p/book/9781138932821.

Bond, P. (2018a) South African and global governance generated in conflict from above and below. In: Everatt, D. (ed.) *Governance in South Africa*. Johannesburg, Wits University Press.

Bond, P. (2018b) African uprisings, labour and ideology in an era of renewed economic crisis. In: Poku, N. & Whitman, J. (eds.) *Africa in the Age of Neoliberalism*. London, Earthscan.

Bonney, N. (2016) Life after Kony: How Uganda's women are rebuilding their lives. *The Guardian*. [Online] Available from: www.theguardian.com/world/2016/aug/02/ life-after-joseph-kony-uganda-women-rebuilding-lives-child-soldiers [Accessed 1st June 2020].

Boseley, S. (2008) Mbeki Aids denial 'caused 300,000 deaths.' *The Guardian*. [Online] Available from: https://www.theguardian.com/world/2008/nov/26/aids-south-africa [Accessed 10th July 2019.]

Bosshard, P. (2002) The World Bank's next white elephant. *The Observer*. [Online] Available from: http://observer.guardian.co.uk/worldview/story/0,,742145,00.html [Accessed 23rd June 2020].

Bosshard, P. (2006) *China Conquers Africa's Hydropower Market*. [Online] Available from: https://www.internationalrivers.org/resources/china-conquers-africa's-hydro power-market-1800 [Accessed 22nd November 2018].

Bosshard, P. (2007) China's role in financing infrastructure in Africa. *International Rivers Network*. [Online] Available from: http://asiandrivers.open.ac.uk/ChinaExim BankAfrica.pdf [Accessed 17th January 2022].

Bosshard, P. (2008) China's environmental footprint in Africa. *Pambazuka News*. [Online] Available from: https://www.pambazuka.org/land-environment/china's-environmental-footprint-africa [Accessed 17th September 2017].

Bosshard, P. (2013a) The World Bank returns to big dams. *International Rivers*. [Online] Available from: http://www.internationalrivers.org/resources/world-bank-returns-to-big-dams-8077 [Accessed 4th January 2015].

Bosshard, P. (2013b) The World Bank is bringing back big, bad dams. *The Guardian*. [Online] Available from: https://www.theguardian.com/environment/blog/2013/jul/16/world-bank-dams-africa [Accessed 18th June 2020].

Bosshard, P. (2016) *Setting the World Bank President Straight on Large Dams*. [Online] Available from: https://www.internationalrivers.org/blogs/227/setting-the-world-bank-president-straight-on-large-dams [Accessed 16th June 2020].

Bossoni, B. (2011) At the shrink's bed: The IMF, the global crisis and the Independent Evaluation Office report. *VOXEU, CEPR*. [Online] Available from: https://voxeu.org/article/imf-s-psychodrama-independent-evaluation-office-report [Accessed 4th December 2021].

Boston Consulting Group. (2012) *Global Wealth 2012: The Battle to Regain Strength*. [Online] Available from: http://piketty.pse.ens.fr/files/BCG2012.pdf [Accessed 22nd May 2020].

Boyce, J. & Ndikumana, L. (2011) *African's Odious Debts: How Foreign Loans and Capital Flight Bled a Continent*. London, Zed Books.

Boyce, J. & Ndikumana, L. (2012) Capital flight from Sub-Saharan African Countries: Updated estimates, 1970–2010. *Political Economy Research Institute (PERI)*. [Online] Available from: https://peri.umass.edu/publication/item/492-capital-flight-from-sub-saharan-african-countries-updated-estimates-1970-2010 [Accessed 22nd November 2021].

Bradlow, D. (2019) An IMF that works for Africa. *Global Governance Project*. [Online] Available from: https://www.globalgovernanceproject.org/an-imf-that-works-for-africa/ [Accessed 9th December 2021].

Brady, D. (2019) Theories of the causes of poverty. *Annual Review of Sociology*. 45, 155–175. [Online] Available from: https://www.annualreviews.org/doi/10.1146/annurev-soc-073018-022550 [Accessed 18th August 2019].

Branigan, T. (2014) Chinese premier declares war on pollution in economic overhaul. *The Guardian*. [Online] Available from: https://www.theguardian.com/world/2014/mar/05/china-pollution-economic-reform-growth-target [Accessed 12th October 2016].

Branigan, T. & Taylor, L. (2014) US and China strike deal on carbon cuts in push for global climate change pact. *The Guardian*. [Online] Available from: https://www.

theguardian.com/environment/2014/nov/12/china-and-us-make-carbon-pledge [Accessed 29th July 2020].

Brautigam, D. (2009) *Dragon's Gift: The Real Story of China in Africa*. Oxford and New York, Oxford University Press.

Brautigam, D. (2009a) China's engagement in African agriculture: 'Down to the Countryside.' *China Quarterly*. 199. [Online] Available from: 10.1017/S0305741009990166 [Accessed 31st July 2020].

Brautigam, D. (2010) *China in Africa: The Real Story: Digging into the Myths and Realities*. [Online] Available from: http://www.chinaafricarealstory.com/2010/09/how-many-africans-are-studying-in-china.html [Accessed 10th June 2011].

Brautigam, D. (2011) *Testimony on China's Growing Role in Africa Before the United States*. [Online] Available from: https://static1.squarespace.com/static/5652847de4b033f56d2bdc29/t/5b75ecb0c2241b9d47a6f6bb/1534454961263/Chinese+Geese+WP+-+V2+.pdfs Senate Committee on Foreign Relations Subcommittee on African Affairs [Accessed 22nd January 2013].

Brautigam, D. (2013) *Rubbery Numbers for Chinese Aid to Africa*. [Online] Available from: http://www.chinaafricarealstory.com/2013/04/rubbery-numbers-on-chinese-aid.html [Accessed 24th May 2019].

Brautigam, D. (2015) *Will Africa Feed China?* New York, Oxford University Press.

Brautigam, D. (2018) China's FOCAC financial package for Africa 2018: Four Facts. *China-Africa Research Initiative*. [Online] Available from: http://www.chinaafrica realstory.com/2018/09/chinas-focac-financial-package-for.html [Accessed 22nd November 2018].

Brautigam, D. & Hwang, J. (2016) *Eastern Promises: New data on Chinese Loans in Africa, 2000 to 2014*, SAIS China-Africa Research Initiative Briefing Paper No. 4. [Online] Available from: https://static1.squarespace.com/static/5652847de4b033f56d2bdc29/t/58ac91ede6f2e1f64a20d11a/1487704559189/ea [Accessed 24th May 2019].

Brautigam, D. & Tang, X. (2011) African Shenzhen: China's special economic zones in Africa. *The Journal of Modern African Studies*. 49 (1), 27–54. [Online] Available from: https://www.jstor.org/stable/23018877 [Accessed 11th June 2019].

Brautigam, D., Hwang, J. & Wang, L. (2015) Chinese financed hydropower projects in Sub Saharan Africa. *Working Paper 8. China Africa Research Initiative (CARI)*. [Online] Available from: https://saiscari.files.wordpress.com/2014/10/sais-cari-brief-8-april-2015-website.pdf [Accessed 11th January 2021].

Brautigam, D., Tang, X. & Xia, Y. (2018) *What Kinds of Chinese 'Flying Geese' are Flying to Africa?* Evidence from Chinese manufacturing firms, Working Paper 17. China Africa Research Initiative (CARI). [Online] Available from: https://static1.square space.com/static/5652847de4b033f56d2bdc29/t/5b75ecb0c2241b9d47a6f6bb/1534454961263/Chin [Accessed 29th May 2020].

Bread for All. (2020) *The Liberian Socfin Plantation SRC Opts Out of Conflict Resolution Process*. [Online] Available from: https://breadforall.ch/the-liberian-socfin-plantation-src-opts-out-of-conflict-resolution-process/ [Accessed 13th October 2021].

Breene, K. (2016) 7 things to know about China's economy. *World Economic Forum*. [Online] Available from: https://www.weforum.org/agenda/2016/06/7-things-to-know-about-chinas-economy/ [Accessed 21st July 2019].

Breeze, V. & Moore, N. (2017) *Why African Students are Choosing China*. [Online] Available from https://www.usnews.com/news/best-countries/articles/2017-06-29/china-second-most-popular-country-for-african-students [Accessed 18th September 2017].

Bretton Woods Project. (2006) *IFC Backs Controversial Ghana Gold Mine*. [Online] Available from: https://www.brettonwoodsproject.org/2006/04/art-531853/ [Accessed 16th June 2020].

Bretton Woods Project. (2010) *Undermining Development? IFIs' Role in Extractive Industries in Disarray*. [Online] Available from: https://www.brettonwoodsproject.org/2010/09/art-566641/ [Accessed 30th October 2021].

Bretton Woods Project. (2011a) *China and the World Bank*. [Online] Available from: https://www.brettonwoodsproject.org/2011/09/art-568894/ [Accessed 22nd May 2020].

Bretton Woods Project. (2011b) *World Bank Increases Extractives Lending Despite Human Rights Abuses*. [Online] Available from: https://www.brettonwoodsproject.org/2011/04/art-567950/ [Accessed 30th October 2021].

Bretton Woods Project. (2011c) *World Bank Policies 'enabling' African Land Grab*. [Online] Available from: https://www.brettonwoodsproject.org/2011/09/art-568890/ [Accessed 19th November 2021].

Bretton Woods Project. (2012a) *The World Bank and Extractives: A Rich Seam of Controversy*. [Online] Available from: https://www.brettonwoodsproject.org/2012/02/art-569560/ [Accessed 30th October 2021].

Bretton Woods Project. (2012b) *World Bank Views on Poverty 'econocentric.'* [Online] Available from: https://www.brettonwoodsproject.org/2012/04/art-569952/ [Accessed 16th June 2020].

Bretton Woods Project. (2012c) *World Bank and Climate Change, Cloudy Forecast for Policy Reform*. [Online] Available from: https://www.brettonwoodsproject.org/2012/12/art-571584/ [Accessed 6th August 2020].

Bretton Woods Project. (2014) *Scaling up Renewable Energy Program* (SREP). [Online] Available from: https://www.brettonwoodsproject.org/2014/11/scaling-renewable-energy-program-srep-3/ [Accessed 9th November 2021].

Bretton Woods Project. (2017) *IFC Investments Implicated in Land Grabs in Africa*. [Online] Available from: https://www.brettonwoodsproject.org/2017/07/ifc-investments-implicated-land-grabs-africa/ [Accessed 18th November 2021].

Bretton Woods Project. (2019) *What are the Main Criticisms of the World Bank and the IMF?* [Online] Available from: https://www.brettonwoodsproject.org/2019/06/what-are-the-main-criticisms-of-the-world-bank-and-the-imf/ [Accessed 16th June 2020].

Bretton Woods Project. (2019a) *The IMF & Climate Change: Can the Fund Help Countries Avoid a 'Climate Minsky Moment'?* [Online] Available from: https://www.brettonwoodsproject.org/2019/10/the-imf-climate-change-can-the-fund-help-countries-avoid-a-climate-minsky-moment/ [Accessed 3rd October 2020].

Briody, D. (2004) *The Halliburton Agenda: The Politics of Oil and Money*. New Jersey, John Wiley & Sons.

Brown, L. R. (2006) *Plan B 2.0: Rescuing a Planet under Stress and a Civilization in Trouble*. New York, W.W. Norton & Company.

Brown, L. R. (2009) *Plan B 4.0: Mobilizing to Save Civilization*. New York, W.W. Norton & Company and the Earth Institute.

Brown, L. R. (2011) *World on the Edge*. New York, W.W. Norton and Company.

Buckley, C. (2015) China burns much more coal than reported. *NY Times*. [Online] Available from: https://www.nytimes.com/2015/11/04/world/asia/china-burns-much-more-coal-than-reported-complicating-climate-talks.html [Accessed 5th November 2018].

Burch, D., Capp, J. & Murphy, S. (2012) Cereal secrets. The world's largest grain traders and global agriculture. *Oxfam*. [Online] Available from: https://www-cdn.oxfam.org/s3fs-public/file_attachments/rr-cereal-secrets-grain-traders-agriculture-30082012-en_4.pdf [Accessed 23rd June 2020].

Burnett, T. & Games, A. (2007) *Who Really Runs the World? The War Between Globalization and Democracy*. New York, Conspiracy Books.

Business and Human Rights Resource Centre. (n.d.) *Apartheid Reparations Lawsuits (re South Africa)*. [Online] Available from: https://www.business-humanrights.org/en/apartheid-reparations-lawsuits-re-so-africa?page=5 [Accessed 19th March 2019].

Cairncross, E. & Kisting, S. K. (2016) Platinum and gold mining in South Africa: The context of the Marikana massacre. *NEW SOLUTIONS A Journal of Environmental and Occupational Health Policy*. 25 (4), 513–534 [Online] Available from: https://www.researchgate.net/publication/288888996_Platinum_and_Gold_Mining_in_South_Africa_The_Context_of_the_Marikana_Massacre [Accessed 28th June 2020].

Cameron-Booth. (2017) Dispatch from African tea convention & exhibition: Kenya's sustainable tea farming vision. *Rainforest Alliance*. [Online] Available from: https://www.rainforest-alliance.org/business/sustainable-farming/dispatch-from-african-tea-convention-exhibition-kenyas-sustainable-tea-farming-vision/ [Accessed 25th July 2020].

Caramel, L. & Thibault, H. (2012) China at the centre of 'illegal timber' trade. *The Guardian*. [Online] Available from: https://www.theguardian.com/environment/2012/dec/11/china-illegal-logging-deforestation [Accessed 22nd May 2020].

Carney, T. (2017) Boeing 'loves' the Export-Import Bank, but Boeing doesn't 'need' the Export-Import Bank. *Washington Examiner*. [Online] Available from: https://www.washingtonexaminer.com/boeing-loves-the-export-import-bank-but-boeing-doesnt-need-the-export-import-bank [Accessed 17th August 2019].

Carrere, R. (2002) The World Bank in the forest. In: *Marketing the Earth. The World Bank and Sustainable Development*. Friends of the Earth/Halifax Initiative. [Online] Available from: https://allafrica.com/view/resource/main/main/id/00010013.html [Accessed 6 July 2022].

Carrington, D. (2019) Why the Guardian is changing the language it uses about the environment. *The Guardian*. [Online] Available from: https://www.theguardian.com/environment/2019/may/17/why-the-guardian-is-changing-the-language-it-uses-about-the-environment [Accessed 8th January 2022].

Carter, B. (2017) *A literature Review on China's Aid. K4D*. [Online] Available from: https://gsdrc.org/wp-content/uploads/2017/10/177_China_aid.pdf [Accessed 10th September 2019].

Casey, J. P. (2019) Into Africa: The US' drive for African rare earth minerals. *Mining Technology*. [Online] Available from: https://www.mining-technology.com/features/into-africa-the-us-drive-for-african-rare-earth-minerals/ [Accessed 10th June 2020].

CBS News. (2018) *The Most Polluted Cities in the World, Ranked.* [Online] Available from: https://www.cbsnews.com/pictures/the-most-polluted-cities-in-the-world-ranked/ [Accessed 4th November 2018].

Center for Public Impact. (2017) *The Bujagali Dam Project in Uganda.* [Online] Available from: https://www.centreforpublicimpact.org/case-study/bujagali-dam-project-uganda [Accessed 8th October 2021].

Center for Strategic and International Studies (CSIS). (2020) *China Power.* [Online] Available from: https://chinapower.csis.org/air-quality/ [Accessed 22nd May 2020].

Central Intelligence Agency (CIA). (2019a) *World Factbook USA.* [Online] Available from: https://www.cia.gov/library/publications/the-world-factbook/geos/us.html [Accessed April 2019].

Central Intelligence Agency (CIA). (2019b) *World Factbook China.* [Online] Available from: https://www.cia.gov/library/publications/the-world-factbook/geos/ch.html [Accessed April 2019].

Central Intelligence Agency (CIA). (2019c) *World Factbook South Africa.* [Online] Available from: https://www.cia.gov/library/publications/the-world-factbook/geos/sf.html [Accessed April 2019].

Central Intelligence Agency (CIA). (2020) *World Factbook: USA.* [Online] Available from: https://www.cia.gov/the-world-factbook/countries/united-states/ [Accessed 19th December 2020].

Central Intelligence Agency (CIA). (2020a) *World Factbook Nigeria.* [Online] Available from: https://www.cia.gov/library/publications/the-world-factbook/geos/ni.html [Accessed April 2019].

Central Intelligence Agency (CIA). (2020b) *World Factbook: Cameroon.* [Online] Available from: https://www.cia.gov/library/publications/the-world-factbook/geos/cm.html [Accessed 24th July 2020].

Central Investigation Agency (CIA). (2020c) *World Factbook China: Economy.* [Online] Available from: https://www.cia.gov/library/publications/the-world-factbook/geos/ch.html [Accessed 6th June 2020].

Central Intelligence Agency (CIA). (2021) *World Factbook: USA.* [Online] Available from: https://www.cia.gov/the-world-factbook/countries/united-states/ [Accessed 19th March 2021].

Chandran, N. (2017) *China Development Aid: How and Where Beijing is Spending its Cash.* [Online] Available from: https://www.cnbc.com/2017/10/13/china-development-aid-how-and-where-beijing-is-spending-its-cash.html [Accessed 28th October 2018].

Chang, A. (2013) When lobbyists literally write the bill. *National Public Radio.* [Online] Available from: https://www.npr.org/sections/itsallpolitics/2013/11/11/243973620/when-lobbyists-literally-write-the-bill [Accessed 18th August 2019].

Charveriat, C. (2001) Bitter coffee: How the poor are paying for the slump in coffee prices. *Oxfam.* [Online] Available from: https://policy-practice.oxfam.org.uk/publications/bitter-coffee-how-the-poor-are-paying-for-the-slump-in-coffee-prices-114002 [Accessed 13th November 2018].

Chatelard, S., Chatelard, G. & Chu, J. M. (2015) Chinese agricultural engagements in Zambia. *Policy brief 04/15. SAIS-CARI.* [Online] Available from: http://investzambia.

zda.org.zm/wp-content/uploads/2019/04/CARI-Chinese-agricultural-engagements-in-Zambia.pdf [Accessed 29th May 2020].

Chen, L. (2018) China, Africa trade volume rises 14% to $170 billion. *China Daily.* [Online] Available from: http://www.chinadaily.com.cn/a/201808/29/WS5b86536ea310add14f388762.html [Accessed 6th June 2019].

Chen, W. & Nord, R. (2017) *A Rebalancing Act for China and Africa; The Effects of China's Rebalancing on Sub-Saharan Africa's Trade and Growth.* [Online] Available from: https://ideas.repec.org/p/imf/imfdep/17-03.html [Accessed 29th May 2020].

Chen, W., Dollar, D. & Tang, H. (2015a) Why is China investing in Africa? Evidence from the firm level. *The Brookings Institution.* [Online] Available from: https://www.brookings.edu/wp-content/uploads/2016/06/Why-is-China-investing-in-Africa.pdf [Accessed 17th September 2017].

Chen, W., Dollar, D. & Tang, H. (2015b) China's direct investment in Africa: Reality versus myth. *The Brookings Institution.* [Online] Available from: https://www.brookings.edu/blog/africa-in-focus/2015/09/03/chinas-direct-investment-in-africa-reality-versus-myth/ [Accessed 29th May 2020].

Chêne, M. (2010) U4 Expert Answer: The impact of corruption on indigenous people. *Transparency International.* 245. [Online] Available from: https://knowledgehub.transparency.org/assets/uploads/helpdesk/245_Impact_of_corruption_on_indigenous_people.pdf [Accessed 9th May 2020].

China Africa Research Initiative (CARI). (2018a) *China-Africa Trade Data (country by country) 1992–2016.* [Online] Available from: http://www.sais-cari.org/data-china-africa-trade/ [Accessed 20th November 2018].

China Africa Research Initiative (CARI). (2018b) *Data: Chinese Workers in Africa.* [Online] Available from: http://www.sais-cari.org/data-chinese-workers-in-africa/ [Accessed 21st December 2018].

China Africa Research Initiative (CARI). (2019a) *Chinese Loans to Africa.* [Online] Available from: http://www.sais-cari.org/research-chinese-loans-to-africa [Accessed 29th May 2020].

China Africa Research Initiative (CARI). (2019b) *Data: Chinese Foreign Aid.* [Online] Available from: http://www.sais-cari.org/data-chinese-foreign-aid-to-africa [Accessed 24th May 2019].

China Africa Research Initiative (CARI). (2019c) *Chinese Agricultural Investments in Africa.* [Online] Available from: http://www.sais-cari.org/data-chinese-agricultural-investments-in-africa [Accessed 29th May 2020].

China Africa Research Initiative (CARI). (n.d.a) *Publications.* [Online] Available from: http://www.sais-cari.org/publications-working-papers [Accessed 8th January 2022].

China Africa Research Initiative (CARI). (n.d.b) *Data: Chinese Global Foreign Aid.* [Online] Available from: http://www.sais-cari.org/data-chinese-global-foreign-aid [Accessed 19th August 2021].

China Daily. (2015) *Full Text: China's Sescond Africa Policy Paper.* [Online] Available from: http://www.chinadaily.com.cn/world/XiattendsParisclimateconference/2015-12/05/content_22632874.htm [Accessed 26th May 2019].

China Daily. (2017) China becomes single largest contributor of Africa's FDI: Report. *Xinhua.* [Online] Available from: http://www.chinadaily.com.cn/world/2017-05/03/content_29189581.htm [Accessed 8th August 2017].

China Labour Bulletin. (n.d.) *Migrant Workers and Their Children*. [Online] Available from: http://www.clb.org.hk/content/migrant-workers-and-their-children [Accessed 1st September 2017].

China Policy. (2017) *Going Global: Between Ambition and Capacity*. [Online] Available from: https://policycn.com/wp-content/uploads/2017/05/2017-Chinas-going-global-strategy.pdf [Accessed 7th June 2020].

Chironga, M., Cunha, L., De Grandis, H. & Kuyoro, M. (2018) *African Retail Banking's Next Growth Frontier*. McKinsey & Company. [Online] Available from: https://www.mckinsey.com/industries/financial-services/our-insights/african-retail-bankings-next-growth-frontier [Accessed 1st June 2020].

Chitonge, H. (2011) A decade of implementing water services reform in Zambia: Review of outcomes, challenges and opportunities. *Water Alternatives*. 4(3). [Online] Available from: http://dlc.dlib.indiana.edu/dlc/bitstream/handle/10535/7724/Art4-3-2.pdf?sequence=1 [Accessed 18th June 2020].

Chomsky, N. & Herman, E. S. (1988) *Manufacturing Consent*. New York, Pantheon Books.

Christian Aid. (2005) Economics of failure: the real cost of 'free' trade for poor countries. *Briefing Paper*. [Online] Available from: https://www.christianaid.org.uk/sites/default/files/2017-08/economics-failure-june-2005.pdf [Accessed 2nd June 2020].

Chuhan-Pole, P., Dabalen, A. & Land, B. (2017) *Mining in Africa: Are Local Communities Better Off*? Africa Development Forum series. Washington, DC, World Bank. [Online] Available from: doi:10.1596/978-1-4648-0819-7 [Accessed 11th October 2021].

Ciochetto, L. (2005) Contemporary advertising in China. *Media Asia*. 32 (1), 47–60.

Ciochetto, L. (2011) *Advertising and Globalization in Brazil, Russia, India and China*. London, Routledge.

Ciochetto, L. (2014) Impact of China on Sub-Saharan Africa's ability to work towards a sustainable future. *The Journal of Global Studies*. 7.

Climate Action Tracker. (n.d.) *Countries*. [Online] Available from: https://climateactiontracker.org/countries/ [Accessed 26th December 2021].

Climate Action. (2018) *China Announces Huge Reforestation Plans*. [Online] Available from: http://www.climateaction.org/news/china-announces-huge-reforestation-plans. [Accessed 29th May 2020].

Climate Central. (2020) *Top 10 Warmest Years on Record*. [Online] Available from: https://www.climatecentral.org/gallery/graphics/top-10-warmest-years-on-record [Accessed 10th June 2020].

Clough, C. (2017) Illicit financial flows to and from developing countries from 2005 to 2014. *Global Financial Integrity*. [Online] Available from: http://www.gfintegrity.org/press-release/new-study-illicit-financial-flows-in-developing-countries-large-and-persistent/ [Accessed 30th July 2018].

Clough, C. (2017a) New Study: Illicit financial flows in developing countries large and persistent. *Global Financial Integrity*. [Online] Available from: https://gfintegrity.org/press-release/new-study-illicit-financial-flows-in-developing-countries-large-and-persistent/ [Accessed 6th June 2020].

CNN. (2018) *Christiane Amanpour Broadened the Definition to 'Military, Industrial, Political and Technological Complex*.' [author viewed]. Broadcast 16 May 2018.

Coalition for Human Rights in Development. (2019) *Uncalculated Risks: Massacre of Workers at the Marikana Mine*. [Online] Available from: https://www.traffickingmatters.

com/wp-content/uploads/2020/02/Uncalculated-Risks-Full-report-cmpr-h-1.pdf [Accessed 28th June 2020].

Colgan, A-L. (2002) Hazardous to health: The World Bank and IMF in Africa. *Pambazuka News*. [Online] Available from: https://www.pambazuka.org/printpdf/9222 [Accessed 15th August 2018].

Compton, R. (2019) The Eskom calamity explained — Energy economist. *BizNews*. [Online] Available from: https://www.biznews.com/thought-leaders/2019/02/12/eskom-calamity-explained-energy-economist [Accessed 23rd July 2019].

Connor, P. (2018) The most common Mediterranean migration paths into Europe have changed since 2009. *Pew Research*. [Online] Available from: https://www.pewresearch.org/fact-tank/2018/09/18/the-most-common-mediterranean-migration-paths-into-europe-have-changed-since-2009/ [Accessed 1st June 2020].

Constantaras, E. (2016) Visualizing China's aid to Africa. *China File*. [Online] Available from: http://www.chinafile.com/infographics/visualizing-chinas-aid-africa [Accessed 21st December 2018].

Conway, E. M. & Oreskes, N. (2010) *Merchants of Doubt: How a Handful of Scientists Obscured the Truth on Issues from Tobacco Smoke to Global Warming*. London, Bloomsbury Press.

Cook, S., Lu, J., Tugendhat, H. & Alemu, D. (2016) Chinese migrants in Africa: facts from fiction in the agri-food sector in Ethiopia and Ghana. *World Development*. 81.

Copson, R. (2000) Africa: US foreign assistance issues. *Congressional Research Service*. [Online] Available from: https://pdf.usaid.gov/pdf_docs/PCAAA814.pdf [Accessed 6th November 2021].

Cordero, J. A., Johnston, J., Montecino, J. A., Ray, R. & Weisbrot, M. (2009) *IMF-Supported Macroeconomic Policies and the World Recession: A Look at Forty-One Borrowing Countries*. [Online] Available from: http://obela.org/system/files/imf-2009-10.pdf [Accessed 10th May 2020].

Corpwatch. (2011) *The True Cost of Chevron: An Alternative Annual Report*. [Online] Available from: http://www.corpwatch.org/sites/default/files/Chevron%202011.pdf [Accessed 20th June 2020].

Cotula, L., Leonard, R., Keeley, J. & Vermeulen, S. (2009) Landgrab or development opportunity?: International investment and international land deals in Africa. *FAO, IIED and IFAD*. [Online] Available from: https://www.ifad.org/documents/10180/a2ea06a0-d0b2-4e99-a9b4-1f23e0491afb [Accessed 13th January 2017].

Coulibaly, B. S., Gandhi, D. & Senbet, L. (2019) Is sub-Saharan Africa facing another systemic sovereign debt crisis? *Brookings*. [Online] Available from: https://www.brookings.edu/research/is-sub-saharan-africa-facing-another-systemic-sovereign-debt-crisis/#footnote-4 [Accessed 16th July 2019]

Council on Foreign Relations. (2017) *China in Africa*. [Online] Available from: https://www.cfr.org/backgrounder/china-africa [Accessed 8th August 2017].

Credit Suisse. (2010) Analysing Chinese grey income. *Asia Pacific Equity Research*. [Online] Available from: https://research-doc.credit-suisse.com/docView?language=ENG&source=ulg&format=PDF&document_id=857531571&serialid=WabTv3n9BdHCgZ3T53I97qLKOv%2BqNcskKT70z4WvV [Accessed 22nd May 2020].

Credit Suisse. (2015) *Global Wealth Report 2015*. [Online] Available from: https://www.credit-suisse.com/ch/en/about-us/research/research-institute/publications.html [Accessed 7th January 2021].

Cruise A. (2017) Good news for elephants: China's legal ivory trade is 'dying' as prices fall. *The Guardian*. [Online] Available from: https://www.theguardian.com/environment/2017/mar/30/chinas-legal-ivory-trade-is-dying-as-prices-fall [Accessed 29th May 2020].

CSIS. (2021) *China Power Project*. [Online] Available from: https://chinapower.csis.org/energy-footprint/ [Accessed 17th March 2021].

Curtis, M. (2017) Honest Accounts. *Curtis Research*. [Online] Available from: https://curtisresearch.org/wp-content/uploads/honest_accounts_2017_web_final.pdf [Accessed 8th January 2022].

D'Alelio, D. (2018) US Aid to fragile states: Where does the money go? *Center for Global Development*. [Online] Available from: https://www.cgdev.org/blog/us-aid-fragile-states-where-does-money-go [28th July 2021].

Dahir, A. L. (2018) *The Growing Membership of a China-Led Development Bank Challenges the IMF-World Bank Orthodoxy*. [Online] Available from: https://qz.com/africa/1273424/kenya-joins-china-led-asian-infrastructure-investment-bank-aiib/ [Accessed 19th February 2019].

Dalton, M., O'Neill, B., Fürnkranz-Prskawetz, A., Jiang L. & Pitkin, J. (2008) Population aging and future carbon emissions in the United States. *Energy Economics*. 30, 642–675. [Online] Available from: https://econpapers.repec.org/article/eeeeneeco/v_3a30_3ay_3a2008_3ai_3a2_3ap_3a642-675.htm [Accessed 22nd May 2020].

Daly, H. (2014) *Use and Abuse of the 'Natural Capital' Concept*. [Online] Available from: https://ourworld.unu.edu/en/use-and-abuse-of-the-natural-capital-concept [Accessed 1st October 2021].

Danaher, K. (2004) *10 Reasons to Abolish the IMF & World Bank*. London, Penguin Random House.

Dasnois, A. (2014) Marikana: World Bank loan undermines Lonmin's arguments, says academic. *GroundUp*. [Online] Available from: https://www.groundup.org.za/article/marikana-world-bank-loan-undermines-lonmins-arguments-says-academic_2426/ [Accessed 28th June 2020].

Davies, N. (2015) Marikana massacre: The untold story of the strike leader who died for workers' rights. *The Guardian*. [Online] Available from: https://www.theguardian.com/world/2015/may/19/marikana-massacre-untold-story-strike-leader-died-workers-rights [Accessed 11th September 2021].

Dawson, T. (2003) On the IMF's role and activities in Africa, Speech by Thomas C. Dawson, Director of External Relations. *IMF*. [Online] Available from: https://www.imf.org/en/News/Articles/2015/09/28/04/53/sp042803

de Tavernier, J. & Thomas, G. (2017) Farmer-suicide in India: debating the role of biotechnology. *Life Sci Soc Policy*. [Online] Available from: doi: 10.1186/s40504-017-0052-z [Accessed 18th November 2021].

Dembele, D. M. (2004) The International Monetary Fund and World Bank in Africa: A 'disastrous' record. *Pambazuka*. [Online] Available from: https://www.pambazuka.org/governance/international-monetary-fund-and-world-bank-africa-disastrous-record [Accessed 13th May 2020].

Deng, T. T. (2017) In China, the water you drink is as dangerous as the air you breathe. *The Guardian*. [Online] Available from: https://www.theguardian.com/global-development-professionals-network/2017/jun/02/china-water-dangerous-pollution-greenpeace [Accessed 22nd May 2020].

Denny, L. & Elliot, C. (2002) US wrecks cheap drugs deal: Cheney's intervention blocks pact to help poor countries after pharmaceutical firms lobby White House. *The Guardian*. [Online] Available from: https://www.theguardian.com/world/2002/dec/21/usa.aids [Accessed 20th June 2020].

Deshmukh, R. & Wu, G. C. (2015) Designing low carbon electricity futures for African and other developing economies. *International Rivers*. [Online] Available from: https://www.internationalrivers.org/sites/default/files/attached-files/intlrivers_low-carbon_small.pdf [Accessed 30th July 2020].

Desilver, D. (2017) U.S. students' academic achievement still lags that of their peers in many other countries. *Pew Research Center*. [Online] Available from: https://www.pewresearch.org/fact-tank/2017/02/15/u-s-students-internationally-math-science/ [Accessed 18th August 2019].

Desilver, D. (2019) 5 facts about the national debt. *Pew Research Center*. [Online] Available from: https://www.pewresearch.org/fact-tank/2019/07/24/facts-about-the-national-debt/ [Accessed 4th September 2021].

Dibie, M. I. (2017) China becomes largest single contributor of Africa's FDI-Report. *Africa News*. [Online] Available from: http://www.africanews.com/2017/05/04/china-becomes-single-largest-contributor-of-africa-s-fdi-report// [Accessed 17th October 2018].

Dixon, R. & Kaiman, J. (2016) Can China's ban on ivory sales save Africa's elephants, or will people keep on buying ivory trinkets? *Los Angeles Times*. [Online] Available from: https://www.latimes.com/world/africa/la-fg-south-africa-elephants-ivory-ban-20161230-story.html [Accessed 29th May 2020].

Dollar, D. (2016) China's engagement with Africa — From Natural Resources to Human Resources. *The Brookings Institution*. [Online] Available from: https://www.brookings.edu/wp-content/uploads/2016/07/Chinas-Engagement-with-Africa-David-Dollar-July-2016.pdf [Accessed 17th October 2018].

dos Santos, Q. (2016) *Chevron's Misplaced Endorsement of Nepotism in Angola*. [Online] Available from: https://www.makaangola.org/2016/06/chevrons-misplaced-endorsement-of-nepotism-in-angola/ [Accessed 7th July 2021].

Downs, E. (2006) *The brookings foreign policy studies: Energy series: China*. [Online] Available from: https://www.brookings.edu/wp-content/uploads/2016/06/12china.pdf [Accessed 8th September 2017].

Doyle. M. (2019) What is the U.S. Export-Import Bank? *American Express*. [Online] Available from: https://www.americanexpress.com/us/foreign-exchange/articles/what-is-the-us-export-import-bank/ [Accessed 20th July 2021].

Dugger, C. (2008) Study cites toll of AIDS policy in South Africa. *New York Times*. [Online] Available from: https://www.nytimes.com/2008/11/26/world/africa/26aids.html [Accessed 10th July 2019].

Dwivedi, G. (2011) Despite evidence, World Bank still promoting water privatisation. *Bretton Woods Project*. [Online] Available from: https://www.brettonwoodsproject.org/2011/11/art-569208/ [Accessed 18th June 2020].

Easterley, W. (2007) Are aid agencies improving? *Brookings Institution*. [Online] Available from: https://www.brookings.edu/wp-content/uploads/2016/06/09foreignaid_easterly.pdf [Accessed 23rd May 2018].

Eboh, C. (2010) *Nigeria Cautions Exxon Mobil on Offshore Oil Spills.* [Online] Available from: https://www.reuters.com/article/nigeria-exxon-idUKLDE65E22C20100615 [Accessed 28th July 2021].

Economist. (6 January 2011) *Africa's Impressive Growth.* [Online] Available from: https://www.economist.com/graphic-detail/2011/01/06/africas-impressive-growth. [Accessed 3rd January 2022].

Economy, E. (2004) *The River Runs Black: The Environmental Challenge to China's Future.* Ithaca, Cornell University Press.

Economy, E. C. & Levi, M. (2014) *By All Means Necessary: How China's Resource Quest is Changing the World.* New York, Oxford University Press.

Edwards, C. (2018) Agricultural subsidies. *Downsizing the Government.* [Online] Available from: https://www.downsizinggovernment.org/agriculture/subsidies [Accessed 10th June 2020].

Egalame, E. N., Nforngwa, E. N. & Akana D. (2017) Illegal logging drives deforestation in Cameroon. *InfoCongo.* [Online] Available from: http://infocongo.org/en/3013-2// [Accessed 13th May 2019].

Egan, M. (2014) Oil milestone: Fracking fuels half of U.S. output. *CNN Business: Investing Guide.* [Online] Available from: https://money.cnn.com/2016/03/24/investing/fracking-shale-oil-boom/ [Accessed 10th June 2020].

EIA. (2013) Mozambique loses a fortune to illegal exports. [Online] Available from: https://eia-international.org/press-releases/mozambique-loses-a-fortune-to-illegal-timber-exports-2/ [Accessed 26 May 2022].

EIA. (2017) *The Rosewood Racket: China's Billion Dollar Illegal Timber Trade and the Devastation of Nigeria's Forests.* [Online] Available from: https://content.eia-global.org/assets/2017/rosewood-racket/PDF/Rosewood+Racket+Report+(High+Res).pdf [Accessed 29th May 2020].

Eicher, C. (2003) *Flashback: Fifty Years of Donor Aid to Africa.* [Online] Available from: https://rmportal.net/framelib/donor-aid-to-african-agriculture.pdf [Accessed 7th November 2021].

EITI. (2021a) *Country Status Against the EITI Rules (2007–2016).* [Online] Available from: https://eiti.org/countries-archive [Accessed 28th June 2020].

EITI. (2021b) *United States.* [Online] Available from: https://eiti.org/united-states-of-america#overview [Accessed 16th October 2021].

Energy Intensive Users Group of Southern Africa (EIUG). (2019) *Membership.* [Online] Available from: http://eiug.org.za [Accessed 19th May 2019].

Environmental Defence, Friends of the Earth, and International Rivers Network. (2003) *Gambling With People's Lives.* [Online] Available from: https://www.foei.org/wp-content/uploads/2015/08/gambling.pdf [Accessed 13th October 2021].

Environmental Investigation Agency (EIA). (2012) *Appetite for Destruction: China's Trade in Illegal Timber.* [Online] Available from: https://eia-international.org/report/appetite-for-destruction-chinas-trade-in-illegal-timber/ [Accessed 31st May 2020].

Environmental Investigation Agency (EIA). (2013) *Oil and Natural Gas in Sub-Saharan Africa.* [Online] Available from: https://www.eia.gov/pressroom/presentations/howard_08012013.pdf [Accessed 25th July 2020].

Eurodad (European Network on Debt and Development). (2006) *World Bank and IMF Conditionality: A Development Injustice*. [Online] Available from: https://eurodad.org/files/pdf/454-world-bank-and-imf-conditionality-a-development-injustice.pdf [Accessed 26th November 2019].

Eurodad. (2011) *Exposing the Lost Billions: How Financial Transparency on a Country by Country Basis can Aid Development*. [Online] Available from: https://archive.globalpolicy.org/the-dark-side-of-natural-resources-st/water-in-conflict/51055-exposing-the-lost-billions-how-financial-transparency-by-multinationals-on-a-country-by-country-basis-can-aid-development.html [Accessed 9th January 2022].

European Environmental Agency. (2018) *World Bank Carbon Trading Scheme the Prototype Carbon Fund*. [Online] Available from: fdd9e197604b7806e15aa25ac9050718 [Accessed 29th June 2020].

European Public Service Union. (2018) *EU Auditors Issue Damning Report on Public-Private Partnerships*. [Online] Available from: https://www.epsu.org/article/eu-auditors-issue-damning-report-public-private-partnerships [Accessed 7th October 2021].

Eurostat. (2018) The EU, USA and China account for almost half the world trade in goods. [Online] Available from: https://ec.europa.eu/eurostat/web/products-eurostat-news/-/DDN-20170824-1?inheritRedirect=true [Accessed 27th September 2018].

EXIM Bank. (2000) *News: EX-IM Bank $300 Million Loan Guarantee Proposed to Finance US Exports to Chad-Cameroon Oil Pipeline System*. [Online] Available from: https://www.exim.gov/news/ex-im-bank-300-million-loan-guarantee-proposed-finance-us-exports-chad-cameroon-oil-pipeline [Accessed 11th October 2021].

Extractive Industries Transparency Initiative (EITI). (n.d.) *Timeline*. [Online] Available from: https://eiti.org/history#eiti-history-timeline [Accessed 29th June 2020].

ExxonMobil. (2019) *The Chad Cameroon Pipeline: Overview*. [Online] Available from: https://corporate.exxonmobil.com/en/Locations/Chad-and-Cameroon/Chad-and-Cameroon-overview [Accessed 5th May 2019].

Eyal, J. & Peh, K. (2010) Unveiling China's impact on African environment. *Energy Policy*. 38, 4729–4730.

False Promises. (2020) *The Alliance for a Green Revolution in Africa*. [Online] Available from: https://www.rosalux.de/fileadmin/rls_uploads/pdfs/Studien/False_Promises_AGRA_en.pdf [Accessed 11th October 2021].

Fan, L. (2010) *Last Train Home*. [Film] Available from: https://zeitgeistfilms.com/sitelets/lasttrainhome/ [Accessed 27th May 2019].

Fan, S. & Saurkar, A. (n.d.) Tracking agricultural spending for agricultural growth and poverty reduction in Africa. *Regional Strategic Analysis and Knowledge Support System (ReSAKSS)*. [Online] Available from: https://www.resakss.org/sites/default/files/pdfs/tracking-agricultural-spending-for-agricultural-gr-1349.pdf [Accessed 2nd June 2020].

Fang, L. (2014) Where have all the lobbyists gone*? The Nation*. [Online] Available from: http://www.thenation.com/article/shadow-lobbying-complex/ [Accessed 25th July 2015].

Feed the Future. (2021) *About*. [Online] Available from: https://www.feedthefuture.gov/about/ [Accessed 12th November 2021].

Fei, D. (2018) *Work, Employment, and Training Through Africa-China Cooperation Zones: Evidence from the Eastern Industrial Zone in Ethiopia*. Working Paper No.

2018/19. China Africa Research Initiative, School of Advanced International Studies, Johns Hopkins University, Washington, DC. [Online] Available from: http://www.sais-cari.org/publications [Accessed 16th October 2019].

Ferguson, J. (2005) Seeing like an oil company: Space, security and global capital in neoliberal Africa. *American Anthropologist.* 107 (3). [Online] Available from: https://doi.org/10.1525/aa.2005.107.3.377 [Accessed 3rd June 2020].

Fisher, W. W. & Rigamonti, C. (2005) The South Africa AIDS controversy — A case study in patent law and policy. *Harvard Law School.* [Online] Available from: https://cyber.harvard.edu/people/tfisher/South%20Africa.pdf [Accessed 26th February 2019].

Fleurant, A., Kuimova, A., Tian, N., Wezeman, P. D. & Wezeman, S. T. (2018) Trends in international arms transfers. *SIPR.* [Online] Available from: https://www.sipri.org/publications/2019/sipri-fact-sheets/trends-international-arms-transfers-2018 [Accessed 7th June 2020].

Fleurant, A., Tian, N., Wezeman, P. D. & Wezeman, S. D. (2017) Trends in world military expenditure, 2016. *SIPRI Factsheet.* [Online] Available from: https://www.sipri.org/publications/2017/sipri-fact-sheets/trends-world-military-expenditure-2016 [Accessed 9th June 2020].

Flynn, D. & Liffey, K. (2015) Insight — China's 'infrastructure for minerals deal gets reality-check in Congo.' *Reuters.* [Online] Available from: http://www.reuters.com/article/congodemocratic-mining-china-idUSL8N0ZN2QZ20150708 [Accessed 12th August 2017].

Food and Agricultural Organization (FAO), IFAD and WFP. (2015) The state of food insecurity in the world, 2015. *Meeting the 2015 International Hunger Targets: Taking Stock of Uneven Progress.* [Online] Available from: https://www1.wfp.org/publications/state-food-insecurity-world-2015 [Accessed 17th May 2019].

Food and Agricultural Organization (FAO). (2009) *The State of Food and Agriculture.* [Online] Available from: http://www.fao.org/3/a-i0680e.pdf [Accessed 2nd June 2020].

Food and Agriculture Organization (FAO). (2012) *The State of Food and Agriculture. Investing in Agriculture for a Better Future.* [Online] Available from: https://www.fao.org/3/i3028e/i3028e00.htm [Accessed 2nd December 2021].

Food and Agricultural Organization (FAO). (2019) *Government Expenditure on Agriculture.* [Online] Available from: http://www.fao.org/economic/ess/investment/expenditure/en/ [Accessed 3rd June 2020].

Food and Agricultural Organization (FAO). (n.d.) *REDD+ Reducing Emissions From Deforestation and Forest Eegradation.* [Online] Available from: http://www.fao.org/redd/en/ [Accessed 25th July 2020].

Forest Legality Initiative. (2014) *China.* [Online] Available from: https://forestlegality.org/risk-tool/country/china-0 [Accessed 27th May 2020].

Forest People's Programme. (2013) *The World Bank's Forest Policy: As the World Bank Reviews its Environmental and Social Standards, A Major Opportunity to Overhaul World Bank Approach to Forests Must not be Missed.* [Online] Available from: https://www.forestpeoples.org/en/topics/forests-policy-opbp-436/news/2013/04/world-bank-s-forest-policy [Accessed 2nd July 2020].

Forsyth, M. (2016) China curbs plans for more coal-fired power plants. *New York Times.* [Online] Available from: https://www.nytimes.com/2016/04/26/business/energy-environment/china-coal.html [Accessed 17th March 2021].

Fox, J. (2010) *Gasland.* [Film].

Frankfurt School and UN Environmental Program (UNEP) Collaborating Center. (2019) *Global Trends in Renewable Energy Investment.* [Online] Available from: https://www.fs-unep-centre.org/global-trends-in-renewable-energy-investment-2019/ [Accessed 29th May 2020].

Freedom House. (2016) *Freedom in the World Report 2016.* [Online] Available from: https://freedomhouse.org/sites/default/files/FH_FITW_Report_2016.pdf [Accessed 14th August 2018].

French, H. (2014) *China's Second Continent. How a Million Migrants are Building a New Empire in Africa.* New York, Alfred A Knopf.

Fridley, D., Lu, H. & Liu, X. (2017) Key China energy statistics 2016, Abstract. *China Energy Group.* [Online] Available from: https://china.lbl.gov/publications/key-china-energy-statistics-2016 [Accessed 17th March 2021].

Friends of the Earth International (FOEI). (2014) *Nine Reasons Why REDD is a False Solution: New Report from Friends of the Earth International.* [Online] Available from: https://redd-monitor.org/2014/10/15/nine-reasons-why-redd-is-a-false-solution-friends-of-the-earth-international/ [Accessed 21st March 2019].

Fritel, J. & Roche, M. (2011) *Goldman Sachs: The Bank that Runs the World.* [Film].

Frosch, D. & Roberts, J. (2011) Pipeline spills put safeguards under scrutiny. *New York Times.* [Online] Available from: https://www.nytimes.com/2011/09/10/business/energy-environment/agency-struggles-to-safeguard-pipeline-system.html?pagewanted=all [Accessed 10th August 2011].

Frynas, J. G. (2001) Corporate and state responses to anti-oil protests in the Niger Delta. *African Affairs.* 100, 27–54, The Royal African Society.

Fund for Peace. (2016) *Fragile States Index 2016: The Book.* [Online] Available from: https://fundforpeace.org/2016/06/27/fragile-states-index-2016-the-book/ [Accessed 10th May 2020].

Fung, C. (2016) *China and the Responsibility to Protect: From Opposition to Advocacy.* United States Institute of Peace. Online. Available from: https://www.usip.org/publications/2016/06/china-and-responsibility-protect-opposition-advocacy [Accessed 22nd May 2020].

G7 Research Group. (2009) *L'Aquila Food Security Initiative.* [Online] Available from: http://www.g8.utoronto.ca/summit/2009laquila/2009-food.html [Accessed 5th September 2021].

GAN Anti-Corruption Business Portal. (2017) *China Corruption Report.* [Online] Available from: http://www.business-anti-corruption.com/country-profiles/china [Accessed 7th September 2017].

Gardner, T. (2021) Exxon, Chevron conceal payments to some governments — Watchdog. *Reuters.* [Online] Available from: https://www.reuters.com/business/energy/exxon-chevron-not-disclosing-payments-some-governments-transparency-group-2021-09-22/ [Accessed 8th November 2021].

Gatehouse, G. (2012) How much will technology boom change Kenya? *BBC News.* [Online] Available from: https://www.bbc.com/news/world-africa-19903839 [Accessed 1st June 2020].

Geffen, N. (2010) *Debunking Delusions: Inside Story of the Treatment Action Campaign (TAC).* Jacana Media, Auckland Park.

Gellman, B. & Poitras, L. (2013) U.S., British Intelligence mining data from nine US internet companies in broad secret program. *Washington Post.* [Online] Available from: https://www.washingtonpost.com/investigations/us-intelligence-mining-data-from-nine-us-internet-companies-in-broad-secret-program/2013/06/06/3a0c0da8-cebf-11e2-8845-d970ccb04497_story.html?utm_term=.848ab3a96f21 [Accessed 2nd November 2018].

George, S. (2007) *Of Capitalism, Crisis, Conversion and Collapse: The Keynesian Alternative*. [Online] Available from: http://www.tni.org/detail_page.phtml?&act_id=17306. [Accessed 11th June 2020].

Ghosh, J. & Sial, F. (2021) A wrong turn for World Bank concessional lending. *Eurodad.* [Online] Available from: https://www.eurodad.org/a_wrong_turn_for_world_bank_concessional_lending [Accessed 16th November 2021].

Gidda, M. (2013) Edward Snowden and the NSA files — Timeline. *The Guardian.* [Online] Available from: https://www.theguardian.com/world/2013/jun/23/edward-snowden-nsa-files-timeline [Accessed 9th June 2020].

Giridharadas, A. (2018) *Winners Take All: The Elite Charade of Changing the World.* New York, Alfred A. Knopf.

Global Financial Integrity (GFI). (2017) *Illicit Financial Flows to and from Developing Countries: 2005–2014*. [Online] Available from: https://www.gfintegrity.org/wp-content/uploads/2017/05/GFI-IFF-Report-2017_final.pdf [Accessed 20th June 2020].

Global Footprint Network. (2019) *Ecological Footprint: China* [Online] Available from http://data.footprintnetwork.org/#/ [Accessed 29th July 2020].

Global Footprint Network. (n.d.a.) *Ecological Footprint.* [Online] Available from: https://www.footprintnetwork.org/our-work/ecological-footprint/ [Accessed 7th January 2021].

Global Footprint Network. (n.d.b.) *Ecological Footprint United States of America.* [Online] Available from: https://data.footprintnetwork.org/#/ [Accessed 29th July 2020].

Global Slavery Index. (2017) *The Global Slavery Index 2016.* [Online] Available from: https://reliefweb.int/report/world/global-slavery-index-2016 [Accessed 1st June, 2020].

Goldberg, M. (2015) *7 Humanity Affirming Charts from the UN's Final MDG's Report.* [Online] Available from: https://www.undispatch.com/7-humanity-affirming-charts-from-the-uns-final-mdg-progress-report/ [Accessed 3rd June 2018].

Goldman, M. (2005) *Imperial Nature: The World Bank and Struggles for Social Justice in the Age of Globalization.* New Haven, Yale University Press.

Gosling, M. 2019. Eskom and the multi-billion rand mega projects that could have saved SA. *Fin24.* [Online] Available from: https://www.fin24.com/Economy/eskom-and-the-multi-billion-rand-mega-projects-that-could-have-saved-sa-20190213 [Accessed 1st June, 2019].

Graetz, N., Friedman, J., Osgood-Zimmerman, A. *et al.* (2018) Mapping local variation in educational attainment across Africa. *Nature.* 555, 48–53 [Online]. Available from: doi:10.1038/nature25761 [Accessed 12th May 2020].

GRAIN. (2019) *Food Sovereignty is Africa's only Solution to Climate Chaos.* [Online] Available from: https://www.grain.org/en/article/6293-food-sovereignty-is-africa-s-only-solution-to-climate-chaos [Accessed 2nd July 2020].

Grant, W. (2009) *Zambia Then and Now: Colonial Rulers and Their African Successors.* London, Routledge.

Gray, R. (2017) China's zombie factories and unborn cities. *BBC World News.* [Online] Available from: http://www.bbc.com/future/story/20170223-chinas-zombie-factories-and-unborn-cities [Accessed 18th September 2017].

Green, F. & Stern, N. (2016) China's changing economy: implications for its carbon dioxide emissions. *Climate Policy.* [Online] Available from: doi:10.1080/14693062.2016.1156515.

Greene, J. (2012) *Riots, Suicides and other Problems at Foxconn's iPhone Factories.* [online] Available from: https://www.cnet.com/news/riots-suicides-and-other-issues-in-foxconns-iphone-factories/ [Accessed 18th August 2017].

Greenpeace. (n.d.) *Everything you Need to Know About Fossil Fuel Subsidies.* [Online] Available from: https://www.greenpeace.org/usa/ending-the-climate-crisis/everything-you-need-to-know-about-fossil-fuel-subsidies/ [Accessed 4th September 2021].

Greenpeace Africa. (2016) *Africa's Forests Under Threat.* [Online] Available from: https://www.greenpeace.org/africa/en/publications/2056/africas-forests-under-threat-2/ [Accessed April 2020].

Greenpeace International. (2012) *Palm Oil's New Frontier: How Industrial Expansion Threatens Africa's Rainforests.* [Online] Available from: https://www.greenpeace.org/usa/wp-content/uploads/legacy/Global/usa/planet3/PDFs/PalmOilsNewFrontier.pdf [Accessed April 2020].

Greenwald, G. (2011) *With Liberty and Justice for Some.* New York, Harry Holt.

Greenwald, G. (2012) New York's top court highlights the meaninglessness and menace of the term 'terrorism.' *Guardian Reprint.* [Online] Available from: https://www.theguardian.com/commentisfree/2012/dec/16/court-terrorism-morales-gangs-meaningless [Accessed 10th June 2020].

Greenwald, G. (2013) NSA collecting phone records of millions of Verizon customers daily. *The Guardian.* [Online] Available from: https://www.theguardian.com/world/2013/jun/06/nsa-phone-records-verizon-court-order [Accessed 10th June 2020].

Greenwald, G. (2014) Congress is irrelevant on mass surveillance: Here's what matters instead. *The Intercept.* [Online] Available from: https://theintercept.com/2014/11/19/irrelevance-u-s-congress-stopping-nsas-mass-surveillance/ [Accessed 18th August 2019].

Greer, J. & Singh, K. (2000) A brief history of transnational corporations. *Corporatewatch.* [Online] Available from: http://www.globalpolicy.org/component/content/article/221/47068.html [Accessed 22nd September 2013].

Gulali, N. (2018) *The World Bank in Africa: An Analysis of World Bank Aid and Programmes in Africa and Their Impact, in The Changing Faces of Development Aid and Cooperation.* [Online] Available from: https://reliefweb.int/report/world/reality-aid-2018-changing-faces-development-aid-and-cooperation [Accessed 8th November 2021].

Guldbrandsen, C. (2011) Why Poverty: Stealing Africa. *BBC 4.* [Online] Available from: https://www.youtube.com/watch?v=WNYemuiAOfU [Accessed 16th June 2020].

Haas, B. (2017) More than 100 Chinese cities now above 1 million people. *The Guardian.* [Online] Available from: https://www.theguardian.com/cities/2017/mar/20/china-100-cities-populations-bigger-liverpool [Accessed 22nd May 2020].

Haley, U. C. V. (2010) No paper tiger: subsidies to China's paper industry from 2002-09. *Economic Policy Institute Briefing paper #264*. [Online] Available from: https://www.epi.org/publication/no_paper_tiger/ [Accessed 27th July 2020].

Halifax Initiative. (2004) *Issue Brief: The World Bank and Water Privatization, The Role of the World Bank in Developing Country Water Privatization*. [Online] Available from: https://halifaxinitiative.org/content/issue-brief-world-bank-and-water-privatization-march-2004 [Accessed 16th June 2020].

Hallam, D. (2003) Falling commodity prices and industry responses: some lessons from the international coffee crisis. *FAO*. [Online] Available from: http://www.fao.org/3/y5117e/y5117e03.htm [Accessed 29th June 2020].

Hansen, J. E. & Sato, M. (2011) *Paleoclimate Implications for Human-Made Climate Change*. [Online] Available from: https://arxiv.org/abs/1105.0968 [Accessed 10th June 2020].

HanShih, T. (2014) China Three Gorges subsidiary banned from World Bank projects. *South China Morning Post*. [Online] Available from: https://www.scmp.com/business/china-business/article/1600881/china-three-gorges-subsidiary-banned-world-bank-projects [Accessed 29th May 2020].

Hartung, W. D. (2010) *Prophets of War: Lockheed Martin and the Making of the Military-Industrial Complex*. New York, Nation Books.

Hatthaway, T. (2010) What is driving dams in Africa. *International Rivers*. [Online] Available from: https://www.internationalrivers.org/resources/what-is-driving-dams-in-africa-1695, https://corporate.exxonmobil.com/en/Locations/Chad-and-Cameroon/Chad-and-Cameroon-overview [Accessed 5th May 2019].

Hatton, C. (2017) China's secret aid empire uncovered. *BBC*. [Online] Available from: https://www.bbc.com/news/world-asia-china-41564841. [Accessed 20th November 2018].

He, L. (2012) The super rich rises as China begins leadership transition. *Forbes*. [Online] Available from: https://www.forbes.com/sites/laurahe/2012/11/07/the-super-rich-rises-as-china-begins-leadership-transition/#62e8cb393fbb [Accessed 22nd May 2020].

Henry J. & Kaiser Family Health Foundation. (2018) *Key Facts About the Uninsured Population*. [Online] Available from: https://www.kff.org/uninsured/fact-sheet/key-facts-about-the-uninsured-population/ [Accessed 18th August 2019].

Hertz, N. (2004) *The Debt Threat*. New York, Harper Business.

Hilton, I. (2010) Review: When a billion Chinese jump. *The Guardian*. [Online] Available from: https://www.theguardian.com/books/2010/jul/17/when-billion-chinese-jump-watts [Accessed 20th September 2017].

Hochberg, F. (2015) *Oversight of The Export-Import Bank of the United States*. [Online] Available from: https://www.govinfo.gov/content/pkg/CHRG-114shrg97305/html/CHRG-114shrg97305.htm [Accessed 16th June 2020].

Holzner, B. & Holzner, L. (2006) *Transparency in Global Change: The Vanguard of the Open Society*. Pittsburgh, University of Pittsburgh Press.

Hook, L. (2013) China's environmental activists. *Financial Times*. [Online] Available from: https://www.ft.com/content/00be1b66-1f43-11e3-b80b-00144feab7de [Accessed 17th September 2017].

Hoover, R. (2001) Pipe Dreams: The World Bank's failed efforts to restore lives and livelihoods of dam-affected people in Lesotho. *International Rivers*. [Online] Available from: https://archive.internationalrivers.org/sites/default/files/attached-files/download_a_2001_report.pdf [Accessed 11th October 2021].

Huang, Y. (2013) *China, the Abnormal Great Power, Carnegie Endowment for International Peace*. [Online] Available from: http://carnegieendowment.org/2013/03/05/china-abnormal-great-power-pub-51112 [Accessed 26th March 2018].

Hue, S. (2019) China still borrows billions in low-cost loans from World Bank, as Trump administration pushes back. *CNBC*. [Online] Available from: https://www.cnbc.com/2019/01/09/china-no-longer-a-poor-nation-still-borrows-billions-from-world-bank.html [Accessed 21st July 2019].

Human Rights Watch. (2011) *'You'll be Fired if you Refuse,' Labor Abuses in Zambia's Chinese State-Owned Copper Mines*. [Online] Available from: https://www.hrw.org/report/2011/11/04/youll-be-fired-if-you-refuse/labor-abuses-zambias-chinese-state-owned-copper-mines [Accessed 11th August 2017].

Humphreys, J., Solomon, A. & Tumusiime, E. (2013) US investment in large-scale land acquisitions in low- and middle-income countries. *Oxfam America Research Backgrounder Series*. [Online] Available from: http://www.oxfamamerica.org/publications/US-investment-in-large-land-acquisitions [Accessed 11th September 2021].

Independent Evaluation Group (IEG) of the World Bank. (2009) *Global Program Review Multi-Donor Trust Fund for the Extractive Industries Transparency Initiative*. [Online] Available from: http://documents.worldbank.org/curated/en/566061468163739415/pdf/599280BR0CODE21c031111110BOX358303B.pdf [Accessed 23rd June 2020].

Independent Evaluation Group (IEG) of the World Bank. (2011) *Assessing IFC's Poverty Focus and Results*. [Online] Available from: https://www.afraca.org/download/general_rf_publications/Effecitveness-of-IFCs-Poverty-Focus-Results-Evaluation-Report-by-Ade-Freeman-et-al.pdf [Accessed 18th June 2020].

Independent Evaluation Office (IEO) of the IMF. (2007) *The IMF and aid to Sub-Saharan Africa*. [Online] Available from: https://www.imf.org/external/np/ieo/2007/ssa/eng/pdf/report.pdf [Accessed 4th December 2021].

Information Office of the State Council. (2010) *China-Africa Cooperation (FOCAC)*. [Online] Available from: http://bw.china-embassy.org/eng/jmwl/t785012.htm [Accessed 29th May 2020].

Infrastructure Consortium for Africa. (2016) *Infrastructure Financing Trends in Africa*. [Online] Available from: https://www.icafrica.org/fileadmin/documents/IFT_2016/Infrastructure_Financing_Trends_2016.pdf [Accessed 11th October 2021].

Ingwe, R., Okoro, J. & Ukwayi, J. K. (2010) The new scramble for Africa: How large-scale acquisition of sub-Saharan Africa's land by multinational corporations and rich countries threatens sustainable development. *Journal of Sustainable Development in Africa*. 12 (3). [Online] Available from: https://www.researchgate.net/publication/235409065_ _The_new_scramble_for_Africa_How_buying_of_large_parcels_of_land_in_sub-Saharan_Africa_threatens_sustainable_development_in_the_region [Accessed 23rd July 2020].

Initiative Pour la Transparence des Industries Extractive (ITIE). (2018) *Democratic Republic of Congo*. [Online] Available from: https://eiti.org/democratic-republic-of-congo [Accessed 5th November 2019].

Inkpen, A. C. & Moffat, M. H. (2011) *The Global Oil & Gas Industry: Management, Strategy & Finance*. Tulsa, Pennwell Books.

Institute of Development Economies Japan External Trade Organization. (n.d.) *ExxonMobil*. [Online] Available from: https://www.ide.go.jp/English/Data/Africa_file/Company/angola04.html [Accessed 8th November 2021].

International Agency for Research on Cancer. (2017) IARC monographs. In: *Some Organophosphate Insecticides and Herbicides*, vol. 112, Glyphosate, pp. 321–412. Lyon, IARC/WHO

International Assessment of Agricultural Knowledge, Science and Technology for Development (IAASTD). (2016) *Agriculture at the Crossroads*. [Online] Available from: https://www.globalagriculture.org/fileadmin/files/weltagrarbericht/EnglishBrochure/BrochureIAASTD_en_web_small.pdf [Accessed 22nd November 2019].

International Energy Agency (IEA). (2014) *Africa Energy Outlook 2014*. [Online] Available from: https://www.iea.org/reports/africa-energy-outlook-2014 [Accessed 29th May 2020].

International Energy Agency (IEA). (2017) *Share of Total Primary Energy Supply China in 2014*. [Online] Available from: http://www.iea.org/stats/WebGraphs/CHINA4.pdf [Accessed 10th August 2017].

International Finance Corporation (IFC). (2007) *IFC Supports Lonmin Expansion and Economic Development of Surrounding Communities*. [Online] Available from: https://pressroom.ifc.org/all/pages/PressDetail.aspx?ID=22290 [Accessed 28th June 2020].

International Institute for Environment and Development (IIED). (2015) *Mozambique: Exploring Options to Improve Practice for Africa's Largest Exporter of Timber to China*. [Online] Available from: https://pubs.iied.org/pdfs/G03947.pdf? [Accessed 18th July 2019].

International Labour Organization (ILO). (2015) *Labour Migration in Africa*. [Online] Available from: https://www.ilo.org/africa/areas-of-work/labour-migration/WCMS_670561/lang--en/index.htm [Accessed 1st June 2020].

International Labour Organization (ILO). (2016) *Child Labour in Africa*. [Online] Available from: https://www.ilo.org/ipec/Regionsandcountries/Africa/WCMS_618949/lang--en/index.htm [Accessed 1st June 2020].

International Monetary Fund (IMF). (2000) *Press Release: HIPC Debt Relief for Uganda Increased to a Total of US$2 Billion: Additional Relief for Uganda's Poverty Reduction Programs*. [Online] Available from: https://www.imf.org/en/News/Articles/2015/09/14/01/49/pr0006 [Accessed 13th November 2018].

International Monetary Fund (IMF). (2013) *China-Africa*. [Online] Available from: https://www.worldbank.org/content/dam/Worldbank/Event/Africa/Investing%20in%20Africa%20Forum/2015/investing-in-africa-forum-china-and-africa.pdf [Accessed 23rd November 2018].

International Monetary Fund (IMF). (2014) *Regional Economic Outlook*: Staying the Course. [Online] Available from: https://www.imf.org/en/Publications/REO/SSA/Issues/2015/10/20/Regional-Economic-Outlook-October-2014-Staying-the-Course-41855 [Accessed 1st June 2020].

International Monetary Fund (IMF). (2017) *MDRI Factsheet*. [Online] Available from: https://www.imf.org/external/np/exr/facts/mdri.htm [Accessed 3rd December 2021].

International Monetary Fund (IMF). (2017a) *Debt Relief Under the Heavily Indebted Poor Countries (HIPC) Initiative*. [Online] Available from: http://www.imf.org/en/About/Factsheets/Sheets/2016/08/01/16/11/Debt-Relief-Under-the-Heavily-Indebted-Poor-Countries-Initiative [Accessed 2nd July 2017].

International Monetary Fund (IMF). (2017b) *The Multilateral Debt Relief Initiative*. [Online] Available from: https://www.imf.org/external/np/exr/facts/mdri.htm [Accessed 2nd July 2017 and 29 May 2020].

International Monetary Fund (IMF). (2017c) *Regional Economic Outlook: Restarting the Growth Engine*. [Online] Available from: https://www.imf.org/en/Publications/REO/SSA/Issues/2017/05/03/sreo0517 [Accessed 2nd June 2020].

International Monetary Fund (IMF). (2021) *Debt Relief Under the Heavily Indebted Poor Countries (HIPC) Initiative*. [Online] Available from: http://www.imf.org/en/About/Factsheets/Sheets/2016/08/01/16/11/Debt-Relief-Under-the-Heavily-Indebted-Poor-Countries-Initiative [Accessed 3rd December 2021].

International Rivers. (2001) *NGO's Tell World Bank Bujagali Dam is "too flawed."* [Online] Available from: https://archive.internationalrivers.org/resources/the-new-great-walls-a-guide-to-china's-overseas-dam-p [Accessed 28th June 2020].

International Rivers. (2004) *World Bank Debars Acres International Limited (Acres)*. [Online] Available from: https://www.internationalrivers.org/resources/world-bank-debars-acres-international-limited-acres-1972 [Accessed 23rd June 2020].

International Rivers. (2007) *The World Bank's Big Dam Legacy*. [Online] Available from: https://www.internationalrivers.org/wp-content/uploads/sites/86/2020/05/the_world_banks_big_dam_legacy.pdf [Accessed 3rd January 2022].

International Rivers. (2010) *Governments and Institutions that Endorse the WCD Recommendations*. [Online] Available from: https://www.internationalrivers.org/resources/governments-and-institutions-that-endorse-the-wcd-recommendations-3463 [Accessed 22nd April 2020].

International Rivers. (2012a) *The New Great Walls: A Guide to China's Overseas Dam industry*. 2nd ed. [Online] Available from: https://www.internationalrivers.org/sites/default/files/attached-files/intlrivers_newgreatwalls_2012_2.pdf [Accessed 22nd May 2020].

International Rivers. (2012b) *The south-north water transfer project*. [Online] Available from: https://www.internationalrivers.org/campaigns/south-north-water-transfer-project [Accessed 22nd May 2020].

International Rivers. (2015) *Community Voices from Lake Turkana*. [Online] Available from: https://www.internationalrivers.org/resources/8475 [Accessed 29th May 2020].

International Rivers. (2016) *World Bank's Kandadji Dam Leaves Niger Communities High and Dry*. [Online] Available from: https://www.internationalrivers.org/node/9518 [Accessed 18th June 2020].

International Rivers. (2017) *China*. [Online] Available from: https://www.internationalrivers.org/programs/china [Accessed 22nd May 2020].

International Rivers. (n.d.) *Bui Dam, Ghana*. [Online] Available from: https://www.internationalrivers.org/resources/bui-dam-ghana-3608 [Accessed 24th July 2019].

Irele, A. & Jeyifo, B. (2010) *The Oxford Encyclopaedia of African Thought*, Vol. 1. New York, Oxford University Press.

Irigoyen, C. (2017) The Bujagali dam project in Uganda. *Center for Public Impact.* [Online] Available from: https://www.centreforpublicimpact.org/case-study/bujagali-dam-project-uganda/ [Accessed 28th June 2020].

Isar, S. (2012) Was the Highly Indebted Poor Country Initiative (HIPCI) a success? *Consilience: The Journal of Sustainable Development.* 9 (1), 107–122.

Isine, O. (2014) Oil spill: Akwa Ibom community locks down ExxonMobil. *Premium Times.* [Online] Available from: https://www.premiumtimesng.com/regional/ssouth-east/164522-oil-spill-akwa-ibom-community-locks-down-exxonmobil.html [Accessed 15th November 2021].

Ismi, A. (2002) The ravaging of Africa: Western neo-colonialism fuels wars. *Plundering of Resources.* [Online] Available from: https://www.policyalternatives.ca/publications/monitor/october-2002-ravaging-africa [Accessed 22nd April 2014].

Ismi, A. (2004) Impoverishing a continent: The World Bank and the IMF in Africa. The Halifax Initiative. [Online] Available from: https://policyalternatives.ca/sites/default/files/uploads/publications/National_Office_Pubs/africa.pdf [Accessed 13th June 2020].

Izvorski, I. (2018) 7 surprising findings about resource-rich sub-Saharan Africa. *Brookings and the World Bank.* [Online] Available from: https://www.brookings.edu/blog/future-development/2018/08/01/7-surprising-findings-about-resource-rich-sub-saharan africa/ [Accessed 12th October 2021].

Jacques, M. (2012) *When China Rules the World.* London, Penguin.

Jafrani, N. (2012) China's growing role in Africa: Myths and facts. *International Economic Bulletin: Weekly, Carnegie Endowment for International Peace.* [Online] Available from: http://carnegieendowment.org/ieb/2012/02/09/china-s-growing-role-in-africa-myths-and-facts [Accessed 28th January 2013].

Jaganathan, J. & Daly, T. (2017) Global refiners brace themselves as China cements its oil market dominance. *Reuters.* [Online] Available from: http://www.reuters.com/article/us-china-oil-refining-idUSKBN1AK0MC [Accessed 5th August 2017].

Jayaram, K., Kassiri, O. & Yuan S. I. (2017) The closest look yet at Chinese economic engagement in Africa. *McKinsey & Company.* [Online] Available from: https://www.mckinsey.com/featured-insights/middle-east-and-africa/the-closest-look-yet-at-chinese-economic-engagement-in-africa [Accessed 30th July 2020].

Jenkins, B., Gilbert, R. & Nelson, J. (2017) The 2030 Water Resources Group: Collaboration and country leadership to strengthen water security. *The Harvard Kennedy School of Corporate Responsibility* Initiative. [Online]. Available from: https://www.hks.harvard.edu/sites/default/files/2030%20WRG%20final.pdf [Accessed 16th November 2021].

Jerome, A., Adjiboloso, S. & Busari, D. 2005. Oil and growth in Africa. Addressing oil related corruption in Africa: Is transparency enough? *Review of Human Factor Studies Special Edition, International Institute for Human Factor Development.* 11 (1), 7–32.

Jiangtao, S. (2012) Upstream dams risk starving Three Gorges of water. *China Morning Post.* cited by Adams, P, Probe International. [Online] Available from: https://journal.probeinternational.org/2012/06/06/dam-fever-threatens-viability-of-three-gorges-dam/ [Accessed 27th June 2020].

Jianqiang, L. (2013) China's new "middle class" environmental protests, China Dialogue. [Online] Available from: https://chinadialogue.net/en/author/liujianqiang/ [Accessed 31 May 2022].

Jiao, M. (2015) WB: China's national poverty line is higher than its new standard. *Beijing Review*. [Online] Available from: http://www.bjreview.com/Opinion/201510/t20151016_800040481.html [Accessed 27th July 2020].

Jiao, Y. (2015a) Chinese agribusiness entrepreneurship in Africa: Case Studies in Ghana and Nigeria. *Policy Brief, 05/2015 SAIS CARI*. [Online] Available from: https://static1.squarespace.com/static/5652847de4b033f56d2bdc29/t/568c4768a2bab8d5752 [Accessed 29th May 2020].

Jubilee Debt Campaign. (2015) The new debt trap: How the response to the last global financial crisis has laid the ground for the next. [Online] Available from: https://jubileedebt.org.uk/wp-content/uploads/2015/07/The-new-debt-trap_07.15.pdf [Accessed 25th July 2020].

Jubilee Debt Campaign. (2018) *Africa's Growing Debt Crisis: Who is the Debt Owed To?* [Online] Available from: https://jubileedebt.org.uk/wp/wp-content/uploads/2018/10/Who-is-Africa-debt-owed-to_10.18.pdf [Accessed 6th August 2020].

Jubilee Plus. (2003) *Real Progress Report on HIPCI*. [Online] Available from: https://www.globalpolicy.org/component/content/article/210/44762.html [Accessed 21st July 2019].

Jurney, C. (2016) Global 2000: The world's largest drug and biotech companies. *Forbes*. [Online] Available from: https://www.forbes.com/sites/corinnejurney/2016/05/27/2016-global-2000-the-worlds-largest-drug-and-biotech-companies/#3f28c3cf1962 [Accessed 10th August 2019].

Kaiser Family Foundation (KFF). (2020) *The U.S. President's Emergency Plan for AIDS Relief (PEPFAR)*. [Online] Available from: https://www.kff.org/global-health-policy/fact-sheet/the-u-s-presidents-emergency-plan-for-aids-relief-pepfar/ [Accessed 19th July 2021].

Kar, D. & Curcio, K. (2011) *Illicit Financial Flows from Developing Countries: 2000-2009 Update with a Focus on Asia*. The Global Financial Integrity, Washington, D.C. [Online] Available from: https://www.gfintegrity.org/wp-content/uploads/2011/12/GFI_2010_IFF_Update_Report-Web.pdf [Accessed 23rd April 2020].

Kar, D. & Freitas, S. (2011) Illicit financial flows from developing countries over the decade ending 2009. *Global Financial Integrity*. [Online] Available from: https://www.gfintegrity.org/storage/gfip/documents/reports/IFFDec2011/illicit_financial_flows_from_developing_countries_over_the_decade_ending_2009.pdf [Accessed 13th November 2018].

Kar, D. & Spanjers, J. (2015) Illicit financial flows from developing countries: 2004–2013. *Global Financial Integrity*. [Online] Available from: https://gfintegrity.org/report/illicit-financial-flows-from-developing-countries-2004-2013/ [Accessed 10th May 2020].

Kazeem, Y. (2017) China doubled its investment spend in Africa in 2016 as US and UK fell. *Quartz Africa*. [Online] Available from: https://qz.com/978419/china-influence-has-an-investor-in-africa-grew-in-2016/ [Accessed 26th March 2018].

Keet, D. (2010) South–South strategic bases for Africa to engage in China. In: Cheru, F. & Obi, C. (eds.) *The Rise of China and India in Africa*. London, Nordic Africa Institute and Zed Books, pp. 21–33.

Kelly, L. & Jordan, J. (2004) The Prototype Carbon Fund: Addressing challenges of globalization — An independent evaluation of the World Bank's approach to global programs. *Operations Evaluation Department (OED) Working Paper Series*. [Online] Available from: https://openknowledge.worldbank.org/handle/10986/20213 [Accessed 5th December 2021].

Kembaro, M. (2012) *The Rise of Low-Cost Android Smartphones in Kenya Could Mean the End for BlackBerry and Nokia*. [Online] Available from: http://www.moseskemibaro.com/2012/07/01/the-rise-of-low-cost-androidsmartphones-in-kenya could-mean-the-end-for-blackberry-and-nokia/ [Accessed 3rd December 2012].

Kenyon, P. (2018) *Dictatorland*. New York, Apollo.

Khadka, N. S. (2018) Is UK barbecue charcoal fuelling global deforestation? *BBC News*. [Online] Available from: https://www.bbc.com/news/science-environment-44880398 [Accessed 24th July 2020].

Kharas, H. (2010) The emerging middle class in developing countries. *OECD Development Center Working Paper*. [Online] Available from: https://www.oecd-ilibrary.org/content/paper/5kmmp8lncrns-en?crawler=true [Accessed I June 2020]

Khumalo, S. (2018) Eskom opens forensic probe into Mesuli and Medupi. *fin24*. [Online] Available from: https://www.fin24.com/Economy/Eskom/eskom-opens-forensic-probe-on-medupi-kusile-20181206 [Accessed 9th May 2019].

Kipp, A. M., Maimbolwa, M., Brault, M. A., Kalesha-Masumbu, P., Katepa-Bwalya, M., Habimana, P., Vermund, S. H., Mwinga, K. & Haley, C. A. (2017) Improving access to child health services at the community level in Zambia: A country case study on progress in child survival, 2000–2013. *Health Policy and Planning*. 32 (17). [Online] Available from: doi:10.1093/heapol/czw141 [Accessed 6th November 2018].

Kisika, S. (2017) You will pay if Kenyans lose Sh3bn in dam project, PS told. *The Star*. [Online] Available from: https://www.the-star.co.ke/news/2017/03/24/you-will-pay-if-kenyans-lose-sh3bn-in-dam-project-ps-told_c1530085 [Accessed 22nd December 2018].

Klein, N. (2006) *This Changes Everything*. New York, Simon & Schuster.

Kobo, O. M. (2013) A new world order? Africa and China, *Current Events in Historical Perspective*. 2 (8). [Online] Available from: http://origins.osu.edu/article/new-world-order-africa-and-china/page/0/2 [Accessed 11th July 2018].

Kolakowski, M. (2020) History of oil prices. *Investopedia*. [Online] Available from: https://www.investopedia.com/history-of-oil-prices-4842834 [Accessed 8th January 2021].

Kosnik, R. L. (2007) The Oil and Gas Industry's Exclusions and Exemptions to Major Environmental Statutes. *Earthworks*. [Online] Available from: https://earthworks.org/cms/assets/uploads/archive/files/publications/PetroleumExemptions1c.pdf [Accessed 10th June 2020].

Kristof, N. (2012) Africa on the rise. *New York Times*. [Online] Available from: https://www.nytimes.com/2012/07/01/opinion/sunday/africa-on-the-rise.html [Accessed 5th March 2013].

Krupnick, A. & Wang, Z. (2013) US Shale Gas Development What Led to the Boom? Issue Brief 13–04. *Resources for the Future*. [Online] Available from: https://media.rff.org/archive/files/sharepoint/WorkImages/Download/RFF-IB-13-04.pdf [Accessed 10th June 2020].

Kuimova, A., Wezeman, P. D. & Wezeman, S. D. (2021) Trends in international arms transfers 2020. *SIPRI*. [Online] Available from: https://sipri.org/sites/default/files/2021-03/fs_2103_at_2020.pdf [Accessed 4th September 2021].

Kuo, L. (2017a) *China is Training Africa's Next Generation of Transportation and Aviation Experts*. [Online] Available from: https://qz.com/1030978/china-is-training-africas-next-generation-of-aviation-and-transport-officials/ [Accessed 7th August 2017].

Kuo, L. (2017b) China opens its first military base in Africa. *Quartz Africa*. [Online] Available from: https://qz.com/1043185/china-has-officially-opened-its-first-overseas-military-base-in-djibouti-in-the-horn-of-africa/ [Accessed 17th September 2017].

Kuo, L. (2017c) Chinese manufacturing may not be moving to Africa all that soon. *Quartz Africa*. [Online] Available from: https://qz.com/africa/1146018/china-in-africa-chinese-manufacturing-not-moving-to-africa-all-that-soon/ [Accessed 21st December 2018].

Lafraniere, S. (2005) Africa tackles graft: With millions in aid play. *New York Times*. [Online] Available from: https://www.nytimes.com/2005/07/06/world/africa/africa-tackles-graft-with-billions-in-aid-in-play.html [Accessed 15th June 2020].

Landau, K. & Eisen, N. (2018) Unhappy anniversary: U.S. withdrawal from the Extractives Industries Transparency Initiative, one year later. *Brookings Institution*. [Online] Available from: https://www.brookings.edu/blog/fixgov/2018/11/16/unhappy-anniversary-u-s-withdrawal-from-eiti/ [Accessed 4th November 2021].

Landler, M. (2014) U.S. and China reach climate accord after months of talks. *New York Times*. [Online] Available from: https://www.nytimes.com/2014/11/12/world/asia/china-us-xi-obama-apec.html [Accessed 23rd May 2020].

Landry, D. G. (2018) *The risks and rewards of Resource-for-Infrastructure deals: Lessons from the Congo's Sicomines Agreement*. Working Paper 16. CARI. [Online] Available from: https://foreignpolicy.com/wp-content/uploads/2018/06/01911-sicomines-workingpaper-landry-v6.pdf [Accessed 29th May 2020].

Larson, C. (2010) China takes first steps in the fight against acid rain. *Yale Environment360*. [Online] Available from: https://e360.yale.edu/features/china_takes_first_steps_in_the_fight_against_acid_rain [Accessed 4th November 2018].

Lau, T. (2019) *Citizens United Explained, Center for Justice*. [Online] Available from: https://www.brennancenter.org/our-work/research-reports/citizens-united-explained [Accessed 8th January 2021].

Laurance, W. (2011) China's appetite for wood takes heavy toll on forests. *Yale Environmental 360*. [Online] Available from: http://e360.yale.edu/features/chinas_appetite_for_wood_takes_a_heavy_toll_on_forests [Accessed 1st September 2017].

Lawrence, F. (2011) The global food crisis: ABCD of food — How the multinationals dominate trade. *The Guardian*. [Online] Available from: https://www.theguardian.com/global-development/poverty-matters/2011/jun/02/abcd-food-giants-dominate-trade [Accessed 23rd April 2020].

Lawrence, F. & Provost, C. (2012) US Food Aid programme criticised as 'corporate welfare' for grain giants. *The Guardian*. [Online] Available from: https://www.theguardian.com/global-development/2012/jul/18/us-multinationals-control-food-aid [Accessed 16th June 2020].

Le Belzic, S. (2012) China's Eximbank Bank: Africa's largest financier looks for an even bigger role. *The Africa Report.* [Online] Available from: https://www.theafricareport.com/6472/chinas-exim-bank-africas-largest-financier-looks-for-an-even-bigger-role/ https://www.theafricareport.com/6472/chinas-exim-bank-africas-largest-financier-looks-for-an-even-bigger-role/ [Accessed 22nd November 2018].

Lee, R. (2006) *Chevron Accused of Tax Evasion by Nigerian Government.* [Online] Available from: https://www.tax-news.com/news/Chevron_Accused_Of_Tax_Evasion_By_Nigerian_Government_____24523.html [Accessed 16th October 2021].

Lee, M. C. (2007) Uganda and China: Unleashing the power of the dragon, in *Current African Issues.* 33, China in Africa, 26–40, Nordiska Afrikainstitutet, Upsala. [Online] Available from: http://docs.mak.ac.ug/sites/default/files/Uganda%20and%20China.pdf [Accessed 30th July 2020].

Leggett, J. A. (2020) The United Nations Framework Convention on Climate Change, the Kyoto Protocol, and the Paris Agreement: A summary. *The Congressional Research Service.* [Online] Available from: https://fas.org/sgp/crs/misc/R46204.pdf [Accessed 10th June 2020].

Leke, A., Lund, S., Manyika, J. & Ramaswamy, S. (2014) *Lions go Global: Deepening Africa's Ties to the United States.* [Online] Available from: https://www.mckinsey.com/featured-insights/middle-east-and-africa/lions-go-global-deepening-africas-ties-to-the-united-states [Accessed 3rd June 2020].

Leke, A., Lund, S., Roxburgh, C. & van Wamelen, A. (2010) *What's Driving Africa's Growth?* McKinsey Quarterly [Online] Available from: https://www.mckinseyquarterly.com/Whats_driving_Africas_growth_26011 [Accessed 6th January 2011].

Lelyveld, M. (2016) China cites rises in coal deaths despite drive to cut output. *RadioFreeAsia.* [Online] Available from: http://www.rfa.org/english/commentaries/energy_watch/china-coal-08152016150446.html [Accessed 18th August 2017].

Lelyveld, M. (2017) China's Oil Import Dependence Climbs as Output Falls, Radio Free Asia. [Online] Available from: https://www.rfa.org/english/commentaries/energy_watch/chinas-oil-import-dependence-climbs-as-output-falls-12042017102429.html [Accessed 26 May 2022].

Lew, L. (2019) Explosions and landslides — The worst industrial accidents in China since 2014. *The South China Morning Post.* [Online]. Available from: https://www.scmp.com/news/china/society/article/3002908/explosions-and-landslides-worst-industrial-accidents-china-2014 [Accessed 22nd May 2020].

Li, G. & Wang, W. (2016) Investing in Africa's agriculture: Solidifying foundation for sustainable and inclusive development. *World Bank.* [Online] Available from: http://documents1.worldbank.org/curated/en/847331472710963734/pdf/108109-REVISED-WP-PUBLIC.pdf [Accessed 2nd July 2020].

Li, X. (2012) Hu's speech at Fifth Ministerial Conference of FOCAC. *China Daily.* [Online] Available from: http://www.chinadaily.com.cn/china/2012-07/19/content_15600866.htm [Accessed 30th July 2020].

Liu, Z. (2016) *China's Emissions Carbon Report 2016: Regional Carbon Emissions and the Implications for China's Low Carbon Development.* [Online] Available from: https://dash.harvard.edu/bitstream/handle/1/29916843/China_Carbon_Emissions_2016_final_web.pdf?sequence=1&isAllowed=y [Accessed 14th November 2018].

Lobe, J. (2007) *Politics: Africa to Get Its Own U.S. Military Command.* [Online] Available from: http://www.ipsnews.net/2007/01/politics-africa-to-get-its-own-us-military-command/ [Accessed 16th June 2020].

Lopes, C. (2013) *Structural Adjustment Policies and Africa — A Reply to Shantayanan Devarajan Economic Commission for Africa.* [Online] Available from: https://www.uneca.org/sites/default/files/LopesWritings/structural_adjustment_policies_and_africacarlos_lopes_response.pdf [Accessed 3rd June 2020].

Lu, D. (2019) China's two-child policy linked to 5 million extra babies in 18 months. *New Scientist.* [Online] Available from: https://www.newscientist.com/article/2214179-chinas-two-child-policy-linked-to-5-million-extra-babies-in-18-months/#ixzz6TLsMe2vw [Accessed 20th July 2020].

Lu, X. (2000) Booty socialism, bureau-preneurs, and the state in transition: organizational corruption in China. *Comparative Politics.* 32 (3), 273–294. [Online]Available from: https://www.jstor.org/stable/422367 [Accessed 20th July 2020].

Lujala, P., Rustad, S. A. & Le Billon, P. (2017) Has the EITI been successful? *Chr. Michelsen Institute.* [Online] Available from: https://www.cmi.no/publications/6300-has-the-eiti-been-successful [Accessed 13th September 2021].

Lyman, P. (2005) China's rising role in Africa: Presentation to the US-China Commission. *The Brookings Institution.* [Online] Available from: https://www.cfr.org/report/chinas-rising-role-africa [Accessed 16th September 2017].

Mackay, F. (2004) Indigenous people's right to free, prior and informed consent and the World Bank's extractive industries review. *Sustainable Development Law and Policy.* 4. [Online] Available from: https://digitalcommons.wcl.american.edu/cgi/view content.cgi?referer=&httpsredir=1&article=1380&context=sdlp [Accessed 2nd July 2020].

Maddow, R. (2019) *Blow Out.* New York, Crown Publishing Group.

Madowo, L. (2018) Should Africa be wary of Chinese debt? *BBC.* [Online] Available from: https://www.bbc.com/news/world-africa-45368092 [Accessed 20th July 2019].

Magnier, M. (2008) China feels the heat of its Olympic ambitions. *Los Angeles Times.* [Online] Available from: http://www.latimes.com/travel/la-trw-china14feb14-story. [Accessed 18th September 2017].

Marcuse, G. (2013) *Waking the Green Tiger. The Rise of China's Green Movement.* [Documentary] Available from https://www.videoproject.org/Waking-the-Green-Tiger.html [Accessed 9th January 2022].

Martin, R., Moyle, B. & Stiles, D. (2015) *Analysis of Ivory Demand Drivers.* [Online] Available from: http://danstiles.org/publications/ivory/43.Analysis%20of%20Demand.pdf [Accessed 20th May 2019.]

Martin-Prével, A. (2014) Corporatising agriculture. *The Bretton Woods Project.* [Online] Available from: https://www.brettonwoodsproject.org/2014/05/corporatising-agriculture/ [Accessed 8th November 2021].

Matthews, C. (2016) Why China's stimulus package was a big mistake. *Fortune.* [Online] Available from: http://fortune.com/2016/01/15/why-chinas-stimulus-package-was-a-big-mistake/ [Accessed 6th August 2017].

Mawdsley, E. (2008) Fu Machu versus Dr Livingston in the dark continent? Representing China, Africa and the West in British Broadsheet Newspapers. *Political Geography.* 27, 509–529.

Mayer, J. (2016) *Dark Money: The Hidden History of the Billionaires Behind the Rise of the Radical Right*. New York, Anchor Books.

Mbow, C., Skole, D., Dieng, M., Justice, C., Kwesha, D., Mane, L., Gamri, E. M., Vordzogbe, V. & Virji, H. (2012) *Challenges and Prospects for REDD+ in Africa: Desk Review Of REDD+ Implementation in Africa*. Copenhagen, GLP-IPO.

McAfee, K. & Murphy, S. (2005) *US Foodaid: Time to get it right*. [Online] Available from: https://www.iatp.org/sites/default/files/451_2_73512.pdf [Accessed 5th December 2021].

McBride, J. (2018) How does the U.S. spend its foreign aid? *Council on Foreign Relations*. [Online] Available from: https://www.cfr.org/backgrounder/how-does-us-spend-its-foreign-aid [Accessed 21st June 2020].

McGarrity, J. & Roberts, C. (2015) China pledges $3.1 bn of climate finance. *China Dialogue*. [Online] Available from: https://www.chinadialogue.net/blog/8208-China-pledges-US-3-1bn-of-climate-finance-/en [Accessed 9th April, 2015].

McKinsey Global Institute (MGI). (2016) *Lions on the Move 11: Realizing the Potential of Africa's Economies*. [Online] Available from: https://www.mckinsey.com/~/media/McKinsey/Featured%20Insights/Middle%20East%20and%20Africa/Realizing%20the%20potential%20of%20Africas%20economies/MGI-Lions-on-the-Move-2-Executive-summary-September-2016v2.ashx [Accessed 1st June 2020].

McKissack, A. & Xu, J. (2011) Chinese macroeconomic management through the crisis and beyond. *Treasury Working Paper, 2011-01*. [Online] Available from: https://static.treasury.gov.au/uploads/sites/1/2017/06/Tsy_WorkingPaper_11_1.pdf [Accessed 5th November 2018].

Meeks, P. (n.d.) Unravelling Tied Aid. Why aid must never be tied to donor country companies at the expense of women and men living in poverty. *Eurodad*. [Online] Available from: https://www.eurodad.org/files/pdf/1546810-unravelling-tied-aid-1516803666.pdf [Accessed 4th July 2020].

Meltzer, A. (2000) The Report of the International Financial Institution Advisory Commission. [Online] Available from: https://www.ifo.de/DocDL/Forum400-focus2.pdf [Accessed 25th January 2022].

Meng, Q. & Bempong, N. E. (2019) *Local Skill Development from China's Engagement in Africa: Comparative Evidence from the Construction Sector in Ghana*. Working Paper No. 2019/22. China Africa Research Initiative, School of Advanced International Studies, Johns Hopkins University, Washington, DC. [Online] Available from: http://www.sais-cari.org/publications [Accessed 16th October 2019].

Millennium Challenge Corporation. (n.d.) *About*. [Online] Available from: https://www.mcc.gov [Accessed 21st July 2021].

Millennium Development Goals Monitor. (2016) *Millennium Development Goals Progress Report of Africa in 2015*. [Online] Available from: http://www.mdgmonitor.org/mdg-progress-report-africa/ [Accessed 1st July 2017].

Milman, O. (2015) James Hansen, father of climate change awareness, calls Paris talks 'a fraud.' *The Guardian*. [Online] Available from: https://www.theguardian.com/environment/2015/dec/12/james-hansen-climate-change-paris-talks-fraud [Accessed 30th July 2019].

Minto, R. & Romei, V. (2012) Chart of the week: Who makes up China's exports local companies or foreign? *Financial Times*. [Online] Available from: http://blogs.ft.com/

beyond-brics/2012/09/10/chart-of-the-week-who-is-making-chinas-exports/ [Accessed 12th October 2016].

Miyazako, M. & Syed, S. (2013) Promoting investment in agriculture for increased production and productivity. *Food and Agriculture Organization, (FAO).* [Online] Available from: http://www.fao.org/3/a-az725e.pdf [Accessed 22nd June 2020].

Mkandawire, T. & Soludo, C. C. (1998) *Our Continent, Our Future: African Perspectives on Structural Adjustment.* Dakar, Council for the Development of Social Science Research in Africa.

Monbiot, G. (2006) The denial industry. *The Guardian.* [Online] Available from: https://www.theguardian.com/environment/2006/sep/19/ethicalliving.g2 [Accessed 9th September 2018].

Monbiot, G. (2009) Toxic assets. *The Guardian.* [Online] Available from: www.monbiot.com/2009/09/22/toxic-assets [Accessed September 2009].

Monbiot, G. (2012) Mitt Romney and the myth of self-created millionaires. *The Guardian.* [Online] Available from: https://www.theguardian.com/commentisfree/2012/sep/24/mitt-romney-self-creation-myth [Accessed 9th June 2020].

Monbiot, G. (2013) Corporate carve up. *The Guardian.* [Online] Available from: https://www.monbiot.com/2013/06/10/corporate-carve-up/ [Accessed 23rd June 2020].

Monbiot, G. (2014) Put a price on nature? We must stop this neoliberal road to ruin, The Guardian. [Online] Available from: https://www.theguardian.com/environment/georgemonbiot/2014/jul/24/price-nature-neoliberal-capital-road-ruin [Accessed 31 May 2022].

Monbiot, G. (2016) We'd never kill an albatross or gorilla: But we let others do it on our behalf. *The Guardian.* [Online] Available from: https://www.theguardian.com/commentisfree/2016/sep/14/extinction-let-others-kill-albatross-gorilla-whale-shark-conumerism [Accessed 23rd July 2020].

Monbiot, G. (2018) The UK government wants to put a price on nature — But that will destroy it. *The Guardian.* [Online] Available from: https://www.theguardian.com/commentisfree/2018/may/15/price-natural-world-destruction-natural-capital [Accessed 11th September 2021].

Moore, M. (2009) Chinese earthquake may have been man-made say scientists. *The Telegraph.* [Online] Available from: https://www.telegraph.co.uk/news/worldnews/asia/china/4434400/Chinese-earthquake-may-have-been-man-made-say-scientists.html [Accessed 22nd May 2020].

Morelle, R. (2013) Deforestation in Africa's Congo Basin rainforest slows. *BBC News.* [Online] Available from: https://www.bbc.com/news/science-environment-23382526 [Accessed 25th July 2020].

Mortished, C. (2010) China backs an outsider for economic glory. *The Times*, republished in the Dominion Post, C16.

Moss, T. (2011) Helping Africa's largest country shed $30 billion in debt. *Center for Global Development.* [Online] Available from: https://www.cgdev.org/topics/nigerian-debt-relief [Accessed 3rd April 2019].

Moyo, D. (2009) *Dead Aid: Why Aid Is Not Working and How There Is a Better Way for Africa.* New York, Farrar Straus & Giroux.

Multidimensional Poverty Index. (2016) *Highlights: Sub Saharan Africa.* [Online] Available from: https://www.ophi.org.uk/wp-content/uploads/MPI2016-AFRICA-HIGHLIGHTS_June.pdf [Accessed 3rd December 2021].

Mustapha, Shakira and Prisson, Annalisa. (2018) Africa's rising debt, Overseas Development Institute. [Online] Available from: https://cdn.odi.org/media/documents/12491.pdf [Accessed 26 May 2022].

Mutume, G. (2005) Industrial countries write off Africa's debt. *United Nations*. [Online] Available from: https://www.un.org/africarenewal/magazine/october-2005/industrial-countries-write-africas-debt [Accessed 25th July 2020.].

Nabeshima, K. & Yusuf, S. (2011) Optimizing urban development, 1–40. [Online] Available from: http://siteresources.worldbank.org/INTEAECOPRO/Resources/3087694-1206446474145/Chapter_1_China_Urbanizes.pdf [Accessed 2nd February 2015].

National Association of Professional Environmentalists (NAPE). (2012) *The Impacts of the Flower Industry on the Environment and Peoples' Livelihoods in Uganda*. [Online] Available from: https://www.nape.or.ug/publications/chemical-management/42-the-impacts-of-flower-industries-to-health-and-environment-pdf/file [Accessed 16th June 2019]

Ndikumana, L. (2017) Curtailing Capital Flight from Africa: The time for action is now. *International Policy Analysis*. [Online] Available from: http://static1.squarespace.com/static/5a0c602bf43b5594845abb81/t/5a2c786be2c483bdd9d7f963/1512863854696/CurtailingCapitalFlight+REPORT.pdf [Accessed 1st June 2020].

Netherlands Environmental Agency (PBL). (2016) *Trends in Global CO² Emissions: 2016 Report*. [Online] Available from: http://edgar.jrc.ec.europa.eu/news_docs/jrc-2016-trends-in-global-co2-emissions-2016-report-103425.pdf [Accessed 7th September 2017].

Newman, C., Page, J. & Tarp, F. (2017) Made in Africa — The future of production on the continent. *World Economic Forum*. [Online] Available from: https://www.weforum.org/agenda/2017/01/made-in-africa-the-future-of-production-on-the-continent/ [Accessed 2nd June 2020].

New York Times. (1996) *Monsanto Agrees to Modify Roundup Ads in New York State*. [Online] Available from: https://apnews.com/d196b9a5bb54637a7b281760b0f7a966 [Accessed 10th June 2020].

New York Times. (2002) *The Hypocrisy of Farm Subsidies*. [Online] Available from: https://www.nytimes.com/2002/12/01/opinion/the-hypocrisy-of-farm-subsidies.html [Accessed 10th June 2020].

New York Times. (2007) ICBC to buy $5.6 billion stake in South African bank. *New York Times*. [Online] Available from: http://www.nytimes.com/2007/10/26/business/worldbusiness/26iht-26icbc.8062473.html [Accessed 8th August 2017].

News24. (2015) *How Ramaphosa Obtained his Wealth*. [Online] Available from: https://www.news24.com/news24/MyNews24/How-Cyril-Ramaphosa-obtained-his-wealth-20150713 [Accessed 1st June 2020].

Nierenberg, D. (2005) *Happier Meals: Rethinking the Global Meat Industry*. Worldwatch Paper. p. 171. Washington, DC, Worldwatch Institute.

Ning, H. (2016) Mozambique faces race against time to end illegal logging. *The Guardian*. [Online] Available from: https://www.theguardian.com/sustainable-business/2016/aug/31/mozambique-illegal-logging-china-timber-deforestation [Accessed 21st March 2019].

Njehu, N. N. (1999) Testimony by: Director 50 Years Is Enough. *U.S. Network for Global Economic Justice*. [Online] Available from: http://www.africa.upenn.edu/Urgent_Action/apic_42999.html [Accessed 8th May 2020].

Njiraini, J. (2014) AGOA: The US–Africa trade dilemma, has the Africa growth and opportunity Act run its course? Africa renewal. *The United Nations*. [Online] Available from: https://www.un.org/africarenewal/magazine/december-2014/agoa-us–africa-trade-dilemma [Accessed 17th June 2020].

O'Neill, J. (2001) *Building Better Global BRICs*. [Online] Available from: https://www.goldmansachs.com/insights/archive/building-better.html [Accessed 10th June 2020].

O'Neill, B. C. & Chen B. (2002) Demographic determinants of household energy use in the United States. *Methods of Population-Environment Analysis: A Supplement to Population and Development Review*. 28, 53–88.

Ogden, T. (2011) Living with the Gates Foundation: A retrospective. *Stanford Social Innovation Review*. [Online] Available from: https://ssir.org/articles/entry/living_with_the_gates_foundationa_retrospective [Accessed 2nd December 2021].

Ogodo, O. & Vidal, J. (2007) Drained of life. *The Guardian*. [Online] Available from: https://www.theguardian.com/society/2007/feb/14/kenya.conservation [Accessed 25th July 2020].

One World Nations Online. (2016) *The 2016 United Nations Human Development Index (HDI) Rankings for All Countries*. [Online] Available from: https://www.nationsonline.org/oneworld/human_development.htm [Accessed 19th March 2021].

Orestes, N. & Conway, E. M. (2010) *Merchants of Doubt: How a Handful of Scientists Obscured the Truth on Issues from Tobacco Smoke to Global Warming*. London, Bloomsbury.

Organization for Economic Cooperation and Development (OECD). (2001) *World Investment Report: The Triad Accounts for Four-Fifths of Global FDI Outflows and Outward Stock*. [Online] Available from: https://www.ifo.de/DocDL/Forum102-sl2.pdf [Accessed 20th June 2020].

OECD and Food and Agricultural Organization (FAO). (2016) *Agricultural Outlook 2016–2025*. [Online] Available from: http://www.fao.org/3/a-bo092e.pdf [Accessed 3rd June 2020].

OECD. (2002) *Foreign Direct Investment for Development Maximising Benefits, Minimising Costs*. [Online] Available from: https://www.oecd.org/investment/investmentfordevelopment/foreigndirectinvestmentfordevelopmentmaximisingbenefitsminimisingcosts.htm [Accessed 16th June 2020].

OECD. (2003) *Aid Effectiveness and Selectivity: Integrating Multiple Objectives into Aid Allocations*. [Online] Available from: http://www.oecd.org/development/effectiveness/18444948.pdf [Accessed 1st June 2020].

OECD. (2014) *Venture Philanthropy in Development: Dynamics, Challenges and Lessons in the Search for Greater Impact*. [Online] Available from: https://www.oecd.org/dev/Venture%20Philanthropy%20in%20Development-BAT-24022014-indd5%2011%20mars.pdf [Accessed 3rd August 2020].

OECD. (2015) *World Investment Report*. [Online] Available from: https://unctad.org/en/PublicationsLibrary/wir2015_en.pdf [Accessed 21st June 2020].

OECD. (2016) *Development Statistics at a Glance: Aid by Region, 2. Africa*. [Online] Available from: https://www.oecd.org/dac/stats/documentupload/2%20Africa%20-%20Development%20Aid%20at%20a%20Glance%202016.pdf [Accessed 2nd December 2017].

OECD. (2018) *Development Aid at a Glance Statistics by Region: Africa.* [Online] Available from: https://www.oecd.org/dac/financing-sustainable-development/development-finance-data/Africa-Development-Aid-at-a-Glance-2018.pdf [Accessed 19th May 2019].

OECD. (2019) *Data: Net ODA.* [Online] Available from: https://data.oecd.org/oda/net-oda.htm [Accessed 1st June 2020].

OECD. (n.d.) *Development Assistance Committee (DAC) Glossary of Key Terms and Concepts.* [Online] Available from: https://www.oecd.org/dac/dac-glossary.htm [Accessed 8th June 2020].

OECD. (n.d.a). *Convention on Combating Bribery of Foreign Public Officials in International Business Transactions and Related Documents.* [Online] Available from: https://www.oecd.org/daf/anti-bribery/ConvCombatBribery_ENG.pdf [Accessed 21st June 2020].

OECD. (n.d.b) *Paris Declaration and the Accra Agenda for Action (AAA).* [Online] Available from: https://www.oecd.org/dac/effectiveness/parisdeclarationandaccra agendaforaction.htm [Accessed 22nd June 2020].

OECD. (n.d.c) *Untying Aid: The Right to Choose.* [Online] Available from: https://www.oecd.org/dac/untied-aid/untyingaidtherighttochoose.htm [Accessed 22nd June 2020].

OECD. (n.d.d). *Aid and Export Credits.* [Online] Available from: https://www.oecd.org/trade/topics/export-credits/aid-and-export-credits/ [Accessed 22nd June 2020].

OECD. (n.d.e). *Paris Declaration and the Accra Agenda for Action (AAA).* [Online] Available from: https://www.oecd.org/dac/effectiveness/parisdeclarationandaccraagendaforaction.htm [Accessed 22nd June 2020].

OECD. (n.d.f). *Guidelines for Multinational Enterprises.* [Online] Available from: https://www.oecd.org/corporate/mne/ [Accessed 3rd July 2020].

OECD. (n.d.g). *OECD Recommendations* (Common Approaches). [Online] Available from: http://www.oecd.org/tad/xcred/oecd-recommendations.htm [Accessed 26th February 2019].

OECD Watch. (2021) *Stocktaking on the OECD Guidelines — First Draft Report* [Online] Available from: http://mneguidelines.oecd.org/OECD-Watch-public-consultation-OECD-Guidelines-for-MNEs.pdf [Accessed 2nd December 2021].

OECD Watch. (n.d.) *United States.* [Online] Available from: https://www.oecdwatch.org/?s=United+States [Accessed 17th November 2021].

Overseas Development Institute (ODI). (2016) *Manufacturing More Than Doubles in Sub-Saharan Africa, Despite Fall in Share of GDP — New Report.* [Online] Available from: https://www.odi.org/news/782-manufacturing-more-doubles-sub-saharan-africa-despite-fall-share-gdp-new-report [Accessed 1st June 2020].

Oxfam. (2011) Land and power: The growing scandal surrounding the new wave of investments in land. *Oxfam briefing Paper 151.* [Online] Available from: https://oxfamilibrary.openrepository.com/bitstream/handle/10546/142858/bp151-land-power-rights-acquisitions-220911-en.pdf;jsessionid=8FB826417BAFCC96AFDD1E9AA328171D?sequence=32 [Accessed 14th May 2019].

Oxfam. (2013) *Reforming the G8's Public — Private Partnership on Agriculture and Food Security.* [Online] Available from: https://www.globalpolicy.org/component/

content/article/217-hunger/52498-reforming-the-g8s-publicprivate-partnership-on-agriculture-and-food-security.html [Accessed 26th May 2019].

Oxfam. (2014) *For Whose Benefit? The G8 New Alliance for Food Security and Nutrition in Burkina Faso.* [Online] Available from: https://www-cdn.oxfam.org/s3fs-public/file_attachments/bn-whose-benefit-burkina-faso-g8-new-alliance-220514-en.pdf [Accessed 19th November 2019].

Oxfam. (2014) *Working for the Few.* [Online] Available from: https://www.oxfam.org/en/research/working-few [Accessed 26th September 2018].

Oxfam. (2016) *The IFC and Tax Havens.* [Online] Available from: https://oi-files-d8-prod.s3.eu-west-2.amazonaws.com/s3fs-public/file_attachments/ifcandtaxhavensen.pdf [Accessed 11th October 2021].

Oxfam International. (2016) Oil, gas and mining transparency initiative facing crisis of relevance and legitimacy. *Oxfam.* [Online] Available from: https://www.oxfam.org/en/press-releases/oil-gas-and-mining-transparency-initiative-facing-crisis-relevance-and-legitimacy [Accessed 23rd November 2020].

Oxfam International. (2018a) *Inequality and Poverty: The Hidden Costs of Tax Dodging.* [Online] Available from: https://www.oxfam.org/en/inequality-and-poverty-hidden-costs-tax-dodging [Accessed 1st June 2020].

Oxfam International. (2018b) *The Paradise Papers: The Hidden Costs of Tax Dodging.* [Online] Available from: https://www.oxfam.org/en/even-it/paradise-papers-hidden-costs-tax-dodging. [Accessed 26th August 2018].

Palitza, K. (2011) Child labour: The tobacco industry's smoking gun. *The Guardian.* [Online] Available from: https://www.theguardian.com/global-development/2011/sep/14/malawi-child-labour-tobacco-industry [Accessed 1st June 2020].

Park, Y. J. (2016) One million Chinese living in Africa. *Perspectives, SAIS.* [Online] Available from: http://www.saisperspectives.com/2016issue/2016/5/12/n947s9csa0ik6kmkm0bzb0hy584sfo [Accessed 29th May 2020].

Pearce, F. (2012) *The Landgrabbers: The New Fight Over Who Owns the Earth.* London, Eden Project Books.

Pearce, F. (2012a) Landgrabbing has more of an impact on the world's poor than climate change, Interview by Tom Templeton. *The Observer.* [Online] Available from: https://www.theguardian.com/world/2012/may/20/fred-pearce-land-grab-interview [Accessed 13th May 2020].

Peck, A. (2012) The World Bank and agriculture. *The Bretton Woods Project.* [Online] Available from: https://www.brettonwoodsproject.org/2012/04/art-569959/ [Accessed 8th November 2021].

Pei, M. (2007) Corruption threatens China's future. *Carnegie Endowment for Peace.* [Online] Available from: https://carnegieendowment.org/2007/10/09/corruption-threatens-china-s-future-pub-19628 [Accessed 22nd May 2020].

Perkins, J. (2004a) Confessions of an Economic Hitman interview. *Democracy Now.* [Online] Available from: https://www.democracynow.org/2004/11/9/confessions_of_an_economic_hit_man [Accessed 15th May 2019].

Perkins, J. (2004b) *Confessions of an Economic Hit Man.* London, Edbury Press.

Pew Research Center. (2014) *Global Attitudes Survey: Greatest Dangers in the World.* [Online] Available from: https://www.pewresearch.org/global/dataset/2014-spring-global-attitudes/ [Accessed 13th May 2019].

Pew Research Center. (2017) *How well off is China's middle class?* [Online] Available from: https://chinapower.csis.org/china-middle-class/ [Accessed 5th November, 2018].

Philanthropy News. (2016) *Gates Foundation to Invest $5 Billion in Africa Over Five Years*. [Online] Available from: https://philanthropynewsdigest.org/news/gates-foundation-to-invest-5-billion-in-africa-over-five-years [Accessed 12th July 2021].

Phillips, T. (2016) China ratifies Paris climate change agreement ahead of G20. *The Guardian*. [Online] Available from: https://www.theguardian.com/world/2016/sep/03/china-ratifies-paris-climate-change-agreement [Accessed 27th July 2020].

Phillips, T. (2017) Cambridge University censorship 'exposes Xi Jinping's authoritarian shift.' *The Guardian*. [Online] Available from: https://www.theguardian.com/uk-news/2017/aug/20/cambridge...egories&utm_term=240162&subid=5396776&CMP=EMCNEWEML6619I2 [Accessed 22nd August 2017].

Pidcock, R. (2016) Analysis: What global emissions in 2016 mean for climate change goals. *Carbon Brief*. [Online] Available from: https://www.carbonbrief.org/what-global-co2-emissions-2016-mean-climate-change [Accessed 10th June 2020].

Pilling, D. (2017) Chinese investment in Africa: Beijing's testing ground. *The Financial Times*. [Online] Available from: https://www.ft.com/content/0f534aa4-4549-11e7-8519-9f94ee97d996 [Accessed 29th May 2020].

Pottinger, L. (2000) Profiling problem projects, Uganda's Bujagali Dam: A case study in corporate welfare. *International Rivers Network*. [Online] Available from: https://www.internationalrivers.org/sites/default/files/attached-files/case_study.pdf [Accessed 18th June 2020].

Prasad, E. (2015) The path to sustainable growth in China. Brookings Institute. [Online] Available from: https://www.brookings.edu/testimonies/the-path-to-sustainable-growth-in-china/ [Accessed 4th November 2018].

Pricewaterhouse Coopers. (2016) *Economic Crime: A South African pandemic: No Sector or Region is Immune*. [Online] Available from: https://www.pwc.co.za/en/assets/pdf/south-african-crime-survey-2016.pdf [Accessed 10th May 2020].

Prins, N. (2014a). *All the Presidents' Bankers: The Hidden Alliances That Drive American Power*. New York, Nation Books/ Bold Type Books.

Prins, N. (2014b). *All the President's Bankers: The Hidden Alliances that drive America's Power*. Radio New Zealand: Saturday Morning, author interview by Kim Hill [Online] Available from: https://www.rnz.co.nz/national/programmes/saturday/audio/2598795/nomi-prins-bankers-and-power [Accessed 1st October 2014].

Prins, N. (2018) *Collusion: How Central Bankers Rigged the World*. New York, Nation Books/Bold Type Books.

Publish What You Pay. (2015) *US Aid Transparency Review*. [Online] Available from: http://www.publishwhatyoufund.org/wp-content/uploads/2016/12/2015-US-Aid-Transparency-Review.pdf [Accessed 22nd June 2020].

Publish What You Pay. (2017) *US Congress Votes Down Anticorruption Rule*. [Online] Available from: https://www.publishwhatyoupay.org/tag/dodd-frank-1504/?post_type=pwyp_news [Accessed 22nd June 2020].

Pye-Smith, C. (2012) Increasing rural unemployment in Sub-Saharan Africa. *CTA Policy Brief*. [Online] Available from: https://brusselsbriefings.files.wordpress.com/2012/02/

no-4-increasing-rural-employment-in-sub-saharan-africa.pdf [Accessed 1st June 2020].

Radelet, S. (2010) Emerging Africa: How 17 countries are leading the way. *Center for Global Development*. [Online] Available from: http://www.cgdev.org/sites/default/files/1424419_file_EmergingAfrica_FINAL.pdf [Accessed 22nd December 2014].

Rakotoarisoa, M. A., Iafrate, M. & Paschali, M. (2007) Why has Africa become a net food importer? Explaining Africa agriculture and food trade deficits. *Food and Agriculture Organization (FAO)*. [Online] Available from: http://www.fao.org/3/a-i2497e.pdf [Accessed 29th June 2020].

Rakotoarisoa, M. A., Iafrate, M. & Paschali, M. (2011) Why has Africa become a net food importer? Explaining Africa agricultural and food trade deficits. *FAO*. [Online] Available from: http://www.fao.org/3/a-i2497e.pdf [Accessed 3rd June 2020].

Ramzy, A. (2012) Simmering discontent: the biggest challenge to social harmony. *Time Magazine*. [Online] Available from: http://world.time.com/2012/06/07/chinas-simmering-discontent-the-biggest-challenge-to-social-harmony/ [Accessed 22nd August 2017].

Raymond, N. (2016) Och-Ziff to pay $412 million to settle U.S. foreign bribery charges. *Reuters*. [Online] Available from: https://www.reuters.com/article/us-sec-och-ziff-capital-corruption-idUKKCN11Z2NW [Accessed 6th September 2021].

Regional Network for Equity in Health in East and Southern Africa. (2018) *Mining and Health: A Health Literacy Module*. [Online] Available from: https://www.equinetafrica.org/sites/default/files/uploads/documents/HL%20module%20Mining%20and%20Health%202018.pdf [Accessed 2nd November 2021].

Reuters. (2017) *China Ban on Ivory Sales Begins Sunday, Aims to Curb Elephant Poaching*. [Online] Available from: https://www.reuters.com/article/us-china-ivory/china-ban-on-ivory-sales-begins-sunday-aims-to-curb-elephant-poaching-idUSKBN1EN0I5 [Accessed 21st July 2019].

Ribiero, D. (2004) An Analysis of the Mphanda Nkuwa Dam Project against the World Commission on Dams guidelines. *International Rivers*. [Online] Available from: https://www.internationalrivers.org/resources/an-analysis-of-the-mphanda-nkuwa-dam-project-against-the-world-commission-on-dams [Accessed 18th December 2018].

Rice, X. (2008) World Bank cancels pipeline deal with Chad after revenues misspent. *The Guardian*. [Online] Available from: https://www.theguardian.com/world/2008/sep/12/worldbank.oil [Accessed 20th November 2020].

Rich, A. (1999) U.S. Exports Arms to the World. *Federation of American Scientists*. [Online] Available from: https://fas.org/asmp/library/articles/resist.html [Accessed 16th June 2020].

Riley, T. (2017) Just 100 companies responsible for 71% of global carbon emissions, study says. *The Guardian*. [Online] Available from: https://www.theguardian.com/sustainable-business/2017/jul/10/100-fossil-fuel-companies-investors-responsible-71-global-emissions-cdp-study-climate-change [Accessed 11th July 2018].

Rizvi, H. (2005) Liberia: Firestone Sued Over "Slave" Plantation. *International Labour Rights Forum*. [Online] Available from: https://laborrights.org/in-the-news/liberia-firestone-sued-over-slave-plantation [Accessed 2nd December 2021].

Rodney, W. (1981) *How Europe Underdeveloped Africa*. Washington DC, Howard University Press.

Rogoff, E. K., Kose, M. A. & Wei, S. J. (2003) Effects of financial globalization on developing countries: Some empirical evidence. *IMF*. [Online] Available from: https://www.imf.org/external/np/res/docs/2003/031703.pdf [Accessed 3rd August 2020].

Rome, A. (2003) 'Give earth a chance': The environmental movement and the sixties. *Journal of American History.* 90 (2). [Online] Available from: doi:10.2307/3659443 [Accessed 10th June 2020].

Romero, M. J. & Ruiz, M. (2011) Exposing the lost billions: How financial transparency on a country by country basis can aid development. *Eurodad*. [Online] Available from: http://eurodad.org/4720/ [Accessed 29th July 2018].

Rosling, H. (2018) *Factfulness*. London, Sceptre.

Ross, A. (2015) Insight: China's 'infrastructure for minerals' deal gets a reality-check in Congo. *Reuters*. [Online] Available from: http://www.reuters.com/article/congo democratic-mining-china-idUSL8N0ZN2QZ20150708 [Accessed 12th August 2017].

Rotberg, R. (2013) *Africa Emerges: Consummate Challenges, Abundant Opportunities*. New York, Wiley.

Ryder, H. (2021) Two China-Africa experts on the stereotypes they're surprised to still be unpacking. *Quartz Africa*. [Online] Available from: https://qz.com/africa/1991048/china-africa-experts-on-the-stereotypes-that-persist/ [Accessed 9th January 2022].

Sachs, J. (2002) *Resolving the Debt Crisis of Low-Income Countries* [Online] Available from: https://www.jstor.org/stable/1209181 [Accessed 23rd July 2020].

Sahara Reporters. (2013) *Tax Evasion: Nigerian Court Orders US Oil Firm ExxonMobil To Pay $83 Million For 2008-NAN*. [Online] Available from: http://saharareporters.com/2013/06/23/tax-evasion-nigerian-court-orders-us-oil-firm-exxonmobil-pay-83-million-2008-nan [Accessed 16th October 2021].

Salbu, S. (1997) Bribery in the global market: A critical analysis of the foreign corrupt practices act. *Washington and Lee Law Review*. [Online] Available from: https://scholarlycommons.law.wlu.edu/cgi/viewcontent.cgi?article=1611&context=wlulr [Accessed 27th August 2021].

Salidjanova, N. (2011) Going out, an overview of China's outward investment. *US-China Economic and Security Review Commission*. [Online] Available from: https://www.uscc.gov/sites/default/files/Research/GoingOut.pdf [Accessed 22nd May 2020].

Salomon, M. & Spanjers, J. (2017) Illicit financial flows to and from developing countries: 2005–2014. *Global Financial Integrity*. [Online] Available from: https://www.gfintegrity.org/report/illicit-financial-flows-to-and-from-developing-countries-2005-2014/ [Accessed 3rd March 2019].

Sanyanga, R. (2014) World Bank insists on Inga 3, skips lessons learned' from past big dams. *International Rivers*. [Online] Available from: https://www.internationalrivers.org/resources/inga-1-and-inga-2-dams-3616 [Accessed 10th June 2019].

Sasson, A. (2012) Food security for Africa: An urgent global challenge. *Agric & Food Secur.* 1 (2). [Online] Available from: https://doi.org/10.1186/2048-7010-1-2 [Accessed 21st June 2020].

Save the Rhino. (2017) *Leading Environmental Organisations in Namibia Hold China Accountable for Increased Wildlife Crime*. [Online] Available from: https://www.savetherhino.org/poaching-crisis/leading-environmental-organisations-in-namibia-hold-china-accountable-for-increased-wildlife-crime/ [Accessed 29th May 2020].

Schlein, L. (n.d.) WHO world water day report. *World Health Organization.* [Online] Available from: https://www.who.int/water_sanitation_health/takingcharge.html [Accessed 3rd July 2020].

Schneidman, W. & Lewis, Z. A. (2012) The African growth and opportunity act: Looking back, looking forward. *Brookings Institution.* [Online] Available from: https://www.brookings.edu/wp-content/uploads/2016/06/agoa_full_report.pdf [Accessed 23rd June 2020].

Schuttenheim, R. (2018) *Climate & Agriculture 1: African Food Imports Increase, While Agricultural Dependence Stays High.* [Online] Available from: http://www.bitsofscience.org/african-food-imports-agriculture-dependence-7906/ [Accessed 11th May 2019].

Seager, A. & Lewis, J. (2007) How top London law firms help vulture funds devour their prey: Indebted poor countries are being taken for millions of dollars in the courts. *The Guardian.* [Online] Available from: https://www.theguardian.com/business/2007/oct/17/debt.law [Accessed 10th June 2020].

Seery, E. & Seghers, J. (2019) Hitting the Target. *Oxfam.* [Online] Available from: https://oxfamilibrary.openrepository.com/bitstream/handle/10546/620721/bp-hitting-the-target-aid-inequality-agenda-080419-en.pdf [Accessed 7th October 2021].

Sen, S. (2012) How financial speculators manipulated the oil and energy markets. *China Dialogue.* [Online] Available from: https://www.chinadialogue.net/article/show/single/en/5215-How-financial-speculators-manipulated-the-oil-and-energy-markets [Accessed 10th June 2020].

Seto, K. (2000) Urban growth in China: Challenges and prospects. [Online] Available from: https://web.stanford.edu/class/cee320/CEE320B/Seto.pdf [Accessed 28th July 2017].

Settle, W., Garba, M. H. & Poisot, A-S. (2014) Reducing pesticide risks to farming communities: Cotton farmer field schools in Mali. *The Royal Society.* [Online] Available from: doi:10.1098/rstb.2012.0277 [Accessed 23rd July 2020].

Shaxon, N. (2007) Oil, corruption and the resource curse. *International Affairs.* [Online] Available from: https://doi.org/10.1111/j.1468-2346.2007.00677.x [Accessed 2nd June 2020].

Shen, Y. & Tang, K. (2019) *Do China-Financed Dams in Sub-Saharan Africa Improve the Region's Social Welfare? A Case Study of the Impacts of Ghana's Bui Dam.* CARI. Working Paper 25/2019 [Online] Available from: https://static1.squarespace.com/static/5652847de4b033f56d2bdc29/t/5cdc2a755fbd1300012a2aa0/1557932662293/WP-2019-04-Tang-Shen-Bui-Dam.pdf [Accessed 29th May 2020].

Shendruk, A. (2019) *A Simple Guide to Who Funds the UN.* [Online] Available from: https://qz.com/1712054/who-funds-the-united-nations/ [Accessed 23rd November 2020].

Sherwood, H. (2016) Saving Africa's elephants: Can you imagine a world without them? *China Dialogue.* [Online] Available from: https://www.chinadialogue.net/article/show/single/en/9244-Sa…&utm_medium=email&utm_term=0_5db8c84b96-2b434b22eb-46046012 [Accessed 14th September 2016].

Shinn, D. H. (2008) *African Migration and the Brain Drain.* [Online] Available from: https://sites.google.com/site/davidhshinn/Home/african-migration-and-the-brain-drain [Accessed 28th October 2018]

Shinn, D. H. (2016) The environmental impact of China's investment in Africa. *Cornell International Law Journal.* 49 (1), Article 2. [Online] Available from: https://scholarship.law.cornell.edu/cilj/vol49/iss1/2 [Accessed 25th July 2020].

Sieber, S. (2015) What is natural economic accounting? *World Economic Forum.* [Online] Available from: https://www.weforum.org/agenda/2015/06/what-is-natural-capital-accounting/ [Accessed 28th September 2019].

Silk, R. (2013) China weighs environmental costs. *Wall Street Journal.* [Online] Available from: https://www.wsj.com/articles/SB10001424127887324879504578597462908226052 [Accessed 27th July 2020].

Skidelsky, R. (2009) The lost continent. *Project Syndicate.* [Online] Available from: https://robertskidelsky.com/2009/06/19/the-lost-continent/ [Accessed 29th May 2020].

Slezak, M. (2017) Barack Obama transfers $500m to Green Climate Fund in attempt to protect Paris deal. *The Guardian.* [Online] Available from: https://www.theguardian.com/us-news/2017/jan/18/barack-obama-transfers-500m-to-green-climate-fund-in-attempt-to-protect-paris-deal [Accessed 10th June 2020].

Smith, D. (2009) The food rush: Rising demand in China and west sparks African land grab. *The Guardian.* [Online] Available from: https://www.theguardian.com/environment/2009/jul/03/africa-land-grab [Accessed 25th July 2020].

Smith, D. (2010) Nigeria to drop Dick Cheney charges after plea bargain. *The Guardian.* [Online] Available from: https://www.theguardian.com/world/2010/dec/15/nigeria-dick-cheney-plea-halliburton [Accessed 6th June 2019].

Snowdon, E. (2019) *Permanent Record.* New York, Metropolitan Books.

Songwe, V. & Winter, D. (2012) *Exports and Export Diversification in Sub-saharan Africa: A Strategy for Post-crisis Growth.* Brookings Africa Growth Initiative, Working Paper 3. [Online] Available from: https://www.brookings.edu/wp-content/uploads/2016/06/12-exports-africa-songwe.pdf [Accessed 3rd June 2020].

Southwestern University of Finance and Economics. (2016) *China Household Finance Survey: The Number of China's Middle Class has been more than 200 million.* [Online] Available from: http://www.chfsdata.org/detail-26,27-181.html [Accessed September 2017].

Sow, M. (2017) Figure of the week: The cost of debt in sub-Saharan Africa. *Brookings* [Online] Available from: https://www.brookings.edu/blog/africa-in-focus/2017/01/26/figure-of-the-week-the-cost-of-debt-in-sub-saharan-africa/ [Accessed 23rd April 2019].

Specter, M. (2014) Seeds of Doubt: An activist's controversial crusade against genetically modified crops. *The New Yorker.* [Online] Available from: https://www.newyorker.com/magazine/2014/08/25/seeds-of-doubt [Accessed 26th June 2020].

Ssempala, R., Ssebulime, K. & Twinoburyo, E. (2020) Uganda's experience with debt and economic growth: an empirical analysis of the effect of public debt on economic growth 1980–2016. *Economic Structures.* 9, 48. [Online] Available from: https://doi.org/10.1186/s40008-020-00224-2 [Accessed 1st October 2021].

Stahl, K. (2016) China's relations with Sub-Saharan Africa. *Istituto Affari Internationali.* [Online] Available from: http://www.iai.it/sites/default/files/iaiwp1622.pdf [Accessed 17th September 2017].

Standard & Poors. (2018) *US GDP Growth Rate by Year.* [Online] Available from: http://www.multpl.com/us-gdp-growth-rate/table/by-year [Accessed 19th July 2018].

Standing, G. (2014) *The Precariat: The New Dangerous Class*. London, Bloomsbury.

Statista. (2020) Degree of urbanization in China from 2008 to 2018. [Online] Available from: https://www.statista.com/statistics/270162/urbanization-in-china/ [Accessed 6th June 2020].

Steffen, D. (2016) *Who are the Niger Delta Avengers. The Maritime Executive*. [Online] Available from: https://www.maritime-executive.com/editorials/who-are-the-niger-delta-avengers [Accessed 2nd December 2021].

Stern, N. (2007) *Stern Review on the Economics of Climate Change*. Cambridge, Cambridge University Press.

Stiglitz, J. (2009) Wall Street's toxic message. *Vanity Fair*. [Online] Available from: https://www.vanityfair.com/news/2009/07/third-world-debt200907. [Accessed 9th June 2020].

Stockholm International Peace Research Institute (SIPRI). (2019) *Military Expenditure by Country 1988–2018, in Constant (2017) US$m*. [Online] Available from: https://www.sipri.org/sites/default/files/Data%20for%20all%20countries%20from%20 1988–2018%20in%20constant%20%282017%29%20USD%20%28pdf%29.pdf [Accessed 24th June 2019].

SIPRI. (n.d.a) *US Arms Exports by Year*. [Online] Available from: http://armstrade.sipri.org/armstrade/html/export_values.php [Accessed 29th July 2020].

SIPRI. (n.d.b) *Arms Transfers to Sudan 1994–2004*. [Online] Available from: www.sipri.org/contents/armstrad/atsud_data.html/view?searchterm=sudan, viewed on April 13, 2007 [Not available 2020].

Stratfor. (2001) *DRC Receives World Bank Loan (O)*. [Online] Available from: https://worldview.stratfor.com/article/drc-receives-world-bank-loan-o [Accessed 22nd December 2018].

Streatfield, J. (2018) Electricity investment in Sub-Saharan Africa: A historical overview and a way forward. *Journal of International Trade and Economics*. [Online] Available from: https://www.usitc.gov/publications/332/journals/electricity_investment_in_ssa-final.pdf [Accessed 28th September 2021].

Structural Adjustment Participatory Review International Network (SAPRIN). (2004) *The Policy Roots of Economic Crisis and Poverty: A Multi-Country Participatory Assessment of Structural Adjustment*. [Online] Available from: http://www.saprin.org/Sapri_Rpt.pdf [Accessed 3rd June 2020].

Sullivan, E. (2018) Nearly 90 elephants found dead near Botswana sanctuary, killed by poachers. *NPR*. [Online] Available from: https://www.npr.org/2018/09/03/644340279/nearly-90-elephants-found-dead-near-botswana-sanctuary-killed-by-poachers [Accessed 5th September 2018].

Sun, Y. (2014a) China's aid to Africa: Monster or messiah? *The Brookings Institution*. [Online] Available from: https://www.brookings.edu/opinions/chinas-aid-to-africa-monster-or-messiah/ [Accessed 21st December 2018].

Sun, Y. (2014b) *Africa in China's Foreign Policy*. John L. Thornton China Center/Africa Growth Initiative paper. [Online] Available from: https://www.brookings.edu/wp-content/uploads/2016/06/Africa-in-China-web_CMG7.pdf [Accessed 18th September 2017].

Sun, Y. (2015a) The Sixth Forum on China-Africa Cooperation: New agenda and new approach? *The Brookings Institution*. [Online] Available from: https://www.

brookings.edu/wp-content/uploads/2016/07/china-africa-cooperation-sun-2.pdf [Accessed 29th November 2018].

Sun, Y. (2015b) Xi and the 6th Forum on China-Africa Cooperation: Major commitments, but with questions. *The Brookings Institution: Africa Growth Initiative*. [Online] Available from: https://www.brookings.edu/blog/africa-in-focus/2015/12/07/xi-and-the-6th-forum-on-china-africa-cooperation-major-commitments-but-with-questions/ [Accessed 21st September 2017].

Sundaram, J., Schwank, O. & von Arnim, R. (2011) *Globalization and Development in Sub-Saharan Africa*. [Online] Available from: https://www.researchgate.net/publication/254455267_Globalization_and_development_in_sub-Saharan_Africa [Accessed 7th May 2020].

Tabuchi, H. (2021) House panel expands inquiry into climate disinformation by oil giants. *New York Times*. Available from: https://www.nytimes.com/2021/09/16/climate/exxon-oil-disinformation-house-probe.html [Accessed 9th January 2022].

Tang, K. (2019) *Lessons from East Asia: Comparing Ethiopia and Vietnam's Early-Stage Special Economic Zone Development*. Working Paper 2019/26, China Africa Research Initiative, School of Advanced International Studies, Johns Hopkins University, Washington, DC. [Online] Available from: https://static1.squarespace.com/static/5652847de4b033f56d2bdc29/t/5cdc2a848165f5c5cfd8ba68/1557932677135/WP-2019-05-Tang-Ethiopia-and-Vietnam-SEZ.pdf [Accessed 30th July 2020].

Taylor, A. (2002) Unpacking China's resource diplomacy, in Africa. In: M. Lee, Melber, H., Naidu, S. & Taylor, I (eds.) *China in Africa*. Nordiska Institutet. [Online] Available from: https://www.researchgate.net/publication/237700606_China_in_afri_C_a [Accessed 4th August 2020]].

Taylor, A. (2014) MAP: The U.S. military currently has troops in these African countries. *Washington Post*. [Online] Available from: https://www.washingtonpost.com/news/worldviews/wp/2014/05/21/map-the-u-s-currently-has-troops-in-these-african-countries/ [Accessed 3rd August 2020].

Taylor, I. (2006) China's oil diplomacy in Africa. *International Affairs*. 82 (5), 937–959. Online. Available from: doi:10.1111/j.1468-2346.2006.00579.x [Accessed 22nd May 2020].

Taylor, I. (2007) *Unpacking China's Resource Diplomacy in Africa*. Center on China's Transnational Relations1 Working Paper 19. [Online] Available from: http://www.cctr.ust.hk/materials/working_papers/WorkingPaper19_IanTaylor.pdf [Accessed 30th July 2020].

Taylor, I. (2009) *China's New Role in Africa*. Boulder, Lynne Rienner Publishers.

The African Union and Economic Commission for Africa. (2015) *Illicit Financial Flows: Report of the High Level Panel on Illicit Financial Flows from Africa*. [Online] Available from: https://www.uneca.org/sites/default/files/PublicationFiles/iff_main_report_26feb_en.pdf [Accessed 26th July 2020].

The Chicago Council on Global Affairs. (2010) *New ActionAid Report Notes Funding Gaps in G8's $22B Food Security Pledge*. [Online] Available from: https://globalfoodforthought.typepad.com/global-food-for-thought/2010/06/new-actionaid-report-notes-funding-gaps-in-g8s-22b-food-security-pledge.html [Accessed 27th June, 2019].

The Corner House, Sinks Watch & Carbon Trade Watch. (2004) *Memorandum to the Inquiry into the International Challenge of Climate Change: UK Leadership in the*

G8 and EU. [Online] Available from: http://www.thecornerhouse.org.uk/resource/memorandum-inquiry-international-challenge-climate-change-uk-leadership-g8-and-eu [Accessed 10th June 2020].

The Earthwatch Institute, World Conservation Union, World Business Council for Sustainable Development & World Resources Institute. (n.d.) *Business and Ecosystems*. [Online] Available from: https://docs.wbcsd.org/2006/11/Ecosystem_Challenges_Business_Implications.pdf [Accessed 8th June 2020].

The Economic Intelligence Unit. (2016) *Democracy Index 2016: Revenge of the 'Deplorables.'* [Online] Available from: https://www.transparency.org.nz/docs/2017/Democracy_Index_2016.pdf [Accessed 1st June 2020].

The Economist. (2000) *Hopeless Africa*. [Online]. Available from: https://www.economist.com/leaders/2000/05/11/hopeless-africa [Accessed 1st June 2018].

The Economist. (2000a) *Hopeless Africa*. [Online] Available from: http://www.economist.com/node/333429 [Accessed 28th January 2015].

The Economist. (2000b) *The Hopeless Continent*. [Online] Available from: www.economist.com/printedition/2000-05-13 [Accessed 28th January 2015].

The Economist. (2010) *A Wealth of Data*. [Online] Available from: https://www.economist.com/finance-and-economics/2010/07/29/a-wealth-of-data [Accessed 1st June 2020].

The Economist. (2010a) *China's Economy: A New Epic. China's New Five-Year Plan is at Odds with Itself*. [Online] Available from: www.economist.com/node17314578 [Accessed 22nd October 2010].

The Economist. (2011) *The Sun Shines Bright: Africa's Hopeful Economies*. [Online]. Available from: http://www.economist.com/node/21541008/ [Accessed 25th January 2015].

The Economist. (2011a) *The Lion Kings: A More Hopeful Continent*. [Online] Available from: http://www.economist.com/node/17853324/print [Accessed 28th January 2015].

The Economist. (2011b) *The Chinese in Africa: Trying to Pull Together. Africans are Asking if China is Making their Lunch or Eating It*. [Online] Available from: http://www.economist.com/node/18586448 [Accessed 8th August 2017].

The Economist. (2011c) *Africa Rising: The Hopeful Continent*. [Online] Available from: http://www.economist.com/node/21541015 [Accessed 27th January 2015].

The Economist. (2012) *The End of Cheap China?* [Online] Available from: https://www.economist.com/blogs/freeexchange/2010/07/china [Accessed 18th September 2017].

The Economist. (2019) *A Failure of Power: Eskom is Turning out the Lights in South Africa*. [Online] Available from: https://www.economist.com/middle-east-and-africa/2019/12/12/eskom-is-turning-out-the-lights-in-south-africa [Accessed 20th November 2020].

The Economist Intelligence Unit. (2014a) *The Impact of the Shale Revolution*. [Online] Available from: http://www.eiu.com/industry/article/151852599/the-impact-of-the-shale-revolution/2014-05# [Accessed 17th June 2020].

The Economist Intelligence Unit. (2014b) *US Vows to Reshape its Relations with Africa*. [Online] Available from: https://www.eiu.com/industry/article/952160879/us-vows-to-reshape-its-relations-with-africa/2014-08-11 [Accessed 3rd July 2020].

The Economist Intelligence Unit. (2017) *China's new NEV rules*. [Online] Available from: http://www.eiu.com/industry/article/1185390902/chinas-new-nev-rules/2017-05-03 [Accessed 18th September 2017].

The FOCAC Reporting Project. (2015) 10 things you need to know about China-Africa relations. *China Africa Research Institute (CARI) and WitsJournalism Africa China Reporting Project.* [Online] Available from: https://www.reporting-focac.com/10-things-you-need-to-know.html [Accessed 26th May 2019].

The Goldman Environmental Prize. (1995) *1995 Goldman Environmental Prize Ceremony: Ken Saro Wiwa.* [Online] Available from: https://www.youtube.com/watch?v=aMUb4LHLYXk [Accessed 1st June 2020].

The Guardian. (2016) *Democracy in Africa: Five Myths Explored.* [Online] Available from: https://www.theguardian.com/global-development/datablog/2016/feb/25/democracy-in-african-countries-five-myths-explored [Accessed 12th May 2018].

The Guardian. (2017) *America Owes China $1tn. That's a Problem for Beijing, and Trump Knows it.* [Online] Available from: https://www.theguardian.com/business/2017/apr/09/us-owes-china-billion-dollars-problem-beijing-trump-knows [Accessed 10th June 2020].

The National Center for Biotechnology Information. (n.d.) *Evaluation of PEPFAR.* [Online] Available from: https://www.ncbi.nlm.nih.gov [Accessed 1st December 2021].

The New Humanitarian (formerly the Integrated Regional Information Networks (IRIN), UN). (2004) *Court Case to Determine Rights of Bushmen.* [Online] Available from: http://www.thenewhumanitarian.org/feature/2004/07/01/court-case-determine-rights-bushmen [Accessed 12th May 2020].

The Observatory of Economic Complexity (OEC). (2017) *China.* [Online] Available from: http://atlas.media.mit.edu/en/profile/country/chn/ [Accessed 18th August 2017].

The Source. (2016) *Chinese Contractor for Beitbridge-Chirunu Highway Banned by World Bank for Corruption.* [Online] Available from: http://source.co.zw/2016/06/chinese-contractor-for-beitbridge-chirundu-highway-banned-by-world-bank-for-corruption/ [Accessed 6th September 2017].

The White House Office of the Press Secretary. (2015) *Factsheet: Power Africa.* [Online] Available from: https://obamawhitehouse.archives.gov/the-press-office/2015/07/25/fact-sheet-power-africa [Accessed 25th April 2020].

Thielman, S. (2016) ExxonMobil under investigation over lucrative Nigerian oil deal. *The Guardian.* [Online] Available from https://www.theguardian.com/business/2016/jun/23/exxonmobil-nigeria-oil-fields-deal-investigation [Accessed 20th July 2021].

Thomson, J. A. (2015) Why genetically modified crops have been slow to take hold in Africa. *The Conversation.* [Online] Available from: https://theconversation.com/why-genetically-modified-crops-have-been-slow-to-take-hold-in-africa-44195 [Accessed June 2020].

Tian, N., Fleurant, A., Kuimova, A., Wezeman, P. D. & Wezeman, S. T. (2018) Trends in world military expenditure, 2017. *Stockholm International Peace Research Institute (SIPRI).* [Online] Available from: https://www.sipri.org/publications/2018/sipri-fact-sheets/trends-world-military-expenditure-2017 [Accessed 29th May 2020].

Time Magazine. (2012) *Africa Rising.* [Online] Available from: http://content.time.com/time/covers/europe/0,16641,20121203,00.html [Accessed 3rd June 2020].

Tobin, D. (2011) Inequality in China: Rural poverty persists as urban wealth balloons. *The Guardian.* [Online] Available from: http://www.bbc.co.uk/news/business-13945072 [Accessed 21st January 2013].

Touissant, E. (2014) Domination of the United States of the World Bank. *Committee for the Abolition of Illegitimate Debt (CADTM)*. [Online] Available from: http://www.cadtm.org/Domination-of-the-United-States-on-the-World-Bank [Accessed 29th December 2018].

Toulmin, C. (2009) *Climate Change in Africa*. London, Zed Books.

Transparency International. (2017) *Corruption Perceptions Index 2016*. [Online] Available from: https://www.transparency.org/en/news/corruption-perceptions-index-2016 [Accessed 10th July 2019].

Transparency International. (2019) *How do you Define Corruption?* [Online] Available from: https://www.transparency.org/what-is-corruption [Accessed 15th March 2019].

Transparency International. (n.d.) (2016) *Corruption Perceptions Index*. [Online] Available from: https://www.transparency.org/en/cpi/2016/index/nzl [Accessed 28th September 2021].

Transport and the Environment. (2018) *EU Ends Target for Food-Based Biofuels But Will Only Halt Palm-Oil Support in 2030*. [Online] Available from: https://www.transportenvironment.org/news/eu-ends-target-food-based-biofuels-will-only-halt-palm-oil-support-2030 [Accessed 17th May 2019].

Treasury Direct. (n.d.) *Debt to the Penny and Who Holds It*. [Online] Available from: https://treasurydirect.gov/govt/reports/pd/debttothepenny.htm [Accessed 18th August 2019].

TRT World. (2020) *Document Trove Shows how 'Africa's richest woman' Stole Fortune*. [Online] Available from: https://www.trtworld.com/business/document-trove-shows-how-africa-s-richest-woman-stole-fortune-33067 [Accessed 20th July 2021].

Turner, G. (2016) The World Bank's dirty finance. *Tax Justice Network*. [Online] Available from: https://www.taxjustice.net/2016/11/01/harmful-finance/ [Accessed 9th May 2019]

Turner, G. (2018) Two years after we exposed Rift Valley Railways, World Bank corruption probe sanctions companies. *Finance Uncovered*. [Online] Available from: https://www.financeuncovered.org/investigations/two-years-exposed-rift-valley-railways-world-bank-sanctions-companies-corruption-probe/ [Accessed 16th June 2020].

Turse, N. (2015a) The US carried out 674 military operations in Africa last year. Did you hear about any of them? *The Nation*. [Online] Available from: https://www.thenation.com/article/archive/us-carried-out-674-military-operations-africa-last-year-did-you-hear-about-any-them/ [Accessed 16th June 2020].

Turse, N. (2015b) The US Military's best-kept secret. *The Nation*. [Online] Available from: https://www.thenation.com/article/archive/the-us-militarys-best-kept-secret/ [Accessed 16th June 2020].

UN Conference on Trade and Development (UNCTAD). (2001) *World Investment Report*. [Online] Available from: https://unctad.org/en/pages/PublicationArchive.aspx?publicationid=656 [Accessed 23rd June 2020].

Union of Concerned Scientists (UCS). (2020) *The 20 Countries that Emitted the Most Carbon Dioxide in 2017*. [Online] Available from: https://www.ucsusa.org/resources/each-countrys-share-co2-emissions [Accessed 10th June 2020].

United Nations (UN). (n.d.) *Global Contract*. [Online] Available from: https://www.unglobalcompact.org [Accessed 4th December 2021].

United Nations. (1992) *United Nations Framework Convention on Climate Change.* [Online] Available from: https://unfccc.int/resource/docs/convkp/conveng.pdf [Accessed 11th August 2020].

United Nations. (2015) *The Millennium Development Goals Report 2015.* [Online] Available from: https://www.un.org/millenniumgoals/2015_MDG_Report/pdf/MDG%202015%20rev%20(July%201).pdfpdf [Accessed 3rd July 2020].

United Nations. (2020) *United Nations Peacekeeping: How We are Funded.* [Online] Available from: https://peacekeeping.un.org/en/how-we-are-funded [Accessed 6th June 2020].

United Nations. (n.d.) *The 17 Goals.* [Online] Available from: https://sdgs.un.org/#goal_section [Accessed 1st June 2020].

United Nations Commission on Trade and Development (UNCTAD). (2004) *Debt Sustainability: Oasis or Mirage?* [Online] Available from: https://unctad.org/en/Docs/gdsafrica20041_en.pdf [Accessed 3rd June 2020].

United Nations Conference on Trade and Development (UNCTAD). (2013) The rise of BRICS and FDI in Africa. [Online] Available from: https://unctad.org/en/PublicationsLibrary/webdiaeia2013d6_en.pdf [Accessed 29 May 2020].

United Nations Conference on Trade and Development (UNCTAD). (2017) *World Investment Report.* [Online] Available from: https://unctad.org/en/PublicationChapters/wir2017ch2_en.pdf [Accessed 29th May 2020].

United Nations Council on Trade and Development (UNCTAD). (2017a) *Key Statistics and Trends in International Trade 2017: Trade Imbalances.*[Online] Available from: https://unctad.org/en/PublicationsLibrary/ditctab2017d6_en.pdf [Accessed 23rd June 2019].

United Nations Department of Economic and Social Affairs (DESA). (2015) World population prospects: Key findings and advance tables. *United Nations.* [Online] Available from: https://esa.un.org/unpd/wpp/Publications/Files/Key_Findings_WPP_2015.pdf [Accessed 20th June 2018].

United Nations Development Program (UNDP). (1990) *Human Development Report 1990.* Oxford, Oxford University Press.

UNDP. (2015) *Human Development Report 2015: Work for Human Development.* [Online] Available from: http://hdr.undp.org/sites/default/files/2015_human_development [Accessed 10th May 2020].

UNDP. (2016) *Human Development Report: Development for Everyone.* [Online] Available from: http://hdr.undp.org/sites/default/files/2016_human_development_report.pdf [Accessed 10th May 2020].

UNDP. (2018) *About Sub-Saharan Africa: Africa at a turning point.* [Online] Available from: https://www.africa.undp.org/content/rba/en/home/regioninfo/ [Accessed 10th May 2020].

UNDP. (n.d.) *Human Development Index.* [Online] Available from: http://hdr.undp.org/en/content/human-development-index-hdi [Accessed 2nd November 2021].

United Nations Educational, Scientific and Cultural Organization (UNESCO) (2016) *Office Dakar and Regional Bureau for Education in Africa.* [Online] Available from: https://unesdoc.unesco.org/ark:/48223/pf0000258981 [Accessed 10th May 2020].

United Nations Office of Drugs and Crime (UNODC). (2016) Almost a third of trafficking victims are children. *UNODC Report*. [Online] Available from: https://www.unodc.org/unodc/en/frontpage/2016/December/almost-a-third-of-trafficking-victims-are-children_-unodc-report.html [Accessed 1st June 2020].

United Nations Treaty Collection. (2021) *The United Nations Convention Against Corruption*. [Online] Available from: https://treaties.un.org/Pages/ViewDetails.aspx?src=IND&mtdsg_no=XVIII-14&chapter=18&clang=_en [Accessed 9th December 2021].

United States Agency for International Development (USAID). (2013) *USAID's Legacy in Agricultural Development*. [Online] Available from: https://www.usaid.gov/sites/default/files/documents/1867/USAID-Legacy-in-Agricultural-Development [Accessed 12th November 2021].

USAID. (2018) *Power Africa Strategic Roadmaps*. [Online] Available from: https://www.usaid.gov/powerafrica/roadmap [Accessed 7th October 2021].

USAID. (2019) *History*. [Online] Available from: https://www.usaid.gov/who-we-are/usaid-history [Accessed 7th June 2020].

USAID. (n.d.a). *What We Do*. [Online] Available from: https://www.usaid.gov/what-we-do/working-crises-and-conflict [Accessed 8th June 2020].

USAID. (n.d.b). *Leveraging Partnerships to Increase Access to Power in Sub-Saharan Africa*. [Online] Available from: https://www.usaid.gov/powerafrica/aboutus [Accessed 21st July 2021].

United States Census Bureau. (2019) *International Programs: International Database*. [Online] Available from: https://www.census.gov/data-tools/demo/idb/informationGateway.php [Accessed 1st June 2020].

United States Census Bureau. (2020) *US Trade in Goods with Africa*. [Online] Available from: https://www.census.gov/foreign-trade/balance/c0013.html#2016 [Accessed 10th May 2020].

United States Department of State. (2017) *Trafficking in Persons Report*. [Online] Available from: https://www.state.gov/reports/2017-trafficking-in-persons-report/ [Accessed 1st June 2020].

United States Energy Information Administration (EIA). (2016) *Hydraulically Fractured Wells Provide Two-Thirds of U.S. Natural Gas Production*. [Online] Available from: https://www.eia.gov/todayinenergy/detail.php?id=26112 [Accessed 11th June 2020].

United States Environmental Protection Agency (EPA). (n.d.) *Global Greenhouse Gas Emissions Data*. [Online] Available from: https://www.epa.gov/ghgemissions/global-greenhouse-gas-emissions-data#Country [Accessed 11th June 2020].

United States Government Accountability Office (GAO). (2014) *Drinking Water: EPA Program to Protect Underground Sources from Injection of Fluids Associated with Oil and Gas Production Needs Improvement*. [Online] Available from: https://www.gao.gov/assets/670/664499.pdf [Accessed 10th August 2019].

Urbina, I. (2011) Regulation lax as gas wells' tainted water hits rivers. *The New York Times*. [Online] Available from: https://www.nytimes.com/2011/02/27/us/27gas.html [Accessed 10th June 2020].

US Census. (2019) *2000: U.S. Trade in Goods with Africa*. [Online] Available from: https://www.census.gov/foreign-trade/balance/c0013.html#2000 [Accessed 30th July 2019].

US Census Bureau. (2017) *Trade in goods with China*. [Online] Available from: https://www.census.gov/foreign-trade/balance/c5700.html [Accessed 5th June 2020].

US Congressional Research Service. (2020) *U.S. Assistance to Sub-Saharan Africa: An overview*. [Online] Available from: https://sgp.fas.org/crs/row/R46368.pdf [Accessed 2nd December 2021].

US Department of Commerce. (2018) *Biennial Report on the Implementation of the African Growth And Opportunity Act*. [Online] Available from: https://ustr.gov/sites/default/files/2018_AGOA_Implementation.pdf [Accessed 4th July 2020].

US Department of Commerce. (n.d.) *U.S. Trade with Sub-Saharan Africa*. [Online] Available from: https://legacy.trade.gov/agoa/pdf/2016%20US-SSA%20Trade%20 One-Pager.pdf [Accessed 2nd December 2021].

US House of Representatives Committee on Financial Services. (2007) Transparency of extractive industries: High stakes for resource-rich countries. *Citizens and International, Business*. 4. Washington, US Government Printing Office.

US International Trade Commission. (2018) *US Trade and Investment with Sub-Saharan Africa*. [Online] Available from: https://www.usitc.gov/publications/332/pub4780.pdf [Accessed 16 November 2021].

US Senate Foreign Relations Committee. (2004) *Combatting Corruption in the Multilateral Banks*. [Online] Available from: https://www.govinfo.gov/content/pkg/CPRT-111SPRT55285/html/CPRT-111SPRT55285.htm [Accessed 28th August 2021].

US Senate Judiciary Committee on Human Rights and the Law. (2008) *The Oil Industry and Human Rights in the Niger Delta*. [Online] Available from: https://www.judiciary.senate.gov/imo/media/doc/08-09-24BasseyTestimony.pdf [Accessed 28th August 2021].

van Luyn, F.-J. (2010) *Rainmakers: China's Environment on the Brink of Disaster*. [Documentary]. Amsterdam.

Varinsky, D. (2018) The $66 billion Bayer-Monsanto merger just got a major green light — But farmers are terrified. *Business Insider*. [Online] Available from: https://www.businessinsider.com/bayer-monsanto-merger-has-farmers-worried-2018-4 [Accessed 4th September 2019].

Vaughan, A. (2016) China tops the WHO list for deadly air pollution, *The Guardian*. Online. Available from: https://www.theguardian.com/environment/2016/sep/27/more-than-million-died-due-air-pollution-china-one-year [Accessed 4th November 2018].

Vidal, J. & Adam, D. (2007) China overtakes US as world's biggest CO^2 emitter. *The Guardian*. [Online] Available from: www.guardian.co.uk/environment/2007/jun/19/china.usnews/print [Accessed 22nd May 2020].

Vidal, J. (2007) UK: Class action starts over toxic waste dumped in Africa. *The Guardian*. [Online] Available from: http://www.corpwatch.org/article.php?id=14292&printsafe=1 [Accessed 15th August 2013].

Vidal, J. (2010) Why is the Gates foundation investing in GM giant Monsanto? *The Guardian*. [Online] Available from: https://www.theguardian.com/global-development/poverty-matters/2010/sep/29/gates-foundation-gm-monsanto [Accessed 22nd April 2020].

Vidal, J. (2010a) Landgrabbing in Africa (1). *China Dialogue*. [Online] Available from: https://www.chinadialogue.net/article/show/single/en/3593--Land-grabbing-in-Africa-1- [Accessed 1st December 2018].

Vidal, J. (2010b) Land-grabbing in Africa (2). *China Dialogue*. [Online] Available from: https://chinadialogue.net/en/business/3594-land-grabbing-in-africa-2/ [Accessed 25th July 2020].

Vidal, J. (2015) Water privatisation: A worldwide failure*? The Guardian.* [Online] Available from: https://www.theguardian.com/global-development/2015/jan/30/water-privatisation-worldwide-failure-lagos-world-bank [Accessed 10th October 2021].

Vidal, J. (2016) Are Gates and Rockefeller using their influence to set agenda in poor states*? The Guardian.* [Online] Available from: https://www.theguardian.com/global-development/2016/jan/15/bill-gates-rockefeller-influence-agenda-poor-nations-big-pharma-gm-hunger [Accessed 2nd December 2021].

Volcovici, V. & Yukhananov, A. (2013) World Bank to limit financing of coal-fired plants. *Reuters.* [Online] Available from: https://www.reuters.com/article/us-worldbank-climate-coal-idUSBRE96F19U20130716 [Accessed 4th December 2021].

Vuylsteke, Y. (2017) Ibrahim Index of African Governance: 2017 IIAG key findings. *The Mo Ibrahim Foundation.* [Online] Available from: http://mo.ibrahim.foundation/news/2017/2017-iiag-key-findings/ [Accessed 8th May 2020].

Walker, B. (2014) How Africa is changing Chinese oil companies. *China Dialogue.* [Online] Available from: https://www.chinadialogue.net/article/show/single/en/7583-How-Africa-is-changing-Chinese-oil-companies [Accessed 16th December 2014].

Wang, L. & Bateman, J. (2018) *China's Medical Aid in Africa: China is Doing More than Building Roads in Africa. It is Curing People.* [Online] Available from: https://thediplomat.com/2018/03/chinas-medical-aid-in-africa/ [Accessed 12th December 2018].

Watts, J. (2010) *When a Billion Chinese Jump: How China will save the world or destroy it.* London, Simon & Schuster.

Weibing, L. (2016) China focus: All major targets of 12th Five Year Plan fulfilled: Premier. *Xinhua.* [Online] Available from: http://news.xinhuanet.com/english/2016-03/05/c_135158992.htm [Accessed 7th September 2017].

Weisbrot, M. & Johnson, J. (2016) Voting share reforms at the IMF. Will it make a difference? *Center for Economic Policy Research.* [Online] Available from: https://ideas.repec.org/p/epo/papers/2016-09.html [Accessed 25th November 2019].

Weisert, D. (2001) Coca Cola in China: Quenching the thirst of a billion. *China Business Review.* 28 (4), 52–56.

Weng, X. (2014) *The Africa–China Timber Trade: Diverse Business Models Call for Specialized Policy Responses.* [Online] Available from: https://www.researchgate.net/publication/284727204_The_Africa-China_timber_trade_Diverse_business_models_call_for_specialized_policy_responses [Accessed 27th May 2019].

Wildau, G. & Mitchell, T. (2016) China income equality among the world's worst. *Financial Times.* [Online] Available from: https://www.ft.com/content/3c521faa-baa6-11e5-a7cc-280dfe875e28?mhq5j=e1[Accessed 17th August 2017].

Williamson, J. (2004) *A Short History of the Washington Consensus.* [Online] Available from: https://www.piie.com/publications/papers/williamson0904-2.pdf [Accessed 7th June 2020].

Wise, T. (2020) Failing Africa's farmers: An impact assessment of the alliance for a Green Revolution in Africa. *Tufts University.* [Online] Available from: https://sites.tufts.edu/gdae/files/2020/10/20-01_Wise_FailureToYield.pdf [Accessed 11th October 2021].

Woetzel, J. (2015) *5 Reasons Why China's Economy won't Collapse.* McKinsey & Company. [Online] Available from: http://mckinseychina.com/5-reasons-why-chinas-economy-wont-collapse/ [Accessed 25th March 2018].

Woods, N. (2008) Governance matters: The IMF and Sub-Saharan Africa. In: Boughton, J. & Lombardi, D. (eds.). Oxford, Oxford University Press.

Woods, N. (2009) Governance matters: The IMF and Sub-Saharan Africa. In: Boughton, J. & Lombardi, D. (eds.) *Finance, Development and the IMF*. Oxford, Oxford University Press.

Woody, C. (2016) Here's the dramatic shift America's thirst for oil has undergone since 2000. *Business Insider*. [Online] Available from: https://www.businessinsider.com.au/change-in-us-oil-imports-since-2000-2016-5?r=US&IR=T [Accessed 30th July 2019].

World Bank (WB). (2004) *Adjustment in Africa*. [Online] Available from: http://documents1.worldbank.org/curated/en/219981468192845881/pdf/multi-page.pdf [Accessed 16th June 2020].

World Bank (WB). (2005) *Where is the Wealth of Nations? Measuring Capital for the 21st Century*. [Online] Available from: https://openknowledge.worldbank.org/handle/10986/7505 [Accessed 10th May 2020].

World Bank (WB). (2012a) *The Natural Capital Accounting Issue Brief*. [Online] Available from: https://www.worldbank.org/en/news/feature/2012/05/07/natural-capital-accounting.print [Accessed 11th June 2020].

World Bank (WB). (2012b) *From Growth to Inclusive Green Growth: The Economics of Sustainable Development*. [Online] Available from: https://www.worldbank.org/en/news/feature/2012/05/09/growth-to-inclusive-green-growth-economics-sustainable-development [Accessed 3rd July 2020].

World Bank (WB). (2013) *Growing Africa: Unlocking the Potential of Agribusiness*. [Online] Available from: http://siteresources.worldbank.org/INTAFRICA/Resources/africa-agribusiness-report-2013.pdf [Accessed 13th September 2019].

World Bank (WB). (2014a) *A Stronger, More Connected World Bank Group*. [Online] Available from: https://openknowledge.worldbank.org/bitstream/handle/10986/16093/32813_ebook.pdf?sequence= [Accessed 13th October 2021].

World Bank (WB). (2014b) *The Little Green Data Book*. Washington, DC.

World Bank (WB). (2015a) *World Bank Announces New Settlement with Gezhouba Group Co. Ltd. press release*. [Online] Available from: http://www.worldbank.org/en/news/press-release/2015/05/29/world-bank-new-settlement-gezhouba-group [Accessed 22nd December 2018].

World Bank (WB). (2015b) *FAQs: Global Poverty Line Update*. [Online] Available from: https://www.worldbank.org/en/topic/poverty/brief/global-poverty-line-faq [Accessed 27th July 2020].

World Bank (WB). (2016a) *Global Regional Prospects*. [Online] Available from: https://www.worldbank.org/content/dam/Worldbank/GEP/GEP2016a/Global-Economic-Prospects-January-2016-Spillovers-amid-weak-growth.pdf [Accessed 10th May 2020].

World Bank (WB). (2016b) *Eskom Investment Support Project*. [Online] Available from: http://projects.worldbank.org/P116410/eskom-investment-support-project?lang=en&tab=overview [Accessed 9th May 2019].

World Bank (WB). (2017a) *Global Outlook: A Fragile Recovery*. [Online] Available from: http://pubdocs.worldbank.org/en/216941493655495719/Global-Economic-Prospects-June- 2017-Global-Outlook.pdf [Accessed 10th May 2020].

World Bank (WB). (2017b) *World Bank in Africa: Overview.* [Online] Available from: https://www.worldbank.org/en/region/afr/overview [Accessed 23rd July 2020].

World Bank (WB). (n.d.) *Who We Are.* [Online] Available from: https://www.worldbank.org/en/who-we-are [Accessed 16th June 2020].

World Bank (WB). (n.d.a) *China: Data: GNI per Capita.* [Online] Available from: https://data.worldbank.org/indicator/NY.GDP.PCAP.CD?locations=CN [Accessed 27th July 2020].

World Bank (WB). (n.d.a1). *Data: Sub Saharan Africa.* [Online] Available from: https://data.worldbank.org/country/ZG [Accessed 16th June 2020].

World Bank (WB). (n.d.a2) *Open Data: World (GDP, Population, School Enrolment-Primary, CO² Emissions, Life Expectancy at Birth, GNI per Capita).* [Online] Available from: https://data.worldbank.org/region/world [Accessed 7th June 2018].

World Bank (WB). (n.d.a3). *World Bank: About.* [Online] Available from: http://www.worldbank.org/en/about [Accessed 9th February 2019].

World Bank (WB). (n.d.b) *China: Data: Poverty.* [Online] Available from: https://data.worldbank.org/country/china?view=chart [Accessed 4th June 2020].

World Bank (WB). (n.d.b1). *Data: World.* [Online] Available from: https://data.worldbank.org/indicator/NY.GDP.MKTP.CD [Accessed 1st July 2020].

World Bank (WB). (n.d.b2) *Open Data: Sub-Saharan Africa (GDP, Population, School Enrolment-Pri¬mary, CO² Emissions, Life Expectancy at Birth, GNI per Capita).* [Online] Available from: https://data.worldbank.org/region/sub-saharan-africa [Accessed 7th June 2018].

World Bank (WB). (n.d.b3). *World Bank Group Finances.* [Online] Available from: https://finances.worldbank.org/Shareholder-Equity/Top-8-countries-voting-power/udm3-vzz9 [Accessed 11th June 2020].

World Bank (WB). (n.d.c) *China: Data: Unemployment.* [Online] Available from: https://data.worldbank.org/indicator/SL.UEM.TOTL.ZS?locations=CN [Accessed 27th July 2020].

World Bank (WB). (n.d.c1) *Open Data: Sub-Saharan Africa: Net Official Development Assistance and Official Aid Received 1960–2018.* [Online] Available from: https://data.worldbank.org/indicator/DT.ODA.ALLD.CD?locations=ZG [Accessed 7th June 2018].

World Bank (WB). (n.d.c2). *Archivists' Chronology 1944–2013.* [Online] Available from: http://pubdocs.worldbank.org/en/186241442500110286/PDF-World-Bank-Group-Archivists-Chronology-1944-2013.pdf [Accessed 16th June 2020].

World Bank (WB). (n.d.c3). *Data US: GNI.* [Online] Available from: https://data.worldbank.org/country/US [Accessed 11th June 2020].

World Bank (WB). (n.d.d) *China: Data: GINI index.* [Online] Available from: https://data.worldbank.org/indicator/SI.POV.GINI?locations=CN [Accessed 27th July 2020].

World Bank (WB). (n.d.d1). *Data US: Life Expectancy.* [Online] Available from: https://data.worldbank.org/country/US [Accessed 11th June 2020].

World Bank (WB). (n.d.d2) *Trading Economics: Sub-Saharan Africa (all income levels) — Net ODA Received per Capita.* [Online] Available from: https://tradingeconomics.com/sub-saharan-africa-all-income-levels/net-oda-received-per-capita-current-us$-wb-data.html [Accessed 2nd June 2020].

World Bank (WB). (n.d.e) *China Urban Population (% of Total Population)* [Online] Available from: https://data.worldbank.org/indicator/SP.URB.TOTL.IN.ZS?locations=CN [Accessed 27th July 2020].

World Bank (WB). (n.d.e1) *Data: SSA: Remittances.* [Online] Available from: https://data.worldbank.org/indicator/BX.TRF.PWKR.DT.GD.ZS?locations=ZG&year_high_desc=false [Accessed 5th September 2021].

World Bank (WB). (n.d.e2). *Data US: GINI Index (World Bank Estimate) United States.* [Online] Available from: https://data.worldbank.org/indicator/SI.POV.GINI?locations=US&view=chart [Accessed 10th June 2020].

World Bank (WB). (n.d.f) *China: Data: Population Over 65.* [Online] Available from: https://data.worldbank.org/indicator/SP.POP.65UP.TO.ZS?locations=CN [Accessed 27th July 2020].

World Bank (WB). (n.d.f1) *World Integrated Trade Solution (WITS): SSA Trade Summary.* [Online] Available from: https://wits.worldbank.org/CountryProfile/en/Country/SSF/Year/2000/Summary [Accessed 2nd June 2020].

World Bank (WB). (n.d.f2). *Data US: GDP.* [Online] Available from: https://data.worldbank.org/country/US [Accessed 11th June 2020].

World Bank (WB). (n.d.g) *World Integrated Trade Solution (WITS): SSA Trade Summary.* [Online] Available from: https://wits.worldbank.org/CountryProfile/en/Country/SSF/Year/2016/Summary [Accessed 2nd June 2020].

World Bank (WB). (n.d.g1). *World GDP.* [Online] Available from: https://data.worldbank.org/indicator/NY.GDP.MKTP.CD [Accessed 29th July 2020].

World Bank (WB). (n.d.g2) *China: Data: Population, GNI, GDP.* [Online] Available from: https://data.worldbank.org/country/CN [Accessed 27th July 2020].

World Bank (WB). (n.d.h) *China GDP Growth (Annual%).* [Online] Available from: https://data.worldbank.org/indicator/NY.GDP.MKTP.KD.ZG?locations=CN-MO [Accessed 27th July 2020].

World Bank (WB). (n.d.h1) *Open Data: Sub-Saharan Africa Foreign Direct Investment.* [Online] Available from: https://data.worldbank.org/indicator/BX.KLT.DINV.CD.WD?locations=ZG [Accessed 2nd June 2020].

World Bank (WB). (n.d.h2). *US Data: Economy and Growth.* [Online] Available from: https://data.world-bank.org/topic/economy-and-growth?locations=US [Accessed 29th July 2020].

World Bank (WB). (n.d.i) *World Integrated Trade Solutions: China.* [Online] Available from: https://wits.worldbank.org/CountryProfile/en/Country/CHN/Year/2016/TradeFlow/Import/Partner/by-country/Product/44-49_Wood/Show/Partner%20Name;MPRT-TRD-VL;MPRT-PRDCT-SHR;AHS-WGHTD-AVRG;MFN-WGHTD-AVRG;/Sort/MPRT-TRD-VL/Chart/top10 [Accessed 5th June 2020].

World Bank (WB). (n.d.i1). *Data US: World Integrated Trade Solution (WITS): US Trade 2000.* [Online] Available from: https://wits.worldbank.org/CountryProfile/en/Country/USA/Year/2000/Summary [Accessed 8th June 2020].

World Bank (WB). (n.d.i2). *Restructuring Paper on a Proposed Project Restructuring of Eskom Investment Support Project.* [Online] Available from: http://documents.worldbank.org/curated/en/945661577445675366/pdf/Disclosable-Restructuring-Paper-Eskom- Investment-Support-Project-P116410.pdf [Accessed 10th May 2020].

World Bank (WB). (n.d.j) *USx: Data: GDP, GNI per Capita.* [Online] Available from: https://data.worldbank.org/indicator/NY.GDP.PCAP.KN?locations=US&view=chart [Accessed 27th July 2020].

World Bank (WB). (n.d.j1). *Data US: World Integrated Trade Solution (WITS): US trade 2016.* [Online] Available from: https://wits.worldbank.org/CountryProfile/en/Country/USA/Year/2016/Summary [Accessed 8th June 2020].

World Bank Operations Evaluation Department. (2000) *The World Bank Forest Strategy: Striking the Right Balance.* [Online] Available from: https://ieg.worldbankgroup.org/sites/default/files/Data/reports/forestry.pdf.

World Health Organization. (WHO) (2014a) *Chemicals of Public Concern.* [Online] Available from: https://apps.who.int/iris/bitstream/handle/10665/178166/9789290232810.pdf;jsessionid=0A7810BAC034BBA94AEA731AC585B5E5?sequence=5 [Accessed 25th July 2020].

World Health Organization (WHO). (2014b) *Preventing Diarrhoea through Better Water, Sanitation and Hygiene, Exposures and Impacts in Low- and Middle-Income Countries.* [Online] Available from: https://apps.who.int/iris/bitstream/handle/10665/150112/9789241564823_eng.pdf?sequence=1 [Accessed 18th June 2020].

WHO. (2019) *Lead Poisoning and Health* [Online] Available from: https://www.who.int/news-room/fact-sheets/detail/lead-poisoning-and [Accessed 28th June 2020].

World Politics Review. (2019) *Why African Countries Maintain Tight Restrictions on Genetically Modified Food.* [Online] Available from: https://www.worldpolitics review.com/trend-lines/27892/why-african-countries-maintain-tight-restrictions-on-genetically-modified-food [Accessed 16th June 2020].

World Trade Organization (WTO). (2018) *Who's WTO is it Anyway?* [Online] Available from: https://www.wto.org/english/thewto_e/whatis_e/tif_e/org1_e.htm [Accessed 25th August 2018].

World Wildlife Fund (WWF). (2012) *China Ecological Footprint Report 2012.* [Online] Available from: https://www.footprintnetwork.org/content/images/article_uploads/China_Ecological_Footprint_2012.pdf [Accessed 27th May 2020].

World Wildlife Fund. (2018a) *Africa Deforestation.* [Online] Available from: http://wwf.panda.org/about_our_earth/deforestation/deforestation_fronts/deforestation_in_the_congo_basin/ [Accessed 5th January 2018].

World Wildlife Fund. (2018b) *Illegal Wildlife Trade.* [Online] Available from: https://www.worldwildlife.org/threats/illegal-wildlife-trade [Accessed 5th January 2018].

Wroughton, L. (2006) Ghana: IFC approves loans to controversial Newmont gold mine in divided vote — local & international. *Business and Human Rights Resource Centre.* [Online] Available from: https://www.business-humanrights.org/en/ghana-ifc-approves-loans-to-controversial-newmont-gold-mine-in-divided-vote-local-intl-ngos-concerned-about-displacement-of-local-residents-environmental-impacts [Accessed 28th June 2020].

Wroughton, L. (2008) World Bank pulls plug on Chad oil pipeline agreement. *Reuters.* [Online] Available from: https://www.reuters.com/article/idUSN09320796._CH_.2400 [Accessed 18th June 2020].

Xia, Y. (2019a) *Wealth from Waste? Chinese Investments and Technology Transfer in the Tanzanian Plastic Recycling Industry.* Working Paper 2019/27, China Africa

Research Initiative, School of Advanced International Studies, Johns Hopkins University, Washington, DC. [Online] Available from: http://www.sais-cari.org/publications [Accessed 29th May 2020].

Xia, Y. (2019b) *Chinese Manufacturing and Agricultural Investment in Tanzania: A Scoping Study*. Working Paper 2019/31, China Africa Research Initiative, School of Advanced International Studies, Johns Hopkins University, Washington, DC. [Online] Available from: http://www.sais-cari.org/publications [Accessed 29th May 2020].

Xia, Y. (2019c) *Chinese Agricultural and Manufacturing Investment in Kenya: A Scoping Study*. Working Paper 2019/30, China Africa Research Initiative, School of Advanced International Studies, Johns Hopkins University, Washington, DC. [Online] Available from: http://www.sais-cari.org/publications [Accessed 29th May 2020].

Xiang Bo. (2017) China becomes single largest contributor of Africa's FDI, report. *Xinhua*. [Online] Available from: http://www.chinadaily.com.cn/world/2017-05/03/content_29189581.htm [Accessed 8th August 2017].

Xiaoyang, T. (2019a) *The Impact of Chinese Investment on Skill Development and Technology Transfer in Zambia and Malawi's Cotton Sector*. Working Paper 2019/23, China Africa Research Initiative, School of Advanced International Studies, Johns Hopkins University, Washington, DC. [Online] Available from: http://www.sais-cari.org/publications [Accessed 31st May 2020].

Xiaoyang, T. (2019b) *Export, Employment, or Productivity? Chinese Investments in Ethiopia's Leather and Leather Product Sectors*. Working Paper 2019/32, China Africa Research Initiative, School of Advanced International Studies, Johns Hopkins University, Washington, DC. [Online] Available from: http://www.sais-cari.org/publications [Accessed16 October 2019].

Xie, L. (2011) China's environmental activism in an age of globalization. *Asian Politics and Policy*. [Online.] Available from: doi:10.1111/j.1943-0787.2011.01256.x [Accessed 16th July 2015].

Xinhua. (2016a) China' car ownership reaches 172 million. *China Daily*. [Online] Available from: https://www.chinadaily.com.cn/business/motoring/2016-01/26/content_23253925.htm [Accessed 12th October 2016].

Xinhua. (2016b) *Chinese Firm to Build 80mln USD Ceramic Tiles Plant in Ghana*. [Online] Available from: http://www.china.org.cn/world/Off_the_Wire/2016-04/13/content_38230906.htm [Accessed 30th July 2020].

Xinhua. (2017) *Facts & Figures: China's fight against poverty*. [Online] Available from http://www.xinhuanet.com/english/2017-05/24/c_136311122.htm [Accessed 7th January 2021].

Yale Environment 360. (2019) *Piling up: How China's ban on importing waste has stalled global recycling*. [Online] Available from: https://e360.yale.edu/features/piling-up-how-chinas-ban-on-importing-waste-has-stalled-global-recycling [Accessed 22nd May 2020].

Yan, S. (2004) *Corruption and Market in Contemporary China*. Ithaca, NY, Cornell University Press.

Yap, C-Y. (2014) China's Hebei Iron & Steel to build plant in South Africa. *Wall Street Journal*. [Online] Available from: https://www.wsj.com/articles/chinas-hebei-iron-steel-to-build-plant-in-south-africa-1410497371 [Accessed 31st May 2020].

Yardley, J. (2008) Chinese are left to ask why schools crumbled. *New York Times*. [Online] Available from: http://www.nytimes.com/2008/05/25/world/asia/25schools.html?mcubz=3 [Accessed 18th September 2017].

Zafar, A. (2007) The growing relationship between China and Sub-Saharan Africa: Macroeconomic, trade, investment and aid links. *The World Bank Research Observer*. 22 (1).

Zhang, C. (2017) *Six Important Environmental Cases*. [Online] Available from: https://www.chinadialogue.net/blog/9715-Six-important-environmental-cases-/en [Accessed 24th March 2018].

Zhang, Y. (2011) The shadow over rural China. *China Dialogue*. [Online]. Available from: www.chinadialogue.net, article number 4098 [accessed 15th February 2011].

Zhang, J., Alon, I. & Chen, Y. (2013) Impacts of China's foreign direct investment in Sub-Saharan Africa. *SSRN*. [Online] Available from: https://papers.ssrn.com/sol3/papers.cfm?abstract_id=2226927 [Accessed 29th May 2020].

Zhao, S. (2011a) The geo-politics of China-African oil. *China Briefing News*. [Online] Available from: http://china-briefing.com/news/2011/04/13/ [Accessed 2nd May 2012].

Zhao, S. (2011b) The China-Angola partnership: A case study of China's oil relations in Africa. *China Briefing News*. [Online] Available from: http://china-briefing.com/news/2011/05/25/ [Accessed 31st August 2017]. doi.org/10.1016/j.eiar.2015.06.008.

Zhou, J. (2015) *Neither 'friendship Farm' nOR 'landgrab', Chinese Agricultural Engagement in Angola*. SAIS-CARI Working Paper 07/2015. [Online] Available from: https://saiscari.files.wordpress.com/2014/10/sais-cari-brief-7-march-20151.pdf [Accessed 29th May 2020].

Zimba, J. (2016) *Itezhi-Tezhi Power Plant Comes On*. [Online] Available from: http://www.daily-mail.co.zm/itezhi-tezhi-power-plant-comes/ [Accessed 18th December 2018].

Index

A
Accra Agenda for Action, 177
acid rain, 81
Action Aid, 38, 42, 176
AES, 189–190
    AES Nile Power (AESNP), 203
Affordable Healthcare Act, 95
African Growth and Opportunity Act (AGOA), 174, 191, 216
African Development Bank (ADB), 29, 46, 50, 118, 135, 180, 187, 189
African Union (AU), 37, 39, 51, 70, 116, 122, 133, 142, 153
    the Maputo Declaration 2003, 142
Africa rising, 3, 18, 30–33, 47, 51
aid (*see* US, China), 2–9, 11, 15, 20–21, 24, 27, 31, 33–34, 36, 38, 40–45, 47–49, 54, 56, 65–66, 91, 93, 105, 111, 114–115, 117, 119–123, 125–131, 133–135, 137, 142, 153–154, 157–159, 164–166, 169, 172–179, 186–188, 191–193, 195, 204–206, 210, 212–217, 219–220
    aid conditions (*see* neoliberalism)
    benefits to donors, 209
    definitions (differing), 128
        OECD, Development Assistance Committee (DAC), 11, 41 128
        USAID or 'overseas development assistance', 128, 175–177
        China, 6, 128
    effectiveness, 24, 216
    justification by land grabbers, 56
    tied aid, 6, 40, 42, 114, 123, 126, 129–130, 133, 153, 176–177
        Helsinki Package on Tied Aid, 129, 176
aid to SSA
    aid and loans to repressive leaders, 48, 159, 209, 213
    aid figures, 129, 216
    aid per capita (SSA), 41–42
    China's aid, 5–6, 36, 40, 114–115, 117, 119, 120–123, 125–126, 128–131, 133–135, 137, 142, 153–154, 213, 216
    recipients profile, 41, 175, 187, 219
    sources of figures (CARI and AidData), 11, 128, 137
    to sectors
        agriculture, 8, 134, 142, 192–193, 204–205
        infrastructure, 6, 43, 65, 114, 119, 123 127, 130–131, 133–134, 142, 154, 192, 204, 213, 215, 219
        manufacturing, 192, 215
    transparency, 66, 119, 130, 133, 153, 169, 177
    USAID (*see* US section)
AidData, 11, 117, 128, 130, 137

AIDS, 22, 25, 28, 30, 52, 127, 167–169, 177
Algeria, 1, 121, 174, 207
Algiers Convention (2003), 51–52
agribusiness, 51, 55, 57, 59, 141, 143, 148, 153, 172, 174–175, 177, 179, 193–194, 205–207, 212–213, 216–217, 219
  use of chemicals, 51, 57, 59
agricultural productivity
  SSA, 36–37, 67, 141–142, 192
  US, 102
American invasion of Iraq, 101
AngloAshantiGold, 22
Angloplats, 184
Angola, 5, 17, 32, 35, 41, 46–48, 78, 116, 121, 124–126, 135–136, 142, 149, 152, 161–163, 168, 174, 184, 191, 200, 212–213
animal migration threats, 59
apartheid (South Africa), 23, 24, 159, 171, 181, 230
arms exporters, 92, 101, 111
arms sales, 116, 122
Asia, 16, 20, 29, 36, 41–42, 60, 62–63, 76–77, 79, 97, 111, 118, 140, 196, 202, 207
attacks on Chinese workers, 117
automobile sectors
  China, 79
  US, 99–100
automobile ownership
  China, 79, 85
  US, 99, 104

B

balance of payments
  China's surplus, 78
  IFFs and the balance of payments crisis, 64
  IFFs from Nigeria, 49
  leakages (deficits), 21, 49, 61, 180, 183–184, 217, 219
Bandung Conference, 114
banking sector,
  China, 145
  SSA, 39
    m-banking, 40
  US, 91, 93–94, 100
    deregulation, 90, 96–98, 103, 213
  World Bank funding, 174
Basel Convention on Hazardous Waste, 58, 91, 195
basic needs, 19, 65, 211
Batoka Gorge dam, 204
Belt and Road Initiative (One Belt One Road), 4, 87, 147
Benin, 46, 147, 200
BHB Billiton, 21, 54, 189, 199
bilateral aid and loan partners, 15, 40–41, 49, 66, 91, 93, 125, 128, 158, 167, 176–177, 184
biocapacity, 10, 80, 104
biodiversity, 60–61, 109, 207
  biodiversity loss, 109
biofuels, 59, 77
Black Economic Empowerment (BEE), 29–30
Boeing, 91, 101–102,
Boston Consulting Group, 72, 162
Botswana, 18, 20, 23, 29, 52, 56, 152
BP, 107, 109
Brautigam, Deborah, 2, 6–9, 11, 17, 36, 39–41, 43, 47, 65, 75, 113–116, 118–119, 121, 123–132, 134–135, 137–141, 149, 153–154, 160, 192, 194, 215
Bretton Woods Institutions (BWIs) (*see* World Bank, IMF), 1–4, 6–9, 15, 18–20, 30–33, 38–41, 46–49, 51, 58, 60, 64–65, 71, 89, 91–92, 97, 126, 135–136, 154, 157–160, 164–167, 170, 172–173, 177, 179–182, 184–187, 191–195, 199, 202–204, 209–210, 212–214, 216–220
    inability to admit failure, 179, 185, 187
    institutional bias against public spending, 194–195
    loans to totalitarian leaders, 181
    neoliberal policies, 8
    policy failures, 173, 184, 187
    poverty elimination in SSA, 7
    pressure to lend, 31
    project failures, 9, 170, 173, 178, 188, 209, 217, 220
bribery, 20–21, 35, 44–45, 51, 56, 74, 99, 117, 160–163, 167–168, 175, 180, 183–184, 188–190, 214, 216

BRICS (Brazil, Russia, India, China and South Africa), 12, 19, 64, 71, 91–92, 126, 154
British American Tobacco, 172
British colonialism
Kenya, 54
South Africa, 54
Bui dam (Ghana), 119, 148 149
Bujagali dam (Uganda), 39, 170, 189–190, 194, 199, 203–204, 219
Burkina Faso, 46–47, 57, 114, 159, 163, 172, 206
Burundi, 17, 28, 47, 212
Bush, George W., 5, 92, 95, 97, 101, 104, 163, 165, 167, 175, 177, 186
Business and Ecosystems Report, 109

C
Cabo Verde, 23, 47
cacao production, 172
Cameroon, 17, 46–47, 60–61, 122, 125, 133, 141, 151–153, 159, 161, 172, 187, 196, 199–201, 208, 212–213, 218
capital flight, 42–45, 159–160, 164, 166, 173, 182, 184, 209, 212, 215–217, 219
climate crisis assistance, 54, 197
carbon (CO_2) emissions, 5, 53–54, 59, 62, 69, 80–82, 85, 104–106, 108–109, 111, 146, 148, 155, 157, 196–197, 199, 200–202, 209, 213, 218, 220
China, 53, 69, 80–82, 85–86, 105–106, 108, 111, 146, 155, 218
EU-28, 81
India, 53
SSA, 59, 148, 196–197, 200–202, 213, 218
US, 5, 80–81, 85, 104–106, 108–109, 111, 157, 197, 209, 218, 220
Carbon Majors Report, 108
carbon sinks, 53, 60, 213
carbon trading 62, 197
cement, 81–82, 150–151
Central African Republic, 17, 28–29, 47, 61, 63, 159, 163, 212
Chad, 17, 26, 36, 46–47, 57, 129, 135, 150, 159, 161–163, 174, 188, 201, 212
Chad–Cameroon pipeline project, 161, 172, 187–188, 196, 199–201, 206, 208
Cheney, Dick, 162
Chevron, 108–109, 116, 161–162, 168, 171, 180, 184, 186, 191–192, 200–201
China, 1–6, 8–9, 11–12, 18–20, 28–29, 33–34, 36, 39–40, 43, 47, 53, 56, 58, 60–61, 63–64, 69–87, 91–92, 98–99, 104–106, 111, 113–155, 170, 213–216, 218–219
12th Five Year Plan, 72, 77
acquisition of US assets, 97
age profile, 74
aid, 6, 11, 36, 114–115, 119–121, 123, 125–126, 128–130, 134–135, 153–154, 213, 215–216, 219–220
anti-corruption campaign (China), 74
automobile ownership, 79, 85
borrowing from WB (IBRD), 76
carbon emissions, 5, 69, 79–82, 85, 104–106, 108–109, 111, 146, 148, 155, 157, 196–197, 199, 200–202, 209, 213, 218, 220
carbon emissions from corporations, 108
China Model, 3, 86, 122–123
Communist Party, 3, 5, 70, 86, 146
coal-burning power stations, 18, 218
condition-free loans and assistance, 123, 220
corruption, 8, 63, 74, 117–118, 126, 145, 152, 215
corruption in tendering processes, 8
democracy and human rights, 70
development, 4–6, 18, 20, 69–71, 75–82, 85–87, 113, 135, 138, 141
ecological footprint, 80–81
environmental impact of development, 4, 79–84, 145
exports from foreign firms, 79
foreign investment, 77–78
foreign-owned enterprises, 79, 87
foreign policy change, 87
GDP, 19, 70, 74–75
GNI per capita, 75
Go Global policy, 4–5, 69
gross national savings rate, 77
health and safety, 73, 83
human rights, 3–4, 70, 75, 86, 115,
human development ranking 71
hydropower, 78, 85, 137

inequality, 72
joined the IMF and WB, 5
market socialism, 3, 69, 87
middle class, 71–72
millionaire households, 72
oil
imports, 76–78, 105, 124–125
domestic production, 76–77
persecution of minorities, 70, 75
policies
Go Global, 4
One Belt One Road, 4
Belt and Road Initiative, 4
province to country model, 120
pollution 69, 74, 76, 80–81–83, 86
cancer villages, 83
poverty, 3, 71–73, 75–76, 86
renewable energy, 77, 147
regional SOEs, 113, 132
social issues, 73
stages of development, 4, 87
trade, 5, 40, 63, 77–78, 98 99, 113–114, 117, 124
trade with US, 78
urban-rural divide, 71–73
voting power in the BWIs institutions, 19, 71
China in SSA, 5, 8–9, 34, 36, 40, 43, 47, 56, 58, 60, 63–64, 76, 78, 101, 113–155, 170, 213–216, 218–219
African Policy, white paper, 115, 133
agricultural demonstration centres, 141–142
aid, 116–117, 120, 125, 129–130, 213, 215–216
beneficial impact on SSA, 2, 6, 8, 60–61, 65, 114, 119–120, 123, 127–8, 130, 134, 136–137, 139–140, 143–144, 147, 154, 216, 219
Chinese companies, 4, 6, 43, 53, 62, 69, 75–76, 78, 79, 83, 87, 108, 113, 117–119, 120–121, 125–127, 130–133, 136–137, 140, 144–154, 169, 215–216, 218, 220
blacklisting of Chinese companies, 118
China Development Bank, 125, 128–129, 134, 142
construction, 76–77, 81–82, 118–119, 121, 126–127, 131–133, 137–138, 142, 144–146, 148, 151, 153
Cultural Revolution, 3, 87
debt relief, 135
deforestation, 60–62, 84, 150–152, 218
demand for ivory, 62–63, 152
development assistance, 5–6, 115, 117, 119, 121, 123, 128–130, 135–136, 141–142, 154, 213, 215, 219–220
ecological footprint in SSA, 146, 153
economic development models, 3, 6, 86–87, 130
2–big development strategy (big companies and big ticket projects), 130
crossing the river by feeling the stones (pioneering new forms of business), 75
flying geese model, 75
market socialism, 87
economic impact on SSA, 2, 8, 34, 39, 53, 61, 79, 114, 119, 135, 137–138, 145–146, 148–149, 154, 218–220
exports to SSA, 36, 122, 124, 140, 153
finance and aid, 123
ecological footprint in SSA since 2000, 153
imports from SSA, 33–34, 40, 57, 61, 77–78, 84, 124–125, 132, 140, 143, 151–153
investment in SSA, 43, 116, 123, 127–128, 130–133, 135–144, 147, 151, 153–155, 194
labour, 36, 120–121, 145–146, 153, 155, 214
land acquisitions, 6, 141, 153
loans to SSA, 5–6, 8, 40, 43, 47, 114–117, 119, 123, 125–131, 134–138, 142, 145, 149, 153–154, 157–158, 213, 215–216, 219–220
low-cost financing and cheap labour for infrastructure, 136
medical assistance, 6, 119–120, 129
New Development Bank, 71, 126
peacekeepers, 122
policies in SSA
win-win, 6, 64, 114–115, 119, 123, 126, 136, 154, 213

non-interference, 70, 114, 116–117, 122, 135, 149, 154, 213
public–private partnerships, 138, 141, 144
special export processing zones, 138–139
private farms, 142–144, 147
project numbers, 135
provincial and private corporations, 113, 145
respect for political sovereignty, 213
trade, 61–63, 77, 114, 116–117, 123–125, 130–131, 133–134, 140, 151–152, 154, 191–192
training and education programmes, 6, 8, 119, 135, 138–140, 143, 213, 219
transportation and power, 132
tendering corruption, 8, 118, 216
China–Africa Cooperation Forum (CACF), 119, 123, 137, 145
China–Africa Cotton project, 142–143
China–Africa Research Initiative (CARI) at John Hopkins University, 8–9, 11–12, 40, 95, 114, 123, 125–126, 128–129, 134, 137–139, 141–142, 147, 153
China–Africa Summits, 115
2000, 115, 123, 130
2006, renamed the Forum on China and Africa Cooperation (FOCAC), 115, 123, 141
2015, 115
China Development Bank, 125, 134,
China Exim Bank, 117, 121, 125–127, 129–130, 132, 135, 137, 142, 145, 148–149, 162
China Model, 3, 86, 122–123
China National Petroleum Company (CNPC), 116, 150,
Chinese investment in sectors, 133–134, 138–139
CIA, 98, 163
Citizens United vs Federal Electoral Commission, 90
climate change, 11, 23, 79–80, 86, 99, 104–106, 108–111, 146, 158, 197–198, 202, 209
climate crisis, 5, 11, 30, 51–55, 59, 61, 64, 66, 86, 104, 106, 108–111, 146–147, 149, 155, 157, 196–198, 206, 209, 213, 218, 220
climate mitigation, 86, 106, 197
coal, 54, 73, 76, 80–81, 83, 104–105, 108–109, 197, 201–202, 220
coal-fired power, 21, 39, 54, 76, 80–81, 147, 188, 198, 201–202, 218
cobalt, 125, 127, 198–199
Coca-Cola, 75, 178
cocoa farming, 27, 37, 149, 174, 208
Cold War, 16, 20, 41, 44–45, 48, 92, 158–159, 175, 177, 181, 188, 214, 217
collusion, 21, 35, 48, 136, 159, 171, 180, 190
colonialism, 4–5, 16, 55, 87, 208
commercial loans, 5, 6, 31, 40–41, 48, 66, 76, 90, 123, 125, 128–129, 137, 142, 166, 172, 174–176, 181, 189, 202, 214–215
commercialisation of nature (WB), 196
Commission for Africa, 42, 44
common approaches to the environment, 146, 195
common but differentiated responsibilities, 105, 198
Comoros, 28
competition between unsubsidised and subsidised products, 212
compliance, 23, 46, 145, 164, 170–171, 174, 180, 186, 217
complicity in corruption, 187
Comprehensive Africa Agriculture Development Programme (CAADP), 37
concessional loans, 5, 40–41, 76, 117, 119, 125, 128–130, 135, 174–176
conditions of employment, 27, 73, 95, 120, 169–170, 209
Congo (Republic of), 28, 35, 78, 125, 159, 162–163
Congo-Brazzaville, 17, 125, 133
ConocoPhillips, 108–109
construction, 34, 76–77, 81–82, 118–119, 121, 126–127, 131–133, 137–138, 142, 144–146, 148, 151, 153, 189–190
consumer goods, 76, 81, 100, 140
consumption, 59, 62, 67, 72, 74, 76–78, 80–82, 84–85, 102–105, 110–111, 185, 204
Convention on International Trade in Endangered Species (1989), 62
corporations (*see* foreign corporations (companies), multinational corporations (MNCs)), 1, 8, 10, 15,

19–20, 27–28, 31, 33, 35, 42, 44, 48, 51, 53, 56, 60, 66, 78, 100, 107, 109–110, 140, 143, 160, 172, 174, 177–180, 183–184, 190–191, 195, 205–206, 208–209, 215–217
bribery, 21, 45, 99, 163, 175, 180, 183
capital flight/transfers, 9, 43–44, 49, 51, 162, 183, 209
collusion with governments, 21, 35, 48, 136, 159, 171, 180, 190
corruption, 8, 21, 22, 35, 45, 167, 180, 186–187, 189–190, 203, 215,
expansion into agriculture, 205, 207, 209–210, 217
corporate-driven development models (*see* public-private-partnerships (PPP)), 169, 193
environmental challenges, 109
food giants, 193
illegal financial flows, *see*: illegitimate/ illegal/illicit financial flows (IFFs)
impunity, 187, 195, 199
influence in US, 90–91, 95–96, 99–100, 103, 110–111, 157
land purchases, 55, 56, 206–207
lobbying, 91, 99–100, 105, 180, 205
profits, 3, 9, 22, 33, 43, 45, 52–53, 100, 110, 157, 169, 172–173, 179, 182–183, 191, 193, 207, 209, 219
regulation/deregulation, 99, 103, 107, 146, 179–180
resource extraction sector, 3, 21, 27, 33, 35, 43, 51–52, 66, 107, 118, 123, 129, 132, 136, 145, 150, 153, 158, 160, 161, 165, 170–171, 179, 182, 191, 195, 197, 198–199, 200, 204, 209, 213, 215, 217, 220
subsidies, 102, 175, 178, 196
tax avoidance/tax evasion, *see*: illegitimate/ illegal/illicit financial flows (IFFs), 3, 9, 22, 30, 33, 35, 44, 100, 183–185, 195, 215, 192, 219
tax havens, 22, 44–45, 48, 79, 100, 183–185, 217
corruption,
China, 8, 51, 63, 116–117, 126, 145, 154, 215
corporations *see also* (illegitimate/ illegal/illicit financial flows (IFFs))
SSA, 3, 17–18, 20, 22, 30, 35, 44–45, 51, 64, 116–117, 126, 136, 154, 159, 184, 188, 190, 212, 215
Corruption Perception Index
Transparency International, 74, 118
Côte d'Ivoire, 17, 27, 47–48, 58, 117, 151, 172, 207, 212
cotton, 36–37, 57, 60, 102, 140, 142–143, 174, 177, 206
coups, 19
covert operations (CIA), 163
crime, 13, 21, 23, 28, 30, 35, 39, 45, 59, 97–98, 171
critically endangered species, eastern gorilla, 63
criticism of China's engagement with SSA in the international media, 114–115
unbalanced reporting, 115
criticism of China's engagement with Darfur and the Chinese response, 116

D

dams, 8, 21, 39, 43, 60, 74, 78, 82, 85, 90, 119, 121, 126, 136–137, 145, 147–149, 153, 155, 170, 191, 194, 202, 203–204, 208, 213, 218, 219
alternative models to large scale dams, 148
Bui (Ghana), 119, 149
Batoka Gorge, 204
Bujagali Dam (Uganda), 39, 170, 189, 194, 199, 203, 219,
China funds dams rejected by other funders, 148
environmental costs, 8, 60, 82, 119, 149, 153, 194, 203
Gilgel Gibe 111 on the Omo River, 148
Grand Ethiopian Renaissance Dam on the Blue Nile, 148
Inga 3 (Congo), 149, 204
Itezhi-Tezhi, 149
Kaibar dam (Sudan), 148
Lower Kafue Gorge Project (Zambia), 148
Merowe Dam on the Nile (North Sudan), 121, 148
Mphanda Nkuwa, (Mozambique), 149
Tekeze (Ethiopia), 149, 204

data mining (US), 90
de Beers (corporation), 56, 184
debt (SSA), 2–3, 7–8, 15, 17–18, 20, 22–25, 30–35, 37, 39–51, 53–54, 58, 61, 64–66, 93, 97, 116, 127, 130, 136, 154, 157–158, 164–166, 170, 173, 175–176, 180–182, 185–186, 189–191, 194–195, 199, 204, 206, 209–217, 219–220
cancellation, 48, 66
entrapment, 20, 64, 181, 209
illegitimate ('odious'), 3, 45, 51, 66, 181–182, 209, 214
legitimate, 45–46, 180
debt relief, 6, 11, 12, 23, 25, 37, 40, 42, 44, 47, 49–51, 65–66, 128, 131, 134–136, 158, 165, 175–176, 182, 186, 210–211, 215, 217, 219
debt relief under HIPCI and MDRI, 3, 6, 8, 12, 23, 37, 44, 46, 49–51, 66, 131, 135–136, 164, 181, 185–186, 217
debt relief programmes
compliance with neoliberal/structural adjustment policies, 23, 36, 40, 49, 53, 164, 186, 217
debt repayment, 22, 24–25, 30–31, 41, 43, 45, 48, 50, 53, 65–66, 93, 116, 127, 134, 157–158, 164, 166, 181–182, 191, 195, 199, 204, 214, 216
burdens of, 24
debt servicing, 3, 7, 23, 34, 39, 43, 47–51, 65–66, 99, 158, 164–166, 181–182, 185, 209, 211–212, 216–217, 219
debt sustainability framework, 164, 186
debt-to-GDP ratio, 35, 48–49, 66, 99, 134, 217
defence spending (US), 92
defensive lending (World Bank), 32, 185
deforestation
China, 84
SSA, 51, 56, 59–62, 66, 84, 150–152, 158, 208, 213, 218
production of charcoal, 62
demand for ivory and rhino horn, 63,
demand for resources (China), 3, 5, 31–32, 34, 39, 40, 61–62, 66, 77–78, 84, 101, 124, 128, 136, 144, 199, 212–213
democracy, 3–4, 18–19, 30, 64, 70, 74–75, 86, 95–96, 115–116, 165
Democracy Index (Economic Intelligence Unit), 19
Democratic Republic of the Congo (DRC), 17, 20, 22, 28, 46, 48, 61, 63, 114, 116, 125–127, 134, 136, 151–152, 159, 160, 162–163, 172, 180, 182, 198–199, 204, 212–213, 215, 218
depleted global resources, 104, 109
deregulation, 2–3, 31, 40, 44–45, 90, 94, 96, 99–101, 103, 157–158, 162, 164, 170, 173, 180, 185, 208–209, 212–213, 215–216, 219
desertification, 53, 56–57, 84, 197
development assistance, 12
BWIs, 7, 9, 20, 186, 188,
China, 115, 119, 121, 128–130, 135, 141–142, 154, 213, 215, 219–220
Development Assistance Committee (DAC) of the OECD, 4, 11–12, 31, 41, 93, 128, 138, 175
Overseas Development Assistance, (USAID), 11, 13, 91, 165
development models, *see* neoliberal policies (structural adjustment policies, (SAPs)), 3, 6, 17, 165
Bread for the World, 149
Cascade Approach, a 'private-finance-first' model, 195
Chinese experimental model, 5, 138, 141, 213
Chinese model, 122–123
Chinese strategies, 75, 120, 138,
fossil fuel-based model (US), 103–105
influx of finance model, 180
low carbon development models, 54, 106, 197
private–public sector engagement model (WB), 177, 179, 189, 194, 217
state-driven development model (gradualist), 2, 20
dictators, 45, 114, 116, 181, 187, 188, 212
Chad, 161
digital technology, 5, 90–92, 100
Djibouti, 47, 134, 137, 163
Dikulushi Copper-Silver Mining Project, 172

displacement of people, 74, 121, 148–149, 154, 158, 170, 190, 201, 204
Dodd–Frank Wall Street Reform and Consumer Protection Act, 98, 180
Doha Agreement, 167

E
Extractive Industries Transparency Initiative (EITI), 127, 153, 160, 180, 186, 195
Extractives For Development policy (E4D), (WB), 160
Ebola, 26
ecological debt, 53–54
ecological footprint, 5, 10, 80, 104, 111
ecological limits, 104
Economic Community of West African States (ECOWAS), 38
Economic Crimes Surveys (Price Waterhouse Coopers), 39, 45
economic development, 1–9, 11, 17–18, 20, 26, 29, 32–33, 39, 44, 48, 51, 62, 64–66, 75–76, 79–81, 85, 87, 92, 104, 128, 137, 142–143, 147, 149, 158, 171, 175, 184, 186–187, 195, 197, 201, 203–204, 209, 211–212, 214, 216–217, 219–220
economic diversification, 36, 66
economic growth, 2–3, 5, 7–8, 17–18, 23–24, 31–34, 36, 47, 49–51, 63–66, 69–70, 74–75, 78–81, 84, 87, 96, 100, 129, 157–158, 165166, 175, 181, 185, 187, 194, 196, 200, 212, 215–216
economic imbalance between West and SSA, 33
economic impact of the US/BWIs on SSA, 1–2, 7–8, 32, 38–39, 154, 157–159, 165–166, 173, 181, 185–187, 191, 194–195, 203, 209, 217–220
economic impact China on SSA, *see* China economic impact on SSA
Economic Intelligence Unit: Democracy Index, 19
economic stagnation (SSA), 8–9, 17, 31–32, 53, 64, 158, 185, 209, 215–217
education (SSA), 7–9, 22, 24–27, 29–30, 34, 37–38, 65, 67, 119, 134, 154, 161, 163–164, 166, 173, 179, 184, 209, 211 213–214, 219
EITI crisis of relevance and legitimacy, 180
electricity shortages, 127, 137
elephant slaughters, 62–63, 153, 218
Emergency Aids Plan (President Bush), 167, 177
employment, 5, 26–28, 30, 36–37, 55–56, 64–66, 71, 73, 91, 94–95, 99, 101, 120, 123, 140, 143, 154, 165, 169–170, 185, 194, 209–212
endangered species, 62–63, 149, 151–153
Enron scandal, 101
environmental activism, 21, 35, 85–86, 103
environmental policies, 51–52, 56, 60, 70, 81, 108–109, 116, 145–147, 149, 153, 155, 158, 171, 190, 195–196, 198–199, 202–203, 208–209, 218, 220
environmental crisis, 11, 51–52, 54, 59, 61, 66, 86, 104, 106–107, 109, 150
  climate crisis, 11, 51, 54, 59, 61, 66, 86, 104, 106–107, 146–147, 149, 155, 196, 198, 206, 209, 218, 220
  risks for corporations, 109–110
environmental policies for overseas projects (China), 145–146, 149, 153, 155,
environmental policies for overseas projects (BWIs), 158, 171, 190, 195–196, 198–199, 202–203, 208–209, 218, 220
environmental impact (of development), 4, 6, 8, 22–23, 38, 51–52, 55, 59–61, 68–70, 80–81, 84, 85, 103–105, 105, 107, 109–110, 137, 145–146, 148–155, 158, 160, 168, 171, 179, 188–189, 194–203, 208–209, 213
environmental issues, 70, 83, 146, 150, 153, 155, 195, 197, 199, 218
environmental pollution, 51, 54, 57–58, 74, 80–83, 86, 107, 145, 150, 158, 168–169, 197, 209, 213, 220
environmental protection, 116, 146, 195, 220
Environmental Protection Agency, 5, 103, 105, 107, 195
Equatorial Guinea, 17, 23, 28, 46–47, 50, 61, 125, 151–152, 161, 163, 187, 200, 212
Equator Principles, 145

Eritrea, 17, 28, 47, 117
erosion, 51, 56–57, 84
Eskom, 21–22, 39, 54, 147, 188–189, 198–199, 201, 218
Ethiopia, 5, 17, 28, 32, 36–37, 41–42, 46, 55–57, 59, 117, 120–122, 125–126, 132–133, 137–139, 148–149, 151, 159, 163, 175, 188, 193, 205, 207
European Union (EU), 12, 29, 38, 40–41, 68, 79, 124, 146–147, 152, 170, 173, 179, 205, 212
export credits, 40–41, 92, 125, 128–130, 176
Export Credit Agencies, 41, 129, 161, 176, 181, 189, 195
  China Exim Bank, 117, 121, 125–127, 129–130, 132, 135, 137, 142, 145, 148–149
  US Exim Bank. 101–102, 162, 176, 191, 201–202, 214
export-driven agricultural policies, 36–37, 54, 192, 204, 208, 217
export-focused manufacturing, 138
export-led growth models, 51, 191, 195
exports, 4, 10, 20, 32, 34–38, 40, 42, 54, 56–58, 60–61, 66, 75, 77–79, 81, 84, 92, 98, 101–102, 108, 111, 116–17, 122, 124, 127, 135, 140, 147, 150–151–154, 157, 164, 172, 174, 183–184, 192–193, 199, 204–205, 208, 212–213, 216–217
Extractive Industries Transparency Initiative (EITI), 127, 153, 160, 180, 186–187
Extractive Industry Review, 195, 197, 199
extreme weather events, 53, 108, 196
ExxonMobil, 105, 108–109, 161, 163, 168, 171, 180, 184, 186, 191–192, 200–201

F

FAO, 12, 38, 55, 178
FDI in SSA, 27, 36, 40, 42–44, 65, 130–133, 138–140, 146, 151, 179
fertiliser use in SSA, 36–37, 58, 60, 67, 142–143, 192
financial deregulation, 3, 31, 40, 44–45, 96, 158, 179–180, 185, 209, 212–213, 215
financial fraud, 21, 45, 97, 183
financial models
  cascade model, private-finance-first, 195
  Public-private-partnerships (PPP)
  state-financed model
financial sectors, 1, 5, 9, 90, 96–98, 100, 111, 133, 158, 165–166, 196, 213
financial transparency, 98, 116, 119, 133, 161
Firestone, 28, 172
food crisis, 55 178, 192, 206
food aid, 38, 54, 175, 193, 205
food imports, 36–37, 67, 153, 174, 192–193
food insecurity, 36, 217
food security, 54, 56, 65, 67, 141, 153, 178, 192, 205–207, 217
foreign agricultural investment, 56, 141–144, 205
foreign corporations (companies), 3–4, 7–10, 15, 19, 21–22, 27, 30, 33, 35, 39, 43–45, 51, 57, 75–76, 81, 118, 131, 133, 135, 157–158, 160–161, 165, 168, 170–173, 179, 182, 184–185, 191, 194–195, 197, 205, 207, 209, 216, 219
Foreign Corrupt Practices Act, 117, 160
foreign direct investment (FDI), 33–34, 36, 42, 78–79, 123, 130–132, 138, 154, 179, 182, 189
foreign expropriation of land, 55
foreign land acquisition, 55–56, 66, 141, 153, 191, 194, 205–207, 209, 213, 219
foreign land investment, 55–56, 143–144, 153, 172, 191, 194, 205–207
Forestry Protocol, 208
Forum on China–Africa Co-Operation (FOCAC), 12, 133, 135, 145
  2000, 115, 119
  2006, 120, 123, 133, 141
  2015, 8, 134, 140
fossil fuels, 103–105, 107, 109, 197, 198
  companies, 90, 99–100, 105, 107–110, 191, 195, 197
  income, 191, 197
  projects, 54, 108–109, 191, 195, 197–198, 218
fossil fuel-based model, 104
fossil fuel-intensive development (South Africa), 54

fossil fuel sector, 5, 80 100, 107–108, 110–111, 191, 195, 197–198, 218
political power, 5, 90, 99–100, 103, 105, 110–111, 197
Foxconn, 73
fracking, 5, 54, 101, 103, 105, 107–108
fragile states, 17–18, 64, 117, 159, 164, 199, 203, 212, 219,
Fragile States Index (previously the Failed States Index), 17
free trade, 140, 174
free trade agreements, 40
funding of coal projects, 54, 76, 147, 198, 201–202, 218, 220
funding of large dams, 60, 82, 121, 137–149, 191, 194–195, 202–204, 208, 218–219

G

G7, 3, 12, 32, 38, 40, 71, 91
G77, 53, 154, 165, 178, 198
G8, 12, 25, 42, 46, 50, 159, 180, 206–207, 218
Gabon, 17, 19, 23, 35, 46, 52, 63, 125, 150, 152
Gaborone Declaration for Sustainability, 16, 52
Gambella National Park, 59
Gambia, 46–47
Gasland, 107
Gates, Bill (Gates Foundation), 103 169
Gates Foundation (GF), 103, 120, 169, 193, 205
promotion of GM seeds, 193
GDP, 2, 12, 16, 18–19, 24, 27, 32–33, 34–39, 44, 47–49, 52, 61, 66, 70, 74–75, 77–78, 83, 87, 96, 98–99, 101, 127, 134, 142, 145, 159, 161, 164–165, 172, 174, 186, 201, 212–213, 217
Gecamines, 160
Ghana, 23, 27–28, 37, 46–47, 52, 55, 119, 122, 129, 134–135, 138, 144, 147, 149, 151, 163, 172, 178, 199, 200, 205
Bui dam (Ghana), 157
Gilgel Gibe 111 Dam, 148
Glass–Segal Act, 96–97
Glencore, 101, 184
Global Corruption Report, 20
global economy, 15, 19, 31, 78, 93, 96–97, 157
global carbon emissions, 69, 8, 197, 213, 218
Global Environmental Facility, 197
global financial crisis (GFC), 4–5, 12, 34, 44, 46, 70, 75, 77–78, 85, 87, 93, 96–97, 101, 124, 136
Global Financial Integrity (GFI), 3, 8, 12, 21, 100, 183, 213
Global Footprint Network, 10
Global Multidimensional Poverty Index, 24
GM seeds, 108, 193, 205–206
Go Global strategy, 4, 5, 69, 78, 87
Going Out strategy of 2001, 123, 147
Goldman Sachs, 33, 91–92, 97, 102
governance, 20, 44, 50, 175
good governance, 18, 133, 160, 165, 188, 190, 214
poor governance, 3, 16, 20, 65, 115–117, 127, 133, 130, 133, 153, 159, 181–182
Grand Ethiopian Renaissance Dam, 148
Grand Inga 3 dam, 204
Great Elephant Census Report, 62, 152
Green Agricultural West Africa Ltd. (GAWA), 142, 144
green credit policy, 145
green economy, 86
greenhouse gas accumulation, 104
greenhouse gases (GHG), 12, 52, 62, 104–106
Greenpeace, 105, 152, 208
gross national income (GNI), 12, 71, 93
growth rates, 3–4, 15, 17, 24, 30, 32–34, 46, 50–51, 74–75, 87, 96, 136, 165, 210, 212, 215
guanxi, 63
Guardian Weekly, 11
Guinea, 17, 28, 46, 212
Guinea Bissau, 17, 28, 46–47, 212

H

habitat destruction, 189
Halliburton, 161–162
Halliburton Loophole, 103
harmful chemical use in Africa, 57
health impacts of neoliberal policies, 6, 9, 23–24, 26, 34, 39, 94, 119–120, 164, 166–169, 219, 166, 173, 211
health and safety, 60, 73, 83, 94, 108, 120–121, 165, 168

healthcare services, 6, 17, 25, 30, 38, 58, 65, 67, 72 (China), 93 (US), 164–166, 173, 211
health costs of contaminated water, 167–168, 199–200
health impacts of mining, 57, 168–169
health services, 6–7, 17, 23–25, 30, 38–39, 65, 67, 72, 93, 164–166, 173, 211, 219
Helsinki Package (to address 'tied aid'), 129, 176
Highly Indebted Poor Country Initiative (HIPCI), 3, 6, 8, 12, 23, 37, 44, 46, 49–51, 66, 131, 135–136, 164, 181, 185–186, 211, 217
high risk/high reward strategy, 202
HIV (*see* AIDs)
HSBC banking scandal, 98
human-centred approach, 211
human-centred model of development (UNDP), 65
human cost of capital flight (Boyce and Ndikumana), 166
human development, 2–3, 8–9, 16–18, 21–24, 29–31, 33–34, 42, 64–66, 69, 81, 89, 93, 115, 119, 158–159, 164–165, 173, 191, 209, 211–212, 214, 219
Human Development Index, 42, 93, 164, 211–212
humanitarian aid, 11, 120, 154, 175
Human Poverty Index (Global Multidimensional Poverty Index), 24
human rights, 3–4, 18, 21–23, 49, 55, 64, 70, 75, 86, 115–116, 120–121, 146, 159, 161, 163, 170–172, 180, 187, 201–202, 207–209, 214
Human Rights Watch, 22, 121
human trafficking, 28
hydropower, 78, 137, 147–148, 170, 194, 197–198, 202
  alternatives, 149, 197, 204
  projects in SSA rejected by West, 148

I

International food crisis (2007–2008), 193
IAASTD, 207
IFC, 172, 184
IFC loans, 192
IFC loan to Lonmin, 171
illegitimate/illegal/illicit financial flows (IFFs), 3, 8–9, 15, 21, 31, 33, 43–45, 49, 51–52, 65–66, 100, 136, 158, 162, 173, 182, 183–184, 209, 212–213, 216
  IFFs as percentage of GDP in SSA, 213
  IFFs exceed aid, 216
illegal logging, 51, 61–62, 151, 213
illegal timber imports (China), 61, 151–152
illegal wood exports to China, 213
illegitimate debt (*see* debt),
IMF (*see* World Bank and BWIS, neoliberal policies/structural adjustment policies (SAPs)), 32, 48, 92–93, 114, 116, 130, 134, 159, 165–166, 176, 180–182, 185–187, 195–196, 198, 210
  IMF and African Development Bank, 50
  IMF loan conditions, 176
  IMF voting allocations, 71
  poverty reduction strategy (PRS), 50, 165, 187, 201
  unable to accept criticism or modify behaviour (*see* World bank), 166, 179
immigration (from China), 121–122
impact of China's exports on trade and manufacturing, 138–140
impact of US agricultural subsidies, 37, 40, 102, 158, 170, 174, 216, 219
inadequate oversight, 17, 74, 118, 121, 145, 187–188, 190, 196, 202–203, 215
independence (SSA), 2, 5, 7, 9, 16, 19, 36, 38, 42, 48, 157, 163, 170, 173, 180, 195
individualism, 96, 111
industrial accidents, 73, 83
industrial agriculture, 58, 102, 173, 204–205, 208
industrialisation, 4, 20, 74, 81, 87, 105, 145
industrial pollution, 58, 74, 81–83, 86, 145, 150
ineffective environmental policies, 51–52, 56, 60, 70, 81, 103, 108–109, 144, 146, 149, 153, 155, 158, 160, 171, 179, 190, 194–196, 198–199, 202–203, 208–209, 218–220

inequality, 4, 17, 24, 29, 32, 72, 93, 94–97, 103, 111, 161, 187, 211–212
infrastructure, 4, 6, 8, 34, 38–39, 42–43, 47, 51, 56, 60, 65–66, 73–74, 77, 79, 82, 87, 93, 98, 107, 114, 119, 121, 123, 126–127, 130–131, 133–139, 141–142, 144, 147–148, 154, 178–192, 194–195, 202, 204, 213, 215, 219–220
infrastructure investment, dams, 126, 137, 148, 191, 194
infrastructure programmes, 82, 137
infrastructure project financing, 126, 130–131
institutional bias against public spending (BWIs), 194–195
insurance, 39, 92, 94, 172
interest-bearing loans, 11, 41, 114, 125, 174
Intergovernmental Panel on Climate Change (IPCC)
  1990 Report, 104–105
  2007 Report, 106
  2014 Report, 81
International Bank for Reconstruction and Development (IBRD), 76, 92
International Centre for Settlement of Investment Disputes, 92
International Development Association (IDA), 76, 92, 175
International Energy Agency, 12, 147, 204
International Finance Corporation (IFC) of the WB, 49, 71, 76, 92, 145, 166, 170–172, 177–178, 184, 187, 189–191, 193, 196, 199–202, 206, 208
international food crisis 2007–2008, 55, 178, 192, 206
International Institute for Environment and Development (IIED), 55, 61
International Labour Organisation (ILO), 27, 172
international migration, 26, 28, 121–122
International Monetary Fund (IMF), 1, 2, 5, 6–10, 12, 15, 19, 31–32, 34, 40–41, 45–46, 48–50, 64, 66, 71, 89, 91–93, 103, 106, 111, 114, 116, 130, 132, 134–135, 144, 157, 159, 165–166, 176, 180–182, 185–187, 191, 194–196, 198, 210–211, 213, 214, 218–219
  defensive lending, 185
international system of enablers, 160, 166, 217
internet-based NGOs, 86
invasion of Iraq (2003), 99, 101
irresponsible lending (*see* profligate lending), 41, 182
Itezhi-Tezhi Dam, 149
ivory, 62–63, 152, 218
Ivory Coast, 26, 125, 208

J
jobs (employment), 17, 27, 36, 42, 65, 70, 120–121, 131, 137, 160, 170–171, 205, 214, 219
Jacques, Martin, 2, 6, 69, 73, 88
Johannesburg, corporate elite, 21, 30, 45
Johnson & Johnson, 108
joint venture partnerships, 4, 35, 75, 79, 87, 136, 138, 140, 147, 149, 161, 163, 200
Jubilee Debt Campaigns, 6, 8, 46–47, 135, 182, 215, 219

K
Kaibar dam, 148
Kenya, 23, 29, 36, 38–41, 47, 52, 55, 57–61, 116–118, 121, 126, 133, 135, 139–140, 148, 151, 159, 163, 174, 188, 190, 205
Kenyan flower industry, 38, 57–59
Khulumani case (South Africa), 171
Kyoto Protocol (1997), 104, 106, 195

L
labour and employment, 27–29, 37, 42, 54, 59, 73, 76–77, 86, 104, 120–123, 136, 141–142, 145, 146, 154–155, 170, 172, 173, 180, 183, 185, 209, 214
labour unrest, 120
Lake Naivasha, 57, 59
lack of due diligence, 160, 171, 188, 190, 202, 209
lack of transparency, 35, 118–119, 127, 133, 153, 160–161, 180, 187–188, 190, 207, 214

Lagos, 178
Lagos Plan of Action, 2, 20
land acquisition, 6, 54–56, 64, 66, 141, 153, 191, 193–194, 205–207, 209–210, 213, 216–219
land reform in South Africa, 55
land sales (SSA), 56, 58, 143, 172–173, 206, 209, 217, 219
large-scale environmental destruction, 145, 198, 199, 204, 209, 213
legitimate financial outflows, 43–44, 182–183
Lehman Brothers, 97–98
Lesotho, 47
Lesotho Highlands Water Project (LHWP), 45, 47, 168, 178, 190, 194, 203, 219
 bribery and corruption, 190
 failure to meet goals, 190
 project flaws, 190
 social and environmental impacts, 190
Liberia, 17, 28, 52, 116, 125, 129, 135, 172, 194, 208
Libya, 1, 56, 162, 164
life expectancy (SSA), 24–25, 30, 168, 200
loan and aid neoliberal conditions (*see* neoliberal policies),
Loango National Park, 150
loans for African small and medium businesses, 138
lobby groups, 90–91, 99–100, 105, 180, 205
Lockheed Martin, 91, 101
London, 43, 97, 101, 141
long term supply contracts, 136
Lonmin mine at Marikana, 22, 27, 35, 170–171
low wages, 3, 27, 38, 43, 67, 94–95, 120–121, 132, 162, 165, 170, 173, 183, 192, 209

M

macroeconomic stability, 123, 186–187
Madagascar, 46–47, 55, 138, 151
major aid donors to SSA, 41
malaria, 22, 26, 120, 166–167, 169
Malawi, 28, 36, 46–47, 140, 143, 159, 172
Mali, 28, 36, 46–47, 55, 60, 122, 159, 163, 165, 170, 177, 205, 207
Mandela, Nelson, 43, 55, 170
manufacturing, 5, 29, 34–36, 39, 66, 77, 78, 80, 94–95, 101, 132–135, 138–140, 191, 192, 215
Marikana mining dispute, 22, 27, 35, 170–171, 199–200
Marikana mine environmental and social problems, 170–171, 196, 199–200
market socialism, 3, 69, 87
Masupha Sole, 45
Mauritania, 22, 28, 35, 46–47, 57, 159, 163
Mauritius, 18–19, 23, 138, 179
McKinsey Global Institute (MGI), 18, 144
Millennium Development Goals (MDG), 12, 22, 24, 26, 31, 36, 49–50, 53, 64, 165, 217
meat consumption, 72, 84, 105
Meltzer report, 93, 165, 182, 187, 210, 214
Merowe Dam, 121, 148
Microsoft, 92, 100, 103, 169
middle classes, 29, 62, 71–72, 75–76, 84, 86, 94, 119
middle-income nations, 71, 75, 76, 92, 187
migrants (Chinese), 29, 121–122, 153, 143
migrant workers, 28, 39, 42, 73
migration patterns, 26, 28–29
military assistance, 5, 11, 20, 40, 91, 116, 122, 128, 145, 163–164, 175, 177
military expenditure, 92–93, 99, 111
military–industrial complex, 5, 90, 92, 95, 101, 177
military, industrial, political and technological complex, 90–91
military missions in SSA (US), 163
military presence, 8, 154, 163, 215, 219
military spending (US), 100
military training, 163–164
Millennium Challenge Corporation, 165
Millennium Development Goals (MDG), 12, 22, 24, 26, 31, 36, 49–50, 53, 64, 165, 217
millionaire households (China), 72
mining, 22, 27–28, 35, 39, 45, 51, 57, 61–63, 66, 73, 120, 125–127, 133,

146, 150, 152, 155, 160, 164, 168, 171–172, 180, 184, 196, 198–199, 204, 208, 213
mining, toxic chemicals, 51, 57, 150, 213
misappropriation of funds, 118–119, 127, 188
misreporting in media about China, 128, 136
Mo Ibrahim Foundation, 18
mobile banking, 39–40
Mobutu Sese Seko, 48, 181
money laundering, 19, 21, 162–163
Movement for the Survival of the Ogoni People (MOSOP), 21
Moyo, Dambisa, 173
Mozambique, 5, 32, 46–47, 52, 55, 61, 63, 147, 149, 152, 163, 178, 207, 213
Mozambique timber exports to China, 61
Mphanda Nkuwa Dam, 149, 204
MTN, 19, 22
Multilateral Debt Relief Initiative (MDRI), 3, 12, 44, 46, 50–51, 65–66, 136, 164, 181, 186, 211, 217
Multilateral Investment Guarantee Agency, 92, 172
multinational corporations (MNCs), 1, 8, 10, 15, 19–20, 28, 31, 35, 42, 44, 48, 51, 53, 56, 60, 78, 100, 109–110, 140, 143, 174, 178–180, 183–184, 190–191, 195, 205–206, 208–209
  misinvoicing of trade, 8, 21, 44–45, 183–184
  tax avoidance, 22, 30, 183–185, 215, 219

N

Native Land Act (South Africa), 55
Namibia, 7, 19, 29, 52, 121, 152–153, 159
natural capital accounting, 15–16, 52, 67, 110, 196, 200, 213
neoliberal policies/conditions (structural adjustment policies, SAPs) (US, BWIS, Paris Club, Washington Consensus), 2–5, 7–10, 15, 23, 27, 30–31, 33–34, 36, 43–44, 46–47, 49–51, 64–67, 90–91, 94, 96–97, 99, 102–103, 111, 130, 138, 154, 157–158, 161–162, 164–167, 170, 172–174, 176, 181–186, 191–192, 195, 205, 207, 209–212, 214–217, 219
  deregulation of trade, 31, 40, 212
  impact on agriculture, 170, 179, 192–193
  impact on manufacturing, 36, 192
  justification, 66
  loss of political and economic sovereignty, 20, 65, 172
neoliberal policy failures, 65, 160, 170–171, 173, 179, 184–186, 209
NEPAD, 13, 37–39, 51, 116
Nestlé, 178, 206, 208
New Alliance for Food Security and Nutrition (NAFSN), 178, 217
  Oxfam criticism, 178–179
New Development Bank (NDB), 71, 126, 154
New Partnership for Africa's Development (NEPAD), 13, 37, 39, 51, 116, 133
Niger, 29, 56, 159, 162–163
Niger Delta, 21, 35, 57, 162, 168, 200
Nigeria, 17, 19–22, 25, 27–28, 32, 35, 41–42, 44, 46, 48–50, 57–58, 116–117, 121, 125–126, 132–133, 135–136, 138, 142, 144, 150–151, 159, 161–162, 163–164, 168, 171, 174–175, 179, 181, 183–184, 191, 200, 205, 208, 212–213
  AIDs, 25
  debt, 35, 46, 48–49, 164, 181, 213
  resource curse, 17, 35, 48, 161
non-government environmental organisations (China), 86
non-government organisations (NGOs), 8, 70, 83, 86, 169, 177, 193, 199, 201–203
non-interference (China), 70, 114, 116–117, 122, 135, 149, 154, 213
NSA, 98

O

Oakland Institute, 55, 206, 207
Obama, Barack (President), 92, 95, 97–98, 105–106, 161, 163, 165, 175, 179, 194, 202, 205, 218
Och-Ziff Capital Management, 45, 162
Ogoni activists, 35

oil
companies, 7, 21, 35, 57, 101, 109, 132, 150, 161, 168, 171, 180, 187, 191, 199–200, 214
crisis (1970s), 4, 41, 46, 100
exporting nations, 34, 41, 46, 49, 61, 136, 161, 183, 212, 200–201
importers (from SSA), 40, 43, 76–78, 101, 105, 77–78, 101, 105, 117, 125–126, 216
pollution, 57, 66, 81, 150, 161, 168, 171, 200–201
sector corruption, 45, 100–101, 161, 163
oil and deforestation, 62, 150
oil as loan collateral (western oil companies), 126
oil for infrastructure exchanges (China), 126, 130–131, 136, 142
One Belt One Road project (Belt and Road Initiative), 4, 6, 87, 147
One China Policy, 5, 114, 129,
open-cast mining, 57
Organisation for African Unity (replaced by the African Union), 20, 51
Organisation for Economic Cooperation and Development (OECD), 1, 13, 20, 91, 94, 96, 111, 119, 129, 146, 160, 166, 174–177, 180, 195
OECD Development Assistance Committee (DAC), 4, 11–12, 31, 41, 93, 128, 138, 175
aid definition, 11, 40–41, 58, 91, 93, 128, 175
aid transparency initiatives
Accra Agenda for Action, 177
Helsinki Package (to address 'tied aid'), 129, 176
Paris Declaration (2005), 177
US failure to sign aid transparency agreements, 177
Overseas Development Assistance (ODA) or aid (US), 11 13, 41
Oxfam, 42, 55, 94, 178–179, 184, 193, 207
report on tax avoidance, 184
report on corporate food giants, 193

P
palm oil production palm oil production, 57, 59, 193–194, 208, 213
pan-African environmental laws, 51
Paris Agreement (2015), 54, 86, 104, 106, 109
goal of 1.50°, 218
Paris Club donors (creditors), 4, 8, 31, 47–50, 64, 93, 127, 131, 135, 181, 214
Paris Declaration (2005) on aid, 66, 177
patronage, 16, 17, 74
Peabody Energy, 108–109
peacekeeping, 70, 122
Peking University Center for Structural Economics, 141
penal state (US), 95
per capita biocapacity, 10, 80, 104
per capita ecological footprint, 10, (China) 80, (US) 104, 111
per capita energy consumption (US), 103
Petrobras, 161
Petronas, 200–201
Pew Research Center, 52, 72
Pfizer, 108
phantom aid, 40, 176, 219
pharmaceutical companies, 25, 103, 108, 166, 167, 177, 219
philanthropy, 102, 103, 169
Phillip Morris, 105, 172
plantation agriculture, 27, 58–60, 62, 141, 172, 208
plastic-recycling, 84, 139, 150
poaching, 62–63, 152–153
Kruger National Park (South Africa), 153
policy and project failure rate, 9, 49, 64, 173, 177–179, 182, 186–187, 209, 217, 220
policy priorities, 23, 34, 38, 93, 128, 101, 131, 165, 169, 175, 187, 192, 202, 212, 215, 218
political and economic sovereignty, 2, 20, 30, 33, 64–65, 69, 158, 209, 213–214, 219
pollution
China, 69, 74, 76, 80, 81–83, 86, 145
SSA, 51, 54, 57, 58–59, 64, 81, 107, 149–150, 158, 165, 168–169, 197, 209, 213, 220
US, 107, 150

poor regulatory oversight, 74, 121
population densities, 29
population increases, 24, 29, 41, 51, 54, 57, 59, 62, 65, 166, 191
population repression, 17, 21, 48, 136, 158, 161, 181, 191, 211–212, 214
population SSA, 16, 19, 23, 32, 36, 71, 212, 214
populist politics, 94
poverty, 3–4, 7, 9–12, 17–18, 22–24, 26–27, 29–32, 34–35, 37, 42, 50–53, 63–65, 67, 71–73, 75–76, 86, 93–96, 103, 111, 114, 116, 122, 126, 161, 164–166, 170, 172–173, 176, 178, 184–188, 193 4, 197–198, 201, 205–206, 212, 214
poverty levels/rates, 4, 15, 17, 24, 30, 32, 35, 71, 75, 95–96
poverty reduction, 18, 185–188, 201, 214
poverty reduction strategy (PRS) (IMF), 50, 165, 176, 187, 201
Power Africa project, 165, 179, 194
power of veto, 10, 19, 91, 93, 114, 159, 214
precariat, 95
President's Emergency Plan For AIDS Relief (PEPFAR), 167, 177
PriceWaterhouseCoopers, 21
  Economic Crimes Surveys, 39, 45
PRISM, 90, 92
private charitable foundations, 102–103, 169, 193, 205
private-public-civil society partnerships (WB), 178
Private-Public Partnership model (PPP), 177–179, 189, 194, 196, 217
  persistence despite problems (BWIs), 210
private equity and hedge funds,
  investment in SSA, 208
  land purchases in SSA, 208
privatisation, 2, 8–9, 25, 31–32, 49–50, 65, 157, 166–168, 170, 173, 176–178, 185, 212, 214, 217, 219
problems with Chinese projects, 60, 118, 120–121, 141, 215
productivity, 6, 10, 34, 36–37, 54, 57, 64, 67, 80, 102, 141–142, 192
product obsolescence, 104
profits, 3, 7, 9, 22, 31, 33, 35, 38, 42–43, 45, 47, 51–53, 55, 60, 63, 75–76, 93, 97–98, 100, 110, 113, 126–127, 129–132, 136, 142, 145, 157–158, 161–162, 167, 169, 172–173, 179, 182–185, 188, 191, 193, 195, 201, 207, 209, 212, 217, 219
profit-driven regional SOEs (China), 113, 132
profits exported, 33, 42, 45, 52, 136
profligate lending, 46, 181, 209, 214, 216
project diversity, 135
project failure, 9, 160, 170, 173, 178, 179, 182, 185, 187–189, 196, 209, 217, 220
protests, 25,
  China, 70, 74, 85–86, 116, 145
  Nigeria, 171,
  SSA, 120, 145–146,
  WB, 32, 186, 199, 202
prototype carbon fund, 106, 197
proxy wars, 163
public health-related projects, 120
public–private partnership (PPP), 13, 138, 144, 170, 177, 179, 194, 196, 205–206, 217

Q

quantitative easing, 97
quasi-states, 16–17

R

Rainmakers, 86
Ramaphosa, Cyril, 22, 30, 35
ratio of debt servicing to GDP, 48–49, 217
  US, 99
RE100, 110
Reducing Emissions from Deforestation and Forest Degradation in Developing Countries (REDD), 62
  alternative to REDD (REDD Monitor and Friends of the Earth), 62
  REDD+, 62
reform of the international economic and political system, 64
reframing the role of the state (IFC), 177
regional trade, 38, 66
rejection of recommendations of the Extractive Industry Review,
  US, 195
  WB, 197, 199

remittances, 27, 34, 39, 41–42, 65, 216
renewable energy, 77, 106, 108, 110, 147, 198–199, 203–204
repayment of profligate loans, 181, 214
Republic of Congo (Congo), 78, 125, 152, 159, 162–163, 200
resources, 27, 78–79, 126, 135–136
  Chinese demand, 3
resource-backed loans, 126, 137
resource boom, 5, 65, 136, 159, 199, 212–213, 215
resource curse, 17, 35, 48, 161, 191, 212, 219
resource depletion, 15, 79, 109, 196–197, 200
resource extraction, 35, 57, 66, 125, 150, 198–200, 213
resource exports (SSA), 33–35, 38, 40, 61, 66, 124, 127, 140, 199
resource extraction, 3, 21, 27, 33, 35, 43, 51–52, 66, 107, 118, 123, 129, 132, 136, 145, 150, 153, 158, 160–161, 165, 170–171, 179, 182, 191, 195, 197, 198–200, 204, 209, 213, 215, 217, 220
resource-rich countries, 17–18, 43, 48, 126, 132, 136, 161, 191, 200, 215
resources for infrastructure, 6, 8, 39, 43, 65, 114, 119, 123, 126–127, 135–136, 142, 154, 213, 215, 219
respiratory diseases, 26
rhino, 63, 153,
Rift Valley Railway, 190
Riggs Bank, 163
rising global temperatures, 108
Rodney, Walter, 9, 31
rogue aid, 130
rosewood trafficking, 151
Roundup, 108
rubber production, 172, 194, 208
rural population (SSA), 24, 25, 27, 54, 62, 164
Russia, 5, 12, 28, 59, 71, 76, 91–92, 122
Rwanda, 17, 32, 46, 52, 167

S

safe drinking water, 26, 30, 72, 83, 167
safety standards, 83, 120–121, 155, 165
sanctions on Chinese companies, 118
São Tomé, 17, 23, 46–47, 114, 212
Saro-Wiwa, Ken, 35
Save the Elephants, 63, 152
Senegal, 46–47, 163, 205
Shell, 21, 35, 109,
Sichuan earthquake, 74, 82
Sicomines Mining project, 127
Sierra Leone, 46, 147, 151, 194, 207–208
Sinohydro Corporation and China Railway Group, 118, 127
slavery, 28, 172
slave trade, 7, 15, 48
Snowden, Edward, 90, 95, 186
social activism, 85–86, 103, 168–169
social and economic stagnation, 8–9, 17, 31–31, 53, 64, 158, 185, 209, 215–217
social and environmental impacts, 188, 190, 201–204
  hydropower projects, 148, 170, 190, 194, 202, 204, 219
  mineral extraction, 54, 57, 62, 169, 170, 184, 199, 213
  oil, 17–18, 21, 35, 57, 62, 66, 109, 150, 155, 161–163, 168, 171, 182, 184, 187, 191, 196, 200–201, 212–213,
social (human) and economic development, 3, 8–9, 17–18, 23–24, 26, 29–31, 48, 50, 60, 64–66, 71, 75, 85–87, 93, 119, 128, 137, 143, 146, 158, 161, 16–165, 173, 175, 195, 201, 203, 209, 211, 215–217
social and environmental sustainability, 2, 23, 145, 152
social unrest, 55, 74, 117
social welfare, 4, 65, 73, 94, 96, 165, 171
societies in transition (China and SSA), 4, 18, 87
SOEs (China), 4, 70, 78, 113, 145–147
soft-power strategy (China), 142
soil erosion, 51, 56–57
solar energy, 77, 80, 147–149, 197–198, 204, 218
Somalia, 1, 17, 19–20, 28, 159, 163–164, 212
Sonangol, 162, 200
South Africa, 7, 12, 19, 21–23, 25, 27–29, 32–35, 39, 43–45, 47–48, 52–58, 63–64, 71, 92, 117–118,, 124–125, 131, 133, 135–136, 140, 143, 145, 147, 149–150, 153–154, 159, 163, 166–167, 169–172, 174, 178–179, 181, 188–189,

190, 193, 196, 198–199, 201–203, 205–206, 212–213, 218
AIDs, 25, 166–167
apartheid, 24, 159, 171, 181
BHB Billiton, 21, 54, 199
Chinese FDI, 125, 131, 133, 140, 145, 147
corporate elite, 21, 39 45
companies, 19, 21–22, 33, 35, 39, 43, 45, 145, 147, 190, 202
comprador role in SSA, 19, 54, 64, 133
corruption, 21–22, 35, 45, 117, 159, 188, 190, 203, 212
Eskom, 21–22, 39, 188–189
Lesotho Highlands Water Project, 45
MTN, 22
Transnet, 22
Energy Intensive Users Group, 39, 202
export of China's polluting activities, 58, 150
ecological problems, 22–23, 52, 54, 63, 150, 154, 188–190, 193, 196, 198–199, 201–203, 206, 218
GDP, 32–33, 39
illegal financial flows, 44
life expectancy, 25
military, 163
Prime Minister Mbeki, 25
renewable energy, 147, 198,
Standard Bank South Africa, 131, 131, 133
trade deficit with China, 124
unemployment, 27
water privatisation, 25, 167, 178, 190
South–North Water Transfer Project, 82
South Somalia, 17, 212
South–South co-operation, 113
South Sudan, 17, 19–20, 28, 47, 78, 150, 159, 163–164, 207, 212
sovereignty, 115
special economic zones (SEZs), 138–139
species extinction, 51, 60, 66, 104, 197, 208, 213, 218
standards of living, 15, 24, 63, 70, 72, 74, 77, 84, 95, 161, 164–165, 172–173, 190–191, 209, 211–212, 215
Standing, Guy, 95
state models
quasi-states (SSA), 16
Western model of the state, 16
state-owned commercial banks, 125
state-owned enterprises (SOEs)/ companies (China), 4, 78, 87, 113, 126, 131–132, 137, 142, 144, 146–147
state-owned enterprises (SOEs)/ companies (SSA), 20, 160, 191, 200
Stealing Africa, 184
Stern Review (2006), 104
Stiglitz, Joseph, 90, 97, 144
Stockholm International Peace Research Institute (SIPRI), 92, 101, 122
structural adjustment policies (SAPs), neoliberal policies, 2, 8–10, 13, 23, 25–26, 30–33, 36, 38, 40, 43, 49, 53, 130, 164, 173, 176, 182, 184–186, 209–210, 214–216
structural adjustment programmes, 10, 23, 31–32, 43, 49, 173, 185–186, 209–210, 214, 216
conditions, 23–25, 30, 32–33, 46, 49, 130, 164, 173, 176, 185–186, 210, 214–216
criticisms, 32, 49, 186, 210
cuts to health and education subsidies, 65, 164, 166, 211
debt repayment, 66, 158
economic growth, 7–8, 66, 158
failures, 32, 173, 184–186, 209
goals
impact of SAPs, 30, 164, 166
induced economic stagnation, 53
loans, 49
wages, 3, 27, 43, 73, 94, 162, 165, 170, 171, 183, 192, 209
Structural Adjustment Participatory Review International Network (SAPRIN), 33–34, 185, 210, 216
Sub-Saharan Africa (SSA), 1–3, 5–11, 13, 15–61, 64–66, 78, 93–94, 101, 113–148, 150–155, 157–202, 204–220
age profile, 29
agriculture, 27, 36–38, 58, 60, 65, 66, 99, 102, 141–144, 172, 191–194, 204–205, 207–208, 216–217, 219

Chinese assistance, 119, 134–135, 140, 142, 144
export–driven policies, 36–38, 51, 54, 58, 60, 67, 192, 204, 208
expenditure, 37–38
government neglect, 37, 141, 191, 204
industrial (plantation) agriculture, 58, 60–62, 172–173, 178, 194, 205, 209–212, 217, 219
balance of payments crisis, 64
bonds, 47, 173
brain drain, 26
child labour, 27, 28, 172
child labour and slavery, 28, 172
child mortality, 22, 24, 26, 169
Chinese private investment in services and manufacturing, 132
climate crisis induced poverty, 53
cuts to subsidies, 3, 8, 24, 36–37, 40, 54, 65–66, 157–158, 170, 192, 206, 211, 216, 219
debt (*see* debt (SSA)),
China–debt cancellation, 215
rising African debt to China, 6, 47, 134–135, 215, 219
debt to BWIs and Paris Club, 2–3, 7–8, 18, 20, 30–33, 39, 40–41, 46, 47–49, 51, 58, 64–65, 97, 135–136, 154, 157–158, 164–166, 173, 180–182, 185–186, 191, 194–195, 199, 204, 209–210, 212–214, 216–217, 219–220
dependency, 31
diaspora, 27, 42
dumping of waste from high-income nations, 58
economic diversification, 36, 66
economic growth, 3, 7–8, 15, 17–18, 23–24, 31–34, 47, 49–51, 64–66, 158, 175, 181, 185, 212, 215
economic impact of China on SSA (*see* China: economic impact on SSA)
education, 8, 9, 25–27, 29–30, 34, 37–38, 65, 67, 129, 134, 154, 161, 164, 166, 173, 179, 184, 209, 211, 213–214, 219
environment, 2, 6, 8–9, 21–23, 38, 51–52, 54, 56–61, 68, 116, 137, 145–146, 148, 150–153, 155, 158, 160, 168, 171, 178–179, 188, 194–202, 206, 209, 211, 213, 218–220
challenges, 52, 57, 66, 116, 197, 209
laws, 51, 59, 61, 153, 206
law violations, 145–146, 151, 171, 188
exports, 32–36, 38, 40, 42, 57, 60–61, 66, 77, 101 124, 138, 140, 150–152, 174, 193, 199, 216
export markets, 124–125, 136, 150–152, 158, 174, 192, 205
FDI in SSA, 27, 36, 40, 42–44, 65, 130–133, 138–140, 146, 151, 179
by private and medium-sized companies (China), 146
food security, 36, 54, 56, 65, 67, 141, 153, 178, 192, 205–207, 217
foreign aid (*see* aid to SSA)
fragile states, 17–18, 20, 64, 117, 159, 164, 199, 203, 212, 219
GDP, 16, 32, 33
as percentage of world GDP, 33, 159, 164, 186
per capita, 24, 32–33
to debt ratios, 47–49, 61, 66, 134
GNI per capita, 33
growth rates, 2–3, 15, 17, 24, 30, 32–34, 46, 50–51, 136, 165, 210, 212, 215
healthcare, 24–25, 30
human trafficking, 28, 44
illegal (illegitimate) financial flows (IFFs), 2, 8–9, 15, 31, 44, 51, 65–66, 136, 158, 173, 183–184, 209, 212–213, 216
infrastructure deficit (SSA), 38, 136, 194, 202
key priorities, 37–38, 67, 141, 206–207, 217
land ownership, 55–56, 172–173, 206–207
leaders' requests, 6, 129, 135, 137

literacy, 26
loans to SSA, 175
loans from private creditors, 47
manufacturing, 34–36, 39, 66, 132–135, 138–140, 191–192
maternal health and mortality, 22, 26
national economic profiles, 32, 34–35, 48, 191
nations, 1, 16, 23, 31
population size, 32
neoliberal policies (*see* structural adjustment policies (SAPs), 3, 37, 157–158, 204
net creditor to the rest of the world, 44, 182, 212, 216
oil exports, 34, 35, 57, 61, 66, 77, 124
political interests, 114
to US, 50, 174, 216
to China, 40, 78, 124
population, 16
population increase, 19, 24, 29–30, 36, 41, 54, 57, 59, 62, 65, 191
poverty, 7, 12, 15, 17, 18, 22–24, 26–27, 29–32, 34–35, 37, 50–53, 63–65, 67, 114, 116, 126, 161, 164–166, 172–173, 176, 178, 184–188, 193, 197–198, 201, 205–206, 212, 214
productivity, 37, 54, 57, 64, 67, 141–142
resource management, 66, 146
role in China's overall global policy, 123
resource extraction, 3, 21, 27, 33, 35, 43, 51–52, 66, 107, 118, 123, 129, 132, 136, 145, 150, 153, 158, 160–161, 165, 170–171, 179, 182, 191, 195, 197–200, 204, 209, 213, 215, 217, 220
slavery, 28, 172
social and economic stagnation, 3, 31, 158, 185, 209, 215–217
sewage, 57–58
state sovereignty, 2, 20, 115, 117, 213, 219
structural adjustment/neoliberal policies in SSA (*see* structural adjustment policies (SAPs),
textile manufacturing, 36, 140, 192
trade with China, 61–63, 77, 114, 116–117, 123–125, 130–131, 133–134, 140, 151–152, 154, 191–192
China in deficit until 2015, 40, 124, 134
SSA deficit with China after 2015, 40, 124
trade with US, 40, 140, 167, 173–174, 191, 193, 212, 216
US in deficit, 40, 174
unequal relationships
trade, 7, 40, 158
with US and BWIs, 214, 216
with Washington Consensus, 66
subsidies to US agriculture/agribusinesses, 36, 174–175, 193, 216
subsidised agribusinesses in high income countries, 55
subsidised products, 102, 158, 170, 174, 212
Sudan, 1, 17, 28, 44, 46–47, 55, 63, 116–117, 120–122, 125–126, 132–133, 148, 150, 159, 206, 212
Suez, 138, 168
Supporting Economic Transformation Programme, 141
sustainable development, 18, 23, 54, 60, 62, 64, 85, 106, 109, 147, 155, 160, 203
sustainable agricultural development, 38, 60, 205–206
sustainable and inclusive growth, 81
sustainable business opportunities, 109, 141
sustainable energy development, 109, 147, 155, 203
Swaziland, 114
System for Environmental and Economic Accounts (*SEEA*), 110

T

Tana High Level Forum on African Security, 44
Tanzania, 5, 9, 35–36, 41, 46–47, 52, 55, 58, 61, 63, 117, 120, 126, 139–140, 152, 175, 178, 207

tariffs
removal of 36, 170, 174, 192
tax avoidance (corporate), 21–22, 30, 33, 44, 183–185, 215, 220
tax havens, 19, 22, 44–45, 48, 79, 100, 179, 183–185, 217
Tekeze dam (Ethiopia), 149
telecommunications, 19, 34, 39, 98
The Africa Compact (G20), 179
The Curse of Gold, 22
The Economist, 3, 31–32, 51, 76, 114, 189
Three Gorges Dam, 82, 137, 149
Tibet, 70
tied aid, 6, 40, 42, 114, 129–130, 158, 166
tied aid to infrastructure (China), 6, 114, 126, 130, 153
tied aid US, 42, 158, 176–177
timber, 60–62, 84, 110, 151–152
Time Magazine, 18, 31–32, 5, 85
tobacco, 27–28, 99, 126, 172, 174
Togo, 159, 200
totalitarian governments, 17, 109, 175, 212
China, 23, 83, 86, 145
totalitarian leaders, 23, 48, 158–159, 181, 214
toxic waste, 51, 57–58, 80, 83, 150, 199
trade
trade liberalisation, 31, 37, 40, 65, 192
trade misinvoicing, 8, 21, 44–45, 183–184
trade policies, unequal trade, 158, 167, 173–174
unequal policies and rules, 7, 19, 31, 33–34, 37–38, 40, 65–66, 138, 212, 219
Trafficking Victims Protection Act, 28
Trafigura, 58, 101
transparency, 20, 35, 130, 133, 158–161, 169, 177, 179–180, 186–190, 192, 207, 214
aid, 66, 153, 177
Bribe Payers Index (Transparency International), 117–119
China, 74, 116, 127
corporations, 35, 98, 192,
Corruption Perception Index (Transparency International), 74, 118
Extractive Industries Transparency Initiative (EITI), 127, 153, 160, 180, 186–187
IMF, 186, 214
Transparency International, 20, 74, 118
US, 98, 177, 186–187
Dodd–Frank Wall Street Reform and Consumer Protection Act, 98, 180
World Bank, 187, 188, 189–190, 214
Trans-Saharan Counterterrorism Initiative (TSCTI), 163
Treatment Action Campaign (TAC), 25
Trump, Donald, 78, 94, 106

U
Union of Concerned Scientists (UCS), 103–104, 108
Uganda, 17, 22, 37, 39, 46–47, 50–51, 58–59, 120, 137, 159, 163, 170, 189–190, 193–194, 202–203
UN Conference on Environment and Development 1992 (Rio de Janeiro), 104
UN Convention against Corruption, 117, 160
UN Declaration of Human Rights, 49, 209
unemployment, 5, 27, 30, 71, 94–95, 99, 101, 169–170, 210, 212
unequal development policies, 7, 157, 173, 208, 212, 214
unequal trade, 38, 40, 66, 158, 173, 212
unfair labour practices, 73, 121
Unilever, 60, 206, 208
United Nations (UN), 13, 109, 119, 122, 213
Declaration of Human Rights, 209
Millennium Development Goals (MDG), 12, 22, 24, 26, 31, 36, 49, 50, 64, 165, 217
Sustainable Development Goals (SDG), 13, 36, 64
United Nations Framework Convention on Climate Change (UNFCCC)
1992, 13, 53, 104, 106, 198
2015, 53, 86, 109, 146, 198
Common but Differentiated Responsibilities, 105, 198

UN General Assembly Resolution on Clean Water Access, 167
UN Global Compact, 146 179, 180
non-compliance, 180
UN Organisations
United Nations Development Programme (UNDP), 1, 13, 23, 16, 24, 65
definition of 'basic needs', 65, 211
United Nations Educational, Scientific and Cultural Organization (UNESCO), 13, 26
UN Food and Agricultural Association (FAO), 12, 38, 55, 178
UN Security Council, 114, 116, 122
UN Peace and Development Fund, 70
UN peacekeeping, 70, 122
United States (US), 1–12, 19–20, 23, 25, 28–29, 36–38, 40–42, 48–49, 53, 56, 66, 70–73, 76–81, 84, 86, 87, 89–111, 114–115, 120, 122, 124, 128, 131, 145–147, 152–154, 157–181, 184–187, 189, 191–197, 199–202, 204–207, 209, 211, 213–216, 217–220
agribusinesses, 51, 55, 57, 143, 174–175, 177, 193, 206–207, 212, 216, 219
agricultural subsidies, 37, 102, 158, 174, 216
aid
aid as grants or concessional loans, 40–41, 167, 174–175
aid objectives, 91, 165, 174, 176
benefits to foreign lenders and corporations, 173, 187, 219
goals, 91, 174–175
humanitarian aid, 11, 175
percentage of GDP, 174
phantom aid, 40, 176, 219
recipients, 41, 175
tied aid, 114, 123, 158, 176
USAID United States Agency for International Development, 11, 13, 91, 165–166, 169, 174–177, 179, 191, 193, 204–206
USAID Transparency Review, 177
US influence over other aid donors, 1, 4, 9–10, 91, 93, 111, 157, 176
US as largest aid donor, 93
atypical democracy, 95
automobile ownership US, 104
carbon emissions, 5, 80, 103, 86, 105–106, 108–109, 111, 157, 197, 200, 209, 213, 218, 220
per capita carbon emissions, 5, 81
climate change denial, 53, 99, 105, 109, 197
Congress (US), 25, 48, 91, 93, 98–99, 165, 180, 187, 210, 214
contribution to BWIs, 93
corporations, 168–169, 180
banking and financial corporations, 90–91, 94, 96, 100
banks, too big to fail, 97–98
deregulation, 3, 94, 99–101, 103, 111, 158, 213
greenwash, 108
lobbyists, 90–91, 99–100, 105, 180, 205
mergers and acquisitions, 90
political power, 5, 90–91, 95–96, 99, 102, 110–111, 180
ecological footprint, 5
per capita ecological footprint, 104, 111
economic size, 4, 9, 19, 71, 81, 89, 96, 98, 103–104, 157
emissions reductions, 86, 105–106
Exim (export-import) Bank, 101–102, 162, 176, 191, 201–212, 214
Extractive Industry Transparency Initiative (EITI), 101, 104, 160
failure to sign the Kyoto Protocol, 104
financial sector (international, includes US), 1, 5, 9, 89, 90–91, 93–94, 96–98, 100, 110–111, 158, 165–166, 174, 178, 196, 213
fossil fuel sector, 5, 90, 99–100, 103–105, 107–111, 191, 195, 197
chemicals, 5, 107
fracking, 5, 54, 101, 103, 105, 107, 174

GFC (Global Financial Crisis), 4–5, 12, 34, 44, 46, 70, 75, 77–78, 85, 87, 90, 96–97, 101, 124, 136
bank bail outs, 77, 97–98
Lehman Brothers, 97–98
healthcare, 94–95
imprisonment rates, 95
influence over WB, IMF, Paris Club, 1, 4, 7, 10, 91–92, 96, 103, 111, 157, 176
international environmental regulations, 5, 103, 107, 195, 199
international political agenda, 6–7, 91, 103, 214, 217
lack of banking regulation, 90, 94, 96–98, 103, 213
middle class, 72
military, 10–11, 20, 90–93, 95–96, 99, 101, 111, 128, 145, 154, 157, 163–164, 177, 219
Monsanto, Roundup, 108, 193, 205–206
national security issues, 100–101, 105, 107, 175
neoliberal policies (*see* structural adjustment policies (SAPs))
political power, 5, 9–10, 19, 90–91, 95, 99, 102, 110–111, 159, 179–180, 197, 211, 214
poverty and inequality, 93–95, 103, 111
private charitable foundations, 102–103
share of world trade, 98
subsidies to fossil fuel companies, 100
surveillance, 90–92, 98, 186
tied aid (*see* aid)
trade deficit with China, 5, 78, 99
trade with SSA, 40, 140, 167, 173–174, 191, 193, 212, 216
US-China co-dependence, 99
US and SSA
AFRICOM (US Africa Command), 163
Africa Compact, 179
African Growth and Opportunity Act (AGOA), 174, 191, 216
aid (*see* aid, USAID), 9, 13, 41–42, 93, 114, 157–158, 164–167, 170, 173, 174–179, 191, 193, 195, 204–206, 209, 214, 219
aid recipients in SSA, 175
dependence on minerals found in SSA, 101
destruction of cotton production in Central and West Africa, 37
exports to SSA, 10, 102, 164, 174, 193, 216
failure to meet aid obligations, 165, 174
failure to uphold environmental policies, 158
FDI in SSA, 179
food aid as corporate welfare, 193
impact of SAPs on SSA, 30, 164, 166
loans to SSA, 3, 9, 20, 191, 74, 157, 162, 172, 174–177, 181, 191, 202, 209, 214
loans to totalitarian leaders, 3, 23, 48, 59, 158–159, 175, 181, 214
Power Africa, 165, 179
trade with SSA, 40, 140, 167, 173–174, 191, 193, 212, 216
trade deficit with SSA, 40, 174
trade deficit with China, 5, 99
training 143, 163–164
troops in SSA, 163
US Treasury, 90, 100
Treasury bonds, 78, 99
weapons sales and military training, 157, 164
US/BWIs
beneficiaries of neoliberal policies, 8, 216
debt entrapment, 20, 64–65, 181, 209, 212
voting power in BWIs, 93
urbanisation
China, 72, 80, 82–83, 145
SSA, 30, 34
urban/rural divide (China), 72–73
urban waste removal, 57
used clothing exports, 192

V

Venezuela, 101
very low levels of human development, 212
veto power (US), 10, 19, 91, 93, 159, 214
veto power in Security Council (China), 114

Vietnam, 51, 63, 139, 193
Voice of an Angry River, 85
voluntarily determined national contributions (IPCC Paris 2015), 53–54
voluntary agreements, 146
  China, 146
  Common Approaches to the Environment (OECD), 195
  Extractive Industries Transparency Initiative (EITI), 180
  Guide on Resource Review Transparency (IMF), 187
  Guidelines for Multinational Enterprises, 180
  UN Global Compact, 180
voting structure of BWIs, 10, 19, 71, 93, 159

W

wages, 27, 38, 73, 94–96, 104, 141
wages and neoliberal policies, 3, 27, 38, 43, 67, 132, 162, 165, 170–171, 173, 183, 192, 209
wages in SSA (China), 120–121
Waking the Green Tiger, 85
Wall Street, 90
Walmart
  undermining basic needs production, 19
War on Terror, 5, 92, 101, 163, 175, 187
Washington Consensus, 1, 3, 30–31, 48, 54, 64, 66, 93, 136, 140, 157, 173, 183, 185, 209, 214, 216
  economic domination, 66
  Failure of structural adjustment policies (*see* neoliberalism), 173
waste, 10, 51, 54, 57–59, 66, 77, 80, 82–84, 139, 150–151, 195, 199, 203
water-borne diseases, 25, 169
water pollution, 51, 54, 57, 81–83, 86, 107, 145, 150, 167–169, 213
water privatisation, 9, 25, 32, 59, 65, 167–168, 177–178, 209, 214, 217
water scarcity, 51, 53, 66, 82, 109, 197
welfare state, 4, 94
Western capitalist nations, 4
Western companies (foreign corporations), 19–20, 22, 42, 45, 56, 66, 75, 79, 81, 100, 108–109, 118, 120–121, 123, 125–126, 131–133, 140, 145–146, 148, 150, 157, 160, 172, 184, 197
Western consumers, 81, 152, 172
Western criticisms of China in SSA, 114–116, 118, 145, 150
Western environmental regulations, 5, 58, 60, 81, 103, 107, 150, 199
Western FDI in Africa, 42–44, 65, 179
Western media bias, 116, 122
Western media reporting, 1, 3, 32, 69, 75, 109, 114–116, 130, 137, 144, 153
whistle-blowers (US), 95
White House, 94, 100
wind and solar energy, 77, 80, 147–149, 197–198, 204
win-win philosophy, 64, 114–115, 119, 123, 126, 136, 154, 213
wood imports (China), 61, 84, 151–152
work-related accidents, 83, 120
World Bank (WB), 4, 15–16, 19–22, 25, 27, 31–34, 35, 39, 41–42, 46–50, 52–53, 56, 58, 60, 64–65, 66, 70–71, 75–76, 83, 87, 89, 91–94, 103, 106, 110, 118, 119, 124–127, 134–135, 137, 148, 157–161, 165–167, 170–173, 175–177, 178–182, 184–206, 208–209, 211, 213, 214, 216–220
  adjustment is working, 185
  audit by the World Commission on Dams in 2003, 202–203
  bias in decision-making, 187, 194–195
  failed policies, 32
  infrastructure report 2010, 194
  lending (*see* International Finance Corporation (IFC))
  knowledge bank of development, 9, 10, 173, 217
  models
    Cascade Approach, a 'private-finance-first', 195
    export-led capitalist growth model, 195
    high-risk/high-reward strategy, 195
    public–private partnerships (PPP), 177–179
    private-public-civil society partnerships, 178

projects
high levels of failure, flaws and corruption, 9, 31, 160–161, 178, 182, 187, 188–189, 194, 203–204
US chooses president of the WB, 93
voting allocations, 6, 10, 19, 71, 93, 153, 159
Where is the Wealth of Nations? (report), 35
WB and IMF (BWIs), when appearing together in a sentence, 1–10, 12–13, 15, 19, 31, 46, 50, 64, 66, 91–93, 103, 106, 111, 123, 165–166, 175–176, 179–181, 185–187, 191, 194–195, 210, 214, 218, 219
World Bank in SSA
construction contracts, 118
debt repayments hinder human development (*see* debt repayments)
environmental policies ineffective, 195–196
failure to uphold environmental policies, 199, 202–203, 218–220
Extractive Industry Review (EIR) recommendations ignored, 197, 199
failures
meeting goals, 185, 187–188, 190, 216
meeting World Commission on Dams guidelines, 184, 203
promoting interests of the poor, 187, 194
structural adjustment policies, 32, 173, 184–186, 209
upholding environmental policies, 158
failures unacknowledged, 10, 209
flawed projects
Bujagali Dam project, 170, 189, 194, 199, 203, 219
Grand Inga dam, 204
Lesotho Highlands Water Project (LHWP), 190, 203
Rift Valley Railway, 190
ideologically driven projects, 7, 178, 209
impunity from harm caused, 187, 195
International Finance Corporation (IFC), 76, 92, 166, 170–172, 177–178, 184, 187, 189–191, 193, 196, 199, 200–202, 206, 208
lack of due diligence, 160, 177, 188
lending, 2, 6–7, 9, 20, 22, 31–32, 39, 41, 46, 76, 160, 166, 175–177, 181–182, 185, 187–188, 192, 194, 196–198, 209, 214, 216–217, 219
lending for fossil fuel extraction and energy, 197, 201, 218, 220
lending for hydropower, 198, 201–202, 218
limited support for alternative energy, 39, 198, 202–203
natural capital accounting, 15, 52, 110, 196, 200, 213
pro-corporate policies, 91, 96, 103, 157, 165, 173, 177, 179, 183, 187, 191, 202, 205, 209–210, 214
project failure rate, 178, 182, 188, 220
promotion of private financing of infrastructure in SSA, 194–195
poverty reduction, 23, 24, 30, 42, 50, 76, 116, 164–165, 185–186, 187–188, 201, 214
priorities, 93, 165, 188, 192
project failures, 160, 170, 178, 182, 190, 204, 216
project failure rate in low income countries (65%–70%), 182
projects funded, 137
Bujagali dam, 39, 170, 189–190, 194, 199, 203, 219
Eskom Power Project, 21–21, 188–189, 201, 218
Fomi dam, 170
Kandadji Dam, 170
Lonmin Mine Marikana, 170–171, 199–200
unsound projects, 31
promotes interests of private sector (corporations), 39, 167, 176, 187, 194, 202, 209, 214
structural adjustment policy failures, 30, 32, 49, 53, 164, 173, 182, 184–186, 192, 209–210, 214, 216
training 173, 217
unable to accept criticism or modify behaviour, 166

World Commission on Dams, 157, 195, 202–203, 219
World Health Organisation (WHO), 57, 83, 169
World Trade Organisation (WTO), 1, 5–7, 8, 13, 19, 25, 32–33, 37–38, 40, 66–67, 70, 79, 91–92, 99, 102–103, 119, 129, 166–167, 170, 176
  Agreement on subsidies and countervailing measures, 129
  China joins WTO in 2001, 5, 70, 79
  Doha summit, 25
  rules biased against SSA, 66
  unequal rules on subsidies, 7, 19, 37, 40, 60, 102, 129, 170
  voting allocations, 19
World Wildlife Foundation (WWF), 152

X
Xi Jinping, 63, 74, 86, 119, 122, 134, 140

Z
Zaire (DRC), 159, 181
Zambia, 23, 25, 35, 46–48, 61, 120–121, 125, 133–134, 138, 143, 148–149, 152, 168, 184, 205
  technology transfer, 143
Zimbabwe, 17, 36, 47, 63, 114, 116, 118, 120, 132, 140, 159, 205, 212
Zuma, Jacob, 22, 30

Lightning Source UK Ltd.
Milton Keynes UK
UKHW022029211222
414230UK00006B/247